Lecture Notes in Artificial Intelligence 12498

Subseries of Lecture Notes in Computer Science

More information about this subseries at http://www.springer.com/series/1244

Max Bramer · Richard Ellis (Eds.)

Artificial Intelligence XXXVII

40th SGAI International Conference
on Artificial Intelligence, AI 2020
Cambridge, UK, December 15–17, 2020
Proceedings

 Springer

Editors
Max Bramer
School of Computing
University of Portsmouth
Portsmouth, UK

Richard Ellis
RKE Consulting
Micheldever, UK

ISSN 0302-9743 ISSN 1611-3349 (electronic)
Lecture Notes in Artificial Intelligence
ISBN 978-3-030-63798-9 ISBN 978-3-030-63799-6 (eBook)
https://doi.org/10.1007/978-3-030-63799-6

LNCS Sublibrary: SL7 – Artificial Intelligence

This Springer imprint is published by the registered company Springer Nature Switzerland AG
The registered company address is: Gewerbestrasse 11, 6330 Cham, Switzerland

Preface

This volume, entitled Artificial Intelligence XXXVII, comprises the refereed papers presented at the 40th SGAI International Conference on Innovative Techniques and Applications of Artificial Intelligence (AI 2020), held in December 2020, in both the technical and the application streams. The conference was organized by the British Computer Society Specialist Group on Artificial Intelligence (SGAI). Because of the COVID-19 pandemic the event was held as a virtual conference using video-conferencing software.

The technical papers included present new and innovative developments in the field, divided into sections on neural nets and knowledge management, and machine learning. This year's Donald Michie Memorial Award for the best refereed technical paper was won by a paper entitled "Exposing Students to New Terminologies While Collecting Browsing Search Data" by O. Zammit (Middlesex University, Malta), S. Smith (Middlesex University, London, UK), D. Windridge (Middlesex University, UK), and C. De Raffaele (Middlesex University, Malta).

The application papers included present innovative applications of AI techniques in a number of subject domains. This year, the papers are divided into sections on Industrial Applications, Advances in Applied AI, and Medical and Legal Applications. This year's Rob Milne Memorial Award for the best refereed application paper was won by a paper entitled "Partial-ACO Mutation Strategies to Scale-up Fleet Optimisation and Improve Air Quality" by Darren M. Chitty (Aston University, UK).

The volume also includes the text of short papers in both streams presented as posters at the conference.

On behalf of the conference Organizing Committee we would like to thank all those who contributed to the organization of this year's program, in particular, the Program Committee members, the Executive Program Committees, and our administrators Mandy Bauer and Bryony Bramer.

September 2020

Max Bramer
Richard Ellis

Organization

AI-2020 Conference Committee

Conference Chair

Max Bramer   University of Portsmouth, UK

Technical Program Chair

Max Bramer   University of Portsmouth, UK

Deputy Technical Program Chair

Jixin Ma   University of Greenwich, UK

Application Program Chair

Richard Ellis   RKE Consulting, UK

Workshop Organizer

Adrian Hopgood   University of Portsmouth, UK

Treasurer

Rosemary Gilligan   SGAI, UK

Poster Session Organizer

Richard Ellis   RKE Consulting, UK

AI Open Mic and Panel Session Organizer

Andrew Lea   University of Brighton, UK

Publicity Organizer

Frederic Stahl   DFKI - German Research Center for Artificial
                              Intelligence, Germany

UK CBR Organizer

Stelios Kapetanakis   University of Brighton, UK

Conference Administrator

Mandy Bauer   BCS, UK

Paper Administrator

Bryony Bramer   UK

Technical Executive Program Committee

Max Bramer (Chair)	University of Portsmouth, UK
Adrian Hopgood	University of Portsmouth, UK
John Kingston	Nottingham Trent University, UK
Jixin Ma (Deputy Chair)	University of Greenwich, UK
Gilbert Owusu	British Telecom, UK

Application Executive Programme Committee

Richard Ellis (Chair)	RKE Consulting, UK
Nadia Abouayoub	SGAI, UK
Rosemary Gilligan	SGAI, UK
Stelios Kapetanakis	University of Brighton, UK
Andrew Lea	University of Brighton, UK
Richard Wheeler	The University of Edinburgh, UK

Technical Program Committee

Per-Arne Andersen	University of Agder, Norway
Farshad Badie	Aalborg University, Denmark
Raed Sabri Hameed Batbooti	Southern Technical University and Basra Engineering Technical College, Iraq
Yaxin Bi	Ulster University, UK
Mirko Boettcher	University of Magdeburg, Germany
Soufiane Boulehouache	University of 20 August 1955 Skikda, Algeria
Max Bramer	University of Portsmouth, UK
Krysia Broda	Imperial College London, UK
Ken Brown	University College Cork, Ireland
Marcos Bueno	Radboud University Nijmegen, The Netherlands
Nikolay Burlutskiy	ContextVision AB, Sweden
Darren Chitty	Aston University, UK
Frans Coenen	The University of Liverpool, UK
Bertrand Cuissart	Université de Caen, France
Ireneusz Czarnowski	Gdynia Maritime University, Poland
Nicolas Durand	Aix-Marseille University, France
Mohamed Gaber	Birmingham City University, UK
Hossein Ghodrati Noushahr	University of Leicester, UK
Peter Hampton	Ulster University, UK
Zina Ibrahim	Kings College London, UK
Joanna Jedrzejowicz	University of Gdansk, Poland
Stelios Kapetanakis	University of Brighton, UK

Navneet Kesher	Facebook, USA
John Kingston	Nottingham Trent University, UK
Carmen Klaussner	MTI Technology, Vietnam
Konstantinos Kotis	University of the Aegean, Greece
Ivan Koychev	University of Sofia, Bulgaria
Nicole Lee	University of Hong Kong, China
Fernando Lopes	Laboratório Nacional de Energia e Geologia, Portugal
Jixin Ma	University of Greenwich, UK
Kyle Martin	Robert Gordon University, Aberdeen, UK
Fady Medhat	University of York, UK
Silja Meyer-Nieberg	Universität der Bundeswehr München, Germany
Roberto Micalizio	Università di Torino, Italy
Daniel Neagu	University of Bradford, UK
Lars Nolle	Jade University of Applied Sciences, Germany
Joanna Isabelle Olszewska	University of the West of Scotland, UK
Daniel O'Leary	University of Southern California, USA
Filipo S. Perotto	Toulouse University, IRIT, France
Fernando Saenz-Perez	Universidad Complutense de Madrid, Spain
Miguel A. Salido	Universitat Politècnica de València, Spain
Sadiq Sani	British Telecom, UK
Rainer Schmidt	University of Rostock, Germany
Frederic Stahl	DFKI - German Research Center for Artificial Intelligence, Germany
Simon Thompson	GFT Group, UK
Jon Timmis	University of Sunderland, UK
M. R. C. van Dongen	University College Cork, Ireland

Application Program Committee

Nadia Abouayoub	BCS-SGAI, UK
Hatem Ahriz	Robert Gordon University, UK
Tony Allen	Nottingham Trent University, UK
Ines Arana	Robert Gordon University, Aberdeen, UK
Mercedes Arguello Casteleiro	The University of Manchester, UK
Juan Carlos Augusto	Middlesex University, UK
Ken Brown	University College Cork, Ireland
Nikolay Burlutskiy	ContextVision AB, Sweden
Xiaochun Cheng	Middlesex University, UK
Sarah Jane Delany	Technological University Dublin, Ireland
Richard Ellis	RKE Consulting, UK
Andrew Fish	University of Brighton, UK
Rosemary Gilligan	University of Hertfordshire, UK
John Gordon	AKRI Ltd., UK
Chris Hinde	Loughborough University, UK
Adrian Hopgood	University of Portsmouth, UK

Contents

Short Technical Stream Papers

Application Papers

Industrial Applications

Advances in Applied AI

Medical and Legal Applications

Short Application Stream Papers

Technical Papers

Exposing Students to New Terminologies While Collecting Browsing Search Data (Best Technical Paper)

Omar Zammit[1]([✉]), Serengul Smith[2]([✉]), David Windridge[2]([✉]), and Clifford De Raffaele[1]([✉])

[1] Middlesex University Malta, Pembroke, Malta
{ozammit,cderaffaele}@ieee.org
[2] Middlesex University, London, UK
{s.smith,d.windridge}@mdx.ac.uk

Abstract. Information overload is a well-known problem that generally occurs when searching for information online. To reduce this effect having prior knowledge on the domain and also a searching strategy is critical. Obtaining such qualities can be challenging for students since they are still learning about various domains and might not be familiar with the domain-specific keywords. In this paper, we are proposing a framework that aims to assist students to have a richer list of keyphrases that are pertinent to a domain under study and provide a mechanism for lecturers to understand what search strategies their students are adopting. The proposed framework includes a Google Chrome Extension, a background and a remote server. The Google Chrome Extension is utilized to collect, process browsing data and generate reports containing keyphrases searched by students. The results of the user evaluation were compared with a similar framework (TextRank). The results indicate that our framework performed better in terms of accuracy of keyphrases and response time.

Keywords: Searching strategy · Keyphrase extraction · Exposing knowledge

1 Introduction

The term *Information Overload* is defined as the problem of navigating the web to search for relevant documents [1,2]. Although search engines aim to reduce the number of documents for a given search, students still have to go through several documents to find the required information. With time students will improve their searching strategy and learn how to formulate proper queries to obtain a reasonable amount of results [2]. Queries are made up of keyphrases that students refine iteratively until the required result is obtained [3]. If few results are found students might think that the wrong search terms were used [4] and therefore a good searching strategy with enough keyphrases is required

© Springer Nature Switzerland AG 2020
M. Bramer and R. Ellis (Eds.): SGAI-AI 2020, LNAI 12498, pp. 3–17, 2020.
https://doi.org/10.1007/978-3-030-63799-6_1

[5]. Unfortunately, various factors can lead to a poor searching strategy; users might find it difficult to formulate correct queries [6] because they lack patience and time [7] or they find it difficult to locate relevant content [8].

Keyphrases are used in information retrieval since they provide a summary of a document's contents [9], having prior domain-specific content knowledge about the domain [10, 11] and a good search strategy [12] is beneficial for students because it will assist them in building the correct keyphrases and find relevant information. The work by Tsai (2009) explained how a good search strategy is crucial for school-related tasks, especially for novice online learners. A novice student is exposed to new keyphrases during lectures and seminars and however, some might be missed or misunderstood. To address such issue Zammit et al. (2019) proposed a framework that performs *Keyphrase assignment* based on the domain being studied by a student. Keyphrase assignment is the process of selecting phrases that best describe a document [9]. And in this study, we are extending the framework introduced by Zammit et al. (2019) and focus mainly on improving the quality of keyphrase assignment, evaluate the effectiveness of the framework by analysing students feedback and provide a central repository containing information about students searching strategies for lecturers to perform data mining.

Following a brief review in Sect. 2 on related work, the paper presents in detail the proposed framework design and implementation in Sect. 3. Section 4 and Sect. 4.2 present and discuss the results obtained from the implementation when the framework was compared with existing solutions and evaluated by students. Lastly, a conclusion is drawn in Sect. 5.

2   Reviewing Existing Approaches

In natural language processing and text mining, keyphrases are also referred to as n-grams and defined as the occurrence of N items in sequence in a given text [15]. N-grams modelling has also been explored and successful in low resource languages like Bengali [16]. Some authors opted to use pre-defined dictionaries to support n-gram creation, in fact Gledec et al. (2019) relied on Croatian online spellcheckers in their study to generate n-grams and also explained how such n-grams can be used in a variety of tasks.

To extract keyphrases from different texts Witten et al. (1999) proposed KEA[1], an algorithm that uses machine learning to build a prediction model using training documents with known keyphrases, and then uses the model to extract keyphrases from unseen documents. Such an approach has a lot of benefits, but it requires training documents. KEA was also used by other researchers to reduce the time spend by students while searching online. Some authors used it to extract keyphrases from educational documents and send them as search queries to Google. The search results obtained then were prioritised based on relevant feedback returned by the students who have previously viewed the result page or domain. Irfan et al. (2012) improved KEA since they stated that it might include noise and irrelevant terms. They proposed Keakat, a system that focuses mainly

---

[1] http://community.nzdl.org/kea/.

on online resources like web pages. The main disadvantage with KEA and its extensions is that it requires training documents that might not be available to student and once trained the algorithm is domain-specific [2].

Some studies used keyphrase extraction to automatically identify and describe documents, Mihalcea (2004) proposed Textrank, a graph-based ranking model for keyphrases and sentence extraction. Although our aim is different from the one proposed by Mihalcea (2004), the fact that the authors are extracting keyphrases using unsupervised learning was considered and such algorithm was used as a benchmark when we evaluated our proposed solution (refer to Sect. 4). A technical solution that takes the personal search history of a student into consideration and provides a holistic view of the domain under study was proposed by Zammit et al. (2019). The issue with such solution is that only uni-grams and bigrams (n-grams having 1 or 2 words) were considered during suggestions and evaluation was done using a quantitative methodology based on data sets rather than taking students activity into consideration.

Similar systems that were explored during this study require collecting data, training process or dependency on external sources. Collecting data in Gledec et al. (2019) was outlined as a major disadvantage while dependency on external online dictionaries [17] is domain-specific and the approach might not be useful in different domains. In this study, we tried to focus on a solution that does not include a data collection process and training models to extract keyphrases.

3 Proposed Approach

A web search session starts with a student query, then the query is processed by the search engine, however, the result may not be satisfactory [20]. Therefore students will repeat this session multiple times, and in every iteration, the query is refined until the intended information is found. Some studies show that queries that students submit in search engines can be collected and used to help students find relevant information the next time they search for something related. In their study Zammit et al. (2019) proposed a framework that collects searched queries and using text enrichment to build a bag-of-words. While searching online, the framework builds keyphrases using various similarity analysis algorithms to find the closest bag-of-words and the results are displayed in a wordcloud. The problem with this framework is that the authors focused on uni-grams and bigrams (n-grams having 1 or 2 words) and a quantitative methodology based on datasets rather considering students search activity. In this study, we are extending the framework proposed by Zammit et al. (2019) and introducing a function which dynamically creates and collects keyphrases in a central repository and allows user-based evaluation during an online search.

A 'Google Chrome Extension' was implemented to collect visited URLs and keyphrases searched by the students (refer to Sect. 3.1). The collected data is pre-processed by the 'Background Server', and predicted results are displayed back to the students in the extension (refer to Sect. 3.2). A 'Monitoring Mechanism' was implemented that sends information about students activity to a Remote

Server, where data is stored into a central location (refer to Sect. 3.3). *The Feedback Loop* depicted in Fig. 1 shows that lecturers can access and use the collected data to perform data mining techniques to learn more about students searching strategies.

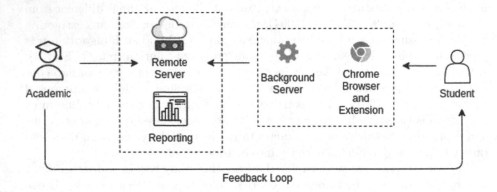

Fig. 1. Solution overview showing feedback loop

3.1 Google Chrome Extension

While Zammit et al. (2019) implemented a Windows Application, in this study to provide better user experience we opted to create a Google Chrome Extension[2] since this will be embedded within the Google Chrome Browser. Once a student visits a web site, using the *chrome.webNavigation* API and HTTP POST requests containing the URL details is sent to a background worker for further processing. Using an interval the extension sends an HTTP GET request to the background worker to get keyphrase suggestions and an overview of what is currently being searched by the student. The extension also allows students to navigate through the suggestions and interact with the wordcloud. Table 1 depicts the main functionality.

3.2 Background Server

The background server is installed on the student's local computer and its main aim is to collect, store and process information about the student's browsing behaviour. Using Python and various libraries, the background server was built on the research done by Zammit et al. (2019) . The server identifies and extract keywords searched by students from search queries, performs text enrichment using Google Search Engine and creates the respective bag-of-words using various Natural Language Processing techniques[3]. For each search done by the

---

[2] https://developer.chrome.com/extensions.
[3] https://www.nltk.org/.

Table 1. Google Chrome Extension Main Functionality

1. *Last Searched Keywords*: Last keywords searched by the student.

2. *Similar Searched Keywords*: Using similarity analysis as suggested by Zammit et al. (2019) this contains a list of similar keywords previously searched by the student.

3. *Word Cloud*: This contains keyphrases related to the domain. The keyphrases are extracted using the function explained in Listing 1. This allows students to be exposed to new terminologies and potential search keyphrases.

4. *Generic Feedback*: Allows students to share if they are finding relevant information.

student, using Cosine Similarity [21], Euclidean Distance [22] and Jaccard Similarity [23] finds related bag-of-words and extracts keyphrases. Keyphrases are then made available to the student in the Google Chrome Extension. The main difference between our study and the framework proposed by Zammit et al. (2019) is the way the keyphrases are extracted to expose students to ontologically pertinent terminologies. All processed data is stored into SQLite[4] since its the same technology used by many browsers [24]. When the background server receives a request that contains a URL visited by the student, it extracts the searched keyword from the query string which takes the form of a key-value pair. There is no common standard of how keywords are included in a URL, therefore the background server was configured to extract keywords from the following web sites:

- Google and Google Scholar.
  https://www.google.com/search?q=computers
- Wikipedia
  https://en.wikipedia.org/wiki/computers
- Stackoverflow (open community for developers)
  https://stackoverflow.com/search?q=computers
- Exlibrisgroup (a solution for higher education)
  https://exlibrisgroup.com/discovery/search?query=computers

A function was created (refer to Listing 1) that can build keyphrases of different sizes from any block of text. In Natural Language Processing and text mining,

---

[4] https://www.sqlite.org/index.html.

such keyphrases are also referred to as n-grams and defined as the occurrence of N items in sequence in a given text [15]. Some studies show how n-grams can grow in quantity leading to a *Curse of Dimensionality* [25] and therefore focusing on the topmost frequent n-grams within a block of text [26] to limit the quantities is recommended. Such functions usually are based on a ranking mechanism that decides which keyphrases are extracted and how important such keyphrases are within the block of text. Such mechanisms can be either unsupervised based on encoding properties from a block of texts or supervised, based on training using sample documents [27]. We opted for an unsupervised approach to avoid the time taken to train the algorithm and the need to have domain-specific documents. Apart from limiting the quantity of extracted n-grams based on their occurrence, we also introduced merging keyphrases based on their intersected words. That is, if the words in a short keyphrase are a subset of the words in a longer keyphrase, the short keyphrase is removed. The function accepts four main parameters; *'text'* the text to extract keyphrases from , *'top'* the amount of keyphrases to extract and the n-gram range from *'start'* to *'end'*.

Listing 1. Extract keyphrases function

```
1   def get_keyphrase_list(text: str, top: int,
2                           start: int, end: int):
3       text = text.lower().replace('\n', ' ')
4       tokens = [x for x in text.split(' ') if x != '']
5       # Variable containing n-grams
6       com = {}
7       for n_grams_count in range(end, start - 1, -1):
8         # Get n-grams for text
9         current = get_ngrams(tokens, n_grams_count)
10        # Get the occurrence of each n-gram
11        cnt = Counter(current)
12        # Determine the mean occurrence value and get
13        # the words having more occurrence than the mean
14        mean = np.mean([x for x in cnt.values()])
15        mean = np.ceil(mean)
16        common =  cnt.most_common()
17        cnt = [[x, b] for x, b in common if b > mean]
18        # Check if the n-gram is already defined
19        for word, count in cnt:
20          # Get similar n-gram entries
21          sims = [x for x in com.keys()
22              if len(set(word.split(' '))
23                .intersection(set(x.split(' ')))) > 0]
24          if len(sims) == 0:
25            com[word] = count
26          else:
27            for sim in sims:
28              com[sim] = com[sim] + count
29      # Return only top words
30      return dict(Counter(com).most_common(top))
```

Long n-grams will impact the performance of the application while short n-grams or unigrams might not cover enough keywords within the domain being researched by a student. Different studies recommend different n-grams values, five [16] and four [17]. Therefore we opted to determine the correct number of n-grams for our solution based on the dictionary accuracy and the datasets described in Sect. 4. A grid-search was performed and n-grams between 1 and 6 were considered. Figure 2 depicts the different accuracies that were obtained and shows that increasing n-grams impacted accuracy until we reached 4. After that accuracy had minimal fluctuations.

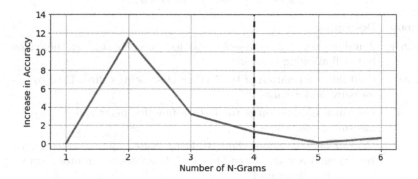

Fig. 2. Impact of n grams on accuracy

3.3   Monitoring Mechanism

Since the Google Chrome Extension is gathering information about students activity, we took the opportunity to normalise the collected data and store it anonymously in a central location on a remote server. We built a remote server and implemented additional functionality in the background server to sent feedback calls whenever the student interacts with the Google Chrome Extension.

Listing 2. Sample Feedback Call

```
1   { "identifier":"1c4d5c8f-78fb-4cc8-ac69-7017ad37ac",
2     "module":"engine.services.interface",
3     "method":"Interface.add_visited_url",
4     "params":{ "url":"https://www.google.com/search?
5           q=support%20vector%20machines
6               &cbf=WORDCLOUD&cbs=machine%20learning
7               &cbt=support%20vector%20machines"
8       },
9     "delta_time":"0:00:01.455315",
10    "call_time":"2020-04-20 13:15:02.727457",
11    "output":"support vector machines"}
```

When students click on a suggested link or visit a URL in the browser, apart from processing the request, a feedback call containing all the information is sent using HTTP POST to the remote server. Listing 2 shows an example of a feedback call of a student that first searched for *'machine learning'* in the Google Browser and then clicked on one of the suggestions predicted by the background server, that is *'support vector machines'*. Table 2 provides more information about what data is collected and sent to the remote server.

Table 2. Feedback Call Details

Attribute	Description
identifier	A unique key that represents a student, keeping student anonymous but still allowing grouping
module	Contains information of the Python class being called. Used to measure performance
method	Contains information of the Python function being called. Used to measure performance
params	Contains details about the URL being visited by the student. The Background Server will add call back functions to monitor from where the call was generated
	– *cbf=WORDCLOUD*: The function clicked by the student (wordcloud in this case)
	– *cbs=machine%20learning*: Keyphrase searched by the student
	– *cbt=support%20vector%20machines*: Keyphrase suggested by the Background Server and clicked by the student
delta_time	The time taken by the Background Server to process the prediction. Used to monitor the performance of the algorithm
call_time	The time when the action was performed by the student
output	The keyphrase clicked or searched by the student

The data collected and stored in the remote server can be used for various tasks. Lecturers can perform data mining techniques and learn more about students search strategies since the data includes the sequence of clicks done and searched keywords by their students. Keyphrases can be mapped with each other and academics can build domain-specific ontologies, since the link between two keyphrases depicts that these two keyphrases are related. Collected data can also be used to evaluate the framework proposed, and to identify what functionalities are being used. Such data can help in improving the usability of the Google Chrome Extension interface.

Figure 3 shows a subset of the collected data for a specific student. The sequence of the collected events shows the approach the student took to find

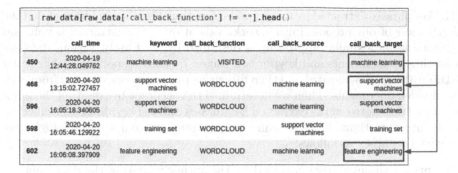

Fig. 3. Student searching approach

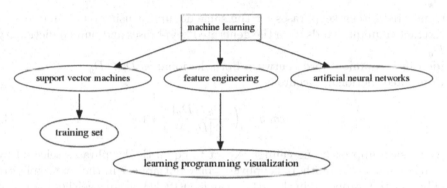

Fig. 4. Keyphrase mappings

the information required. The student started by searching the term *'machine learning'* and then clicked on some of the suggestions extracted by the Google Chrome Extension. our framework exposed the student to new terminologies related to the domain, like *Support Vector Machine* and *Feature Engineering*. The Google Chrome Extension suggested many more keyphrases in this case, but the student clicked on the keyphrases that he deemed are related to the domain. Since such data exist one can visualise the links between keyphrases and build domain-specific ontologies. Figure 4 shows how the data collected about the student was converted into links using a visualisation library[5] in Python.

4   Evaluation

4.1   Computational Experiment Results

To protect the privacy of students that were involved in the evaluation, they were instructed to switch to *'Incognito'* mode or stop the background server if they require to search sensitive information. In the evaluation, we measured the validity

---

[5] https://www.graphviz.org/.

of the keyphrases extracted by the proposed function described in Listing 1 and the effectiveness of our proposed framework. Validation of the extracted keyphrases was done using a similar approach, as described by [9]. Firstly, various datasets consisting of documents and keyphrases chosen by their respective author (refer to Table 3) were downloaded and then fifteen keyphrases were extracted from each downloaded documents. Then we determined the accuracy by counting the number of matches between the extracted keyphrases and the keyphrases specified by the document authors. Since we aim to expose students to new terminologies, we measured accuracy as follows:

1. Identified all keyphrases specified by the author related to the document.
2. Extracted unique words from the author keyphrases and build a dictionary D_k.
3. Generated fifteen keyphrases for the same document using our framework.
4. Extracted unique words from the generated keyphrases and build a dictionary D_g.
5. Identified common words between both dictionaries $D_k \cap D_g$.
6. Computed dictionary accuracy

$$accuracy = \left(\frac{|D_k \cap D_g|}{|D_k|} \right) * 100 \qquad (1)$$

With such approach one cannot expect to equal the keyphrases selected by the author since some authors keyphrases may not appear in the text explicitly [9]. The function proposed in this study can identify keyphrases neither identified nor included by the author. Therefore we cannot measure the accuracy effectively and to resolve this issue TextRank [19] was used as a benchmark since it is an unsupervised approach for keyphrases and sentence extraction. Using a Python implementation of the TextRank algorithm[6] we extracted keyphrases from the downloaded datasets computed the accuracy and validated our proposed function.

Table 3. Datasets used for evaluation

Dataset Reference	File Count	Timings		Total Phrases	Accuracy (%)	
		Function	TextRank		Function	TextRank
gollapalli2014 [28]	547	00:00:00	00:00:14	2278	31.62	36.59
hulth2003 [29]	1990	00:00:01	00:00:57	11783	23.43	40.59
aquino2015 [30]	1640	00:00:16	00:11:03	96337	**71.84**	43.98
kim2010 [31]	243	00:00:12	00:04:46	33490	**72.47**	63.65
krapivin2009 [32]	2301	00:02:20	00:49:29	306774	**85.81**	78.88
nguyen2007 [33]	209	00:00:08	00:03:10	22814	**80.28**	73.20
schutz2008 [34]	1231	00:00:22	00:10:57	104449	**68.79**	57.50
witten2005 [9]	29	00:00:14	00:06:38	15329	**91.70**	84.28

---

[6] https://pypi.org/project/pytextrank/.

While calculating accuracy we also measured the time taken by both algorithms to extract keyphrases, since within the Google Chrome Extension (refer to Sect. 3.1) results are displayed in real-time, response time has to be considered because it will affect the student experience. The results obtained are listed in Table 3 and depicts the following:

1. *Dataset Reference*: The dataset name and the reference.
2. *Files Count*: The total number of files that were processed by both algorithms.
3. *Timings*: The total time taken by the algorithm to complete the keyphrase extraction. Where *Function* refers to our proposed function.
4. *Total Phrases*: The total number of keyphrases extracted from the documents. The algorithms were configured to extract a maximum of fifteen keyphrases. Fewer keyphrases can occur when the document text is not long enough.
5. *Accuracy*: The dictionary accuracy obtained by both algorithms. Where *Function* refers to our proposed function.

When compared to TextRank, on the majority of the datasets, our approach obtained a better accuracy in a shorter time. Both metrics are dependent on the structure of the document, in fact on some datasets, TextRank performed better. On the other hand, amongst other factors, the response time is dependent on the level of complexity of the algorithm but overall our proposed function is faster.

4.2   Student Feedback Evaluation

To evaluate the effectiveness of the proposed framework we selected ten students, five reading a BSc in Computer Science and five reading an MSc in Business Information System Management. We installed our framework on their personal computer and monitored the activity for two months. During the two months, the students had several small assignments and lectures. From the collected data, we managed to understand how many times the students relied on the suggestions given by our framework to find the required information. This was achieved by counting the number of success callbacks received by the remote server. When a student searched a keyphrase in Google Search Engine, the Google Chrome Extension will display the suggested keyphrases. The actions followed were grouped into three categories. Figure 5 shows the quantity as a percentage of all the collected data followed by a description of all categories.

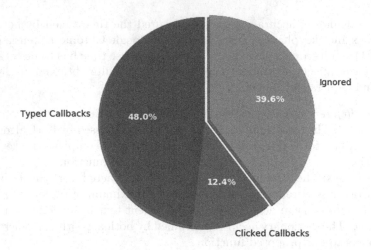

Fig. 5. Overview of callback data

A *'Clicked callback'* is when a student takes into consideration one of the suggestions provided by the Google Chrome Extension by clicking the suggested link and follows the search result page. A *'Typed callback'* is when a student instead of clicking the suggested link types manually the suggestion in Google Search Engine. These two callbacks can be considered as a success since the student took into consideration the suggestion provided by the Google Chrome Extension. Student can also *'ignore'* the suggestions provided by the Google Chrome Extension. Although this is not considered a success callback, it does not mean that the framework failed in this instance. It might be that the student found what he was looking for without the need to refer to the suggestions. Or the student took into consideration the suggestion but formulated and searched a different keyphrase. Figure 5 shows that more than 60% of the instances students relied on the suggestions provided by our framework since they either clicked or searched the suggestions manually. Considering that the remaining 40% have a probability of false negatives the results obtained by the framework produced promising results in assisting students.

5   Conclusion

Having a good search strategy and prior-domain knowledge is crucial for students to find relevant information while they are doing online research. In this study, we proposed a framework that builds on existing technologies to assist students and help them in formulating rich queries. A Google Chrome Extension was implemented together with a local background server that collects students browsing activities, identifies the student searched keywords and predicts pertinent content. The function proposed is capable of extracting keyphrases of different dimensions in real-time. All collected data is also sent to a remote server where lecturers can connect and perform data-mining techniques to learn more about different student searching strategies. An evaluation was done using popular datasets, and comparing the results with similar studies, while qualitative evaluation was done using a user-based approach. Future research should continue evaluating our framework and used by students enrolled in different courses to enrich the collected dataset. The results of this study clearly show that our framework performed better than similar benchmarks studies.

References

1. Maes, P.: Agents that reduce work and information overload. Commun. ACM **37**, 30–40 (1994). https://doi.org/10.1145/176789.176792
2. Kilbride, J., Mangina, E.: Automated keyphrase extraction: assisting students in the search for online materials. In: Szczepaniak, P.S., Kacprzyk, J., Niewiadomski, A. (eds.) AWIC 2005. LNCS (LNAI), vol. 3528, pp. 225–230. Springer, Heidelberg (2005). https://doi.org/10.1007/11495772_35
3. Usta, A., Altingovde, I.S., Vidinli, I.B., Ozcan, R., Ulusoy, O.: How K-12 students search for learning? Analysis of an educational search engine log. In: SIGIR 2014 - Proceedings of 37th International ACM SIGIR Conference on Research and Development in Information Retrieval, pp. 1151–1154. ACM (2014). https://doi.org/10.1145/2600428.2609532
4. Barr, E., Bird, C., Hyatt, E., Menzies, T., Robles, G.: On the shoulders of giants. In: Proceedings of FSE/SDP Workshop on Future of Software Engineering Research FoSER 2010, vol. 41(4), pp. 23–27 (2010). https://doi.org/10.1145/1882362.1882368
5. Sheeja, N.K.: An analytical study of medical students' interaction with internet and online resources. Int. J. Inf. Dissem. Technol. **5**(3), 167–170 (2015)
6. Kroustallaki, D., Kokkinaki, T., Sideridis, G.D., Simos, P.G.: Exploring students' affect and achievement goals in the context of an intervention to improve web searching skills. Comput. Hum. Behav. **49**, 156–170 (2015). https://doi.org/10.1016/j.chb.2015.02.060
7. Wu, D., Cai, W.: An empirical study on Chinese adolescents' web search behavior. J. Doc. **72**, 435–453 (2016). https://doi.org/10.1108/JD-04-2015-0047
8. Zhou, M.: SCOOP: a measurement and database of student online search behavior and performance. Brit. J. Educ. Technol. **46**(5), 928–931 (2015). https://doi.org/10.1111/bjet.12290
9. Witten, I.H., Paynter, G.W., Frank, E., Gutwin, C., Nevill-Manning, C.G.: KEA: Practical automated keyphrase extraction. In: Design and Usability of Digital Libraries: Case Studies in the Asia Pacific, pp. 129–152. IGI Global (2005)
10. Monchaux, S., Amadieu, F., Chevalier, A., Mariné, C.: Query strategies during information searching: effects of prior domain knowledge and complexity of the information problems to be solved. Inf. Process. Manag. **51**(5), 557–569 (2015). https://doi.org/10.1016/j.ipm.2015.05.004
11. Sanchiz, M., Chin, J., Chevalier, A., Fu, W.T., Amadieu, F., He, J.: Searching for information on the web: impact of cognitive aging, prior domain knowledge and complexity of the search problems. Inf. Process. Manag. **53**(1), 281–294 (2017). https://doi.org/10.1016/j.ipm.2016.09.003

12. Chen, K.T.C.: University EFL students' use of online English information searching strategy. Iran. J. Lang. Teach. Res. **8**(1), 111–127 (2020)
13. Tsai, M.J.: Online Information Searching Strategy Inventory (OISSI): a quick version and a complete version. Comput. Educ. **53**(2), 473–483 (2009). https://doi.org/10.1016/j.compedu.2009.03.006
14. Zammit, O., Smith, S., De Raffaele, C., Petridis, M.: Exposing knowledge: providing a real-time view of the domain under study for students. In: Bramer, M., Petridis, M. (eds.) SGAI 2019. LNCS (LNAI), vol. 11927, pp. 122–135. Springer, Cham (2019). https://doi.org/10.1007/978-3-030-34885-4_9
15. Ribeiro, J., Henrique, J., Ribeiro, R., Neto, R.: NoSQL vs relational database: a comparative study about the generation of the most frequent N-grams. In: 2017 4th International Conference on System and Informatics, ICSAI 2017, vol. 2018-January, pp. 1568–1572. Institute of Electrical and Electronics Engineers Inc., June 2017. https://doi.org/10.1109/ICSAI.2017.8248535
16. Ahmad, A., Rub Talha, M., Ruhul Amin, M., Chowdhury, F.: Pipilika N-Gram viewer: an efficient large scale N-Gram model for Bengali. In: 2018 International Conference on Bangla Speech and Language Processing, ICBSLP 2018. Institute of Electrical and Electronics Engineers Inc., November 2018. https://doi.org/10.1109/ICBSLP.2018.8554474
17. Gledec, G., Soic, R., Dembitz, S.: Dynamic N-Gram system based on an online croatian spellchecking service. IEEE Access **7**, 149988–149995 (2019). https://doi.org/10.1109/ACCESS.2019.2947898
18. Irfan, R., Khan, S., Khan, I.A., Ali, M.A.: KeaKAT - an online automatic keyphrase assignment tool. In: Proceedings of 10th International Conference on Frontiers of Information Technology FIT 2012, pp. 30–34 (2012). https://doi.org/10.1109/FIT.2012.14
19. Mihalcea, R.: Graph-based ranking algorithms for sentence extraction, applied to text summarization. In: Proceedings of EMNLP, vol. 85, p. 20 (2004). https://doi.org/10.3115/1219044.1219064
20. Kim, J.Y., Collins-Thompson, K., Bennett, P.N., Dumais, S.T.: Characterizing web content, user interests, and search behavior by reading level and topic. In: WSDM 2012 - Proceedings of 5th ACM International Conference on Web Search Data Mining, pp. 213–222. ACM, New York (2012). https://doi.org/10.1145/2124295.2124323
21. Chaithanya, K., Reddy, P.V.: A novel approach for document clustering using concept extraction. Int. J. Innov. Res. Adv. Eng. **3** (2016)
22. Mesquita, D.P.P., Gomes, J.P.P., Souza Junior, A.H., Nobre, J.S.: Euclidean distance estimation in incomplete datasets. Neurocomputing **248**, 11–18 (2017)
23. Niwattanakul, S., Singthongchai, J., Naenudorn, E., Wanapu, S.: Using of Jaccard coefficient for keywords similarity. Lect. Notes Eng. Comput. Sci. **1**, 380–384 (2013)
24. Flowers, C., Mansour, A., Al-Khateeb, H.M.: Web browser artefacts in private and portable modes: a forensic investigation. Int. J. Electron. Secur. Digit. Forensics **8**(2), 99–117 (2016). https://doi.org/10.1504/IJESDF.2016.075583
25. Fan, J., Fan, Y.: HIGH-Dimensional classification using features annealed independence rules. Ann. Stat. **36**(6), 2605–2637 (2008). https://doi.org/10.1214/07-AOS504
26. Havrlant, L., Kreinovich, V.: A simple probabilistic explanation of term frequency-inverse document frequency (TF-IDF) heuristic (and variations motivated by this explanation). Int. J. Gen. Syst. **46**(1), 27–36 (2017). https://doi.org/10.1080/03081079.2017.1291635

27. Joorabchi, A., Mahdi, A.E.: Automatic subject metadata generation for scientific documents using Wikipedia and genetic algorithms. In: ten Teije, A., et al. (eds.) EKAW 2012. LNCS (LNAI), vol. 7603, pp. 32–41. Springer, Heidelberg (2012). https://doi.org/10.1007/978-3-642-33876-2_6

28. Gollapalli, S.D., Caragea, C.: Extracting keyphrases from research papers using citation networks. In: Proceedings of the National Conference on Artificial Intelligence, vol. 2, pp. 1629–1635 (2014)

29. Hulth, A.: Improved automatic keyword extraction given more linguistic knowledge. In: Proceedings of the 2003 Conference on Empirical Methods in Natural Language Processing, EMNLP 2003, pp. 216–223. Association for Computational Linguistics (2003). https://doi.org/10.3115/1119355.1119383

30. Aquino, G., Lanzarini, L.: Keyword identification in Spanish documents using neural networks. J. Comput. Sci. Technol. **15**(2), 55–60 (2015)

31. Kim, S.N., Medelyan, O., Kan, M.Y., Baldwin, T.: SemEval-2010 task 5: automatic keyphrase extraction from scientific articles. In: ACL 2010 - SemEval 2010–5th Proceedings of International Workshop on Semantic Evaluation, pp. 21–26. Association for Computational Linguistics (2010)

32. Krapivin, M.: Large Dataset for Keyphrase Extraction. Technical Report May 2008, University of Trento (2008)

33. Nguyen, T.D., Kan, M.-Y.: Keyphrase extraction in scientific publications. In: Goh, D.H.-L., Cao, T.H., Sølvberg, I.T., Rasmussen, E. (eds.) ICADL 2007. LNCS, vol. 4822, pp. 317–326. Springer, Heidelberg (2007). https://doi.org/10.1007/978-3-540-77094-7_41

34. Schutz, A.T.: Keyphrase extraction from single documents in the open domain exploiting linguistic and statistical methods.Master of Applied Science (MAppSc) (2008)

Neural Nets and Knowledge Management

Symbolic Explanation Module for Fuzzy Cognitive Map-Based Reasoning Models

Fabian Hoitsma[1], Andreas Knoben[1], Maikel Leon Espinosa[2],
and Gonzalo Nápoles[1(✉)]

[1] Department of Cognitive Science and Artificial Intelligence, Tilburg University,
Tilburg, The Netherlands
g.r.napoles@uvt.nl
[2] Department of Business Technology, University of Miami, Herbert Business School,
Coral Gables, USA

Abstract. In recent years, pattern classification has started to move from computing models with outstanding prediction rates to models able to reach a suitable trade-off between accuracy and interpretability. Fuzzy Cognitive Maps (FCMs) and their extensions are recurrent neural networks that have been partially exploited towards fulfilling such a goal. However, the interpretability of these neural systems has been confined to the fact that both neural concepts and weights have a well-defined meaning for the problem being modeled. This rather naive assumption oversimplifies the complexity behind an FCM-based classifier. In this paper, we propose a symbolic explanation module that allows extracting useful insights and patterns from a trained FCM-based classifier. The proposed explanation module is implemented in Prolog and can be seen as a reverse symbolic reasoning rule that infers the inputs to be provided to the model to obtain the desired output.

Keywords: Fuzzy cognitive mapping · Recurrent neural networks · Interpretability · Symbolic reasoning

1 Introduction

When assessing methods related to pattern classification [8] several factors can be considered. The most popular ones are their predictive accuracy, speed (model building versus predicting/usage speed), robustness, and scalability. Less attention has been given to the concept of interpretability (often referred to as transparency or explainability without any distinction). Overall, the literature reports a lack of transparency found while employing certain machine learning algorithms in real-life problems [17]. Some challenges to consider are (1) how we should interpret such models, (2) how to certify they are transparent in their decisions, (3) make sure the results are both fair and statistically valid, and (4)

F. Hoitsma and A. Knoben—Contributed equally to the paper.

M. Bramer and R. Ellis (Eds.): SGAI-AI 2020, LNAI 12498, pp. 21–34, 2020.
https://doi.org/10.1007/978-3-030-63799-6_2

be prepared for an imminent request from governments about Artificial Intelligence regulations [2] (e.g. companies using intelligent systems might be asked to provide explanations to automated decisions).

More and more data scientists have become aware of the relevance of interpretability [7], and more attempts to lighting existing black-box models have been researched. The recent trends have focused on creating second (post-hoc) models to explain the first black-box model. For example, there exist post-hoc methods to visualize aspects of deep neural networks such as the features and the representations they have learned [14,15]. Similarly, we have the SHapley Additive exPlanations (SHAP) methods, which belong to the class of models called "additive feature attribution methods" where the explanation is expressed as a linear function of features. SHAP is a game-theoretic approach to explain the output of any machine learning model. It connects optimal credit allocation with local explanations using the classic Shapley values from game theory and their related extensions [6]. However, post-hoc methods are far from being a silver bullet. As stated in [12], post-hoc methods sometimes produce unreliable or misleading explanations. Therefore, it would make sense to create or improve inherently interpretable models.

Fuzzy Cognitive Maps (FCMs) are knowledge-based recurrent neural networks [3] that can be used for building intrinsically interpretable reasoning models. This technique has proven useful for modeling complex systems [5], for solving pattern classification problems [10] and in the forecasting time series type of problems [13]. The idea is to have a system represented by a weighted directed digraph, where the nodes represent specific subsystems (variables, or features), while the weighted and directed edges express the direction and strength of the causal relations among them. While FCMs are not necessarily black boxes (in comparison to neural networks), understanding these models might be challenging when the problem domain is described by a dense network.

In this paper, we propose a symbolic explanation module for FCM-based models that allows extracting useful insights and patterns. The idea relies on using Prolog in collaboration with an FCM-based model that has been previously trained. The module itself can be seen as a reverse reasoning procedure that infers the symbolic values of a given subset of input variables and the desired outcome. We used Prolog to implement our symbolic explanation module since it allows expressing pattern matching rules with little effort. The simplicity and expressiveness of Prolog make it very attractive to handle rules. For example, the developers of the IBM Watson System [4] have reported using it to express pattern matching rules over the parse trees and other annotations (such as named entity recognition results). Besides, we calculate a confidence degree for each rule that combines the possible information loss when translating the numerical representations into symbolic ones with the prediction accuracy. The effectiveness of our proposal is illustrated with the aid of a case study that is modeled with an FCM-based classifier.

The rest of the manuscript is organized as follows. Section 2 presents the underpinnings of FCMs and describes an automatic construction procedure for

FCM-based classifiers. Section 3 introduces the symbolic explanation module proposed in this paper. Section 4 illustrates the usability of the proposal through a case study while Sect. 5 concludes the paper.

2   Recurrent Reasoning Module

In this section, we describe how to construct and train FCM-based classifiers. In this paper, these models are referred to as the *recurrent reasoning module* to be coupled with the symbolic reasoning mechanism.

2.1   Fuzzy Cognitive Maps

Fuzzy Cognitive Maps (FCMs) are knowledge based recurrent neural networks consisting of concepts and causal relationships [3,9]. To overcome the limitations of traditional cognitive map models, the causal relationships between concepts in FCMs are weighted in the [1, 1] interval [3]. This way, FCMs are capable of representing the direction and intensity of the causal relationships. Each concept has a well-defined meaning, as opposed to a neuron in traditional neural networks [9]. Each neural concept C_i has an activation value in each iteration. Therefore, the state of an FCM-based model in a given iteration is defined as the activation values of the neurons in that iteration.

The initial activation values are either determined by experts or computed from data [9]. Equation (1) shows the reasoning rule used to produce the next activation value of neuron C_i from its current state,

$$a_{ki}^{(t+1)} = f_i\left(\sum_{j=1}^{P} w_{ji} a_{kj}^{(t)} \right), i \neq j \tag{1}$$

where P is the number of neural concepts in the network, k is the index of the initial activation vector, w_{ji} is the weight of the relationship from neural concept C_j to C_i, and $f_i(\cdot)$ is the transfer function. Equation (2) shows a simplified version of the generalized sigmoid transfer function,

$$f_i(x) = l_i + \frac{u_i - l_i}{(1 + e^{-\lambda_i(x - h_i)})} \tag{2}$$

such that $\lambda_i > 0$ and $h_i \in \mathbb{R}$, where λ_i controls the slope of the sigmoid transfer function and h_i the offset [9]. Moreover, l_i and u_i are the minimal and maximal activation values of the neural concept, respectively.

2.2   Construction and Learning

In this subsection, we will explain how to build and train an FCM-based classifier, which is the recurrent reasoning module to be coupled with the symbolic explanation routine. The FCM-based classifier described in this section was proposed by Nápoles et al. [9] and allows integrating expert knowledge with the knowledge derived from historical data. This means that the matrix regulating the interaction between the input neurons (denoted by W^I) can be determined by experts in the domain. This matrix will not be modified during the learning process, thus allowing for the human-machine interaction while serving as a tool to counter the bias on the historical data.

If this knowledge is not available, then W^I can be replaced with the correlation coefficients in multiple regression models [9]. Equation (3) shows how to compute the weight connecting two input neurons,

$$w_{ji} = \frac{K \sum_k x_{ki} x_{kj} - \sum_k x_{ki} \sum_k x_{kj}}{K(\sum_k x_{kj}^2) - (\sum_k x_{kj})^2}, w_{ji} \in W^I \tag{3}$$

where K is the number of instances in the training set and x_{ki} is the value of the i-th variable of the k-th instance.

The second weight matrix that makes up W is denoted with W^O. This matrix contains the weights regulating the interaction between the input neurons and the output ones. Figure 1 portrays the architecture of an FCM-based classifier involving three inputs neurons and two decision classes.

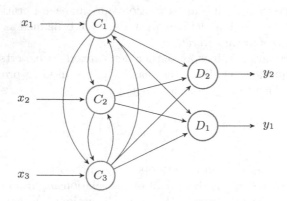

Fig. 1. FCM-based classifier comprised of three input neurons (C_1, C_2, C_3) and two decision neurons (D_1, D_2) denoting the decision classes.

In this model, the W^O matrix will be derived from the historical data such that the training data set has the form $[X, Y]$. X is a matrix containing the instances described by problem variables, which take values in the $[0, 1]$ interval. It will be used to activate the input neurons. Moreover, Y is a matrix containing the actual values for the output variables.

Firstly, we need to determine the $\psi^{(T)}(X)$ matrix, which contains the activation values of input neurons after performing T iterations of the inference process on X in Equation (1). This matrix captures the system semantics as expressed by the interaction between the variables. Equation (4) shows how to compute W^O using a powerful inverse learning rule,

$$W^O = (\psi^{(T)}(X))^+ F^-(Y) \tag{4}$$

where $(\cdot)^+$ denotes a Moore-Penrose inverse of a matrix. $F^-(Y)$ is a matrix that contains the inverse of the transfer functions of the output nodes. Equation (5) shows the inverse of the sigmoid transfer function,

$$f_i^{-1}(y) = \frac{\ln(-1 - y) + h_i \lambda_i}{\lambda_i}. \tag{5}$$

After training the FCM-based classifier, it might be necessary to normalize the weights, so they are in the $[-1, 1]$ interval.

3 Symbolic Explanation Module

In this section, we present a symbolic explanation module that helps understand how the predictions of the FCM-based classifier presented in the previous section are made. Firstly, we describe how to translate the numerical inputs and outputs into symbolic IF-THEN rules. Secondly, we write a Prolog routine to handle the symbolic rules and derive the conclusions.

3.1 Symbolic Knowledge Representation

After computing the most likely decision class for each instance with the FCM-based classifier, we need to transform the activation values into symbolic representations. This can be accomplished using fuzzy logic [18]. Activation values are mapped to the following fuzzy sets: *very low* (VL), *low* (L), *medium* (M), *high* (H), and *very high* (VH). The number of fuzzy sets defines the level of granularity attached to the symbolic knowledge representations. The finer the granularity, the more precise the symbolic representations.

In this approach, each fuzzy set is associated with a membership function, which defines the extent to which an object belongs to the set. A membership function $\mu_S(x)$ gives the membership degree in the $[0, 1]$ interval of an object x within set S [18]. Therefore, a membership degree of zero can be understood as the object certainly not belonging to a set, whereas a membership degree of one means the object certainly belongs to a set.

In this paper, we use the Gaussian membership function [11] since this function allows for smoother transitions between intervals when compared to a triangular or trapezoidal membership function. Equation (6) shows the mathematical formulation of this function and its parameters,

$$\mu_S(x) = e^{-\frac{(x-m)^2}{2k^2}} \tag{6}$$

where m is the central value and $k > 0$ is the standard deviation. In this paper, the parameters associated with the Gaussian membership functions are estimated according to the distribution of the activation values of the neurons. For example, if we observe that most activation values are in the $[0, 0.5]$ interval, then we should build either more fuzzy sets on that region or build Gaussian membership functions with higher coverage of that region. This means that the linguistic terms are relative to the activation values of the neurons. This process was done manually using histograms as a way to involve experts in the data granulation process, but it can be automated in future research efforts.

3.2   Generating Explanations

After granulating the activation space, we can build fuzzy rules to produce counterfactual explanations. Each rule will be associated with a certainty degree that allows quantifying the extent to which the expert can trust on that rule and the explanations generated with it. More specifically, we are interested in producing explanations with the form: "Which values should the variables $x_i \in Q$ have taken to produce the output y_l?". In this case, the expert is requested to provide the set of variables $Q \subset X$ to be investigated.

The set of fuzzy rules has the following form: IF x_1 is s_1 with certainty $\mu_{s_1}(x_1)$ AND ... AND x_i is s_i with certainty $\mu_{s_i}(x_i)$ ... AND ... AND x_M is s_M with certainty $\mu_{s_M}(x_M)$ THEN y_j with certainty $\mu_{y_j}(d_j)$. In such rules, $\mu_{s_i}(x_i)$ is the membership degree x_i to the fuzzy set $s_i \in S$, with S being the set of all fuzzy sets while d_j is the activation value of the output neuron associated to the j-th decision class. Moreover, we assume that $s_i = \text{argmax}_{s_l \in S}\{\mu_{s_l}(x_i)\}$ and consequently that $\mu_{s_i}(x_i) = \max_{s_l \in S}\{\mu_{s_l}(x_i)\}$. Finally, we compute a certainty value ψ_k for each rule. The certainty degrees of rules are computed with a t-norm over the membership degrees of the antecedent components multiplied by the certainty of producing the j-th decision class. Equation (7) formalizes this idea with the t-norm being the minimum,

$$\psi_k = \min\{\mu_{s_1}(x_1), \cdots, \mu_{s_M}(x_M)\} * \mu_{y_j}(d_j). \tag{7}$$

Notice that the result of the t-norm reflects the certainty of the knowledge representation, whereas the maximum of the output values represents the certainty of an instance being classified.

The next step concerns the creation of the Prolog knowledge base used to generate the explanations. Therefore, we need to convert the fuzzy rules into Prolog rules with the form: input($[[s_1, \mu_{s_1}(x_1)], \ldots, [s_i, \mu_{s_i}(x_i)], \ldots, [s_M, \mu_{s_M}(x_M)]$, $\psi_k]$) :- output($[y_j, d_j]$). Moreover, we should declare the output predicates as facts that will be activated dynamically during querying.

The last step is related to querying. When presenting a query, we should retract all predicates previously activated while asserting the facts to be explored. This can be done with the predicates `retractall` and `assertz`, respectively. Likewise, we should instantiate the input variables we know beforehand with their corresponding symbolic terms and the expected output. The variables in the query are reserved for collecting the answers of the query, namely, the variables in Q and the certainty of the instantiation.

4   Experiments

Looking to showcase our model, we worked with a dataset[1] containing diagnostic measurements as input variables and a diabetes diagnosis as output variables. The collected data is from females aged 21 and above from the Pima Indian population, close to Phoenix, Arizona in the United States of America. This population has a higher than average incidence rate of diabetes. The diagnostic measurements are as follows: *number of pregnancies* (x_1), *glucose* (x_2), *blood pressure* x_3, *skin thickness* (x_4), *insulin level* (x_5), *body mass index* (BMI) (x_6), *diabetes pedigree function* (DPF) (x_7), and *age* (x_8). The binary output variable is the decision class on whether or not the patient has diabetes, 0 and 1 being the negative and positive decision classes, respectively.

Firstly, the values of the variables were normalized so they are in the $[0,1]$ interval. The decision class will be replaced with a set of two numerical values, where the negative decision class is translated into $(0.8, 0.2)$ and the positive decision class is translated into $(0.2, 0.8)$. These values are also used in the sigmoid function in Eq. (2) such that $l_i = 0.2$ and $u_i = 0.8$, which prevent the inverse in Eq. (5) from producing infinite values. Moreover, the slope λ_i was set to 2.0 while the offset h_i was set to 0.

The dataset was divided into a training set used to build the model. The training set contains 80% of the data while the remaining 20% is used to test the FCM-based classifier. The test instances are used to build the knowledge base. As explained in Sect. 2.2, the weights connecting the input neurons are determined as the coefficients of multiple regression models, calculated as shown in Eq. (3). The weights connecting the input neurons with the output ones are calculated using the Moore-Penrose inverse. After the learning phase is done, the FCM-based classifier reported accuracy of 76.62% on the test set, which is in line with the results reported in the literature [16].

As mentioned in Sect. 3.2, we determined the parameters of the Gaussian membership functions manually. Firstly, we obtained the histograms for input variables to visualize the distribution of the activation values, as shown in Fig. 2. To determine appropriate parameters, we looked at the probability density across the histogram. We gave membership functions for sets enclosing activation values with higher probability densities smaller standard deviations and a mean value that is closer to adjacent membership functions. This resulted in the membership functions as shown in Fig. 3. The test instances from the dataset were used to build the knowledge base in Prolog.

As a first scenario, let us suppose we want to find the values for *BloodPressure* and *InsulinLevel*, while the values for the other input variables are known: *Pregnancies* is high, *Glucose* is high, *SkinThickness* is very low, *BMI* is very high, *DPF* is medium, and *Age* is medium. We know that the outcome should be positive. Using this setting, we can write a query fixing these values while asking for the values of *BloodPressure* and *InsulinLevel* as well as the certainty degrees. After running the query, the Prolog program returns that *BloodPressure*

---

[1] https://www.kaggle.com/uciml/pima-indians-diabetes-database.

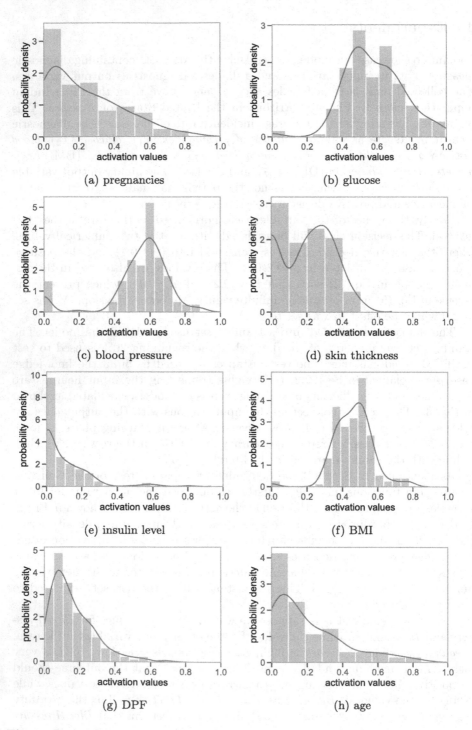

Fig. 2. Probability density functions of input variables. These variables are used to activate the input neurons in the FCM-based model.

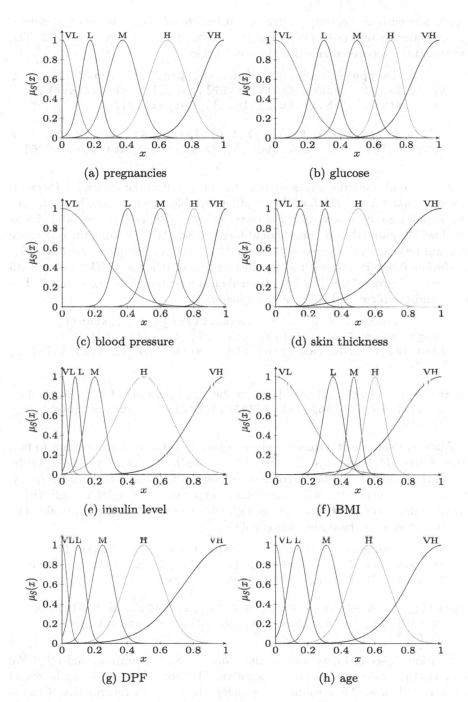

Fig. 3. Gaussian membership functions used to transform the numerical input-output vector into symbolic knowledge representations.

is very low with a certainty degree of 1.0 and *InsulinLevel* is very low with a certainty degree of 0.964. The entire rule has a certainty degree of 0.772. The query and the recovered rule are displayed below.

```
retractall(output()), assertz(output([pos,_])),input([[h,_],[
    h,_],[BloodPressure,CertaintyBP],[vl,_],[InsulinLevel,
    CertaintyIL],[vh,_],[m,_],[m,_], Certainty])

input([[h,0.946],[h,0.834],[vl,1.0],[vl,0.941],[vl,0.964],[vh
    ,0.989],[m,0.91],[m,0.898],0.772]) :- output([pos,0.726])
.
```

As a second scenario, let us suppose we want to find the values for *Pregnancies*, *InsulinLevel*, and *BMI*, while the other variables are known: *Glucose* is very low, *BloodPressure* is low, *SkinThickness* is low, *DPF* is very low, and *Age* is very low. We know the outcome should be negative. After running the query, the program returns that *Pregnancies* is very low with a certainty degree of 0.851, *InsulinLevel* is very low with a certainty degree of 0.964 and *BMI* is low with a certainty degree of 0.812. The entire rule has a certainty degree of 0.907. The query and the recovered rule are given below.

```
retractall(output()), assertz(output([neg,_])),input([[
    Pregnancies,CertaintyPreg],[vl,_],[l,_],[l,_],[
    InsulinLevel,CertaintyIL],[BMI,CertaintyBMI],[vl,_],[vl,_
    ], Certainty])

input([[vl,0.851],[vl,1.0],[l,0.799],[l,0.814],[vl,0.964],[l
    ,0.812],[vl,0.756],[vl,0.892],0.907]) :- output([neg
    ,1.0]).
```

Another example of a query is given below. In this scenario, we want to find *Pregnancies*, *BMI*, and *Age*. The linguistic values for the other variables can be seen in the code below. The outcome should be positive. After running the query, *Pregnancies* is very high with a certainty degree of 0.598, *BMI* is high with a certainty degree of 0.656, and *Age* is high with a certainty degree of 0.569. The certainty degree of the entire rule is 0.428.

```
retractall(output()), assertz(output([pos,_])),input([[
    Pregnancies,CertaintyPreg],[m,_],[m,_],[m,_],[m,_],[BMI,
    CertaintyBMI],[l,_],[Age,CertaintyAge], Certainty])

input([[vh,0.598],[m,0.959],[m,0.9],[m,0.651],[m,0.812],[h
    ,0.656],[l,0.675],[h,0.569],0.428]) :- output([pos
    ,0.552]).
```

In a fourth scenario, we want to find *Glucose*, *Skin Thickness*, and *DPF*. We know that the outcome should be negative. The linguistic values can be found in the code below. After running the query, the program returns that *Glucose* is medium with a certainty degree of 0.728, *Skin Thickness* is medium with a certainty degree of 0.769, and *DPF* is low with a certainty degree of 0.914. The entire rule has a certainty degree of 0.625.

```
retractall(output()), assertz(output([neg,_])),input([[l,_],[
    Glucose,CertaintyGluc],[m,_],[SkinThickness,CertaintySkin
    ],[vl,_],[h,_],[DPF,CertaintyDPF],[l,_], Certainty])
```

```
input([[l,0.876],[m,0.728],[m,0.932],[m,0.769],[vl,0.964],[h
    ,0.72],[l,0.914],[l,0.953],0.625]) :- output([neg,0.668])
```

Figure 4 shows the average membership degrees of the antecedent components of fuzzy rules. Observe that linguistic terms are computed following the max-membership principle, and hence, only the maximal membership values in

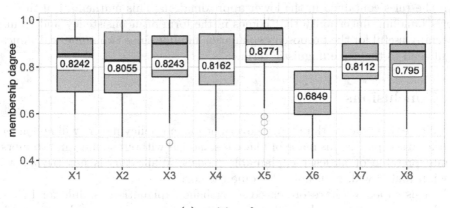

(a) positive class

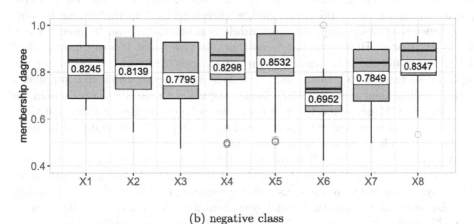

(b) negative class

Fig. 4. Average membership degree values of the antecedent components. These values provide an indicator into how well each antecedent component fits their respective linguistic terms. In this figure, the variables describing the problem are encoded as follows: *number of pregnancies* (X1), *glucose* (X2), *blood pressure* (X3), *skin thickness* (X4), *insulin level* (X5), *body mass index* (BMI) (X6), *diabetes pedigree function* (DPF) (X7), and *age* (X8).

each case are used to compute this statistic. The membership degrees of the antecedent components are used in Eq. (7) to determine the confidence of the fuzzy rules. Overall, the confidence values are acceptable in most cases, although they significantly dispersed across the fuzzy rules.

There is no hesitation that the subsequent research effort should be oriented to improving the certainty of the fuzzy rules. On one hand, we could increase the granularity level, but it would come at the cost of having more linguistic terms. Ideally, we should be able to reach a trade-off between the certainty of the rules and the number of fuzzy sets used the describe the antecedents of the rule. This can be modeled as a multi-objective optimization problem. On the other hand, we could use rough set theory [1] such that we can generate the explanations from the rules contained in the lower approximation. This mathematical theory allows handling uncertainty that comes in the form of inconsistency and seems especially useful for the proposed explanation module since two numerical values might lead to the same linguistic term.

5   Conclusions

We believe that, sooner than later, governments and policymakers will no longer be able to accept systems made of black-box models without significant attempts at interpretable or at least explainable models. While this is not trivial, we envision that it will, eventually, become the norm.

In this paper, we have presented a symbolic explanation module for FCM-based reasoning models that allows producing counterfactual explanations. A set of fuzzy rules is translated into Prolog rules such that we can easily make queries to exploit the implicit knowledge representations. In the current format, the proposed symbolic explanation module is agnostic and can be used for any black-box model. However, that is neither our vision nor the ultimate goal of the research avenue this paper attempted to open. Instead, we prefer for the explanation module to be attached to a reasoning model in which all components have a well-defined meaning while being aligned with the problem domain. In that sense, FCM-based models will continue to be our center of attention since their structural complexity—when modeling problems having many variables— makes it difficult to be understood as a whole.

As a future study, we will focus on encoding the weight matrix into the rules, such that we can use that added information to generate deeper explanations. In that way, our model would not just allow producing counterfactual explanations but also elucidating how the model goes from a state to another. Likewise, we should improve the confidence of the rules. This can be accomplished by increasing the granularity of the symbolic knowledge representations while determining the extent to which each rule conflicts with the others.

References

1. Bello, M., Nápoles, G., Vanhoof, K., Bello, R.: Methods to edit multi-label training sets using rough sets theory. In: Mihálydeák, T., et al. (eds.) IJCRS 2019. LNCS (LNAI), vol. 11499, pp. 369–380. Springer, Cham (2019). https://doi.org/10.1007/978-3-030-22815-6_29
2. Goodman, B., Flaxman, S.: European union regulations on algorithmic decision-making and a "right to explanation". AI Mag. **38**(3), 50–57 (2017)
3. Kosko, B.: Fuzzy cognitive maps. Int. J. Man-Mach. Stud. **24**(1), 65–75 (1986)
4. Lally, A., Fodor, P.: Natural language processing with prolog in the IBM Watson system. Assoc. Logic Programm. (ALP) Newsl. 9 (2011)
5. León, M., Nápoles, G., Bello, R., Mkrtchyan, L., Depaire, B., Vanhoof, K.: Tackling travel behaviour: an approach based on fuzzy cognitive maps. Int. J. Comput. Intell. Syst. **6**(6), 1012–1039 (2013). https://doi.org/10.1080/18756891.2013.816025
6. Mangalathu, S., Hwang, S.H., Jeon, J.S.: Failure mode and effects analysis of RC members based on machine-learning-based SHapley additive explanations (SHAP) approach. Eng. Struct. **219**, 110927 (2020). https://doi.org/10.1016/j.engstruct.2020.110927. http://www.sciencedirect.com/science/article/pii/S0141029620307513
7. Montavon, G., Lapuschkin, S., Binder, A., Samek, W., Müller, K.R.: Explaining nonlinear classification decisions with deep Taylor decomposition. Pattern Recogn. **65**, 211–222 (2017). https://doi.org/10.1016/j.patcog.2016.11.008. http://www.sciencedirect.com/science/article/pii/S0031320316303582
8. Nápoles, G., Leon Espinosa, M., Grau, I., Vanhoof, K., Bello, R.: Fuzzy cognitive maps based models for pattern classification: advances and challenges. In: Pelta, D.A., Cruz Corona, C. (eds.) Soft Computing Based Optimization and Decision Models. SFSC, vol. 360, pp. 83–98. Springer, Cham (2018). https://doi.org/10.1007/978-3-319-64286-4_5
9. Nápoles, G., Jastrzębska, A., Mosquera, C., Vanhoof, K., Homenda, W.: Deterministic learning of hybrid fuzzy cognitive maps and network reduction approaches. Neural Netw. **124**, 258–268 (2020)
10. Nápoles, G., Papageorgiou, E., Bello, R., Vanhoof, K.: Learning and convergence of fuzzy cognitive maps used in pattern recognition. Neural Process. Lett. **45**(2), 431–444 (2017). https://doi.org/10.1007/s11063-016-9534-x
11. Reddy, C.S., Raju, K.: An improved fuzzy approach for COCOMO's effort estimation using Gaussian membership function. J. Softw. **4**(5), 452–459 (2009)
12. Rudin, C.: Stop explaining black box machine learning models for high stakes decisions and use interpretable models instead. Nat. Mach. Intell. **1**(5), 206–215 (2019). https://doi.org/10.1038/s42256-019-0048-x
13. Salmeron, J.L., Froelich, W.: Dynamic optimization of fuzzy cognitive maps for time series forecasting. Knowl.-Based Syst. **105**, 29–37 (2016). https://doi.org/10.1016/j.knosys.2016.04.023. http://www.sciencedirect.com/science/article/pii/S0950705116300752
14. Samek, W., Müller, K.-R.: Towards explainable artificial intelligence. In: Samek, W., Montavon, G., Vedaldi, A., Hansen, L.K., Müller, K.-R. (eds.) Explainable AI: Interpreting, Explaining and Visualizing Deep Learning. LNCS (LNAI), vol. 11700, pp. 5–22. Springer, Cham (2019). https://doi.org/10.1007/978-3-030-28954-6_1

15. Selvaraju, R.R., Cogswell, M., Das, A., Vedantam, R., Parikh, D., Batra, D.: Grad-CAM: Visual explanations from deep networks via gradient-based localization. Int. J. Comput. Vis. **128**(2), 336–359 (2019). https://doi.org/10.1007/s11263-019-01228-7

16. Sisodia, D., Sisodia, D.S.: Prediction of diabetes using classification algorithms. Procedia Comput. Sci. **132**, 1578–1585 (2018). https://doi.org/10.1016/j.procs.2018.05.122. http://www.sciencedirect.com/science/article/pii/S1877050918308548. International Conference on Computational Intelligence and Data Science

17. Wood, D.A., Choubineh, A.: Transparent machine learning provides insightful estimates of natural gas density based on pressure, temperature and compositional variables. J. Nat. Gas Geosci. **5**(1), 33–43 (2020). https://doi.org/10.1016/j.jnggs.2019.12.003. http://www.sciencedirect.com/science/article/pii/S2468256X20300031

18. Zadeh, L.A.: Fuzzy sets. Inf. Control **8**(3), 338–353 (1965)

Overlap Training to Mitigate Inconsistencies Caused by Image Tiling in CNNs

Yu An[1]([⊠]), Qing Ye[2], Jiulin Guo[3], and Ruihai Dong[1]

[1] Insight Centre for Data Analytics, University College Dublin, Dublin, Ireland
yu.an@insight-centre.org
[2] Key Laboratory of Tectonics and Petroleum Resources, Ministry of Education, China University of Geosciences, Wuhan, China
[3] C&C Reservoirs, Brunel House, Reading, UK

Abstract. This paper focuses on the problem of inconsistent predictions of modern convolutional neural networks (CNN) at patch (i.e. sub-image) boundaries. Limited by the graphics processing unit (GPU) resources, image tiling and stitching countermeasure have been applied for most megapixel images, that is, cutting images into overlapping tiles as CNN input, and then stitching CNN outputs together. However, we found that stitched (i.e. recovered) predictions have discontinuous grid-like noise. We propose a simple yet efficient overlap training framework to mitigate the inconsistent prediction at patch boundaries without changing the model architecture while improving the stability, robustness of the model. We have applied our solution to various CNNs (such as U-Net, DeepLab, RCF) and tested them on two real-world datasets. Extensive experiments suggest that the new framework is sufficient in reducing inconsistency and outperform these countermeasures. The source code and coloured figures are made publicly available online at: https://github.com/anyuzoey/Overlap-Training.git.

Keywords: Convolutional neural networks · Computer vision · Image segmentation · Fault recognition

1 Introduction

Convolutional neural networks (CNNs) and its recent variations have led to extraordinary performances in various computer vision tasks. In general, CNN models take image pixel as inputs and use multiple convolutional layers and pooling layers to capture image features. The intermediate layers need to be stored in the CNN calculation process. The memory size required by the model is proportional to the number of input pixels [29]. Limited by the memory capacity of the graphics processing unit (GPU), in many scenarios, CNN cannot directly

Supported by Science Foundation Ireland SFI/12/RC/2289_P2.

use the entire original size image as input, especially megapixel images (e.g. seismic images). There are two main countermeasures: one of them is to down-sample the input image, but it will considerably lose local details. Not suitable for tasks such as fault recognition that make extensive use of local details. Another prevailing countermeasure is to cut out the original size image as sub-images (usually called patches) as model inputs and stitch the outputs.

We found that this image cutting off-dealing-stitching approach will create discontinuous and grid-like noise (see black arrows in Fig. 1) on the stitched out-puts of several trained fault recognition networks. Because the patch predictions on the top, bottom, or left and right are inconsistent, the original continuous geological fault is marked as discontinuous. Geological faults are the planar or gently curved fractures in the earth's crust. The relative displacement of rocks on opposite sides of the fracture is usually related to the occurrence of earth-quakes [11]. Fault recognition is a critical process for seismic data interpreters to understand the subsurface geological structure. For seismic data interpreters, fault recognition (i.e. identify and label certain types of discontinuous reflections) is a manual process, which highly depends on data quality and experience, and usually takes several months.

The discontinuities and grid-like noise greatly affect the user experience of the fault recognition application. A single threshold cannot fix it as it can not effectively distinguish between noise and potential faults among all data. Since the grid-like noise only appears at the boundary position, we call it the boundary effect. These effects are underestimated and rarely discussed in the literature. Only a few relevant studies have suggested methods (proved using their datasets) that might attenuate the boundary effect: use the largest possible patch size [14,22]; pad extra zeros [15,17]; or increase the number of overlapping pixels [14,25]. These methods are either very complicated to use and cannot be widely applied, or add a considerable redundancy and cannot fundamentally solve the problem. We will review and discuss these methods in detail in Sect. 2.

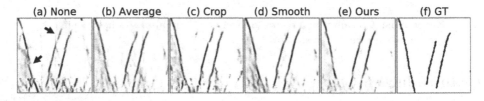

Fig. 1. Examples of different image stitching techniques on the Thebe dataset. (a) None, images are cropped into non-overlapping patches as CNN input. The final pre-diction after stitching can clearly distinguish the traces of image stitching. (b) Average, the prediction of pixels in overlapping areas is averaged. (c) Crop, crop the boundary pixels of the patch according to the number of the overlapping pixels. (d) Smooth, the prediction of each patch first is multiplied by 2D spine window (i.e. position-related 2D weight) (e) Ours (f) Manual interpolation by an expert as ground truth. Coloured vision is available in the code link.

In this paper, we propose a novel overlap training framework to mitigate the boundary effect that we discovered in fault recognition CNNs. The framework uses a simple yet efficient overlap constraint to handle the boundary information better, to improve consistency of CNN prediction in the boundary position, and also the overall performance of the fault recognition application. Our framework obtained the state-of-the-art performance compared with related solutions (see Sect. 4.4 and 4.5).

The rest of this article is organised as follows: Sect. 2 reviews related literature on tiling and stitching techniques, potential causes of boundary effects, and the recommended solutions. Section 3 details our proposed framework, the datasets used and the CNN architectures we tested. In Sect. 4, we provide experimental results and analysis of the proposed method and then summarise in Sect. 5.

2   Related Work

Since the breakthrough of the AlexNet [19] in the 2012 ILSVRC (ImageNet Large-Scale Visual Recognition Challenge), the CNN has achieved the state-of-the-art results in various computer vision tasks (such as image classification [12,31], image segmentation [5–8], edge detection [20,32]). With the development of imaging technology and explosive growth of data, we have encountered more and more large-scale image processing tasks (e.g. remote sensing image processing). Nevertheless, it is unlikely to store large-scale intermediate layers because of the limited GPU resources. For higher accuracy, it is commonly recommended to crop overlapping tiles (i.e. patches) as inputs, and then use averaging [2,24,25] or weighted sum [9,27] or cropping to stitch model predictions. Figure 1 provides an example of different image stitching methods on the fault recognition dataset. Details of the dataset will be introduced later in Sect. 3.1.

Improvements made by applying these image stitching approaches imply that model outputs are not consistent in the overlapping area or more specifically, the boundary area. This situation conflicts with the common assumption that CNN is translation equalvariance or sometimes called translation invariance (that is, CNN can successfully identify the target object, regardless of the position of the object in the image.) [10,16,18]. Moreover, this also means that simple post-processing like image stitching can not fundamentally find and solve the problem.

A few recent studies link this boundary effect with zero padding [14,15,17] and non-unary stride (i.e. stride > 1) operation [3,14] in CNNs. Zero-padding is the default setting for convolutional layers, which pad zeros on the boundary of the input feature map to control output dimensions. If no zero is padded (i.e. 'valid' padding), convolution output will be smaller than the input dimension. 'Same' padding is used to make convolution output remains the same dimensions as input. In convolution layers, boundary pixels are less supported than the relative centre pixels [17]. For instance, a 3 × 3 'same' padding convolution, one output pixel is the dot product between the learnable kernel and corresponding nine pixels in input feature maps. Thus, for the top-left pixel, the corresponding nine pixels contain five zeros. Therefore, when more convolution stacked, zeros are propagated closer and closer to centre pixels, which result in larger boundary effect [17]. For non-unary stride operation, such as 2×2 Max-pooling operation, that is, downsampling the input by selecting the maximum value among four adjacent pixels, will directly lose information and even change output value for shifted inputs.

Some researches recommended using the largest possible patches to reduce boundary effect, because the larger the patch size, the fewer zero-padding pixels compared to the total patch pixels [14,22]. However, the improvement in model accuracy may not be mainly caused by the reduction of zero-padding, but is related to a larger overlapping area. Besides, there are also tasks like our fault recognition application, in which very large patch size may result in a less generalised model.

From the perspective that CNN can exploit absolute spatial location, two state-of-the-art studies discuss similar boundary effects and also point to zero-padding [15,17]. [15] proposed that CNN obtains absolute spatial information through zero-padding to improve accuracy in position-related tasks. Their experiments proved that increase padding value in convolution layer from 0 to 2 could consistent improve model accuracy. Similar but different, [17] proposed that absolute spatial information can be removed by add zero padding. They named this solution as 'FULL' convolution. For the standard 3×3 convolution, 'FULL' convolution is equivalent to padding $= 2$. Authors suggested replacing 'same' padding or 'valid' padding to 'FULL' padding and add extra zero-padding for residual connections to avoid encoding absolute spacial location. This solution is proved to give higher accuracy on image classification tasks and image matching tasks. Although the main conclusions of the two studies conflict, they both agree that extra zero-padding can improve model performance. In this paper, we compared our proposed framework with this zero-padding solution in Sect. 4.4 and achieved better performance. Besides, our framework is a more flexible solution that does not require modification of the model architecture, including the padding settings in convolution layers and the input size.

3   Proposed Framework

In this section, we describe our proposed overlap training framework in detail, see Fig. 2. In general, pixel-level classification problems (e.g. image segmentation) use batches of paired images and masks to train CNNs. The difference between the predictions and the masks are used to update parameters through back-propagation. However, the model trained in this standard approach does not predict consistently at the overlap region of two adjacent patches. We believe that although the absolute position of the target object in the two overlapping patches shifted, the model output should follow the facts, that is, the overlapping region should obtain consistent predictions. Therefore, we propose a constraint to limit the difference between the two predictions in the overlapping region. We construct pairs of overlapping images as inputs and add an overlap loss as the constraint to force the model to predict the overlapping region more consistently. More precisely, in the image preprocessing stage, we prepare pairs of left and right overlapping input images ($Input_{left}$ and $Input_{right}$) and their corresponding masks (GT_{left} and GT_{right}), and the overlapping part accounts for half of the patch size. Thus, $4 \times batchsize$ images are generated at each iteration. A batch of $Input_{left}$ and a batch of $Input_{right}$ are sequentially inputted into one CNN model to obtain predictions $Pred_{left}$ and $Pred_{right}$, respectively. In addition to calculating loss ($loss_{left}$ and $loss_{right}$) between the model prediction and the corresponding masks, we also define and add an $loss_{overlap}$ that will compare the differences between the model predictions in the overlapping area (i.e. $Overlap_{left}$ and $Overlap_{right}$). Here, we introduced two hyper-parameters: N and α, where N means that the overlap loss is added only after the Nth epoch, and α represents the weight of the overlap loss. The total loss l_{total} is the weighted sum of three losses, see Eq. 1.

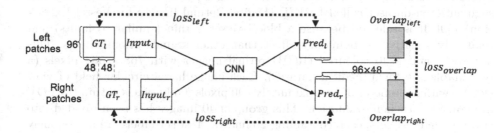

Fig. 2. The overlap training framework

The overlap loss we added may have a certain degree of conflict with the standard loss ($loss_{left}$ and $loss_{right}$). We observe that if the overlap loss is not added, the difference of the predictions in the overlap region between two adjacent patches will increase and then level off. The reason for this phenomenon is that in the early stage of training, the model has not yet learned useful features (weights are close to zeros), resulting in the model output close to zero, just like random noise. Therefore, prematurely adding the overlap loss is equivalent to continuous attack model using a large amount of noise or wrong labels. Thus, the convergence of the model is delayed. However, we also do not recommend adding the overlap loss too late. Firstly, it will make the training time longer. Secondly, one of the purposes of adding overlap loss is to alleviate the overfitting of the model, therefore to improve its generalisation. If the overlap loss is added too late, the model cannot be prevented from overfitting because it is already overfitting. Therefore, we recommend using a hyper-parameter to indicate the appropriate time step to add the overlap loss.

$$loss_{total} = \begin{cases} loss_{left} + loss_{right} + \alpha loss_{overlap}, & epoch > N \\ loss_{left} + loss_{right}, & otherwise \end{cases} \qquad (1)$$

3.1 Datasets

The fault recognition dataset: Thebe is a large-scale 3-dimensional public dataset, which contains the original seismic reflection dataset of the Thebe gas field in the NW shelf of Australia and the corresponding fault labels labelled by experts from Fault Analysis Group, University College Dublin. This dataset contains 1,803 consecutive grey-scale seismic images and corresponding mask image (i.e. fault labels) with height and width of 1,537 and 3,174 pixels. Each seismic image sampled at 12.5-m intervals is a vertical slice of the subsurface. Faults are labelled by polylines and converted to masks with a line width of approximately 8 pixels. First 900 pairs of seismic images and masks are the training set, the following 200 pairs are the validation set, and the last 703 pairs are the test set.

In addition to the primary fault recognition dataset, we also apply our proposed framework on a medical dataset, purely for testing its generalisation ability instead of pursuing a state-of-the-art result. It is a publicly available blood vessel segmentation dataset called DRIVE (Digital Retinal Images for Vessel Extraction) [30]. It is selected because a blood vessel is thin (similar to faults) and relatively sensitive to boundary effect than other segmentation objects. This dataset contains 40 coloured (RGB) retinal images with 768×584 pixels (a reasonable size for a medical dataset). Each image has a circular field of view (FOV) with a diameter of approximately 540 pixels. Only pixels within the FOV are considered when evaluation. This group of 40 images has been divided into training and test sets, each containing 20 images. Test set labels are not publicly available, and test set performance can be acquired by upload prediction to the official website. In our experiment, we split the 20 training images into the train (16 images) and validate set (4 images) for hyper-parameter search.

3.2 Applied Convolutional Neural Networks

For fault recognition, we consider it as either image segmentation or edge detection task. Thus, we apply this framework to these two types of CNNs (image segmentation models: U-Net [23] and DeepLab V3+ [5–8] with a MobileNet V2 [13, 26] encoder, edge detection model: RCF (Richer convolution features) [20]) In this paper, we will observe whether our proposed framework is valid on these three models and whether they have the same improvement trend. We briefly reviewed the three models mentioned above and introduced our modifications.

The U-Net model is a classic image segmentation network, which removes the fully connected layer of the classic VGG16 network [28] as an encoder, and then adds a symmetric decoder and shortcuts to locate the boundary positions accurately. Here, we remove a few convolution layers and reduce feature maps in each convolution layer because our input patch size is much smaller than the original U-Net input size. A sigmoid layer is added at the end of the network to give soft classification outputs range from 0 to 1.

The DeepLab V3+ model is a advanced image segmentation network [8]. It stacks more convolutional layers and uses the atrous spatial pyramid pooling (ASPP) to obtain long-distance information, which implies a larger reception field, thereby improving the accuracy of the model. A larger reception field, however, may lead to a more significant boundary effect. Limited by GPU resources, we select MobileNet V2 as the backbone encoder. Similarly, a sigmoid layer is added to the outputs of this model to give target object probability.

The RCF model is a classic edge detection network, which is also modified from the classic VGG16 network and another edge detection network called HED (Holistic edge detection) [32]. The classic VGG16 network contains five stages of convolution layers divided by four Max-pooling layers and some fully-connected layers. RCF replaces these fully-connected layers by up-sample layers, convolution layers and one sigmoid layer. The model has a total of six outputs, including five prediction maps up-sampled to the input dimension from the feature map obtained from the convolutional layers of each stage, and another prediction map obtained by fusing the five prediction maps. All six feature maps learn parameters by weighted binary cross-entropy. The last output is used as the final prediction output of the model.

3.3 Overlap Loss

Binary cross-entropy (Eq. 2) is used for all three CNN models listed above. l_n stands for loss of the nth pixel, w_n represents the weights. $\hat{y}_n$ stands for model prediction while y_n stands for the ground truth value (0 or 1). Here, w_n is equal to 1 for all pixels (n) in the two segmentation models, while RCF use Eq. 3 to calculate weights. In Eq. 3, Y stands for the total number of pixels of the input image. $|Y_-|$ and $|Y_+|$ represents negative pixels (i.e. label = 0) and positive pixels (i.e. label = 1) respectively.

$$l_n = -w_n \left[y_n \cdot \log \hat{y}_n + (1 - y_n) \cdot \log (1 - \hat{y}_n) \right] \tag{2}$$

$$w_n = \begin{cases} |Y_+|/|Y|, & y_n = 0 \\ |Y_-|/|Y|, & y_n = 1 \end{cases} \tag{3}$$

In our overlap training framework, $loss_{left}$ and $loss_{right}$ in Fig. 2 remain the original binary cross-entropy. Since they are log loss, we define the $loss_{overlap}$ as a log version of mean absolute error (see Eq. 4) so that the range for hyperparameter search should be small. Also, we believe a symmetric loss will be beneficial as the boundary position in one patch is the centre position (i.e. better predicted) in the opposite patch. It can be easily implemented using the detach function in PyTorch, see Eq. 5.

$$logMAE = -log(1 - abs(prediction - target)) \tag{4}$$

$$loss_{overlap} = logMAE(Overlap_{left}, Overlap_{right}.detach()) \\ + logMAE(Overlap_{right}, Overlap_{left}.detach()) \tag{5}$$

4   Experiments

In this section, we first detail the general training settings of the experiments. Then, the evaluation method used is introduced. Finally, three different experiments were designed to systematically and comprehensively test and analyse the performance of our overlap training framework.

4.1   Training Setup

For a fair comparison, model setting like input size (96×96 pixels), overlap size (48 pixels), batch size (128 individual images if without overlap while 64 pairs if with overlap), validation loss monitors: learning rate (lr) scheduler (factor = 0.1, patient = 5) and early stopping scheduler (patient = 10) is consistent among all experiments. Optimiser settings (Adam for segmentation network with initial lr of 0.01, SGD optimiser for RCF with initial lr of 1e–6 and momentum of 0.9, weight decay of 0.0002) is consistent for the same architecture. Unless specified, random seed is 1. All images are recovered by smooth stitching [9] and evaluated on the area of interest. We selected the hyper-parameters N and α that obtained the best validation set results through a grid search. The last layer is used to calculate the overlap loss for the edge detection model.

Thebe dataset is a highly imbalanced dataset. The expert only label faults that they are certain to be geological faults in the area of interest. A sliding window of size 96×96 with a stride of 48 pixels and a filter (fault pixels $> 3\%$) are used to generate the left patches. The corresponding right patches are obtained by right shifting left patches 48 pixels. Overall, $181,029 \times 2$ and $64,317 \times 2$ pairs (i.e. image and mask) of patches as the training set and the validation set, respectively.

For the DRIVE dataset, we divide the original training set (20 images) into the train (16) and validation (4) set. We augment each instance three times using basic methods: horizontal flip, vertical flip, rotate $180°$. We also augment each training instance using the commonly used Contrast-Limited Adaptive Histogram Equalization (CLAHE) transform [4,21]. A sliding window of 96×96 pixels with a stride of 24 pixels is used to generate more patches. Overall, $33,440 \times 2$ half overlap pairs of patches and $6,688 \times 2$ pairs of patches are generated for training and validating sets. Since DRIVE dataset is an RGB dataset, we modify U-Net and DeepLab V3+ to take 3 channel input instead of 1 channel. We did not modify model architecture or generate more training patches to optimise the test set performance.

4.2   Evaluation Metrics

We apply the evaluation method used by the public edge detection BSDS500 dataset [1], which can give comprehensive summarise of soft classification (0 to 1 probability) performance. Given 99 thresholds, this evaluation method calculates precision, recall, F1 score 99 times for each test set image. Thereby, eight evaluation results can be obtained, which are Threshold, Recall, Precision, fixed contour threshold (ODS), Best_Recall, Best_Precision, per-image best threshold (OIS), average precision (AP). The first four metrics are optimal on the entire test set level while the next three represents the average of the per-image optimal precision, recall, F1 score, respectively. AP is the area under the precision-recall curve (AUCPR). Three global evaluation results ODS, OIS, AP, are the primary evaluation metrics for comparison. The ground-truth of the DRIVE test set, however, is not disclosed, test set evaluation result (i.e. mean, maximum, minimum F1 score) is obtained by uploading binary masks.

4.3 Exp1: Can Overlap Training Improve Accuracy, Stability?

The primary focus of this framework is to improve the performance of our fault recognition application. Here, we hypothesis that using overlap training framework can improve model accuracy and stability. Model stability is evaluated by the standard deviation of the three random initialisation. The benchmarks for this experiment (named with the suffix of '_w/o') are the models that have not been trained with our framework. The experimental group, that is, the models obtained by overlap training, are named suffix of '_w'.

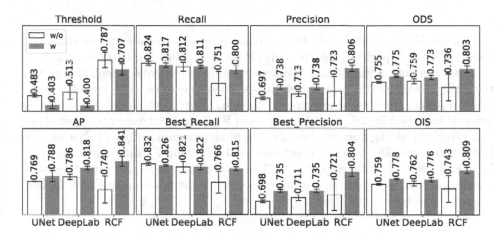

Fig. 3. Exp1: Thebe test set performance

According to Fig. 3, overlap training can bring consistent accuracy improvements among the three architectures. For both image segmentation architectures (U-Net and DeepLab), the use of overlap training framework has improved all global metrics, including ODS by about 2.7% and 1.8%, OIS by 2.5% and 1.9%, and AP by 2.5% and 4.1%. The overlap training framework is particularly prominent for the improvement of the model RCF. The two recall metrics and the two precision metrics are significantly improved by approximately 6.5% and 11.5%, respectively. These improvements lead to a significant improvement of the global evaluation metrics ODS and OIS by approximately 9%, and metric AP rise from

0.74 to 0.841, soaring by almost 14%. Besides, our framework also improves model stability, which is proved by the consistent decreases of standard deviations. According to visual examples in Fig. 4, our framework can provide cleaner predictions even when compared to smooth stitching.

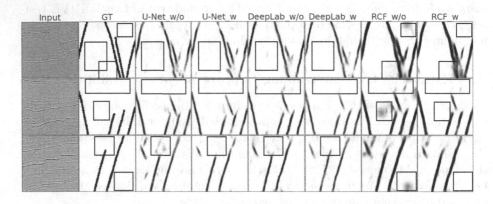

Fig. 4. Exp1: Three Thebe test set examples of the Thebe dataset.

To test the generalisation ability of our proposed framework, we also perform the same experiment on the DRIVE dataset. Since the DRIVE dataset is an image semantic segmentation problem, we only tested two segmentation architectures, namely U-Net and DeepLab. As shown in Table 1, for model U-Net, overlap training increases the average F1 value by 4%, in which the maximum F1 value is increased by 2%, and the minimum F1 value is increased by more than 7%. Overlap training does not improve DeepLab as significantly as U-Net on the DRIVE dataset. The average, maximum, and minimum F1 values are improved by 1%, 0.2%, and 0.8%, respectively. This experiment once again validates our conclusion that using overlap training framework can train models with higher accuracy and better robustness.

Table 1. Exp1: DRIVE test set performance

Model	F1 mean	F1 max	F1 min
U-Net_w/o	0.7650	0.8318	0.6389
U-Net_w	**0.7984**	**0.8492**	**0.6858**
DeepLab_w/o	0.7829	0.8313	0.7628
DeepLab_w	**0.7905**	**0.8329**	**0.7688**

4.4 Exp2: How Overlap Training Affect Boundary Inconsistency?

We designed a mean absolute error versus distance experiment to investigate how the overlap training framework improves the boundary effect and how it performs compared to the state-of-the-art solution. We define the distance is the maximum value of the horizontal and vertical distance from the patch centre, see Fig. 5. Here, we use all non-overlap patches from the area of interest of the Thebe test set. For each architecture, the baseline (i.e. no overlap training) is drawn with a dashed line, and the model trained with overlap framework is shown with a solid line, see Fig. 6. The dot lines, which named with "fullconv", are the state-of-the-art solution suggested by the related work [15,17]. The "fullconv" solution set zero-padding = 2 for every standard 3×3 convolution and pad extra zeros before all residual connections. Due to the large number of residual connections used in the DeepLab MobileNet v2 [26], change to "fullconv" solution is very complicated, so we have not modified this architecture.

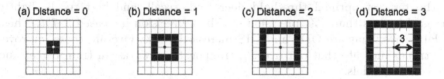

Fig. 5. Exp2: An 8×8 pixels patch example of distance masks. The distance represents $Max(h_i, v_j)$, where h_i and v_j is the horizontal and vertical distance between pixel (i, j) to the patch centre (i.e. the dot). The pixels marked black are the pixels with the same corresponding distance from the centre of the patch. For each distance, the mean absolute error of all test set patches on the corresponding pixels is calculated.

According to Fig. 6, our overlap training method, obtained the lowest mean absolute error on all three architectures, especially at the patch boundary (i.e. around 30 pixels away from patch centre). Compared with the "FULL" convolution solution, our overlap training solution not only can easier apply to different models but also achieved lower mean absolute error.

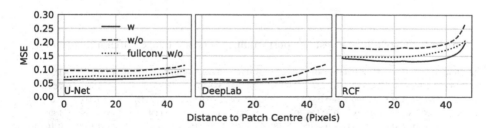

Fig. 6. Exp2: mean absolute error versus the distance to the centre of the patch on the three models: U-Net (left), DeepLab(middle), RCF(right)

4.5   Exp3: Is Overlap Training Better Than Stitching?

We hypothesis that our overlap training framework improves consistently across different image stitching methods. We evaluate this hypothesis on both the dataset and DRIVE dataset using architecture U-Net. According to Table 2 and 3, overlap training consistently improves test set performance among different image stitching methods, in which apply overlap training on crop stitching increase performance the most. In Table 2, overlap training significantly improves the minimum F1 score by 7.339%, 16.886%, 20.937% when applying smooth stitching, average stitching, crop stitching, respectively. Meanwhile, improve the maximum F1 score by 1–2% and improve the average F1 score by 2–6%. The significant improvements on the minimum F1 score indicate our framework is more robust to outlier images.

Similarly, different image stitching method also improves Thebe test set performance, see Table 3. Although the image stitching method is different. The trends for all metrics except AP are the same. When applying overlap training, the test set optimal threshold decreased, recall, and best recall slightly decreased by less than 1%, precision and best precision increased 3 7%. Thus, two F1 scores, that are ODS and OIS increased 1–3%. Overall, these improvement trends indicate that our overlap training framework can train better and more robust models.

Table 2. Exp3: DRIVE test set performance across 3 image stitching method

Method	Model	**F1 mean**	F1 max	F1 min
Smooth	U-Net_w/o	0.7650	0.8318	0.6389
	U-Net_w	+4.366%	+2.095%	+7.339%
Average	U-Net_w/o	0.7729	0.8385	0.6008
	U-Net_w	+2.424%	+1.110%	+16.886%
Crop	U-Net_w/o	0.7496	0.8234	0.5805
	U-Net_w	+6.290%	+2.950%	+20.937%

Table 3. Exp3: Thebe test set performance across 3 image stitching method

Method	Model	Threshold	Recall	Precision	ODS	Best_Recall	Best_Precision	OIS	AP
Smooth	U-Net_w/o	0.4900	0.8288	0.6919	0.7542	0.8367	0.6929	0.7580	0.7691
	U-Net_4_0.5	-24.490%	-0.334%	+5.294%	+2.656%	-0.910%	+5.344%	+2.416%	-0.390%
Average	U-Net_w/o	0.4500	0.8112	0.6955	0.7489	0.8221	0.6943	0.7528	0.7898
	U-Net_4_0.5	-24.444%	-0.250%	+3.585%	+1.779%	-0.348%	+3.339%	+1.618%	+0.164%
Crop	U-Net_w/o	0.5100	0.8292	0.6639	0.7374	0.8400	0.6638	0.7416	0.7102
	U-Net_4_0.5	-23.529%	-1.012%	+7.650%	+3.618%	-0.937%	+7.014%	+3.353%	-1.866%

5   Conclusion

In this paper, we focus on reducing the boundary effect discovered in the fault recognition application. The boundary effect caused by inconsistent predictions between adjacent overlapping tiles. A simple yet effective overlap training framework is proposed. This framework reduces the boundary effect by preparing pairs of left and right overlapping input patches and adding a constraint on the prediction difference of overlapping positions. Extensive experiments have proved that our framework can provide consistent performance improvements on various CNNs (such as U-Net, DeepLab, RCF) and different domain datasets (such as Thebe, DRIVE). Finally, compared with state-of-the-art solutions that deal with the boundary effect, our overlap training framework is not only easier to apply to different models but also achieved smaller error.

References

1. Arbeláez, P., Maire, M., Fowlkes, C., Malik, J.: Contour detection and hierarchical image segmentation. IEEE Trans. Pattern Anal. Mach. Intell. **33**(5), 898–916 (2011). https://doi.org/10.1109/TPAMI.2010.161
2. Audebert, N., Le Saux, B., Lefèvre, S.: Semantic segmentation of earth observation data using multimodal and multi-scale deep networks. In: Lai, S.-H., Lepetit, V., Nishino, K., Sato, Y. (eds.) ACCV 2016. LNCS, vol. 10111, pp. 180–196. Springer, Cham (2017). https://doi.org/10.1007/978-3-319-54181-5_12
3. Azulay, A., Weiss, Y.: Why do deep convolutional networks generalize so poorly to small image transformations? J. Mach. Learn. Res. **20**, 1–25 (2019)
4. Buslaev, A., Parinov, A., Khvedchenya, E., Iglovikov, V.I., Kalinin, A.A.: Albumentations: fast and flexible image augmentations (2018)
5. Chen, L.C., Papandreou, G., Kokkinos, I., Murphy, K., Yuille, A.L.: Semantic image segmentation with deep convolutional nets and fully connected CRFs (2014)
6. Chen, L.C., Papandreou, G., Kokkinos, I., Murphy, K., Yuille, A.L.: Deeplab: semantic image segmentation with deep convolutional nets, atrous convolution, and fully connected CRFs (2016)
7. Chen, L.C., Papandreou, G., Schroff, F., Adam, H.: Rethinking atrous convolution for semantic image segmentation (2017)
8. Chen, L.-C., Zhu, Y., Papandreou, G., Schroff, F., Adam, H.: Encoder-decoder with atrous separable convolution for semantic image segmentation. In: Ferrari, V., Hebert, M., Sminchisescu, C., Weiss, Y. (eds.) ECCV 2018. LNCS, vol. 11211, pp. 833–851. Springer, Cham (2018). https://doi.org/10.1007/978-3-030-01234-2_49
9. Chevalier, G.: Smoothly-blend-image-patches (2017). https://github.com/Vooban/Smoothly-Blend-Image-Patches
10. Cohen, T.S., Welling, M.: Group equivariant convolutional networks (2016)
11. Fossen, H.: Structural Geology. Cambridge University Press (2010). https://doi.org/10.1017/CBO9780511777806
12. He, K., Zhang, X., Ren, S., Sun, J.: Deep residual learning for image recognition (2015)
13. Howard, A.G., et al.: MobileNets: efficient convolutional neural networks for mobile vision applications (2017)

14. Huang, B., Reichman, D., Collins, L.M., Bradbury, K., Malof, J.M.: Tiling and stitching segmentation output for remote sensing: basic challenges and recommendations (2018)
15. Islam, M.A., Jia, S., Bruce, N.D.B.: How much position information do convolutional neural networks encode? (2020)
16. Kauderer-Abrams, E.: Quantifying translation-invariance in convolutional neural networks (2017)
17. Kayhan, O.S., van Gemert, J.C.: On translation invariance in CNNs: convolutional layers can exploit absolute spatial location (2020)
18. Kondor, R., Trivedi, S.: On the generalization of equivariance and convolution in neural networks to the action of compact groups (2018)
19. Krizhevsky, A., Sutskever, I., Hinton, G.E.: ImageNet classification with deep convolutional neural networks. In: Proceedings of the 25th International Conference on Neural Information Processing Systems, vol. 1, pp. 1097–1105. NIPS-12, Curran Associates Inc., Red Hook, NY, USA (2012)
20. Liu, Y., Cheng, M.M., Hu, X., Wang, K., Bai, X.: Richer convolutional features for edge detection (2016)
21. Luo, Z., Zhang, Y., Zhou, L., Zhang, B., Luo, J., Wu, H.: Micro-vessel image segmentation based on the AD-UNet model. IEEE Access **7**, 143402–143411 (2019)
22. Reina, G.A., Panchumarthy, R., Thakur, S.P., Bastidas, A., Bakas, S.: Systematic evaluation of image tiling adverse effects on deep learning semantic segmentation. Front. Neurosci. **14**, 65 (2020). https://doi.org/10.3389/fnins.2020.00065. https://www.frontiersin.org/articles/10.3389/fnins.2020.00065
23. Ronneberger, O., Fischer, P., Brox, T.: U-Net: convolutional networks for biomedical image segmentation. In: Navab, N., Hornegger, J., Wells, W.M., Frangi, A.F. (eds.) MICCAI 2015. LNCS, vol. 9351, pp. 234–241. Springer, Cham (2015). https://doi.org/10.1007/978-3-319-24574-4_28
24. Roth, H.R., et al.: An application of cascaded 3D fully convolutional networks for medical image segmentation (2018)
25. Saito, S., Yamashita, T., Aoki, Y.: Multiple object extraction from aerial imagery with convolutional neural networks. Electron. Imaging **2016**(10), 1–9 (2016)
26. Sandler, M., Howard, A., Zhu, M., Zhmoginov, A., Chen, L.C.: MobileNetV2: inverted residuals and linear bottlenecks (2018)
27. Shi, Y., Wu, X., Fomel, S.: SaltSeg: automatic 3D salt segmentation using a deep convolutional neural network. Interpretation **7**, SE113–SE122 (2019). https://doi.org/10.1190/int-2018-0235.1
28. Simonyan, K., Zisserman, A.: Very deep convolutional networks for large-scale image recognition (2014)
29. Siu, K., Stuart, D.M., Mahmoud, M., Moshovos, A.: Memory requirements for convolutional neural network hardware accelerators. In: 2018 IEEE International Symposium on Workload Characterization (IISWC), pp. 111–121. IEEE, Raleigh, NC (2018)
30. Staal, J., Abramoff, M., Niemeijer, M., Viergever, M., Ginneken, B.: Ridge-based vessel segmentation in color images of the retina. IEEE Trans. Med. Imaging **23**, 501–9 (2004). https://doi.org/10.1109/TMI.2004.825627
31. Tan, M., Le, Q.V.: EfficientNet: rethinking model scaling for convolutional neural networks (2019)
32. Xie, S., Tu, Z.: Holistically-nested edge detection (2015)

The Use of Max-Sat for Optimal Choice of Automated Theory Repairs

Marius Urbonas, Alan Bundy$^{(\boxtimes)}$, Juan Casanova, and Xue Li

University of Edinburgh, Edinburgh, UK
marius.urbonas.edu@gmail.com, A.Bundy@ed.ac.uk

Abstract. The ABC system repairs faulty Datalog theories using a combination of abduction, belief revision and conceptual change via reformation. Abduction and Belief Revision add/delete axioms or delete/add preconditions to rules, respectively. Reformation repairs them by changing the *language* of the faulty theory. Unfortunately, the ABC system overproduces repair suggestions. Our aim is to prune these suggestions to leave only a Pareto front of the optimal ones. We apply an algorithm for solving Max-Sat problems, which we call *the Partial Max-Sat algorithm*, to form this Pareto front.

Keywords: Faulty logical theory repair · Max-Sat · Reformation · Belief revision · Abduction · Datalog theories · Automated theorem proving

1 Introduction

We model the environment as a logical theory. Such a theory will need to be repaired when: errors are detected; the environment changes; or it needs to be re-tuned to cope with new tasks. The ABC system repairs faulty logical theories [9]. It is given a theory, $\mathbb{T}$, as a set of axioms in the decidable logic Datalog [2], and some observations $\mathbb{S}$, represented as a pair of sets of ground propositions. One set, $\mathcal{T}(\mathbb{S})$, is of propositions observed to be true of the environment and the other, $\mathcal{F}(\mathbb{S})$, of those observed to be false. $\mathbb{T}$ is used to make predictions about the environment. When these predictions conflict with the observations in $\mathbb{S}$, the ABC system applies a sequence of repairs to $\mathbb{T}$ until it is fault free. ABC is unique in repairing the *language* of $\mathbb{T}$ as well as the axioms.

$\mathbb{T}$'s predictions are wrong if it proves something in $\mathcal{F}(\mathbb{S})$ (incompatibility) or fails to prove something in $\mathcal{T}(\mathbb{S})$ (insufficiency). The ABC system then tries to repair $\mathbb{T}$ either by adding/deleting axioms, deleting/adding preconditions to rules

M. Urbonas was funded by a studentship from the Student Awards Agency Scotland, A. Bundy was funded by EPSRC grant F14R10199 and J. Casanova by an EPSRC CDT in Data Science and a Brainnwave studentship. We are grateful to Joshua Knowles for suggesting this project, and to several anonymous reviewers for suggestions that improved the paper.

M. Bramer and R. Ellis (Eds.): SGAI-AI 2020, LNAI 12498, pp. 49–63, 2020.
https://doi.org/10.1007/978-3-030-63799-6_4

or changing $\mathbb{T}$'s language. Language changes are implemented by reformation [1] and consist of splitting/merging predicates or constants, or adding/deleting arguments of predicates. Unfortunately, ABC produces too many repair options. In this paper, we describe and evaluate the use of Partial Max-Sat to detect and prune sub-optimal repairs. *Optimal repairs*, are those that minimise the number of any remaining or newly introduced faults. Our hypothesis then is:

> *Our Partial Max-Sat based algorithm prunes sub-optimal repairs from ABC's output. It usually terminates successfully with a significantly smaller set of fault-free, optimal repaired theories.*

The results supporting this claim are discussed in Sect. 5.

Note that a Pareto-front is required because there are conflicting requirements on the repair process. Repairing an incompatibility reduces the number of theorems in order to remove the false one. Repairing an insufficiency, on the other hand, increases the number of theorems to add the true but unprovable one. So, there may be multiple incomparable and conflicting optimal repairs.

Several of the algorithms we use have worst-case exponential complexity in time and/or space. These complexities do not compound and our scaling experiment at the end of Sect. 2.4 shows a quadratic time complexity.

The ABC system is not intended to be a stand-alone system, but to be a component of a larger system, for instance, with sensors, planners, actuators, etc. The wider context will help address some of the current gaps in ABC, e.g., Where do the observations come from? How to choose the best optimal, fault-free repairs? How to assign meaningful names to newly created concepts?

2   Background

We first describe the ABC system. We define: what we mean by a fault; the Datalog theories that ABC repairs; SL Resolution, which ABC uses for deduction; the repair operations it uses; and we illustrate the overproduction problem that this paper addresses.

2.1   Faults as Reasoning Failures

Both incompatibility and insufficiency arise from reasoning failures: mismatches between the theorems of a theory $\mathbb{T}$ and the observations of the environment $\langle \mathcal{T}(\mathbb{S}), \mathcal{F}(\mathbb{S}) \rangle$. A *ground proposition* is a formula of the form $P(C_1, \ldots, C_n)$, where P is an n-ary predicate and the C_is are constants. So, ideally:

$$R \in \mathcal{T}(\mathbb{S}) \implies \mathbb{T} \vdash R \qquad R \in \mathcal{F}(\mathbb{S}) \implies \mathbb{T} \not\vdash R$$

That is, the true ground propositions are theorems of $\mathbb{T}$ and the false ones are not. The language of $\mathbb{T}$ is given in Definition 2 and the inference system in Sect. 2.3.

Definition 1 (Incompatible and Insufficient)

Incompatible: $\mathbb{T}$ *is* incompatible *with* $\mathbb{S}$ *iff* $\exists R.\ \mathbb{T} \vdash R \wedge R \in \mathcal{F}(\mathbb{S})$.
  Insufficient: $\mathbb{T}$ *is* insufficient *for* $\mathbb{S}$ *iff* $\exists R.\ \mathbb{T} \nvdash R \wedge R \in \mathcal{T}(\mathbb{S})$.

The ABC system detects and repairs both kinds of faults.

2.2 Datalog Theories

To ensure termination of proof search, it is convenient to limit the ABC System to a decidable logic. Datalog theories are not only decidable but are sufficiently expressive to admit a wide range of practical applications. Although reformation has been implemented for richer logics [1,11]. Datalog is a logic programming language consisting of Horn clauses in which there are no functions except constants. We represent clauses in Kowalski normal form: an implication between a conjunction of the negated propositions and a disjunction of the positive propositions, i.e., in Kowalski normal form, a clause: $\neg Q_1 \vee \ldots \vee \neg Q_m \vee R_1 \vee \ldots \vee R_n$ is represented as:

$$Q_1 \wedge \ldots \wedge Q_m \implies R_1 \vee \ldots \vee R_n$$

In Horn clauses $n = 0$ or $n = 1$, so they fit one of the four forms in Definition 2.

Definition 2 (Datalog Formulae)
Let the language of a Datalog theory $\mathbb{T}$ be a triple $\langle \mathcal{P}, \mathcal{C}, \mathcal{V} \rangle$, where $\mathcal{P}$ are the propositions, $\mathcal{C}$ are the constants and $\mathcal{V}$ are the variables. We will adopt the convention that variables are written in lower case, and constants and predicates start with a capital letter[1]. A proposition is a formula of the form $P(t_1, \ldots, t_n)$, where $t_j \subset \mathcal{C} \cup \mathcal{V}$ for $1 \leq j \leq n$, i.e., there are no compound terms. Let $R \in \mathcal{P}$ and $Q_i \in \mathcal{P}$ for $0 \leq i \leq m$ in $\mathbb{T}$. R is called the head of the clause and the conjunction of the Q_is forms the body.

Implication: $(Q_1 \wedge \ldots \wedge Q_m) \implies R$. *These usually represent the rules of* $\mathbb{T}$.
Assertion: $\implies R$. *These usually represent the facts of* $\mathbb{T}$.
Goals: $Q_1 \wedge \ldots \wedge Q_m \implies$. *These usually arise from the negation of the conjecture to be proved and from subsequent subgoals in a derivation.*
Empty Clause: $\implies$. *This represents false, which is the target of a refutation-style proof. Deriving it, therefore, represents success in proving a conjecture.*

Repairs operate on the language of $\mathbb{T}$ and on both its implications and assertions.
  The Datalog *safety* condition requires that every variable that appears in the head of a clause also appears in the body. Variables in the head but not the body are called *orphans*[2]. There are other Datalog restrictions, but these are to make

---

[1] The opposite of the Prolog convention.
[2] Although orphans cannot appear in a well-formed Datalog theory, we define them here because they may be created temporarily during the repair process, so must be identified and then eliminated by subsequent repairs.

it behave efficiently as a programming language and we do not need to adopt them. As we will see, despite these restrictions, Datalog is sufficiently expressive for many practical applications.

A small Datalog theory is given in Example 1. The axioms assert that all birds can fly and are feathered, penguins are birds, and Tweety and Polly are both birds.

Example 1 (Tweety Theory). $\mathbb{T}_{Tw}$ *consists of the following set of axioms:*

$$Bird(x) \implies Fly(x) \tag{1}$$
$$Bird(x) \implies Feathered(x)$$
$$Penguin(y) \implies Bird(y) \tag{2}$$
$$\implies Penguin(Tweety)$$
$$\implies Bird(Polly) \tag{3}$$

2.3   Deduction by SL Resolution

Deduction in Datalog is decidable but exponential. So, if there is no proof of a conjecture, the search will eventually terminate without success, so we can be sure that the conjecture is not a theorem. Such finite failure is important for detecting insufficiencies, so was one of the technical reasons for choosing Datalog.

However, if the minimal proof is long then the search for it could exhaust the available resources. Fortunately, in many practical applications, the number of rules is small compared to the facts[3]. So proofs are quite short, even when the number of axioms is large. Resolution proofs work by refutation: the conjecture to be proved is negated and added to the axioms. If the empty clause, $\implies$, is derived then the conjecture has been proved by *reductio ad absurdum*. In Horn clauses, the negated conjecture takes the form of a goal clause. For deduction, we use SL Resolution [8], a deductive rule that is particularly well suited to fault diagnosis. A single SL Resolution step takes the following form:

$$\frac{\bigwedge_{k=1}^{i-1} R_k \wedge \boxed{R_i} \wedge \bigwedge_{k=i+1}^{n} R_k \implies}{(\bigwedge_{k=1}^{i-1} R_k \wedge \bigwedge_{k=1}^{m} Q_k \wedge \bigwedge_{k=i+1}^{n} R_k)\sigma \implies} \quad \bigwedge_{k=1}^{m} Q_k \implies \boxed{P} \tag{4}$$

where the highlighted $\boxed{R_i}$ is the selected goal, the highlighted $\boxed{P}$ is the rule head it is resolved with and σ is the most general substitution of terms for variables that will make P and R_i identical. Note that, to prevent the same variable appearing in both the selected proposition and the head of the axiom, the variables in the axiom should be renamed to new variables. To aid readability, we will do this conservatively.

---

[3] Personal communication from Frank van Harmelen. Based on the LOD-a-lot survey of the Linked Open Data cloud, he estimates that of 23.8 billion unique statements only 565 million could be classified as rules - the rest being facts, i.e., rules make up just under 2% of the total. For more detail, see https://frankvanharmelen.home. blog/2020/07/13/2-makes-all-the-difference-on-the-lod-cloud/ Accessed 14 July 20.

A SL Resolution refutation on Horn clauses takes the form of a linear sequence of SL Resolutions steps (4) in which a goal in each goal clause is resolved with either the head of an implication (rule) or an assertion (fact). This has the advantage that we can apply any repair directly to the axiom involved in either the current or an earlier SL Resolution step in the current branch, so we do not need to inherit the repair back up through derived clauses to an axiom. This advantage is inherited by restricting to Datalog, as all its formulae are Horn clauses, which is the second technical reason for choosing Datalog.

Example 2 uses SL Resolution to infer $Fly(Tweety)$. The highlighting is explained in Sect. 2.4.

Example 2. *We use* $\mathbb{T}_{Tw}$ *from Example* 1.

$$
\cfrac{\cfrac{\cfrac{Fly(Tweety) \implies}{\boxed{Bird(Tweety)} \implies}}{Penguin(Tweety) \implies}}{\implies}
\quad
\begin{array}{l}
Bird(x) \implies Fly(x) \\
Penguin(y) \implies \boxed{Bird(y)} \\
\implies Penguin(Tweety)
\end{array}
\tag{5}
$$

2.4 Repair Operations

Incompatibility and insufficiency faults are diagnosed and repaired in a dual way. $\mathcal{F}(\mathbb{S})$ and $\mathcal{T}(\mathbb{S})$ are both finite sets. The ABC system tries to prove each member of these sets. If a member of $\mathcal{F}(\mathbb{S})$ is proved then we have discovered an incompatibility. Similarly, if a member of $\mathcal{T}(\mathbb{S})$ is not proved then we have discovered an insufficiency. Incompatibilities can be repaired by blocking the unwanted proof. Insufficiencies can be repaired by unblocking a wanted, but failed proof.

The repair operations used by the ABC system are listed in Definitions 3 and 4. They are drawn from the literature on abduction and belief revision, plus our own work on reformation. Note that a single repair application may not produce a fault-free theory. Several applications may be required.

New applications, however, occasionally reveal the opportunity or necessity of new kinds of repair operations or the generalisation of existing operations. So, the space of repair operations seems open-ended and we make no claim to have exhausted the possibilities. In fact, given the unbounded nature of ingenuity, we doubt that an exhaustive classification of repair operations exists or, even if one did, that it could be *proved* to be exhaustive.

Definition 3 (Repair Operations for Incompatibility). *In the case of incompatibility, the unwanted proof can be blocked by causing any of the resolution steps to fail. Suppose the targeted resolution step is between a goal* $P(s_1, \ldots, s_n)$ *and an axiom Body* $\implies$ $P(t_1, \ldots, t_n)$, *where each* s_i *and* t_i *pair can be unified. Possible repair operations are as follows:*

Belief Revision 1: *Delete the targeted axiom.*

Belief Revision 2: *Add an additional precondition to the body of an earlier rule axiom which will become an unprovable subgoal in the unwanted proof.*

Reformation 1: *Rename P in the targeted axiom to the new predicate P'.*

Reformation 2: *Increase the arity of all occurrences P in the axioms by one. Ensure, recursively, that the new arguments, s_{n+1} and t_{n+1}, in the targeted occurrence of P, are not unifiable.*

Reformation 3: *For some i, suppose s_i is C. Since s_i and t_i unify, t_i is either C or a variable. Change t_i to the new constant C'.*

Definition 4 (Repair Operations for Insufficiency). *In the case of insufficiency, the wanted but failed proof can be unblocked by causing a currently failing resolution step to succeed. Suppose the chosen resolution step is between a goal $P(s_1, \ldots, s_m)$ and an axiom $Body \implies P'(t_1, \ldots, t_n)$, where either $P \neq P'$ or, for some i, s_i and t_i cannot be unified. Possible repair operations are:*

Abduction 1: *Add a new axiom whose head unifies with the goal $P(s_1, \ldots, s_m)$.*

Abduction 2: *Locate the rule whose body proposition created this goal and delete this proposition from the rule.*

Reformation 4: *Replace $P'(t_1, \ldots, t_n)$ in the axiom with $P(s_1, \ldots, s_m)$.*

Reformation 5: *Suppose s_i and t_i are not unifiable. Remove the ith argument from all occurrences of P'.*

Reformation 6: *If s_i and t_i are not unifiable, then they are unequal constants, say, C and C'. Either (a) rename all occurrences of C' in the axioms to C or (b) replace the offending occurrence of C' in the targeted axiom by a new variable.*

Note that we disallow repairs that would change $\mathbb{S}$. This is because $\mathbb{S}$ consists of *observations* of the environment. Our goal is to repair the theory $\mathbb{T}$ so that it predicts our observations $\mathbb{S}$ of the environment - not the other way around. There is also the practical consideration that if a predicate, say, $P(C) \in \mathcal{T}(\mathbb{S})$, were changed to, say, $P(C, Normal)$ and $P(C, Abnormal)$ then we would have no basis to say whether either of them belonged to $\mathcal{T}(\mathbb{S})$ or $\mathcal{F}(\mathbb{S})$. This would make it difficult to track the progress of a sequence of repairs. This restriction is implemented by a mechanism that protects nominated predicates and constants from being changed by repairs [9].

A repair of an incompatibility can be illustrated with $\mathbb{T}_{Tw}$ from Example 1 and the refutation in Example 2. Suppose we observe that $Tweety$ cannot fly, i.e., that $Fly(Tweety) \in \mathcal{F}(\mathbb{S})$. Since refutation Example 2 proves $Fly(Tweety)$, we have an incompatibility. Suppose we decide to break the unwanted refutation Example 2 at the highlighted resolution step. One repair suggestion is to apply Reformation 2 from Definition 3. This will give the repaired theory $\nu(\mathbb{T}_{Tw})^4$:

---

[4] Pronounced 'new $\mathbb{T}_{Tw}$'.

$$Bird(x, \boxed{Normal}) \implies Fly(x)$$
$$Bird(x, \boxed{y}) \implies Feathered(x)$$
$$Penguin(y) \implies Bird(y, \boxed{Abnormal})$$
$$\implies Penguin(Tweety)$$
$$\implies Bird(Polly, \boxed{Normal})$$

where *Normal* and *Abnormal* are two new constants. $Fly(Tweety)$ is no longer a theorem of this repaired theory.

The naming of these two new constants was suggested by the observation that new constants introduced by repair Reformation 2, i.e. by giving P a new argument, often distinguish two kinds of P, where the abnormal kind was from the axiom in the now broken resolution step.

These repair operations have been applied to a wide range of examples, some of which can be found in Table 1. In addition, we have evaluated the scalability of the ABC system by applying it to the alignment of two commercial databases with sample sizes up to 1020 entries[5]. Known misalignments were put into $\mathcal{F}(\mathbb{S})$ and the remainder into $\mathcal{T}(\mathbb{S})$. The time taken to find all repairs for a sample was shown to be a quadratic function of the size of the sample, so the ABC system was shown experimentally to have a feasible computational complexity.

2.5   Overproduction of Repair Suggestions

The main problem with the theory repair mechanism outlined in Sect. 2.4, is overproduction, i.e., it makes too many repair suggestions. *The contribution of this paper is a Partial Max-Sat-based mechanism for pruning sub-optimal repair suggestions.* To illustrate the problem, let us consider some of the other repair suggestions that the ABC system generates for repairing the incompatibility in the theory $\mathbb{T}_{Tw}$ from Example 1.

Note that the ABC system can break the unwanted proof in Example 2 at each of the 3 resolution steps, and those steps can be broken using each of the 5 repair operations described in Definition 3, sometimes in more than one way. For the purposes of analysis, let us additionally assume the observations $Feathered(Tweety) \in \mathcal{T}(\mathbb{S})$ and $Fly(Polly) \in \mathcal{T}(\mathbb{S})$. Note that both $Feathered(Tweety)$ and $Fly(Polly)$ are theorems of $\mathbb{T}$. So a new insufficiency will be introduced if either of them is not a theorem of the repaired theory $\nu(\mathbb{T})$. Consider the following repair suggestions to $\mathbb{T}$.

Belief Revision 1: Delete axiom (2), for instance. Note that, *Feathered* (*Tweety*) is no longer a theorem, so this deletion will cause an insufficiency.

Belief Revision 2: Add an additional precondition to the body of axiom (2). User interaction is required to suggest a suitable precondition. Also, *Feathered(Tweety)* is no longer a theorem, so this repair will also cause an insufficiency.

---

[5] The details are subject to NDA, so have been anonymised.

Reformation 1: Rename *Bird* in axiom (2) to the new predicate *Bird'*. Note that *Feathered(Tweety)* is no longer a theorem, which causes the same insufficiency as in the previous two repairs. If, instead, *Bird* in axiom 1 were renamed, then *Fly(Polly)* would cease to be a theorem which would cause a different insufficiency.

Reformation 2: This is the repair described in Sect. 2.4. Note that *Feathered(Tweety)* and *Fly(Polly)* are still theorems, so this repair avoids the insufficiencies caused by the other four repairs.

Reformation 3: This is not applicable to axiom (2), but could be applied to axiom (3) to rewrite it to $\implies Penguin(Tweety')$. Note that *Feathered(Tweety)* is no longer a theorem. In addition, a new incompatibility will be caused if it is observed that $Fly(Tweety') \in \mathcal{F}(\mathbb{S})$.

Without pruning sub-optimal repairs, the ABC System makes 10 repair suggestions for this faulty theory. For incompatibilities with several or longer unwanted proofs, the number of repair suggestions can be much more. The pruning mechanism described in Sect. 4, will prune all but the Reformation 2 repair described in Sect. 2.4.

3   Pruning out Sub-optimal Repairs

The ABC System is applied to Datalog theories, whereas Partial Max-Sat, which is the main component of our pruning mechanism, and similar Sat-based algorithms, are designed for propositional logic. The theory behind reducing Datalog-like theories to propositional ones is well known, but is briefly discussed in Sect. 3.1. This is followed by a brief introduction to Partial Max-Sat in Sect. 3.2 and how we use it in Sect. 4.

3.1   Turning First-Order Theories into Propositional Logic

All Datalog theories can be converted into equivalent propositional ones. Note that if we ground all axioms in a theory $\mathbb{T}$ by instantiating their variables in all possible ways with constants we will get another theory $Ground(\mathbb{T})$ in which all the axioms are variable-free Horn clauses. Since Datalog theories have no non-nullary functions, $Ground(\mathbb{T})$ has only a finite number of axioms. Moreover, $Ground(\mathbb{T})$ has a model iff $\mathbb{T}$ has one [6]. We can view $Ground(\mathbb{T})$ as a propositional theory, so SAT-related algorithms can be applied to it to solve $\mathbb{T}$ problems. Since every occurrence of each variable in $\mathbb{T}$ must be instantiated in $|\mathcal{C}|$ ways then this grounding is an exponential process in time and space.

Definition 5 (Grounding a Datalog Theory)

$$Ground(\mathbb{T}) = \{\phi\sigma \mid \phi \in \mathbb{T} \land \sigma : \mathcal{V} \mapsto \mathcal{C}\}$$

The *Ground* function is illustrated in Example 3.

Example 3 (Grounding a Theory). *Let* $\mathbb{T}_{pqr}$ *be the following set of axioms* :

$$P(x) \implies Q(x), \implies P(A), \implies R(B)$$

Then $Ground(\mathbb{T}_{pqr})$ *is the set:* $\{P(A) \implies Q(A), P(B) \implies Q(B), \implies P(A), \implies R(B)\}$

3.2 Partial Max-Sat

Partial Max-Sat $(pMaxSat)$ specifies the problem in which given two arguments, φ_h and φ_s, denoting sets of ground hard and soft clauses respectively, the goal is to find all assignments of truth values to them such that: (a) all clauses in φ_h are satisfied, i.e., have a model, and (b) the maximum number of clauses in φ_s are satisfied. We use Herbrand models instead of Tarskian models. Herbrand [6] has shown that a theory has a Tarskian model iff it has a Herbrand model. A Herbrand model that meets this specification is called *optimal*.

Definition 6 (Optimal Herbrand Models)
A Herbrand model assigns a truth value to each propositional variable. In our case these are the ground propositions created by the Ground function.
  The Herbrand Base $\mathcal{HB}(\mathbb{T})$ *of a Datalog theory* $\mathbb{T}$ *is:*

$$\mathcal{HB}(\mathbb{T}) = \{P(t_1, \ldots, t_n)\sigma | \sigma : \mathcal{V} \mapsto \mathcal{C} \wedge P(t_1, \ldots, t_n) \subset \mathcal{P}\}$$

The Herbrand Models $\mathcal{HM}(\mathbb{T})$ *of* $\mathbb{T}$ *are subsets of* $\mathcal{HB}(\mathbb{T})$ *for which*

$$\forall \alpha \in \mathbb{T}, \forall hm \in \mathcal{HM}(\mathbb{T}). \; hm \models \alpha$$

A Herbrand Model $hm \in \mathcal{HM}(\mathbb{T})$ *is* optimal *iff*

$$\forall \beta \in \varphi_h. \, hm \models \beta \quad \wedge \quad \forall hm' \in \mathcal{HM}(\mathbb{T}).$$
$$|\{(\beta) \in \varphi_s | hm \models (\beta)\}| \; \geq \; |\{(\beta \implies) \in \varphi_s | hm' \models (\beta)\}| \qquad (6)$$

Let $pMaxSat$ be an algorithm, specified in Definition 7, that returns the size of the subset of φ_s that is *not satisfied* by an optimal Herbrand model. Note that, as a consequence of (6), this size will be the same for all such models.

Definition 7 (Partial Max-Sat Specification)

$$pMaxSat(\varphi_h, \varphi_s) = |\{(\beta) \in \varphi_s | hm \not\models (\beta)\}|$$

where hm *is any optimal Herbrand Model.*

We augmented the ABC system with a third-party Partial Max-Sat solver [7], based on the Fu and Malik algorithm [3].

3.3   Evaluating Fitness of Repairs

This section discusses which repairs are considered to be sub-optimal and how to detect them using automated reasoning.

We want to find repairs $\nu(\mathbb{T})$ of a faulty $\mathbb{T}$ so as to maximise the size of $\{\phi \in \mathcal{T}(\mathbb{S}) | \nu(\mathbb{T}) \vdash \phi\}$ and minimise the size of $\{\phi \in \mathcal{F}(\mathbb{S}) | \nu(\mathbb{T}) \vdash \phi\}$. It will not, in general, be possible to achieve both of these requirements with a single repair, so we need to find all repairs ν that are optimal wrt some measures of these potentially conflicting requirements.

3.4   Pareto Optimality

It suffices to define what it means for one theory to strictly dominate another. The Pareto front of optimal repairs is then just the maximal set of repairs such that no member is strictly dominated by any other repair. Any repair not in the Pareto front is sub-optimal.

We will first need to define the insufficiency set $\mathcal{IS}(\mathbb{T}, \mathbb{S})$ of members of $\mathcal{T}(\mathbb{S})$ that are *not* theorems and the incompatibility set $\mathcal{IC}(\mathbb{T}, \mathbb{S})$ of members of $\mathcal{F}(\mathbb{S})$ that *are* theorems.

Definition 8 (The Incompatibility and Insufficiency sets). *Let:*

$$\mathcal{IS}(\mathbb{T}, \mathbb{S}) = \{\phi \in \mathcal{T}(\mathbb{S}) | \mathbb{T} \nvdash \phi\} \quad \wedge \quad \mathcal{IC}(\mathbb{T}, \mathbb{S}) = \{\phi \in \mathcal{F}(\mathbb{S}) | \mathbb{T} \vdash \phi\}$$

Then we can define when one repair strictly dominates another.

Definition 9 (Strictly Dominated Repair). *Given two repairs ν_k and ν_j, ν_j is strictly dominated by ν_k iff:*

$$|\mathcal{IS}(\nu_k(\mathbb{T}), \mathbb{S})| \leq^* |\mathcal{IS}(\nu_j(\mathbb{T}), \mathbb{S})| \quad \wedge \quad |\mathcal{IC}(\nu_k(\mathbb{T}), \mathbb{S})| \leq^* |\mathcal{IC}(\nu_j(\mathbb{T}), \mathbb{S})|$$

$\leq^*$: *one of the signs has to be a strict inequality.*

Example 4 (Strict Domination). *We compare two of the repairs of $\mathbb{T}_{Tw}$ in Definition 1 from Sect. 2.5. Let ν_{b1} be the deletion of axiom (1) and ν_{r2} be the addition of an argument to Bird. Where:*

$$\mathcal{T}(\mathbb{S}) = \{Feathered(Tweety), Fly(Polly)\} \quad \wedge \quad \mathcal{F}(\mathbb{S}) = \{Fly(Tweety)\}$$

Then $\mathcal{IC}(\nu_k(\mathbb{T}), \mathbb{S})$ is empty for both repairs and $\mathcal{IS}(\nu_k(\mathbb{T}), \mathbb{S})$ is empty for ν_{r2}, but for ν_{b1}, $\mathcal{IS}(\nu_k(\mathbb{T}), \mathbb{S}) = \{Feathered(Tweety), Fly(Polly)\}$. Therefore, ν_{r2} strictly dominates ν_{b1} and, hence, ν_{b1} is sub-optimal.

4   Pruning mechanism

The pruning mechanism provides a way to reduce the search space of repairs of a given faulty theory in an automatic way. The inputs to the pruning mechanism are given by the ABC theory-repair algorithm: a Datalog-like theory $\mathbb{T}$,

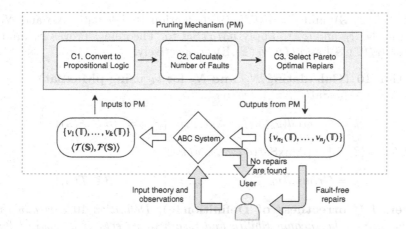

Fig. 1. The components (C1–C3) of the pruning mechanism repair, where $\mathbb{T}$ is a Datalog-like theory, $\{\nu_1, ..., \nu_k\}$ is a set of repairs generated by the ABC algorithm, $\langle \mathcal{T}(\mathbb{T}), \mathcal{F}(\mathbb{T}) \rangle$ are the observations from the environment and the output is a set of optimal, fault-free repairs.

a set of repairs $\{\nu_1, \nu_2, \ldots, \nu_k\}$ and a pair of sets of environmental observations $\langle \mathcal{T}(\mathbb{S}), \mathcal{F}(\mathbb{S}) \rangle$. The output is the sub-set of repair suggestions that are Pareto optimal: $\{\nu_{n_1}, \ldots, \nu_{n_j}\}$.

Figure 1 shows the high-level components of the mechanism. At each step the ABC system generates a set of repairs of a faulty theory. C1 applies each generated repair and converts the resulting Datalog-like theory to propositional logic using *Ground* (see Sect. 3.1). C2 is the central part of the mechanism, which uses *pMaxSat* to determine how many faults were fixed by each repair ν, and how many new faults it introduces to the repaired theory $\nu(\mathbb{T})$. In C3 the set of Pareto optimal repairs are returned to the cycle as (possibly only partially) repaired Datalog theories. This process is repeated on the repaired theories until no faults remain or no further repairs are generated. Any fault-free theories are returned to the user. $\mathbb{S}$ remains unchanged throughout.

Even though, given unbounded resources, the constituent processes of this cycle each terminate, there is the possibility of non-termination of the whole cycle. ABC might reach a situation in which faults still remain, but each repair of them fails to decrease the overall number of faults. This can happen because, as we saw in Sect. 2.5, a repair can introduce new faults when fixing an old one. This has not happened in any of our test examples, but it remains a theoretical possibility. It is this kind of whole cycle non-termination that gives rise to the 'usually' caveat in our hypothesis.

4.1 The use of Partial MAX-SAT for Determining Optimal Repairs

Definition 9 is used to determine whether a repair ν_k is sub-optimal and should be pruned. This requires us to calculate the sizes of incompatibility and insufficiency sets: $|\mathcal{IC}(\nu_k(\mathbb{T}), \mathbb{S})|$ and $|\mathcal{IS}(\nu_k(\mathbb{T}), \mathbb{S})|$. Definition 10 calculates N_C and N_S by specifying the φ_h and φ_s to apply $pMaxSat$ to. Theorem 1 proves N_C and N_S to be $|\mathcal{IC}(\nu_k(\mathbb{T}), \mathbb{S})|$ and $|\mathcal{IS}(\nu_k(\mathbb{T}), \mathbb{S})|$, respectively.

Definition 10 (Calculating N_C and N_S for ν_k using pMaxSat)
  Let $N_C = \mathrm{pMaxSat}(\varphi_h, \varphi_s)$, *where:*

$$\varphi_h = Ground(\nu_k(\mathbb{T})) \quad \wedge \quad \varphi_s = \{\beta \implies |\beta \in \mathcal{F}(\mathbb{S})\}$$

Let $N_S = |\mathcal{T}(\mathbb{S})| - \mathrm{pMaxSat}(\varphi_h, \varphi_s)$, *where:*

$$\varphi_h = Ground(\nu_k(\mathbb{T})) \quad \wedge \quad \varphi_s = \{\beta \implies |\beta \in \mathcal{T}(\mathbb{S})\}$$

Theorem 1 (Correctness of Definition 10). *Definition 10 correctly calculates the size of the incompatibility and insufficiency sets of a repaired theory* $\nu_k(\mathbb{T})$, *i.e.*

$$N_C = |\mathcal{IC}(\nu_k(\mathbb{T}), \mathbb{S})| \wedge N_S = |\mathcal{IS}(\nu_k(\mathbb{T}), \mathbb{S})|$$

Proof Summary. The proofs for N_C and N_S are similar. First apply the definitions of φ_h given in Definition 10. Use Definition 7 to apply the definitions of N_C and N_S. Then use Definition 8 to show the equivalences, appealing to the consistency of Datalog theories.

5   Evaluation

In this section we evaluate the hypothesis:

> *Our Partial Max-Sat based algorithm prunes sub-optimal repairs from ABC's output. It usually terminates successfully with a significantly smaller set of fault-free, optimal repaired theories.*

By construction, the Pareto-fronts generated by the Partial Max-Sat based filter consist solely of optimal repairs. Table 1 shows the result of repairing a test set of 10 faulty theories[6]. It shows the reductions in size between the set of repair suggestions originally generated by the ABC system and these Pareto-fronts.

No one standard benchmark test set is available that could be used to evaluate the diverse abilities of the ABC system. In order to show the generality of our techniques and avoid bias in the evaluation, these test examples were instead drawn from benchmark test and development sets used in research papers in a diverse range of areas of AI, including non-monotonic reasoning, belief revision, etc.

As previously noted, even these optimal repairs may not eliminate all the faults in the input theory. Further rounds of repair may be required to the resulting partially repaired theories. The size reductions are given for only the first round of repairs. This recursive process may be viewed as a search tree, where

---

[6] Plus our development example 1.

the nodes are labelled with theories and the arcs between them with optimal repairs. For success, we require only one branch of this search tree to terminate with a leaf node labelled with a fault-free theory, but sometimes multiple fault-free theories are found. Table 1 shows that success was achieved in all 10 examples.

The columns of Table 1 give the following statistics:

Name: The names of the 10 faulty theories in our test set, plus Tweety (1)[7].
#A: The number of axioms in each faulty theory.
#Unfil: The number of first-round, unfiltered repair suggestions.
#Fil: The size of the Pareto front after the first round. The percentages in parentheses indicate the reduction achieved.
#H and #S: The size of the initial hard and soft clause sets.
#PV: The size of the initial propositional variable set.
Time: The average, over 3 runs, of the time (μs) to generate a fault-free theory.
Succ(n): n is the number of fault-free theories generated, if any.
Reference: The citations of the source of the example, with a note on any adaptions.

Note that the repair process terminates with success for all our 11 examples. The size reduction achieved by our filtering process varies widely from 0% to 93%.

Table 1. Experimental results showing the comparison between the first-round of repairs using the baseline unfiltered ABC system vs. the pruning mechanism.

Name	#A	#Unfil	#Fil	#H	#S	#PV	Time	Succ(n)	Reference
CapOf	3	14	12 (15%)	29	4	18	575 ms	Y (12)	[1]
TooManyMums	3	14	14 (0%)	29	3	19	188 ms	Y (14)	[1]
Tweety	5	10	1 (90%)	8	3	8	158 ms	Y (1)	[14]
MarriedWoman	5	12	6 (50%)	8	2	8	159 ms	Y (6)	From Ex. 3.6 [5]
Researcher	5	13	5 (62%)	9	2	10	154 ms	Y (5)	From Example 1 [13]
Swan	6	20	11 (45%)	8	4	9	1940 ms	Y (54)	[4]
Bat	6	12	4 (67%)	11	4	14	4199 ms	Y (24)	[16]
SuperPenguin	6	16	14 (13%)	6	2	6	164 ms	Y (14)	From Example 3.1 [5]
BuyStock	8	20	18 (10%)	15	2	16	156 ms	Y (18)	From Example 3.3 [5]
SuperPenguin_v2	8	20	12 (40%)	12	4	12	169 ms	Y (12)	From Example 3.1 [5]
BuyStock_v2	10	27	2 (93%)	26	4	23	6260 ms	Y (2)	From Example 3.3[a] [5]

[a] Adapted by adding goodPrice (Blockbuster) and closing (Blockbuster) as suggested in [5]; ontology should infer that you should not buy stocks of a company which has good stock price but is closing down.

[7] Space limitations prohibit us from giving the axioms for each of these theories, except for the Tweety example (1). The remaining theories can be found online at https://github.com/MariusUrbonas/AutomatedPruningMechanismForTheoryRepairs.

This variation can be partially explained by the number of fault-free theories that are eventually returned - where a large number of fault-free repairs exist, then at least that number of repair sequences are needed to find them all. *From these results we conclude that our hypothesis has been empirically confirmed.*

6   Conclusion

The ABC system automates the repair of faulty Datalog theories. It detects faults in a theory $\mathbb{T}$ by testing it against observations of the environment $\mathbb{S}$, represented as a pair of sets of ground propositions $\langle \mathcal{T}(\mathbb{S}), \mathcal{F}(\mathbb{S}) \rangle$, where $\mathcal{T}(\mathbb{S})$ is a set of true ground propositions and $\mathcal{F}(\mathbb{S})$ is a set of false ones. A fault can be an incompatibility, where $\mathbb{T} \vdash \phi$ for some $\phi \in \mathcal{F}(\mathbb{S})$, or an insufficiency, where $\mathbb{T} \nvdash \phi$ for some $\phi \in \mathcal{T}(\mathbb{S})$. ABC repairs theories by a combination of abduction, belief revision and reformation.

Unfortunately, the ABC system overproduces repair suggestions. In this paper, we describe a pruning mechanism based on Partial Max-Sat, which outputs a Pareto front of optimal repair suggestions. Our empirical results confirm that, by pruning out sub-optimal repair suggestions, this mechanism significantly reduces the number of repair suggestions while retaining repairs that lead to a successful outcome of a fault-free theory. Further details can be found in [15].

Inductive Logic Programming [12] also constructs logic programs from positive and negative examples and can invent new intermediate predicates to complete recursive programs. The main differences between ILP and the ABC system is that: ABC repairs faulty theories, which may not be recursive programs; it can change the arity of predicates; split/merge constants, predicates and preconditions. We are currently working with Muggleton's team to apply both techniques to the modelling of virtual bargaining [10], which will provide a vehicle to further compare and contrast them.

In future work, we intend to explore the application of similar pruning mechanisms to richer logics, including some of those for which we have previously implemented reformation [1,11]. When these logics are not decidable or when examples require infeasible run times, we will need to impose resource limits. These limits might mean that we sometimes fail to detect incompatibilities or misclassify an insufficiency. But it will still be useful to find a subset of all incompatibilities or to repair a false insufficiency so that the repaired theory finds a shorter proof of it. It is also the case that for large enough problems the Partial Max-Sat algorithm might not terminate in a feasible amount of time. We will look into using intermediate solutions.

References

1. Bundy, A., Mitrovic, B.: Reformation: a domain-independent algorithm for theory repair. Technical report. University of Edinburgh (2016)
2. Ceri, S., Gottlob, G., Tanca, L.: Logic Programming and Databases. Surveys in Computer Science. Springer, Berlin (1990). https://doi.org/10.1007/978-3-642-83952-8

3. Fu, Z., Malik, S.: On solving the partial MAX-SAT problem. In: Biere, A., Gomes, C.P. (eds.) SAT 2006. LNCS, vol. 4121, pp. 252–265. Springer, Heidelberg (2006). https://doi.org/10.1007/11814948_25

4. Gärdenfors, P.: Knowledge in Flux: Modeling the Dynamics of Epistemic States. MIT Press, Cambridge (1988)

5. Alejandro Gómez, S., Ivan Chesnevar, C., Simari, G.R.: Reasoning with inconsistent ontologies through augmentation. Appl. Artif. Intell. $24(1–2)$, 102–148 (2010)

6. Herbrand, J.: Researches in the theory of demonstration. In: van Heijenoort, J. (ed.) From Frege to Goedel: A Source Book in Mathematical Logic, 1879–1931, pp. 525–581. Harvard University Press, Cambridge (1930)

7. Ignatiev, A., Morgado, A., Marques-Silva, J.: PySAT: a python toolkit for prototyping with SAT oracles. In: Beyersdorff, O., Wintersteiger, C.M. (eds.) SAT 2018. LNCS, vol. 10929, pp. 428–437. Springer, Cham (2018). https://doi.org/10.1007/978-3-319-94144-8_26

8. Kowalski, R.A., Kuehner, D.: Linear resolution with selection function. Artif. Intell. **2**, 227–60 (1971)

9. Li, X., Bundy, A., Smaill, A.: ABC repair system for datalog-like theories. In: 10th International Joint Conference on Knowledge Discovery, Knowledge Engineering and Knowledge Management, vol. 2, pp. 335–342. SCITEPRESS, Seville, Spain (2018). https://doi.org/10.5220/0006959703350342

10. Misyak, J., Noguchi, T., Chater, N.: Instantaneous conventions: the emergence of flexible communicative signals. Psychol. Sci. $27(12)$, 1550–1561 (2016)

11. Mitrovic, B.: Repairing inconsistent ontologies using adapted reformation algorithm for sorted logics. UG4 Final Year Project, University of Edinburgh (2013)

12. Muggleton, S., Lin, D., Pahlavi, D., Tamaddoni-Nezhad, A.: Meta-interpretive learning: application to grammatical inference. In: Proceedings of the 22nd International Conference on Inductive Logic Programming. Springer, Dubrovnik, Croatia (2012). http://ida.felk.cvut.cz/ilp2012/wp-content/uploads/ilp2012_submission_14.pdf

13. Rodler, P., Eichholzer, M.: On the usefulness of different expert question types for fault localization in ontologies. In: Wotawa, F., Friedrich, G., Pill, I., Koitz-Hristov, R., Ali, M. (eds.) IEA/AIE 2019. LNCS (LNAI), vol. 11606, pp. 360–375. Springer, Cham (2019). https://doi.org/10.1007/978-3-030-22999-3_32

14. Strasser, C., Antonelli, G.A.: Non-monotonic logic. In: Zalta, E.N. (ed.) The Stanford Encyclopedia of Philosophy, Summer 2019 edn. Metaphysics Research Lab, Stanford University, Stanford, California (2019)

15. Urbonas, M.: A heuristic approach for guiding automated theory repair for the ABC theory repair system. University of Edinburgh UG4 Project Dissertation (2019)

16. Wan, H., Zhang, H., Xiao, P., Huang, H., Zhang, Y.: Query answering with inconsistent existential rules under stable model semantics. In: AAAI'16: Proceedings of the Thirtieth AAAI Conference on Artificial Intelligence, pp. 1095–1101. AAAI, Phoenix, Arizona, USA (2016)

Machine Learning

Mining Interpretable Rules for Sentiment and Semantic Relation Analysis Using Tsetlin Machines

Rupsa Saha$^{(\boxtimes)}$ (ID), Ole-Christoffer Granmo (ID), and Morten Goodwin (ID)

Centre for AI Research, University of Agder, Grimstad, Norway
{rupsa.saha,ole.granmo,morten.goodwin}@uia.no

Abstract. Tsetlin Machines (TMs) are an interpretable pattern recognition approach that captures patterns with high discriminative power from data. Patterns are represented as conjunctive clauses in propositional logic, produced using bandit-learning in the form of Tsetlin Automata. In this work, we propose a TM-based approach to two common Natural Language Processing (NLP) tasks, viz. Sentiment Analysis and Semantic Relation Categorization. By performing frequent itemset mining on the patterns produced, we show that they follow existing expert-verified rule-sets or lexicons. Further, our comparison with other widely used machine learning techniques indicates that the TM approach helps maintain interpretability without compromising accuracy – a result we believe has far-reaching implications not only for interpretable NLP but also for interpretable AI in general.

Keywords: Natural language processing · Rule mining · Artificial Intelligence · Interpretable AI · Sentiment analysis · Semantic analysis

1 Introduction

The proliferation of Machine Learning (ML) and Artificial Intelligence (AI) techniques has led to their widespread use in critical and non-critical everyday technology. Many of these AI-based systems lack interpretability, i.e., the ability to explain their actions in forms understandable to humans. Without proper explanations, detecting and correcting erroneous behavior becomes more complicated, with some consequences being harsher than others, such as people being incorrectly denied bail and dubious financial decisions being taken. As a result, trust in the systems suffers [25].

Another justification for making AI interpretable is to aid researchers and engineers in improving their models. By leveraging information on where and why a model fails, a model can more easily be debugged. For instance, perhaps one of the most persuasive reasons for using AI versus human reasoning is that machines have the potential of being unbiased. Unfortunately, limited interpretability impedes the ability to detect and rectify bias encoded into a model, thus leading to biased systems falsely being advertised otherwise [17].

© Springer Nature Switzerland AG 2020
M. Bramer and R. Ellis (Eds.): SGAI-AI 2020, LNAI 12498, pp. 67–78, 2020.
https://doi.org/10.1007/978-3-030-63799-6_5

Despite the increasing attention to the importance of interpretable AI, there are still few interpretable ML techniques available that work well for complex problems, compared to the alternative. Currently, there are two main approaches: a) Model-based approaches, where interpretability is intrinsic through a simple and describable model; and b) Post-hoc approaches that extract explanations from a trained model. There are concerns that model-based approaches may not reach sufficiently high predictive accuracy. On the other hand, post-hoc processing also suffers from the fact that the explanations acquired is, at best, an approximation of what the model has learned. It is not enough for a method to be highly accurate – the extracted explanations must also be relevant [21].

By relying on standard ML techniques, Natural Language Processing (NLP) is also afflicted by this interpretability-accuracy conflict. There are several approaches to pattern recognition in NLP, here listed in the order of increasing loss of interpretability: rule-based pattern-recognition system, statistical (TF-IDF) [14] methods, linear classifiers [2], and neural network models employing vector space representations of words [4]. Basic neural network architectures are further enhanced using, e.g., convolution, pooling, and grammatical information [6,28]. In this work, however, we propose to use the recently introduced Tsetlin Machine for NLP, showing that it can address both interpretability and high accuracy.

Tsetlin Machines: Tsetlin Machines are a new pattern recognition approach, which provides an interpretable approach to ML [9]. A Tsetlin Machine constructs human-understandable patterns in the form of conjunctive clauses in propositional logic, each of which has high discriminating power. More recently, Phoulady [23] proposed a weighted scheme that increases the discrimination power of the clauses by assigning them weights, modified by a learning mechanism to combat false positives and encourage true positives. While the performance of Tsetlin Machines in image recognition, pattern discrimination and regression compares well to state-of-the-art machine learning techniques [1,10,23], the method also provides smaller memory footprint and faster inference in reported cases than more traditional neural network-based models [10,32]. Furthermore, Tsetlin Machines have been shown to be fault-tolerant, being able to completely mask stuck-at faults [27]. Inherent interpretability makes Tsetlin Machines a promising candidate for the cause of interpretable AI. Indeed, conjunctive clauses have turned out to be well-suited for human interpretation, while still allowing complex nonlinear patterns to be formed [31].

Paper Contributions: In this paper, we explore the properties of the Tsetlin Machine when applied to NLP through a study on sentiment analysis and semantic relation analysis. We focus on the linguistic patterns obtained by means of the clauses, to identify their informativeness and interpretability. We compare these clauses with expert-crafted rules wherever available to better judge them against an established standard. We also show that we can maintain interpretability while achieving competitive accuracy, and suggest areas for further research based upon our findings.

2 Related Work

As mentioned earlier, one way of bringing interpretation to ML is via a post-hoc model that explains an initial black-box model. Unfortunately, such explanations are often not reliable, and can be misleading, since there is often an unknown degree of approximation involved [25]. It is often impossible for an explanation to be completely faithful unless it is the complete description of the model itself. Yet, an explanation must correspond to how the model behaves when an instance is being predicted. Importantly, local fidelity does not imply global fidelity: features that are globally important may not be important in the local context. While global fidelity would imply local fidelity, identifying globally faithful explanations that are interpretable remains a challenge for complex models [24]. Ultimately, models that are inherently interpretable are preferred, since they are true to the computation undertaken by the model [25].

Previous work on interpretability for NLP has primarily focused on text classification problems, though none involve models that can organically explain the decisions. Ribeiro [24] proposed a model-agnostic approach by employing an interpretable model of the predictions of black box models, where the interpretable model describes the actions of the classifier locally (i.e., for the instance being classified). Another approach, by Samek [26], is to use heat maps to obtain information about how much each hidden element contributes to the prediction, and build connections between the input and the output from that. Hancock et al. [11] developed a framework in which annotators provided a natural language explanation for each label, and these annotations were used to create a weakly supervised larger training set, that ultimately trained a classifier capable to classifying text along with an explanation for the same. Finally, a hybrid generative-discriminative method for text classification is used by Liu [18] to arrive at a novel generative explanation framework that can generate reasonable explanations using information inferred from raw texts.

There has been very little research done in terms of exploring Tsetlin Machine capabilities for NLP. Berge et al. [5] proposed a Tsetlin Machine-based approach to learn human-interpretable rules from medical data. The approach is able to successfully carry out text categorization based on presence or absence of unique medical terminology.

3 Tsetlin Machine for NLP Tasks

3.1 General Classification and Learning Using Tsetlin Machines

Introduced in the early 1960s, a Tsetlin automaton (TA) is a deterministic automaton that learns the optimal action among the set of actions offered by an environment. It performs the action associated with its current state, which triggers a reward or penalty based on the ground truth. The state is update accordingly, so that the TA progressively shifts focus towards the optimal action [30].

A Tsetlin Machine consists of a collection of such TAs, which together create complex propositional formulae using conjunctive clauses. It takes a vector $X = (x_1, \ldots, x_o)$ of Boolean features as input, to be classified into one of two classes, $y = 0$ or $y = 1$. Together with their negated counterparts, $\bar{x}_k = \neg x_k = 1 - x_k$, the features form a literal set $L = \{x_1, \ldots, x_o, \bar{x}_1, \ldots, \bar{x}_o\}$.

A Tsetlin Machine pattern is formulated as a conjunctive clause C_j, formed by ANDing a subset $L_j \subseteq L$ of the literal set:

$$C_j(X) = \bigwedge_{l_k \in L_j} l_k = \prod_{l_k \in L_j} l_k. \tag{1}$$

E.g., the clause $C_j(X) = x_1 \wedge x_2 = x_1 x_2$ consists of the literals $L_j = \{x_1, x_2\}$ and outputs 1 iff $x_1 = x_2 = 1$.

The number of clauses employed is a user set parameter n. Half of the clauses are assigned positive polarity. The other half is assigned negative polarity. The clause outputs are combined into a classification decision through summation and thresholding using the unit step function $u(v) = 1$ **if** $v \geq 0$ **else** 0:

$$\hat{y} = u\left(\sum_{j=1}^{n/2} C_j^+(X) - \sum_{j=1}^{n/2} C_j^-(X)\right). \tag{2}$$

In other words, classification is performed based on a majority vote, with the positive clauses voting for $y = 1$ and the negative for $y = 0$. The classifier $\hat{y} = u(x_1 \bar{x}_2 + \bar{x}_1 x_2 - x_1 x_2 - \bar{x}_1 \bar{x}_2)$, for instance, captures the XOR-relation (illustrated in Fig. 1).

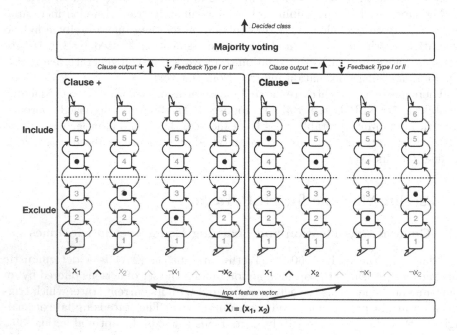

Fig. 1. The Tsetlin Machine architecture

Each TA in a clause $C_j(X)$ decides whether to *Include* or *Exclude* a specific literal l_k in the clause (Fig. 1). Learning which literals to include is based on reinforcement: Type I feedback produces frequent patterns, while Type II feedback increases the discrimination power of the patterns.

Tsetlin Machines learn on-line, processing one training example (X, y) at a time:

Type I feedback is given stochastically to clauses with positive polarity when $y = 1$ and to clauses with negative polarity when $y = 0$. Each clause, in turn, reinforces its TAs based on: (1) its output $C_j(X)$; (2) the action of the TA – *Include* or *Exclude*; and (3) the value of the literal l_k assigned to the TA. Two rules govern Type I feedback:

- *Include* is rewarded and *Exclude* is penalized with probability $\frac{s-1}{s}$ whenever $C_j(X) = 1$ and $l_k = 1$. This reinforcement is strong (triggered with high probability) and makes the clause remember and refine the pattern it recognizes in X.[1]
- *Include* is penalized and *Exclude* is rewarded with probability $\frac{1}{s}$ whenever $C_j(X) = 0$ or $l_k = 0$. This reinforcement is weak (triggered with low probability) and coarsens infrequent patterns, making them frequent.

Above, parameter s controls pattern frequency.

Type II feedback is given stochastically to clauses with positive polarity when $y = 0$ and to clauses with negative polarity when $y = 1$. It penalizes *Exclude* with probability 1 whenever $C_j(X) = 1$ and $l_k = 0$. Thus, this feedback produces literals for discriminating between $y = 0$ and $y = 1$.

3.2 Tsetlin Machines in NLP

Figure 2a shows a snapshot of the training and testing mechanism in a Tsetlin Machine setup for NLP, and how a global and local interpretation of the task is obtained from the clauses. As seen, the Tsetlin Machine takes as input a Boolean feature vector $D_i = [f_1, f_2, \ldots, f_o] \in \{0, 1\}^o$ (Fig. 2a: Training Feature Vectors). Here, D_i refers to a specific input text, while each feature f_k represents the presence/absence of a specific unigram or bigram in D_i.

The feature vector, in turn, is further processed by the clauses $C_1^+, \ldots, C_{\frac{n}{2}}^+$ and $C_1^- \ldots, C_{\frac{n}{2}}^-$. Each clause captures a specific linguistic sub-pattern as a conjunction of literals: $C_a = f_1 \land \ldots \land f_4 \land \neg f_6 \land \ldots$ (Fig. 2a: Clauses Learnt by Tsetlin Machine).

During learning, a larger T along with an increase number in the number of clauses leads to more specific clauses. That is, each clause embodies very particular sub-patterns without much overlap between clauses. The evidence for a sample to belong to a class is aggregated and thresholded for the output. A subset of clauses learnt by the Testlin Machine actively participates in the decision making process for a particular sample, leading us to a local description of said sample (Fig. 2a: Local Description shows $C_a, C_b, C_c \ldots$ making the prediction). For further details of Tsetlin Machine learning, the reader may refer to [9].

---

[1] Note that the probability $\frac{s-1}{s}$ is replaced by 1 when boosting true positives.

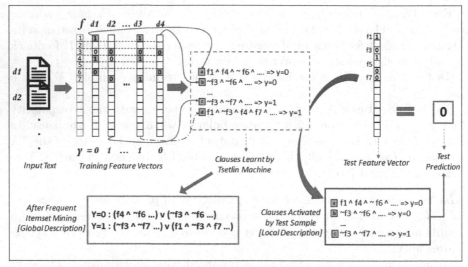

(a) Mechanism of Interpretable Rule Mining using Tsetlin Machines

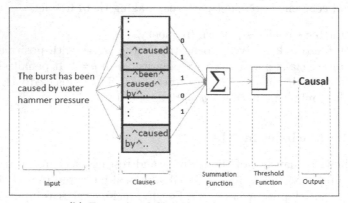

(b) Example of Classification using TM

Fig. 2. Tsetlin Machine for NLP Tasks

In the process of arriving at clauses that best describe the training data, the Tsetlin Machine picks out features that are deemed most important for decision making. In our work, features are simply unigrams and bigrams. Since the literals are initialized at random, in a single epoch of training, there are some inconsequential literals selected as part of one or more clauses, along with the important ones. To preserve interpretability of rules for text classification, we take advantage of the Tsetlin Machine's propensity towards frequently occurring sub-patterns. We perform a frequent itemset mining [3] of clauses over multiple epochs, and arrive at a set of representative sub-clauses (Fig. 2a: Global Description). As discussed subsequently in Sect. 5, these representatives hold up well to linguistic scrutiny.

4 Experimental Setup

In this work, we have used two standard datasets: the SemEval 2010 Semantic Relations dataset [12] and the Sentiment140 Twitter dataset [8].

The SEMEVAL-2010 Task 8 focused on identifying semantic relations between pairs of nominals in text. The dataset contains 10,717 annotated examples, each of which has one of the following ten relation classes: Cause - Effect (S:CE), Instrument - Agency (S:IA), Product - Producer (S:PP), Content - Container (S:CC), Entity - Origin (S:EO), Entity - Destination (S:ED), Component - Whole (S:CW), Member - Collection (S:MC), Message - Topic (S:MT) and Other.

The Sentiment140 dataset contains 1.6 million English language tweets, annotated as Positive and Negative. The dataset is stripped of emoticons to force classifiers to learn from other features, i.e. the words only.

In order to better judge whether the Tsetlin Machine can discern between the important parts of the text and the non-important, we purposefully do not do further preprocessing in the form of stopword or punctuation removal, in either dataset.

For the SemEval dataset, since it is composed of multiple classes, we compare each class separately, in a binary classification setup (i.e., one-vs-all), as well as the full dataset in a multi-class setup. We use a standard Tsetlin Machine model[2], as described by Berge [5] for each experiment. For experiments involving binary classification of SemEval dataset, the Tsetlin Machine was configured to use 40 clauses, a threshold value(T) of 15 and s-value of 3.9 as hyperparameters. For the multi-class classification, we used 1500 clauses, since there was a lot more information to be learnt, with a T of 800. In case of the Sentiment140 dataset, we use 4000 clauses, with the same T and s as before.

5 Analysis of Interpretability Provided by Tsetlin Machines

The interpretability of the Tsetlin Machine approach lies in the clauses produced. Examining the clauses learnt and activated establishes why each text was classified the way it was. In this section, we explore the clauses obtained in the experiments to better judge their relevancy in terms of providing a linguistic explanation. During training, the Tsetlin Machine arrives at a set of clauses using the features provided, which together gives a description of the task in general. During testing, however, each sample only activates a subset of all the

---

[2] Python implementation of Tsetlin Machine based classifier: code retrieved from https://github.com/cair/pyTsetlinMachine.

clauses, and these clauses define the classification problem with respect to that particular sample only.

We begin with instances that contain a Cause-Effect relationship in the SemEval data. While there may be other factors, the presence of one or more unambiguous causal connective is enough to classify a sentence as being a causal sentence [34]. Hence, we can hypothesize that the presence or absence of such words will be a major feature in classifying sentences as causal or non-causal.

Obtaining a frequent itemset from the clauses from over 300 runs of the proposed classifier, an overview of the task Cause-Effect vs All classification becomes clearer in the form of propositional logic:

$$\text{Sentence\_Contains}(\,(caused\_by) \vee (causes) \vee (triggered\_by) \vee (resulted\_in) \vee$$
$$(been\_caused\_by) \vee (radiating\_from) \vee (lead\_to) \vee \ldots) \implies \text{Class}(Cause - Effect).$$

The findings mirror existing expert-verified lexicons [7, 34] for the same task, with the literals present in the above description matching those termed by the researchers as "causal connectives".

While the above encapsulates the global description of the classification, it does not entirely hold true in the local context of a single sample. When classifying a single instance, like "The burst has been caused by water hammer pressure" shown in Fig. 2b, the clauses activated (grayed) provide a local explanation of the classification.

Similar results are seen for Entity-Destination relationship, where the description takes the following form:

$$\text{Sentence\_Contains}(\,(into\_the) \vee (sent\_to) \vee (delivered\_to) \vee (donated\_to) \vee$$
$$(put\_inside) \vee (shipped\_to) \vee (added\_to) \vee \ldots) \implies \text{Class}(Entity - Destination).$$

For the Sentiment140 Dataset, the frequent subclauses are compared against a range of standard Twitter Sentiment Analysis lexicons. The various manual and semi-automatically created sources used are: AFINN-111 [22], Affect Intensity Lexicon [19], EmoLex [20], NRC Hashtag Lexicon [16], LIWC [29], Bing Liu's opinion lexicon [13], MPQA subjective lexicon [33], Sentiment Composition Lexicon [15].

The extent of overlap between existing lexicons and Tsetlin Machine sub-patterns (created by training the Tsetlin Machine) is highlighted in Table 1. We observe high overlap with almost all lexicons, confirming that the Tsetlin Machine-based approach can indeed arrive at a linguistic description of the classification task at hand.

In summary, the frequent itemset of clauses contribute to global interpretability, while sub-clauses that contribute to the final decision of a particular example relates to local interpretability of the task in hand. Moreover, the obtained clauses mimic expert-crafted rules, especially with less complexity than similar approaches (such as decision trees or random forest).

Table 1. Coverage of Various Lexicons by Tsetlin Machine Clauses

Lexicon	Source: Twitter	Mode of creation	Size of $L_D{}^*$	L_D Coverage
AFINN-111	Yes	Manual	1363	87.97%
Affect Intensity	Yes	Manual	18719	83.55%
EmoLex	No	Manual	6272	85.30%
NRC Hashtag	Yes	Automatic	29249	85.68%
LIWC	No	Automatic	1771	92.20%
Bing Liu	No	Manual	1048	83.21%
MPQA	No	Manual	473	87.53%
SCL-NMA	No	Manual	1339	84.17%

$^*L_D = Lexicon \cap Dataset$

Apart from the advantages of being interpretable, a major motivation behind using a Tsetlin Machine-based approach is to not sacrifice performance for interpretability. In order to compare with existing methods, we use SVM (RBF kernel), Random Forest (RF), Gaussian Naive Bayes (NB), and CNN-LSTM. While the first three are vanilla methods, we include CNN-LSTM to compare our work with an ensemble neural network model as well. Standard Python implementations with Scikit-Learn and Keras were employed. For the CNN-LSTM model, we used a one-dimensional Convolutional layer of filter size 64 with MaxPooling, and an unidirectional LSTM layer of output size 100, along with a dense layer with sigmoid activation. In case of the Random Forest Classifier, we used 100 trees with a maximum depth of two. Table 2 records the accuracy obtained by

Table 2. Comparing results of Tsetlin Machine-based Classifier vs Baseline Approaches on SemEval-2010 Task 8 data and Sentiment140 data. Best results for each dataset are in bold

Data	Tsetlin Machine	SVM	RF	NB	CNN LSTM
S:CE	**93.5**	92.3	86.3	86.9	87.11
S:IA	**95.1**	94.0	91.9	89.9	93.2
S:PP	**92.5**	90.7	89.8	86.3	91.13
S:CC	91.6	**96.23**	90.4	90.7	92.89
S:EO	**92.75**	91.6	87.4	86.5	90.45
S:ED	92.5	**94.5**	89.3	88.8	88.4
S:CW	89.75	87.8	86.3	85.9	**90.37**
S:MC	**92.75**	91.1	88.4	86.8	91.02
S:MT	**93.3**	92.2	89.1	86.4	92.02
S:All	**50.20**	44.9	29.05	39.9	46.7
Sent140	69.4	**69.7**	62.52	60.5	49.9

the proposed Tsetlin Machine-based classifier on both datasets, in comparison
to those by other algorithms as baseline.

Table 3. Comparison of average training times (in thousand seconds) for individual
datasets using Tsetlin Machines, CNN-LSTM and SVM

Method	Dataset		
	Tsetlin Machine	CNN LSTM	SVM
SemEval	2.41	3.85	8.62
Sentiment140	4.06	8.27	19.30

Table 3 reports the average time to train taken by the Tsetlin Machine versus
CNN-LSTM and SVM on the two datasets, with the Tsetlin Machine and CNN-
LSTM each being trained over 100 epochs, in a multi-threaded DGX2 setup.
The Tsetlin Machine based architecture consistently trains faster compared to
other methods.

In conclusion, our findings suggest that the Tsetlin Machine-based approach
produces results comparable to other standard text classification methodologies,
and also has comparable training times to neural networks.

6   Conclusion

In this work, we explore the usage of an interpretable Tsetlin Machine-based
approach to text categorization. We conclude that the clauses arrived at by
the Tsetlin Machine for taking the categorization decision, gives us a global
description of the task during training and a local description while testing.
The linguistic structures indicated by the clauses are sufficiently similar to those
arrived at by human experts, thus ensuring that the success of the model is not
merely based on statistical findings that are unrelated to the language. Consequently, Tsetlin Machine-based methods may also enable researchers to arrive
at an understanding of the data and the task even when subject experts are not
available. Apart from allowing a level of transparency into the decision process
in this manner, which is hard to obtain with more conventional methods, the
Tsetlin Machine is also shown to perform at par with baseline approaches, both
in terms of accuracy and training time. Moreover, the interpretability of the
learning process ensures effective triage even when the model makes a mistake.

As a continuation of this work, we aim to investigate how the usage of a feature set enriched by grammatical and semantic information (as in [12]) affects the
performance of our proposed approach. We also plan to explore experimentally
whether the recently introduced convolutional Tsetlin Machine architecture [10]
delivers on the promise of producing even more informative clauses, specifically
for NLP applications. In general, how to make the obtained clauses increasingly
human-interpretable is an object of open discussion and research.

In conclusion, our novel approach to text categorization using a Tsetlin Machine shows promising interpretable results in certain core tasks of NLP. We believe that further studies into more varied NLP tasks (sequence labelling, entity resolution, question answering) can highlight the power of the approach, and pave the way for more interpretable NLP by artificially intelligent systems.

References

1. Abeyrathna, K.D., Granmo, O.C., Zhang, X., Jiao, L., Goodwin, M.: The regression Tsetlin machine - a novel approach to interpretable non-linear regression. Philos. Trans. R. Soc. A **378**(2164), 20190165 (2019)
2. Aggarwal, C.C., Zhai, C.: Mining Text Data. Springer, Boston (2012)
3. Agrawal, R., Srikant, R., et al.: Fast algorithms for mining association rules. In: Proceeding of the 20th International Conference Very Large Data Bases, VLDB, vol. 1215, pp. 487–499 (1994)
4. Bengio, Y., Ducharme, R., Vincent, P., Jauvin, C.: A neural probabilistic language model. J. Mach. Learn. Res. **3**(2), 1137–1155 (2003)
5. Berge, G.T., Granmo, O.C., Tveit, T.O., Goodwin, M., Jiao, L., Matheussen, B.V.: Using the Tsetlin machine to learn human-interpretable rules for high-accuracy text categorization with medical applications. IEEE Access **7**, 115134–115146 (2019)
6. Collobert, R., Weston, J., Bottou, L., Karlen, M., Kavukcuoglu, K., Kuksa, P.: Natural language processing (almost) from scratch. J. Mach. Learn. Res. **12**(8), 2493–2537 (2011)
7. Girju, R.: Automatic detection of causal relations for question answering. In: Proceedings of the ACL 2003 Workshop on Multilingual Summarization and Question Answering, vol. 12, pp. 76–83. Association for Computational Linguistics (2003)
8. Go, A., Bhayani, R., Huang, L.: Twitter sentiment classification using distant supervision. CS224N Proj. Rep. Stanford **1**(12), 2009 (2009)
9. Granmo, O.C.: The Tsetlin Machine - A Game Theoretic Bandit Driven Approach to Optimal Pattern Recognition with Propositional Logic. arXiv preprint arXiv:1804.01508 (2018)
10. Granmo, O.C., Glimsdal, S., Jiao, L., Goodwin, M., Omlin, C.W., Berge, G.T.: The convolutional Tsetlin machine. arXiv preprint arXiv:1905.09688 (2019)
11. Hancock, B., Bringmann, M., Varma, P., Liang, P., Wang, S., Ré, C.: Training classifiers with natural language explanations. In: Proceedings of the 56th Annual Meeting of the Association for Computational Linguistics Conference, vol. 2018, p. 1884. NIH Public Access (2018)
12. Hendrickx, I., et al.: Semeval-2010 task 8: multi-way classification of semantic relations between pairs of nominals. In: Proceedings of the Workshop on Semantic Evaluations: Recent Achievements and Future Directions, pp. 94–99. Association for Computational Linguistics (2009)
13. Hu, M., Liu, B.: Mining and summarizing customer reviews. In: Proceedings of the Tenth ACM SIGKDD International Conference on Knowledge Discovery and Data Mining, pp. 168–177. ACM (2004)
14. Jones, K.S.: A statistical interpretation of term specificity and its application in retrieval. J. Doc. **28**(1), 11–21 (2004)
15. Kiritchenko, S., Mohammad, S.M.: The effect of negators, modals, and degree adverbs on sentiment composition. arXiv preprint arXiv:1712.01794 (2017)

16. Kiritchenko, S., Zhu, X., Mohammad, S.M.: Sentiment analysis of short informal texts. J. Artif. Intell. Res. **50**, 723–762 (2014)
17. Lipton, Z.C.: The mythos of model interpretability. arXiv preprint arXiv:1606.03490 (2016)
18. Liu, H., Yin, Q., Wang, W.Y.: Towards explainable NLP: a generative explanation framework for text classification. arXiv preprint arXiv:1811.00196 (2018)
19. Mohammad, S.M.: Word affect intensities. In: Proceedings of the 11th Edition of the Language Resources and Evaluation Conference (LREC-2018), Miyazaki, Japan (2018)
20. Mohammad, S.M., Turney, P.D.: Crowdsourcing a word-emotion association lexicon. Comput. Intell. **29**(3), 436–465 (2013)
21. Murdoch, W.J., Singh, C., Kumbier, K., Abbasi-Asl, R., Yu, B.: Interpretable machine learning: definitions, methods, and applications. arXiv preprint arXiv:1901.04592 (2019)
22. Nielsen, F.Å.: A new anew: evaluation of a word list for sentiment analysis in microblogs. arXiv preprint arXiv:1103.2903 (2011)
23. Phoulady, A., Granmo, O.C., Gorji, S.R., Phoulady, H.A.: The weighted tsetlin machine: compressed representations with weighted clauses. arXiv preprint arXiv:1911.12607 (2019)
24. Ribeiro, M.T., Singh, S., Guestrin, C.: Why should i trust you? explaining the predictions of any classifier. In: Proceedings of the 22nd ACM SIGKDD International Conference on Knowledge Discovery and Data Mining, pp. 1135–1144. ACM (2016)
25. Rudin, C.: Stop explaining black box machine learning models for high stakes decisions and use interpretable models instead. Nat. Mach. Intell. **1**(5), 206 (2019)
26. Samek, W., Wiegand, T., Müller, K.R.: Explainable artificial intelligence: understanding, visualizing and interpreting deep learning models. arXiv preprint arXiv:1708.08296 (2017)
27. Shafik, R., Wheeldon, A., Yakovlev, A.: Explainability and dependability analysis of learning automata based AI hardware. In: IEEE 26th International Symposium on On-Line Testing and Robust System Design (IOLTS). IEEE (2020)
28. Socher, R., et al.: Recursive deep models for semantic compositionality over a sentiment treebank. In: Proceedings of the 2013 Conference on Empirical Methods in Natural Language Processing, pp. 1631–1642 (2013)
29. Tausczik, Y.R., Pennebaker, J.W.: The psychological meaning of words: LIWC and computerized text analysis methods. J. Lang. Soc. Psychol. **29**(1), 24–54 (2010)
30. Tsetlin, M.L.: On behaviour of finite automata in random medium. Avtom I Telemekhanika **22**(10), 1345–1354 (1961)
31. Wang, T., Rudin, C., Velez-Doshi, F., Liu, Y., Klampfl, E., MacNeille, P.: Bayesian rule sets for interpretable classification. In: 2016 IEEE 16th International Conference on Data Mining (ICDM), pp. 1269–1274. IEEE (2016)
32. Wheeldon, A., Shafik, R., Yakovlev, A., Edwards, J., Haddadi, I., Granmo, O.C.: Tsetlin machine: a new paradigm for pervasive AI. In: SCONA Workshop at Design, Automation and Test in Europe (DATE 2020) (2020)
33. Wilson, T., Wiebe, J., Hoffmann, P.: Recognizing contextual polarity in phrase-level sentiment analysis. In: Proceedings of Human Language Technology Conference and Conference on Empirical Methods in Natural Language Processing (2005)
34. Xuelan, F., Kennedy, G.: Expressing causation in written english. RELC J. **23**(1), 62–80 (1992)

Personalised Meta-Learning for Human Activity Recognition with Few-Data

Anjana Wijekoon[(✉)] [iD] and Nirmalie Wiratunga [iD]

School of Computing, Robert Gordon University, Aberdeen AB10 7GJ, Scotland, UK
{a.wijekoon,n.wiratunga}@rgu.ac.uk

Abstract. State-of-the-art methods of Human Activity Recognition (HAR) rely on a considerable amount of labelled data to train deep architectures. This becomes prohibitive when tasked with creating models that are sensitive to personal nuances in human movement, explicitly present when performing exercises and when it is infeasible to collect training data to cover the whole target population. Accordingly, learning personalised models with few data remains an open challenge in HAR research. We present a meta-learning methodology for learning-to-learn personalised models for HAR; with the expectation that the end-user only need to provide a few labelled data. These personalised HAR models benefit from the rapid adaptation of a generic meta-model using provided few end-user data. We implement the personalised meta-learning methodology with two algorithms, Personalised MAML and Personalised Relation Networks. A comparative study shows significant performance improvements against state-of-the-art deep learning algorithms and other personalisation algorithms in multiple HAR domains. Also, we show how personalisation improved meta-model training, to learn a generic meta-model suited for a wider population while using a shallow parametric model.

Keywords: Personalisation · Human Activity Recognition · Meta-learning · Few-shot learning

1 Introduction

Machine Learning research in HAR has a wide range of high impact applications in gait recognition, fall detection, orthopaedic rehabilitation and general fitness monitoring. A HAR dataset consists of sensor data streams collected from multiple persons. Unavoidably, sensors capture personal traits and nuances in some activity domains more than others, typically with activities that involve higher degrees of freedom. Thus, learning a single reasoning model to recognise the set

This work was part funded by SELFBACK, a project funded by the European Union's H2020 research and innovation programme under grant agreement No. 689043. More details available at http://www.selfback.eu.

of activity classes using a HAR dataset can be challenging, which calls for the personalisation.

We propose it is more intuitive to treat a "person-activity" pair as the class label. Accordingly, each person's data can be viewed as a dataset in its own right, and the HAR task involves learning a reasoning model for the person. Learning from only specific persons' data has shown significant performance improvements in early research with both supervised learning and active learning methods [4, 13]. But these methods require considerable amounts of data obtained from the end-user, periodical end-user involvement and model re-training. Also, current state-of-the-art Deep Learning algorithms require a large number of labelled data instances to avoid under-fitting.

Here we explore the "person-activity" classes concept but attempt to learn with a limited number of data instances per class. Accordingly, it becomes a few-shot classification task [10,14] where the aim is to learn a classifier with one or few labelled data instances for each class. Meta-learning methods are the state-of-the-art in few-shot classification for image recognition [2,6]. In a nutshell, meta-learning is described as learning-to-learn, where a wide range of tasks abstract their learning to a meta-model, such that, it is transferable to any unseen task. Meta-learning algorithms such as MAML [2] and Relation Networks (RN) [12] implement this methodology for few-shot classification, by learning generic models, and rapidly adapting to new tasks with only a few instances of data.

The concept of learning-to-learn aligns well with personalisation where, modelling a person can be viewed as a single task; whereby the meta-model must help learn a model that is rapidly adaptable to a new person. We propose "personalised meta-learning" to create personalised models, by leveraging a small amount of sensing data (i.e. calibration data) extracted from a person. Accordingly, in this paper, we make the following contributions,

1. Formalise Personalised Meta-Learning and implement with two algorithms, Personalised MAML and Personalised RN;
2. Perform a comparative evaluation with 3 HAR datasets representing a wide range of activity domains; and
3. Visualise how personalisation methodology enhanced the training and testing of meta-learners.

Importantly, we show that personalised meta-learning achieve significant performance improvement with simple shallow parametric models that only require a limited amount of labelled data compared to conventional DL models.

2   Related Work

Human Activity Recognition (HAR) is an active research challenge, where Deep Learning (DL) methods claim the state-of-the-art [7,17]. Learning a generalised reasoning model adaptable to many user groups is a unique transfer learning challenge in the HAR domain. Given access to large quantities of end-user data, early research has achieved improved performance by learning personal models [1]. Follow on work attempts to reduce the burden on end-user, by adopting active learning [4] and multi-task [11] methods that rely on periodical model re-training and continuous user involvement. Recent advancements in few-shot learning are adopted as an approach to personalisation in Personalised Matching Networks (MN^p) [8]. MN^p learns a parametric model, that is learning to match, leveraging a few data instances from the same user.

Meta-Learning or "learning-to-learn" is the learning of a generalised classification model that is transferable to new learning tasks with only a few instances of labelled data. In recent research it is interpreted mainly in three optimisation approaches; firstly, similarity optimised meta-learners like Relation Networks (RN) [12]; secondly, model optimised meta-learners like SNAIL [5]; and finally, adaptation optimised meta-learners like MAML [2]. MAML including its variants (FOMAML [2], Reptile [6]) and RN [12] are "model-agnostic", where parametric feature learners are interchangeable. In contrast, model optimised meta-learners, such as SNAIL [5] and MANN [9], where meta-learning is achieved using specific neural network constructs such as LSTM and Neural Turing Machine [3]. Also model optimised meta-learners require from very deep parametric models to learn meta properties [5]. Accordingly, we prefer model-agnostic methods in a HAR application, where heterogeneous sensor modalities may require different feature learners. While MN [14] is seen as a similarity optimised meta-learning, RN is not limited by a similarity metric and more generalisable to many new tasks. In contrast to MAML, RN has the potential to perform Open-ended HAR, by modelling the classification task as a matching task, similar to Open-ended MN [10]. In this paper, we implement personalised meta learning for HAR with the two model-agnostic meta-learners; MAML and RN.

3   Methods

Given a dataset, $\mathcal{D}$, Human Activity Recognition (HAR) is the learning of the feature mapping θ between data instances, x, and activity classes, y, where y is in the set of activity classes, $\mathcal{C}$. In HAR, each data instance in $\mathcal{D}$ belongs to a person, p. Given the set of data instances obtained from person p is $\mathcal{D}^p$, $\mathcal{D}$ is the collection of data instances from the population $\mathcal{P}$ (Eq. 1). As before, all data instances in $\mathcal{D}^p$ will belong to a class in $\mathcal{C}$.

$$\mathcal{D} = \{\mathcal{D}^p \mid p \in \mathcal{P}\} \text{ where } \mathcal{D}^p = \{(x, y) \mid y \in \mathcal{C}\} \tag{1}$$

Notably, looking at any two individuals performing the same set of exercises, we see how sensor data capture personal nuances. For instance in Fig. 1, we visualise 2-dimensional compressed pressure mat data (using PCA) of 7 exercise class for 3 persons to exhibit significant differences in data distributions.

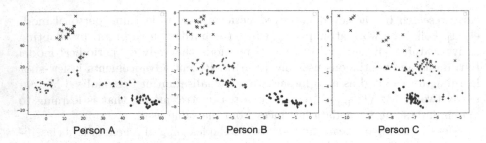

Fig. 1. Data distribution visualisation with PCA for 3 persons from MEx dataset

3.1 Personalised Meta-Learning for HAR

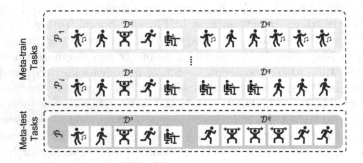

Fig. 2. Personalised meta-learning tasks design for HAR

Meta-learning for few-shot classification can be defined as optimising a generic parametric model over many few-shot tasks (i.e. meta-train), that is able to rapidly adapt to any unseen few-shot task (i.e. meta-test). Here, a few-shot classification task has a "support set", $\mathcal{D}^s$, and a "query set", $\mathcal{D}^q$. The support set represents the training data, with only one or few representatives data instances for each class, and query set is the test data.

Personalised meta-learning for HAR is the learning of a meta-model θ from a population $\mathcal{P}$ while treating activity recognition for a person as an independent few-shot classification task. We propose the task design in Fig. 2 for personalised meta-Learning. Given a dataset $\mathcal{D}$, for population $\mathcal{P}$, we create tasks such that, each "person-task", $\mathcal{P}_i$, only contains data from a specific person, p. We randomly select a $K^s \times |\mathcal{C}|$ number of labelled data instances from person p stratified across activity classes, $\mathcal{C}$, such that there are K^s amount of representatives for each class. We follow a similar approach when selecting a query set, $\mathcal{D}^q$, for $\mathcal{P}_i$. Typically $\mathcal{D}^q$ has no overlap with $\mathcal{D}^s$ similar to a train/test split in supervised learning. Given that existing HAR datasets are not strictly few-shot learning datasets, there can be a few or many data instances available to be sampled for the query set, $\mathcal{D}^q$. Each resulting "person-task" is learning to classify the set of "person-activity" class labels.

At test time, the test person, $\hat{p}$, provides a few seconds of data for each activity class while being recorded by recommended sensor modalities, which forms the support set, $\mathcal{D}^s$, of the person-task, $\hat{\mathcal{P}}$. Thereafter, the meta-model, in conjunction with the support set, predicts the class label for each query data instance, x_i^q, in $\mathcal{D}^q$. After deployment, $\mathcal{D}^q$ is created from the continuous stream of sensor data captured when the test person perform activities in real life. It is noteworthy that, contrary to conventional meta-learning, all personal models and the meta-model are learning to classify the same set of activity classes $\mathcal{C}$, but of different persons (i.e. "person-activity"). Therefore, it is seen as a few-shot classification problem with a $|\mathcal{C}| \times |\mathcal{P}|$ number of classes. Personalised meta-learning is a methodology adaptable with any meta-learner to perform personalised HAR, and next, we show how with two meta-learners, MAML and RN.

3.2 Personalised MAML

Algorithm 1. Personalised MAML Training

Require: $p(\mathcal{P})$: HAR dataset; distribution over persons

Require: $\alpha, \beta, e, n, gs, meta\_gs$
1: randomly initialise θ
2: **for** $i = 0$ **to** e **do**
3:    Sample n person-tasks $\mathcal{P}_i \sim p(\mathcal{P})$
4:    **for all** $\mathcal{P}_i$ **do**
5:      $\mathcal{D}^s = \{(x,y) \in \mathcal{P}_i : |\mathcal{D}^s| = K^s \times |\mathcal{C}|\}$
6:      **for** $i = 0$ **to** gs **do**
7:        Compute $\nabla_\theta \mathcal{L}_{\mathcal{P}_i}(\theta)$ w.r.t. $\mathcal{D}^s$
8:        Compute updated parameters: $\theta_i = \theta - \alpha \nabla_\theta \mathcal{L}_{\mathcal{P}_i}(\theta)$
9:      **end for**
10:     $\mathcal{D}^q = \{(x,y) \in \mathcal{P}_i : \mathcal{D}^s \cap \mathcal{D}^q = \emptyset, |\mathcal{D}^q| = K^q \times |\mathcal{C}|\}$
11:     Compute $\mathcal{L}_{\mathcal{P}_i}(\theta_i)$ w.r.t $\mathcal{D}^q$
12:    **end for**
13:    Meta-update: $\theta \leftarrow \theta - \beta \nabla_\theta \sum_{\mathcal{P}_i \sim p(\mathcal{P})} \mathcal{L}_{\mathcal{P}_i}(\theta_i)$
14: **end for**

Algorithm 2. Personalised MAML Testing

Require: $\mathcal{D}^s$ for test person $\hat{\mathcal{P}}$ obtained via micro-interactions,

Require: θ
1: Initialise $\hat{\theta} = \theta$
2: **for** $i = 0$ **to** $meta\_gs$ **do**
3:    Compute $\nabla_{\hat{\theta}} \mathcal{L}_{\mathcal{P}_i}(\hat{\theta})$ w.r.t. $\mathcal{D}^s$
4:    Compute updated parameters: $\hat{\theta}' = \hat{\theta} - \alpha \nabla_{\hat{\theta}} \mathcal{L}_{\mathcal{P}_i}(\hat{\theta})$
5: **end for**
6: **for all** $\mathcal{D}_i^q$ **do**
7:    predict $y_i^q = \hat{\theta}'(\mathcal{D}_i^q)$
8: **end for**

MAML [2] is a versatile adaptation optimised meta-learner applicable to any parametric classifier model optimised with Gradient Descent (GD). Personalised MAML ($MAML^p$) for HAR is optimised to learn the generic model (i.e. meta-model), θ, such that it is adaptable to any new person encountered at test time. Task design for $MAML^p$ follows the personalised meta-learning methodology. K^s number of data instances per activity class is selected to form the support set, $\mathcal{D}^s$ of a person-task, and all remaining data instances are considered the query set, $\mathcal{D}^q$. More formally, given there are K instances per "person-activity", $K^q = (K - K^s)$ and $\mid \mathcal{D}^q \mid = K^q \times \mid \mathcal{C} \mid$.

$$\mathcal{L}_{\mathcal{P}_i}(\theta_i) = \sum_{x^q, y^q \sim \mathcal{D}_q} y^q \log \theta_i(x^q) + (1 - y^q) \log(1 - \theta_i(x^q)) \tag{2}$$

We present the training of Personalised MAML in Algorithm 1. At each training epoch, a set of person-tasks are sampled where each optimises its person-task-model, θ_i. θ_i is trained with $\mathcal{D}^s$ using one or few steps of GD (gs). The meta-modal, θ is then trained using GD (referred to as the meta-update) using the total losses computed by the trained person-task-models, θ_i, against their respective $\mathcal{D}^q$ using categorical cross-entropy as in Eq. 2. Over the meta training epochs, e, the goal is to learn a generic model by encapsulating the learning experiences of many person-task models (measured by the loss), such that θ that can be rapidly adapted to a new person.

A meta-test person $\hat{p}$, not seen during training, uses their support set, $\mathcal{D}^s$ to train a personalised parametric classifier model $\hat{\theta}$, initialised by the meta-model θ. Here the number of personalisation training epochs is referred to as the meta-gradient steps ($meta\_gs$). After personalisation, $\hat{\theta}$ is used to classify query instances, $\mathcal{D}^q$ as in Algorithm 2. We note that we prefer First-Order MAML when implementing Personalised MAML, which is computationally less intensive, yet achieves comparable performances in comparison to MAML [2].

3.3   Personalised RN

Relation Network (RN) [12] is a few-shot meta-learning algorithm that *learns-to-match* or *similarity optimised*. The goal of RN learning is to learn a generic parametric model suitable for many tasks. In contrast to MAML, this parametric model is not a classifier. Instead, it maps data from any tasks to a discriminatory feature space (discriminated by similarity distance). Once personalised using the personalised meta-learning methodology, Relation Networks RN^p learns a matching, generalisable to any new person encountered at test time. The meta-task design for RN^p is similar to $MAML^p$, where the support set, $\mathcal{D}^s$, and the query set $\mathcal{D}^q$, is selected from the same person. Meta-training instance for person-task, $\mathcal{P}_i$, is created by combining each data instance x_i^q, in $\mathcal{D}^q$, with the support set, $\mathcal{D}^s$ as described below.

$$\mathcal{L}_{\mathcal{P}_i}(\theta_i) = \sum_{x^q, y^q \sim \mathcal{D}_q} \parallel \theta_f, \theta_r(x^q, \mathcal{D}^s) - y^q \parallel_2^2 \tag{3}$$

During training (Algorithm 3), RN^p learns to match x_i^q to a matching instance in $\mathcal{D}^s$ (matched by activity label). A parametric model, θ_f transforms each instance in $\mathcal{D}^s$ to a feature vector; and when $K^s > 1$ prototypical representatives are calculated for each person-activity class by calculating the average feature vector of K^s number of representatives. Next each representative, is paired with feature transformed x_i^q (using θ_f) to create $\mid \mathcal{C} \mid$ number of pairs.

The parametric model, θ_r then predict the similarity of the paired instances. With the personalised approach, the similarity is always estimated against ones own data in the support set. The network is trained end to end for e number of epochs, using mean squared error loss as in Eq. 3. Here the output of θ_r is of size 1 which is expected to be 1 if a matching pair or 0 if not matching pair. A meta-test person $\hat{p}$, not seen during training, can use trained RN^p to match a query instance to a support set instance in $\mathcal{D}^s$ provided during calibration. And therein use the class of the matched support instance as the predicted class label (Algorithm 4).

Algorithm 3. Personalised RN Training

Require: $p(\mathcal{P})$: HAR dataset; distribution over persons
Require: α
1: randomly initialise θ_f and θ_r
2: **for** $i = 0$ to e **do**
3:   Sample n person-tasks $\mathcal{P}_i \sim p(\mathcal{P})$
4:   **for all** $\mathcal{P}_i$ **do**
5:     $\mathcal{D}^s = \{(x,y) \in \mathcal{P}_i : |\mathcal{D}^s| = K^s \times |\mathcal{C}|\}$
6:     $\mathcal{D}^q = \{(x,y) \in \mathcal{P}_i : |\mathcal{D}^q| = K^q \times |\mathcal{C}|, \mathcal{D}^s \cap \mathcal{D}^q = \emptyset\}$
7:     **for all** x_i^q **do**
8:       Create train data instance $(x_i^q, \mathcal{D}^s)$
9:     **end for**
10:   **end for**
11:   Compute $\nabla \mathcal{L}_{\mathcal{P}_i}(\theta_f, \theta_r)$ w.r.t. train data instances of size $n \times K^q \times |\mathcal{C}|$
12:   Update $(\theta_f, \theta_r) \leftarrow (\theta_f, \theta_r) - \alpha \nabla_{\theta_f} \mathcal{L}_{\mathcal{P}_i}(\theta_f, \theta_r)$
13: **end for**

Algorithm 4. Personalised RN Testing

Require: Support set $\mathcal{D}^s$ for test person $\hat{\mathcal{P}}$,
Require: θ_r, θ_f
1: **for all** x_i^q **do**
2:   predict $y_i^q = \theta_f, \theta_r(\mathcal{D}_i^q, \mathcal{D}^s)$
3: **end for**

---

4 Evaluation

We compare the performance of **personalised MAML** ($MAML^p$) and **personalised RN** (RN^p) against the baselines listed below;

DL: Best performing Deep Learning algorithm from benchmarks published in [15]
MN: Few-shot Learning classifier Matching Networks from [14]
MN^p: Personalised Matching Networks from [8]
MAML: Model-Agnostic Meta-Learner [2]
RN: Relation Networks [12]

4.1 Datasets and Pre-processing

We use three data sets to create 9 single modality sensing experiments. MEx[1] is a Physiotherapy Exercises dataset complied with 30 participants performing 7

---

[1] https://archive.ics.uci.edu/ml/datasets/MEx.

exercises. A depth camera (DC), a pressure mat (PM) and two accelerometers on the wrist (ACW) and the thigh (ACT) provide four sensor data streams creating four experiments. PAMAP2[2] dataset contains 8 Activities of Daily Living recorded with 8 participants. Three accelerometers on the hand (H), the chest (C) and the ankle (A) provide three sensor data streams creating 3 experiments. SELFBACK[3] is a HAR dataset with 9 activities. These activities are recorded with 33 participants using two accelerometers on the wrist (W) and the thigh (T), creating 2 experiments.

A sliding window method is applied to each sensor data stream to obtain labelled data instances. The window size of 5 seconds is applied for all 9 datasets and an overlap of 3, 1 and 2.5 for data sources MEx, PAMAP2 and SELFBACK, resulted in 30, 76 and 88 data instance per person-activity on average. A few pre-processing steps are applied to data instances, adapted from previous work [15]. Resulting input sizes for θ_f of RN and θ of MAML are $(5 \times 12 \times 16)$, $(5 \times 16 \times 16)$ and $(5 \times 3 \times 60)$ for DC, PM and AC modalities respectively.

4.2 Experiment Design

We use the DL results for MEx from previous work and for comparability we implement the same 1D-CNN-LSTM architectures for PAMAP2 and SELF-BACK datasets (see [15] for details). We use a 1 layer dense network with 1200 units as the feature learners of each algorithm. RN relation learner is a 3 layer network with 1 2D convolutional layer, and 2 dense layers. All networks use batch normalisation for regularisation. $MAML$, $MAML^p$, RN and RN^p algorithms are trained for 100, 100, 300 and 300 epochs respectively. MN and MN^p experiments are created and trained according to [8].

Meta-learning task designs in the conventional and personalised settings are created with $K^s = 5$. Also, we apply Leave-One-Person-Out (LOPO) train test split where the data from one person is used to create meta-test tasks the rest to create meta-train tasks. Accordingly, meta-test tasks for $MAML$ and RN are comparable to meta-test person-tasks for $MAML^p$ and RN^p. The meta-train and meta-test tasks are created while maintaining class balance; accordingly, we report the accuracy of each experiment averaged over the number of person folds. Since LOPO experiment results that are not normally distributed, non-parametric statistical hypothesis test (Wilcoxon signed-rank test for paired samples) is used to evaluate statistical significance at 95% confidence and highlight the best performances in bold text.

4.3 Results

Table 1 presents the comparative performances for 4 experiments on the exercise recognition task using the MEx modalities. We remind that a MEx experiment creates a few-shot classification setting, where one "person-activity" class

---

[2] http://archive.ics.uci.edu/ml/datasets/pamap2+physical+activity+monitoring.
[3] https://archive.ics.uci.edu/ml/datasets/selfBACK.

has only 30 data instances, and there are $30 \times 7 = 210$ classes. Overall, personalised meta-learning models significantly outperformed DL and conventional meta-learning algorithms. Notably, with visual data, DC and PM, the best performance is achieved by the adaptation optimised personalised meta-learner $MAML^p$, in contrast, accelerometer modalities prefer the similarity optimised RN^p. It is noteworthy that the personalised few-shot learning algorithm MN^p achieves comparable performance against $MAML^p$ with the ACT modality, and also outperform RN^p with DC and PM modalities. Overall, with ExRec, we observe the importance of personalisation and demonstrate that personalised meta-learners successful adapt to new unseen persons with few-data.

Table 1. Performance comparison with MEx for exercise recognition

Algorithm	MEx$_{ACT}$	MEx$_{ACW}$	MEx$_{DC}$	MEx$_{PM}$
DL	0.9015	0.6335	0.8720	0.7408
MN	0.9073	0.4620	0.5065	0.6187
MN^p	0.9155	0.6663	0.9342	0.8205
$MAML$	0.8673	0.6525	0.9629	0.9283
$MAML^p$	0.9106	**0.6834**	**0.9795**	**0.9408**
RN	0.8770	0.5184	0.7628	0.6714
RN^p	**0.9444**	**0.6899**	0.8533	0.7553

Table 2. Performance comparison with SELFBACK and PAMAP2 for HAR

Algorithm	SB$_T$	SB$_W$	PMP$_H$	PMP$_C$	PMP$_A$
DL	0.7880	0.6997	0.7505	0.7878	0.8075
MN	0.8392	0.7669	0.6625	0.7536	0.7361
MN^p	0.9124	**0.8653**	0.7484	**0.8548**	**0.8330**
$MAML$	0.8398	0.7532	0.7593	0.7626	0.6830
$MAML^p$	0.8625	0.8075	**0.8037**	0.7822	0.7256
RN	0.9334	0.8276	0.7818	0.8170	0.7527
RN^p	**0.9487**	0.8528	0.7868	0.8294	0.7761

In comparison to MEx experiments, a PAMAP2 or SELFBACK experiment do not create a strict few-shot classification setting (with 76 and 88 data instances per "person-activity" class). We compare their performance using personalised methodology against conventional DL and few-shot learning methods (Table 2). These experiments help to understand if improvements we observe in MEx experiments can be reproduced in a not-strictly few-shot classification setting. Results show that at least one personalised meta-learner has outperformed the DL performance. Also, personalised meta-learners have outperformed conventional meta-learners in 4 out of 5 experiments except for PMP_H where RN^p and RN performances are comparable. In 2 of the 5 experiments, personalised meta-learners significantly outperformed MN^p. Notably, all experiments achieve their best performance with personalised algorithms, further confirming the significance of personalisation in different domains of HAR. The failure to outperform DL methods with PMP_A is attributed to the more considerable amount of data available for training. Also, all 5 experiment use accelerometer data, where MN^p's simple similarity metric is proven to be sufficient to discriminate significant similarity relations between different classes.

Considering all 9 experiments, we find that visual data prefer the adaptation optimised meta-learner (i.e. $MAML^p$) and experiments with inertial data prefer similarity optimised meta-learners (i.e. MN^p and RN^p). Overall, these results highlight that in a *few-shot setting*, personalisation strategy introduced in this paper has elevated the conventional meta-learners significantly while using shallow feature learners. Personalisation has positively contributed towards eliminating the need for deep parametric models that require an extensive labelled data collection for training. This result is highly significant outcome in the domain of HAR, where even a comprehensive data collection fails to cover all possible personal nuances a recognition model may encounter during deployment.

5   Conventional vs. Personalised Meta-Learners

In this section, we explore meta-learner training to exhibit how personalisation methodology attribute to an improved performance we observed in Sect. 4.3.

5.1   MAML vs. MAML^p

We first investigate the performance improvements achieved by $MAML^p$ over $MAML$. Here we compare three variants, $MAML$ where meta-train and test tasks are created disregarding any personal identifiers; $MAML^p$, as described in Sect. 3.2; and person-aware $MAML$. Here person-aware $MAML$ can be seen as a lazy personalisation of MAML where a meta-train task support set is sampled from multiple persons. Still, the representatives for one exercise class is from one person. The query set will also have data from a single person who may not have been selected to form the support set. This method still preserves the concept of "person-activity" only at the class label level, but not over the entire support set level. LOPO evaluation methodology is used to split the train and test persons and create 30 folds.

We visualise the impact of model adaptation in both, $K^s = 1$, and $K^s = 5$, settings on the MEx$_{PM}$ dataset in Figs. 3 and 4. All experiment design details are similar to Sect. 4.2. Here we plot mean test-task accuracy (please note different ranges in the y-axis) evaluated after every 10 meta-train epochs. At each evaluation point, the meta-test support set is used to adapt the current meta-model for 10 steps. During each adaptation step, we record accuracy using the meta-test query set. Through this process, we can observe the performance of a partially optimised meta-model when being adapted at the test time at increasing adaptation steps.

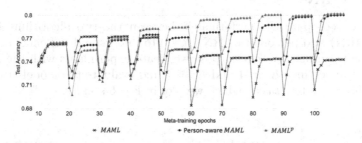

Fig. 3. MAML vs. person-aware MAML vs. MAML^p with MExp$_{PM}$ when $K^s = 1$

Results. $MAML^p$ and person-aware $MAML$ significantly outperformed $MAML$ when $K^s = 1$, and $K^s = 5$. When comparing $MAML^p$ and person-aware $MAML$, $MAML^p$ algorithm achieves a more generic meta-model even before performing meta-test adaptation (1st evaluation at each evaluation point); this is most significant in the $K^s = 1$ setting. These observations verify the advantage of creating personalised tasks. Even with the person-aware $MAML$ algorithm where a task contains data from multiple people, a "person-activity" only containing data from one person has allowed learning a more generic meta-model as seen in comparison to $MAML$.

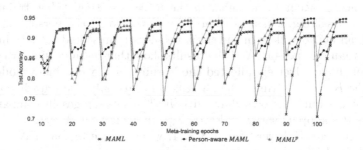

Fig. 4. MAML vs. person-aware MAML vs. MAML^p with MExp$_{PM}$ when $K^s = 5$

Another indication of the significance of personalisation is found when investigating $MAML$ performance over the training epochs. $MAML$ meta-test accuracy after adaptation is not improved over the training epochs, and $MAML$ meta-test accuracy before meta-test adaptation declines consistently. It is most significant when $K^s = 5$, which indicates that the meta-model learned with $MAML$ is not generalisable when an activity class in a meta-train task support set contains data from multiple people. In comparison, meta-model learned with $MAML^p$, performs well on meta-test tasks, even before adaptation.

5.2 RN vs. RN^p

Similarly, we compare the performance between the two algorithms Relation Networks (RN) and personalised RN (RN^p) to understand the effect of personalisation on training. For this purpose we create experiments with the MEx_{PM} dataset in two settings $K^s = 1$ and $K^s = 5$ and evaluate the model at every 10 epochs using meta-test tasks, which we plot in Fig. 5a and b.

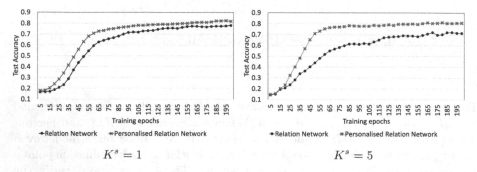

Fig. 5. RN vs. RN^p with MEx_{PM} meta-model tested at every 10 meta-train epochs

Personalisation has significantly improved the meta-training process indicated by the consistently increasing meta-testing accuracy of RN^p over RN. The difference in accuracy is higher in the $K^s = 5$ setting. When training RN in the $K^s = 5$ setting, a task is created by disregarding the person parameter; as a result, an activity class in the supports set is represented by data instances from more than one person. And the results show that learning similarities from many people have adversely affected the learning of the RN meta-model. Similarly, in the $K^s = 1$ setting, when a task contains only one data instance per class, learning from ones own data with RN^p is advantages in comparison to RN, where the support set includes multiple persons. Notably, $K^s = 5$ performance is significantly lower than $K^s = 1$, which suggests that RN^p and RN both find it is challenging to optimising a feature learner when many instances are present in the support set. Overall, these results confirm the strong presence of personal nuances in sensor data, that need to be considered when creating classification models for exercise recognition.

6   Discussion

While RN^P does not require model-retraining, obtaining the activity class label for a given query involves a complex inference process as discussed in Sect. 3.3.

We calculate the average time elapsed for obtaining a prediction on the MEx_{ACT} query data instance, using both algorithms in a computer with 8GB RAM and 3.1 GHz Dual-Core processor. While $MAML^p$ takes 0.0156 ms for a single prediction, RN^p takes 2.4982 ms when $K^s = 1$ and 3.7218 ms when $K^s = 5$. A HAR algorithm should be able to recognise activities as they are performed in real-time for the best user experience. Thus, minimal computational requirements and latency are also critical considerations for edge device deployment. In comparison, $MAML^p$ inference is a simple classification task but requires post-deployment model re-training that also computationally demanding.

A limitation of $MAML^p$ is the inability to perform open-ended HAR. Originally both $MAML$ and RN perform zero-shot image classification [2,12] with a fixed class length. Specifically, $MAML$ is restricted to performing multi-class classification with a soft-max layer. Open-ended HAR requires dynamic expansion of the decision layer as the user adds new activities in addition to the activities that are already included. Few-shot classifiers such as Matching Networks (MN) [14] does not have a strict decision layer which inspired Open-ended MN [16] for Open-ended HAR. Similarities of RN to MN presents the opportunity to improve Open-ended HAR, which we will explore in future.

When a Personalised Meta-Learning model is trained and embedded in the fitness application, there is an initial configuration step that is required for collecting the calibration data (i.e. support set) of the end-user. The end-user will be instructed to record a few seconds of data for each activity using the sensor modalities synchronised with the fitness application. This step is similar to demographic configurations users perform when installing new fitness applications (on-boarding). After that, this support set will be used by the algorithm either to re-train the model ($MAML^p$) or for comparison (RN^p). Notably, both $MAML^p$ and RN^p provide the opportunity to provide new calibration data if the physiology or preferences of the user change over time.

7   Conclusion

In this paper, we presented *personalised meta-learning*, a methodology optimised for personalisation of Human Activity Recognition (HAR) using only a few labelled data. This is achieved by treating the "person-activity" pair in a HAR dataset as an activity class, where each class now has only a few instances of data for training. We implement personalised meta-learning with two meta-learners for few-shot classification personalised MAML ($MAML^p$) and personalised Relation Networks (RN^p) where a meta-model is learned, such that it can be rapidly adapted to any person not seen during training. Both algorithms require only a few instances of calibration data from the end-user to personalised the meta-model. At deployment, $MAML^p$ uses calibration data for model re-training and RN^p uses calibration data directly for matching (without re-training). Our evaluation with 9 experiments shows that both algorithms achieve significant performance improvements in a range of HAR domains while outperforming state-of-the-art deep learning and conventional meta-learning algorithms. We highlight that personalisation achieves higher meta-model generalisation, compared to conventional methods, allowing rapid adaptation. Importantly we find, real-time inference with $MAML^p$ is significantly faster with fewer memory requirements compared to RN^p where calibration data need to be retained in memory.

References

1. Berchtold, M., Budde, M., Gordon, D., Schmidtke, H.R., Beigl, M.: ActiServ: activity recognition service for mobile phones. In: International Symposium on Wearable Computers (ISWC) 2010, pp. 1–8. IEEE (2010)
2. Finn, C., Abbeel, P., Levine, S.: Model-agnostic meta-learning for fast adaptation of deep networks. In: Proceedings of the 34th ICML, vol. 70, pp. 1126–1135 (2017). JMLR. org
3. Graves, A., Wayne, G., Danihelka, I.: Neural turing machines. arXiv preprint arXiv:1410.5401 (2014)
4. Longstaff, B., Reddy, S., Estrin, D.: Improving activity classification for health applications on mobile devices using active and semi-supervised learning. In: 2010 4th International Conference on Pervasive Computing Technologies for Healthcare, pp. 1–7. IEEE (2010)
5. Mishra, N., Rohaninejad, M., Chen, X., Abbeel, P.: A simple neural attentive meta-learner. arXiv preprint arXiv:1707.03141 (2017)
6. Nichol, A., Achiam, J., Schulman, J.: On first-order meta-learning algorithms. arXiv preprint arXiv:1803.02999 (2018)
7. Ordóñez, F.J., Roggen, D.: Deep convolutional and lstm recurrent neural networks for multimodal wearable activity recognition. Sensors 16(1), 115 (2016)
8. Sani, S., Wiratunga, N., Massie, S., Cooper, K.: Personalised human activity recognition using matching networks. In: Cox, M., Funk, P., Begum, S. (eds.) Case-Based Reasoning Research and Development. ICCBR 2018. Lecture Notes in Computer Science, vol. 11156, pp. 339–353. Springer, Cham (2018). https://doi.org/10.1007/978-3-030-01081-2_23
9. Santoro, A., Bartunov, S., Botvinick, M., Wierstra, D., Lillicrap, T.: Meta-learning with memory-augmented neural networks. In: International Conference on Machine Learning, pp. 1842–1850 (2016)
10. Snell, J., Swersky, K., Zemel, R.: Prototypical networks for few-shot learning. In: Advances in Neural Information Processing Systems, pp. 4077–4087 (2017)
11. Sun, X., Kashima, H., Ueda, N.: Large-scale personalized human activity recognition using online multitask learning. IEEE Trans. Knowl. Data Eng. 25(11), 2551–2563 (2012)
12. Sung, F., Yang, Y., Zhang, L., Xiang, T., Torr, P.H., Hospedales, T.M.: Learning to compare: relation network for few-shot learning. In: Proceedings of the IEEE Conference on CVPR, pp. 1199–1208 (2018)
13. Tapia, E.M., et al.: Real-time recognition of physical activities and their intensities using wireless accelerometers and a heart rate monitor. In: 2007 11th IEEE International Symposium on Wearable Computers, pp. 37–40. IEEE (2007)
14. Vinyals, O., Blundell, C., Lillicrap, T., Wierstra, D., et al.: Matching networks for one shot learning. In: Advances in Neural Information Processing Systems, pp. 3630–3638 (2016)
15. Wijekoon, A., Wiratunga, N., Cooper, K.: Mex: Multi-modal exercises dataset for human activity recognition. arXiv preprint arXiv:1908.08992 (2019)

16. Wijekoon, A., Wiratunga, N., Sani, S., Cooper, K.: A knowledge-light approach to personalised and open-ended human activity recognition. Knowl. Based Syst. **192**, 105651 (2020)
17. Yao, S., Hu, S., Zhao, Y., Zhang, A., Abdelzaher, T.: Deepsense: a unified deep learning framework for time-series mobile sensing data processing. In: Proceedings of the 26th International Conference on World Wide Web, pp. 351–360 (2017)

CostNet: An End-to-End Framework
for Goal-Directed Reinforcement Learning

Per-Arne Andersen$^{(\boxtimes)}$ ⓘ, Morten Goodwin ⓘ, and Ole-Christoffer Granmo ⓘ

Department of ICT, University of Agder, Grimstad, Norway
{per.andersen,morten.goodwin,ole.granmo}@uia.no

Abstract. Reinforcement Learning (RL) is a general framework concerned with an agent that seeks to maximize rewards in an environment. The learning typically happens through trial and error using explorative methods, such as ϵ-greedy. There are two approaches, model-based and model-free reinforcement learning, that show concrete results in several disciplines. Model-based RL learns a model of the environment for learning the policy while model-free approaches are fully explorative and exploitative without considering the underlying environment dynamics. Model-free RL works conceptually well in simulated environments, and empirical evidence suggests that trial and error lead to a near-optimal behavior with enough training. On the other hand, model-based RL aims to be sample efficient, and studies show that it requires far less training in the real environment for learning a good policy.

A significant challenge with RL is that it relies on a well-defined reward function to work well for complex environments and such a reward function is challenging to define. Goal-Directed RL is an alternative method that learns an intrinsic reward function with emphasis on a few explored trajectories that reveals the path to the goal state.

This paper introduces a novel reinforcement learning algorithm for predicting the distance between two states in a Markov Decision Process. The learned distance function works as an intrinsic reward that fuels the agent's learning. Using the distance-metric as a reward, we show that the algorithm performs comparably to model-free RL while having significantly better sample-efficiently in several test environments.

Keywords: Reinforcement Learning · Markov decision processes · Neural networks · Representation learning · Goal-directed Reinforcement Learning

1 Introduction

Goal-directed reinforcement learning (GDRL) separates the learning into two phases, where phase one aims to solve the goal-directed exploration problem (GDE). To solve the GDE problem, the agent must determine at least one viable path from the initial state to the goal state. In phase two, the agent uses the

© Springer Nature Switzerland AG 2020
M. Bramer and R. Ellis (Eds.): SGAI-AI 2020, LNAI 12498, pp. 94–107, 2020.
https://doi.org/10.1007/978-3-030-63799-6_7

learned path to find a near-optimal path. The two phases iterate until the agent policy is converged.

Reinforcement learning (RL) classifies into two categories of algorithms. Model-free RL learns a policy or a value-function by interaction with the environment and succeeds in various simulated areas, including video-games [19,25], robotics [12,15], and autonomous vehicles [7,24], but comes at the cost of efficiency. Specifically, model-free approaches suffer from low sample efficiency and are a fundamental limitation for application in real-world physical systems.

On the other hand, Model-based reinforcement learning (MBRL) aims to learn a predictive model of the environment to increase sample efficiency. The agent samples from the learned predictive model, which reduces the required interaction with the environment. However, it is challenging to achieve good accuracy of the predictive model for many domains, specifically for high complexity environments. With high complexity comes high modeling error (model-bias) and it is perhaps the most common problem for unstable and collapsing policies in model-based RL. Recent work in model-based RL focuses primarily on learning high-dimensional and complex predictive models with graphics as part of the MDP. This complicates the model severely and limits long-horizon predictions as the prediction-error increases exponentially.

This paper address this issue with a combination of GDRL and MBRL by learning a predictive model and a distance model that describes the distance between two states. The learned predictive model abstracts the state-space to distance between state and goal, which reduce the state-complexity significantly. The learned distance is applied to the reward-function of Deep Q Learning (DQN) [18] and accelerates the learning effectively. The proposed algorithm, CostNet, is an end-to-end solution for goal-directed reinforcement learning where the main contributions are summarized as follows.

1. CostNet for estimating the distance between arbitrary states and terminal states,
2. modified objective for DQN for efficient goal-directed reinforcement learning, and
3. the proposed method demonstrates excellent performance in simulated grid-like environments.

The paper is organized as follows. Section 2 details the preliminary work for the proposed method. Section 3 presents a detailed overview of related work. Section 4 introduces CostNet, a novel algorithm for cost-directed reinforcement learning. Section 5 thoroughly presents the results of the proposed approach, and Sect. 6 summarizes the work and propose future work in Goal-Directed Reinforcement learning.

2   Background

Model-based reinforcement learning builds a model of the environment to derive its behavioral policy. The underlying mechanism is a Markov Decision Process

(MDP), which mathematically defines the synergy between state, reward, and actions as a tuple $M = (S, A, T, R)$, where $S = \{s_n, \ldots, s_{t+n}\}$ is a set of possible states and $A = \{a_n, \ldots, a_{t+n}\}$ is a set of possible actions. The state transition function $T : S \times A \times S \rightarrow [0, 1]$, which the predictive model tries to learn is a probability function such that $T_{a_t}(s_t, s_{t+1})$ is the probability that current state s_t transitions to s_{t+1} given that the agent choses action a_t. The reward function $R : S \times A \rightarrow \mathbb{R}$ where $R_{a_t}(s_t, s_{t+1})$ returns the immediate reward received on when taking action a in state s_t with transition to s_{t+1}. The policy takes the form $\pi = \{s_1, a_1, s_2, a_2, \ldots, s_n, a_n\}$ where $\pi(a|s)$ denotes chosen action given a state. Model-based reinforcement learning divides primarily into three categories: 1) Dyna-based, 2) Policy Search-based, and 3) Shooting-based algorithms in which this work concerns Dyna-based approaches. The Dyna algorithm from [26] trains in two steps. First, the algorithm collects experience from interaction with the environment using a policy from a model-free algorithm (i.e., Q-learning). This experience is part of learning an estimated model of the environment, also referred to as a predictive model. Second, the agent policy samples imagined data generated by the predictive model and update its parameters towards optimal behavior.

Autoencoders are commonly used in supervised learning to encode arbitrary input to a compact representation, and using a decoder to reconstruct the original data from the encoding. The purpose of autoencoders is to store redundant data into a densely packed vector form. In its simplest form, an autoencoder consists of a feed-forward neural network where the input and output layer is of equal neuron capacity and the hidden layer smaller, used to compress the data. The model consists of an encoder $Q(z|X)$, latent variable distribution $P(z)$, and decoder $P(\hat{X}|z)$. The input X is a vector that represents only a fraction of the ground truth. The objective is for the autoencoder to learn the distribution of all possible training samples, including data not in the training data, but nevertheless, part of the distribution $P(X)$. The final objective for the model is $\mathbb{E}[logP(X|z)] - D_{KL}[Q(z|X)\|P(z)]$, where the first term denotes the reconstruction loss, similar to standard autoencoders and the second term the distance between the estimated latent-space and the ground truth space. The ground truth latent-space is difficult to define, and therefore it is assumed to be a Gaussian, and hence, the learned distribution should also be a Gaussian.

3   Related Work

Pioneering work of the goal-directed viewpoint of reinforcement learning, uniformly suggests that pre-processing of the state-representation (i.e., model-based RL) and careful reward modeling is the preferred method to perform efficient GDRL. The following section introduces related work in GDRL and relevant model-based reinforcement learning methods[1].

---

[1] The reader is referred to [20] for an in-depth survey of MBRL-based methods.

3.1   Goal-Directed Reinforcement Learning

Earlier studies have contributed significantly to improve the abilities to solve reinforcement learning problems with a goal-directed approach. Perhaps the most well-known study of the Goal-Directed Reinforcement Learning problem begins with Koenig and Simmons [13]. Their approach splits the problem into two phases, known as Goal-directed exploration (GDEP) and knowledge exploitation. The study finds that the convergence of GDRL-based $\hat{Q}$- and Q-learning closely relates to the state representation and volume of prior knowledge. Furthermore, their work shows that computationally intractable problems are tractable with minor modifications to the state- representation.

Braga and Araújo apply GDRL in [5], using temporal-difference learning to collect prior knowledge and to create a reward and penalty surface explaining the environment dynamics. The map acts as an expert advisor for the TD algorithm and proves the policy performance. Their work shows that the concept of GDRL works well in grid-based environments and includes significantly better sample efficiency compared to Q Learning.

In [17], the authors study the importance of reward function and initial Q-values for GDRL. The authors thoroughly studied the effect of different initial states of the Q-table and found it challenging to design a generic algorithm for initially setting optimal parameters. However, they found that initial values impact the performance and sample efficiency considerably. Furthermore, the author shows that adding a *goal bias leads to much faster learning* and recommends an *adjustable continuous reward function*. More recently, Debnath et al. propose a hybrid approach, formalized as a GDRL problem, where the first phase optimizes a predictive model of the environment with samples from a model-free reinforcement learning policy. The second phase exploits the learned predictive model to improve the policy further, similar to [3]. The authors show that GDRL-based algorithms accelerate learning and improve sample efficiency considerably [6].

3.2   Model-Based Reinforcement Learning

The Model-Ensemble Trust-Region Policy Optimization (ME-TRPO), formally proposed by [14], is a Dyna-based algorithm for learning a predictive model. The ME-TRPO method uses an ensemble of neural networks to form the predictive model, which significantly reduces model-bias, increasing its generalization abilities. The ensemble individually trains using single-step L2 loss in a supervised setting. After training of the algorithm, the authors use Trust-Region Policy Optimization from [22] as the model-free approach. The work shows significantly faster convergence in several continuous control tasks.

The ME-TRPO method extends to Stochastic Lower Bound Optimization (SLBO) [16]. In comparison, SLBO modifies the single-step L2 loss to multi-step L2-norm loss to the train ensemble predictive model. The authors present a mathematical framework for the guaranteed monotonic improvement of the predictive model.

In [10], the authors analyze previous methods and their capability to generalize well for longer time horizons. Their analysis suggests that the performance is good for shorter time horizons, but exponentially decrease as uncertainty appears when predicting longer rollouts. The proposed algorithm is called Model-based Policy Optimization (MBPO) and balance a trade-off between sample efficiency and performance. The paper suggests a prediction horizon between and 1–15 states, up to 200 states. In conclusion, MBPO shows that model-based approaches can outperform state-of-the-art model-free reinforcement learning when tuning appropriately.

4   CostNet for Goal-Directed RL

CostNet is a combination of four disciplines in Deep Learning, 1) Goal Directed RL [13], 2) Model-Based RL [27], and 3) Variational Autoencoders [11] and forms a novel approach for learning the cost between states modeled after an MDP. The algorithm accumulates training data from using expert systems or random sampling. For systems where safety is a priority, it is advised to perform sampling according to manually defined risk constraints at the cost of increased sample complexity [3].

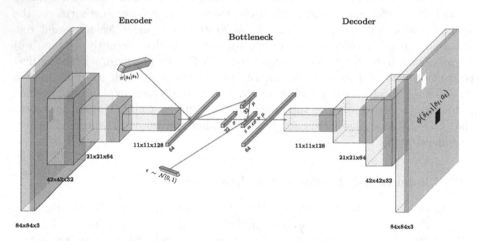

Fig. 1. The encoder-latent-decoder architecture for learning a compact representation of states. The model is a convolutional variational autoencoder with three layers of convolutions before the latent-vector computation. The input is a state s_t. The latent-space, z forms from an estimated μ, and σ, mean and standard-deviation respectively, from a Gaussian. The $\epsilon \sim N$ denotes sampling using the reparametrization trick, as described in [11]. On the right-hand side, the estimated latent-variable z reconstructs into the future state $\hat{s}_{t+1}$

The initial phase of training revolves around training a predictive model of the environment. Recent work indicates that state-of-the-art models suffer from sever policy drift after a few predictions [2,8,10], and CostNet is no exception. Therefore, the problem is redefined to learning only the one-step prediction under a policy $\phi(\hat{s}_{t+1}|s_t, a_t)^\pi$, where ϕ denotes the predictive model. The predictive model is a variational autoencoder (VAE), where the goal is to map input (state) to latent-vectors that describes best possible describe the input. Figure 1 illustrates the proposed structure for the encoder-latent-decoder model for CostNet. The input is an image of an arbitrary state, and the hidden layers are convolutions with 32, 64, and 128 filters, a kernel size of 2, and a stride of 2 with ReLU activation, respectively. The latent-vector size is 64 neurons, but it is highly advised to fine-tune these hyper-parameters as the required embedding capacity varies on the state-complexity.

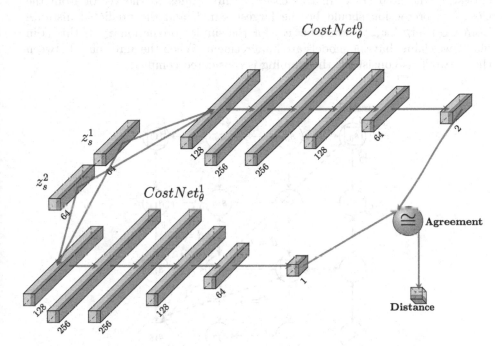

Fig. 2. The proposed CostNet architecture. There are in-total two inputs, z_s^1 and z_s^2, that represent encoded states (see Figure 1. The inputs are sent through two streams (models), $CostNet_\theta^0$, and $CostNet_\theta^1$, and learns two separate objectives using MSE. During training, both networks must agree on the answer for gradients to contribute in a positive direction. When both networks predict the same state to be closest to the goal state, the training is completed. The hidden layers are regular fully-connected with ReLU activation. The output for $CostNet_\theta^0$ activates with softmax, and $CostNet_\theta^1$ with sigmoid activation.

The model-based approach to encode states as is developed as a method to improve the performance of the feed-forward neural network. Figure 2 shows the proposed architecture for the CostNet algorithm and consists of two models with different objectives. The first model, CostNet_θ^0, predicts which of the two states are closest to the goal, $state_A$, or $state_B$. The output is a vector that describes the probability of both $state_A$ and $state_B$ being closest to the goal. The second model, CostNet_θ^1, predicts the absolute distance to a goal state as a real number between 0 and 1, where 0 is at the goal state, and 1 is at maximum possible distance. Both networks train using mean squared error (MSE) loss, where the labels stem from the experience-buffer and the distance label from a backtracking algorithm. The predictions are considered correct (reliable) when there is an agreement between both networks, i.e. that CostNet_θ^0 correctly predicts which of $state_A$ or $state_B$ is closest, and CostNet_θ^1 predict the actual distance.

To exemplify, consider the inputs z_s^1 ($state_A$) and z_s^2 ($state_B$) where z_s^1 is closest to the goal state. In this case, the first index in the vector from the CostNet_θ^0 prediction should be the largest signal, and the predicted distance from CostNet_θ^1 for z_s^1 should be less for the similar prediction z_s^1. If this is in place, we claim that the models are in agreement. When the agreement between the networks is consistent, the training is considered complete.

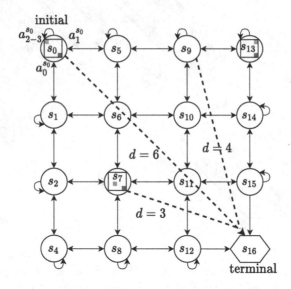

Fig. 3. Illustration of the reformulation of the model-based MDP problem. State 0, 7, and 13 illustrate the usual state complexity for each node in the MDP graph; a pixel-based (full-state) representation. CostNet, on the other hand, simplifies the state nodes to only a single metric: **distance**. This simplifies the complexity of the state-space significantly, and for GDRL-based approaches is sufficient representation.

Figure 3 shows how the MDP is reduced to only focus on the distance to the goal-state. In regular MDP's the whole state information is represented at each node, illustrated by the inner square in state $s_0, s_7,$ and s_{13}. However, in this work, the MDP nodes only try to model the distance from one node to an arbitrary goal node. The problem with this formulation is that 1) there may be many goal states, and 2) agent must visit a goal state at least once. Therefore, the goal-directed approach works best in environments with less stochasticity in terms location of the goal states.

Algorithm 1: CostNet with Deep Q-Learning

Result: Optimized policy π given a set of states S, actions A)

1 **Hyperparameters**: Discount factor $\gamma \in [0 \ldots 1]$, Learning-rate $\alpha \in [0 \ldots 1]$, and Drift threshold $\psi \in [0 \ldots 1]$

2 **Assumptions:** Experience-Replay (ER) from expert-system or random sampling, Ω

3 **while** *training* **do**

4   Train predictive model $\phi(\hat{s}_{t+1}, z_t | s_t, s_{t+1}, a_t)$ from ER using objective $\mathbb{E}[log P(X|z)] - D_{KL}[Q(z|X)\|P(z)]$

5   **if** $\phi < \psi$ **then**

6   Train first supervised CostNet C_θ^1 using $z_t, \hat{z}_{t+1}$ from $\phi(z_t|s_t)$ and $\phi(\hat{z}_{t+1}|\hat{s}_{t+1})$ with MSE loss.

7   Train second supervised CostNet C_θ^2 using z_t from $\phi(z_t|s_t)$ with MSE loss.

8   **if** $C_\theta^1 \cong C_\theta^2$ *for most predictions (agreement)* **then**

9   training = false

10   **end**

11   **end**

12 **end**

13 **while** *training DQN* **do**

14   Choose action a based on ϵ-greedy Execute a at state s and get s_{t+1}, r Perform Q-Update:

15     $L_i(\theta_i) = \mathbb{E}_{s,a,r,s' \sim \rho(.)}\left[(y_i - Q(s,a;\theta_i))^2 \right]$ where $y_i = \frac{r}{1-C_\theta^2} + \gamma \max_{a'} Q(s',a';\theta_{i-1})$

16 **end**

Predictive Model. The algorithm is summarized in the following line-by-line procedure. (Line 1) Initialize hyper-parameters for γ, α, and ψ where the drift-threshold evaluates for n future predictions. When the algorithm is consistently below the threshold, training is complete. (Line 4) Train the predictive model using the ER-buffer using the objective from [11] where $Q(z|X)$ is the encoder to latent-space, $P(z)$ is the distribution of latent-space, and $P(X|z)$ is the decoder distribution. The object splits into two terms. The first term is the reconstruction loss (MSE), and the second term computes the KL distance between the predicted latent distribution $Q(z|X)$ and the assumed normal distributed space $P(z) \sim N(0,1)$. (Line 5) when the predicted model is below the drift-threshold ψ, the training concludes.

CostNet. (Line 6, Line 7) The CostNet$_\theta^0$ model trains with encoded states z_t and z_{t+1} as input and produces a vector that predicts a probability for each of the states being closest to the goal state. A second model, CostNet$_\theta^1$ predicts the distance for a single state, and when the predictions align consistently, the training concludes[2]. (Line 13) The training CostNet is complete, and regular model-free RL is performed, using DQN [18] respectively.

Model-Free RL. (Line 14, Line 15) The agent performs regular sampling to accumulate ER for training. The training is performed similarly to [18], but modifies the reward signal to account for the distance from the goal state. When the distance signal is weak, the agent receives little reward and otherwise large rewards for states close to the goal state.

5   Results and Discussion

The CostNet algorithm is tested in four environments, CartPole-v1 from [4], DeepRTS GoldCollect [1][3], and DeepMaze StaticNoWalls [2][4]. The experiments compare CostNet to DQN [18], and PPO [23] for 1000000 timesteps during 100 experiments for statistical analysis of the results[5].

5.1   Results

Table 1. Hyper-parameters of CostNet algorithm

Parameter	Value
Learning Rate (DQN)	0.01
Discount Factor (DQN)	0.95
ER-Size (DQN)	5000
Optimizer	Adam
Optimizer Learning Rate	0.001
Drift-Threshold ψ	0.3

The hyper-parameters for CostNet are shown in Table 1. Figure 4 shows the environments used in the experiments. The first environment is CartPole, a common benchmark for exploratory reinforcement learning research. The objective is to balance a pole on a cart for 500 timesteps at which the episodes end. The second environment is DeepRTS Gold-Collect, a simple environment where the goal is to accumulate as much gold as possible for 5 min. The optimal episodic reward for this environment is 1000. Finally, the DeepMaze StaticNoWalls environment is an 11×11 grid structure where the goal is located at a fixed position. The reward for DeepMaze is the length of the maze because the agent and goal are located at opposite corners.

---

[2] CostNet$_\theta^x$ where θ is the parameters that are optimized for the model.
[3] The DeepRTS environment is available at: https://github.com/cair/deep-rts.
[4] The DeepMaze environment is available at: https://github.com/cair/deep-maze.
[5] The experiments are available here https://github.com/cair/CostNet.

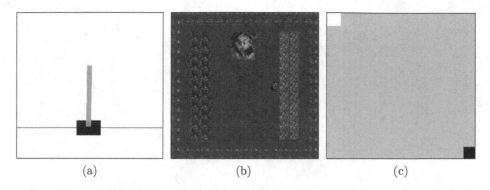

(a)   (b)   (c)

Fig. 4. Illustration of the experiments. (a) Cart Pole. Goal is to balance the pole until terminal state occurs. (b) DeepRTS GoldCollect. Gather as much gold as possible in a time-frame of 5 min. (c) DeepMaze. The player (white) must enter the terminal state (black) in shortest possible time.

Figure 5 compares the performance of CostNet against two competing algorithms, DQN and PPO. Several parameters for the drift-threshold parameter ψ is tested, but a value of 0.3 seems to be stable across several environments. The PPO algorithm uses the parameters defined in [23] and for DQN in [19]. Cost-Net shows significantly better performance across all environments in terms of variance, seen clearly in the DeepMaze environment results. The primary reason for this is that the algorithm starts with a relatively good idea of the underlying environment dynamics from learning the predictive model. Furthermore, in terms of raw performance, the CostNet agent starts at near-optimal performance in some environments, such as the DeepRTS Gold-Collect environment. There are still challenges to be investigated, such as preventing divergence if the policy is already doing good behavior. Another problem is that CostNet demands initial data from expert systems which, is not possible in all environments. Regardless of these challenges, the algorithm is a good leap in the right direction and clearly CostNetwith a modified DQN reward-function, significantly increases the agent's performance, especially in more complex environments such as Deep RTS.

5.2   Discussion

This paper's contribution shows that it is possible to learn distances between states in an MDP reliably and that the learned distance is useful for generic reward functions. The significance of applicability for CostNet spans across several disciplines. **Games** are perhaps the most obvious application for the algorithm as it is not always trivial to design reward functions generic enough to describe every state a complex MDP. While the proposed algorithm also suffers from generalization for multi-objective environments, it is still more accurate in learning reward functions compared to manually crafted functions. **Industry** the CostNet algorithm is applicable to the industry, especially in areas where

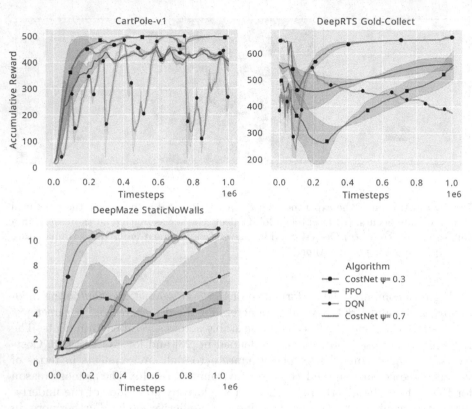

Fig. 5. A comparison of PPO (square), DQN (circle), CostNet (unmarked and diamond) performance in CartPole, DeepRTS, and Deep Maze environment. The y-axis shows the accumulated reward, and the x-axis is at which timestep. Every experiment runs for 100 episodes for 1 million timesteps. CostNet shows outstanding performance compared to fully model-free variants in two of three environments. In CartPole, PPO is superior, but CostNet closely follows. The experiments show that increasing the drift-threshold ψ also decreases performance and are an indication that CostNet impacts performance positively.

the goal is stationary for all timesteps. One example is grid-warehousing, where agents operate on an A-to-B objective. However, upholding safety is a big concern when using RL-based algorithms, and therefore, GLDR-based approaches should be used with care.

6   Future Work and Conclusion

One question that merits future investigation is how to define optimal encode the state-space into latent-vectors. Using VAE is efficient, but still suffers from severe policy-shift for many-step future predictions. The proposed method is generic and should yield significant benefits from encoders that surpass VAE. Specifically, the VQ-VAE2 [21] shows promise, surpassing VAE in several disciplines.

It would be interesting to see the effect VQ-VAE's discrete latent representation has on the overall performance when calculating state-to-state distances.

Another enticing direction for future work is analytical work for the Cost-Net architecture. The algorithm shows promising results empirically, which is often the case for deep reinforcement learning, but it remains future work to analytically prove the algorithm. Furthermore, in the extension of this work, the goal is to test the algorithm in many environments such as the MuJoCo, Atari Arcade, and DeepMind Lab environment to investigate its capabilities to generalize.

CostNet is a novel architecture for accelerating model-free reinforcement learning by combining goal-directed reinforcement learning and model-based reinforcement learning. The hybrid approach learns a predictive model, similar to [9], but learns a simpler model, CostNet, which captures only the distance between any given state and a terminal state. The algorithm outperforms DQN and PPO in several environments and shows outstanding stability during learning. Furthermore, CostNet shows promise for several disciplines, including games, industry, and autonomous driving. The hope is that future studies will lead to many more successes.

References

1. Andersen, P., Goodwin, M., Granmo, O.: Deep RTS: a game environment for deep reinforcement learning in real-time strategy games. In: 2018 IEEE Conference on Computational Intelligence and Games (CIG), pp. 1–8 (aug 2018). https://doi.org/10.1109/CIG.2018.8490409
2. Andersen, P.-A., Goodwin, M., Granmo, O.-C.: The dreaming variational autoencoder for reinforcement learning environments. In: Bramer, M., Petridis, M. (eds.) SGAI 2018. LNCS (LNAI), vol. 11311, pp. 143–155. Springer, Cham (2018). https://doi.org/10.1007/978-3-030-04191-5_11
3. Andersen, P., Goodwin, M., Granmo, O.: Increasing sample efficiency in deep reinforcement learning using generative environment modelling. Expert Syst. (2020). https://doi.org/10.1111/exsy.12537
4. Brockman, G., et al.: OpenAI Gym. arxiv preprint arXiv:1606.01540 (2016). http://arxiv.org/abs/1606.01540
5. de S. Braga, A.P., Araújo, A.F.R.: Goal-directed reinforcement learning using variable learning rate. In: de Oliveira, F.M. (ed.) SBIA 1998. LNCS (LNAI), vol. 1515, pp. 131–140. Springer, Heidelberg (1998). https://doi.org/10.1007/10692710_14
6. Debnath, S., Sukhatme, G., Liu, L.: Accelerating goal-directed reinforcement learning by model characterization. In: IEEE International Conference on Intelligent Robots and Systems, pp. 8666–8673. Institute of Electrical and Electronics Engineers Inc., December 2018. https://doi.org/10.1109/IROS.2018.8593728
7. Grigorescu, S., Trasnea, B., Cocias, T., Macesanu, G.: A survey of deep learning techniques for autonomous driving. J. Field Robot. 37(3), 362–386 (2020). https://doi.org/10.1002/rob.21918

8. Ha, D., Schmidhuber, J.: Recurrent world models facilitate policy evolution. In: Bengio, S., Wallach, H., Larochelle, H., Grauman, K., Cesa-Bianchi, N., Garnett, R. (eds.) Advances in Neural Information Processing Systems, Montréal, CA, vol. 31, pp. 2450–2462. Curran Associates Inc., September 2018. http://papers.nips.cc/paper/7512-recurrent-world-models-facilitate-policy-evolution.pdf

9. Hafner, D., et al.: Learning latent dynamics for planning from pixels. In: Chaudhuri, K., Salakhutdinov, R. (eds.) Proceedings of the 36th International Conference on Machine Learning, ICML 2018, Long Beach, CA, USA, vol. 97, pp. 2555–2565. PMLR, June 2019. http://proceedings.mlr.press/v97/hafner19a/hafner19a.pdf

10. Janner, M., Fu, J., Zhang, M., Levine, S.: When to trust your model: model-based policy optimization. In: Wallach, H., Larochelle, H., Beygelzimer, A., Alché-Buc, F., Fox, E., Garnett, R. (eds.) Proceedings of the 33rd Conference on Neural Information Processing Systems (NeurIPS), Vancouver, BC, Canada, pp. 12519–12530. Curran Associates Inc., June 2019. http://papers.nips.cc/paper/9416-when-to-trust-your-model-model-based-policy-optimization.pdf

11. Kingma, D.P., Welling, M.: Auto-encoding variational Bayes. In: Proceedings of the 2nd International Conference on Learning Representations, December 2013. https://doi.org/10.1051/0004-6361/201527329

12. Kober, J., Bagnell, J.A., Peters, J.: Reinforcement learning in robotics: a survey. Int. J. Robot. Res. **32**(11), 1238–1274 (2013). https://doi.org/10.1177/0278364913495721

13. Koenig, S., Simmons, R.G.: The effect of representation and knowledge on goal-directed exploration with reinforcement-learning algorithms. Mach. Learn. **22**(1/2/3), 227–250 (1996). https://doi.org/10.1023/A:1018068507504

14. Kurutach, T., Clavera, I., Duan, Y., Tamar, A., Abbeel, P.: Model-ensemble trust-region policy optimization. In: 6th International Conference on Learning Representations, Vancouver, BC, Canada (2018). https://openreview.net/forum?id=SJJinbWRZ

15. Levine, S., Finn, C., Darrell, T., Abbeel, P.: End-to-end training of deep visuomotor policies. J. Mach. Learn. Res. **17**(1), 1334–1373 (2016). http://www.jmlr.org/papers/volume17/15-522/15-522.pdf

16. Luo, Y., Xu, H., Li, Y., Tian, Y., Darrell, T., Ma, T.: Algorithmic framework for model-based reinforcement learning with theoretical guarantees. In: Proceedings, 8th International Conference on Learning Representations (ICLR) (2018). https://openreview.net/forum?id=BJe1E2R5KX

17. Matignon, L., Laurent, G.J., Le Fort-Piat, N.: Reward function and initial values: better choices for accelerated goal-directed reinforcement learning. In: Kollias, S.D., Stafylopatis, A., Duch, W., Oja, E. (eds.) ICANN 2006. LNCS, vol. 4131, pp. 840–849. Springer, Heidelberg (2006). https://doi.org/10.1007/11840817_87

18. Mnih, V., et al.: Playing Atari with deep reinforcement learning. Neural Inf. Process. Syst. (2013). http://arxiv.org/abs/1312.5602

19. Mnih, V., et al.: Human-level control through deep reinforcement learning. Nature **518**(7540), 529–533 (2015). https://doi.org/10.1038/nature14236

20. Polydoros, A.S., Nalpantidis, L.: Survey of model-based reinforcement learning: applications on robotics. J. Intell. Robot. Syst. **86**(2), 153–173 (2017). https://doi.org/10.1007/s10846-017-0468-y

21. Razavi, A., van den Oord, A., Vinyals, O.: Generating diverse high-fidelity images with VQ-VAE-2. In: Wallach, H., Larochelle, H., Beygelzimer, A., Alché-Buc, F., Fox, E., Garnett, R. (eds.) Advances in Neural Information Processing Systems, Vancouver, BC, Canada, vol. 32, pp. 14837–14847. Curran Associates Inc. (2019). http://papers.nips.cc/paper/9625-generating-diverse-high-fidelity-images-with-vq-vae-2

22. Schulman, J., Levine, S., Abbeel, P., Jordan, M., Moritz, P.: Trust region policy optimization. In: Bach, F., Blei, D. (eds.) Proceedings of the 32nd International Conference on Machine Learning. Proceedings of Machine Learning Research, Lille, France, vol. 37, pp. 1889–1897. PMLR (2015). http://proceedings.mlr.press/v37/schulman15.html

23. Schulman, J., Wolski, F., Dhariwal, P., Radford, A., Klimov, O.: Proximal policy optimization algorithms. arxiv preprint arXiv:1707.06347 (2017). http://arxiv.org/abs/1707.06347

24. Shah, S., Dey, D., Lovett, C., Kapoor, A.: AirSim: high-fidelity visual and physical simulation for autonomous vehicles. In: Hutter, M., Siegwart, R. (eds.) Field and Service Robotics. SPAR, vol. 5, pp. 621–635. Springer, Cham (2018). https://doi.org/10.1007/978-3-319-67361-5_40

25. Silver, D., et al.: Mastering the game of Go with deep neural networks and tree search. Nature **529**(7587), 484–489 (2016). https://doi.org/10.1038/nature16961

26. Sutton, R.S.: Dyna, an integrated architecture for learning, planning, and reacting. ACM SIGART Bull. **2**(4), 160–163 (1991). https://doi.org/10.1145/122344.122377

27. Sutton, R.S., Barto, A.G.: Reinforcement Learning: An Introduction, 2 edn.. A Bradford Book, Cambridge, MA, USA (2018). https://dl.acm.org/doi/book/10.5555/3312046

A Novel Multi-step Finite-State Automaton for Arbitrarily Deterministic Tsetlin Machine Learning

K. Darshana Abeyrathna[1]([⊠]), Ole-Christoffer Granmo[1], Rishad Shafik[2], Alex Yakovlev[2], Adrian Wheeldon[2], Jie Lei[2], and Morten Goodwin[1]

[1] Centre for Artificial Intelligence Research, University of Agder, Grimstad, Norway
{darshana.abeyrathna,ole.granmo,morten.goodwin}@uia.no
[2] Microsystems Research Group, School of Engineering,
Newcastle University, Newcastle upon Tyne, UK
{rishad.shafik,alex.yakovlev,adrian.wheeldon,jie.lei}@newcastle.ac.uk

Abstract. Due to the high energy consumption and scalability challenges of deep learning, there is a critical need to shift research focus towards dealing with energy consumption constraints. Tsetlin Machines (TMs) are a recent approach to machine learning that has demonstrated significantly reduced energy usage compared to neural networks alike, while performing competitively accuracy-wise on several benchmarks. However, TMs rely heavily on energy-costly random number generation to stochastically guide a team of Tsetlin Automata (TA) to a Nash Equilibrium of the TM game. In this paper, we propose a novel finite-state learning automaton that can replace the TA in TM learning, for increased determinism. The new automaton uses multi-step deterministic state jumps to reinforce sub-patterns. Simultaneously, flipping a coin to skip every d'th state update ensures diversification by randomization. The d-parameter thus allows the degree of randomization to be finely controlled. E.g., $d = 1$ makes every update random and $d = \infty$ makes the automaton completely deterministic. Our empirical results show that, overall, only substantial degrees of determinism reduces accuracy. Energy-wise, random number generation constitutes switching energy consumption of the TM, saving up to 11 mW power for larger datasets with high d values. We can thus use the new d-parameter to trade off accuracy against energy consumption, to facilitate low-energy machine learning.

1 Introduction

State-of-the-art deep learning (DL) requires massive computational resources, resulting in high energy consumption [18] and scalability challenges [5]. There is thus a critical need to shift research focus towards dealing with energy consumption constraints [7]. Tsetlin Machines [10] (TMs) are a recent approach to machine learning (ML) that has demonstrated significantly reduced energy usage compared to neural networks alike [21]. Using a linear combination of conjunctive clauses in propositional logic, the TM has obtained competitive performance in

© Springer Nature Switzerland AG 2020
M. Bramer and R. Ellis (Eds.): SGAI-AI 2020, LNAI 12498, pp. 108–122, 2020.
https://doi.org/10.1007/978-3-030-63799-6_8

terms of accuracy [3, 4, 11], memory footprint [11, 21], energy [21], and learning speed [11, 21] on diverse benchmarks (image classification, regression and natural language understanding). Furthermore, the rules that TMs build seem to be interpretable, similar to the branches in a decision tree (e.g., in the form **if** X **satisfies** condition A **and not** condition B **then** Y = 1) [4]. The reported small memory footprint and low energy consumption make the TM particularly attractive for addressing the scalability and energy challenge in ML.

Recent Progress on TMs. Recent research reports several distinct TM properties. The TM can be used in convolution, providing competitive performance on MNIST, Fashion-MNIST, and Kuzushiji-MNIST, in comparison with CNNs, K-Nearest Neighbor, SVMs, Random Forest, Gradient Boosting, BinaryConnect, Logistic Circuits and ResNet [11]. The TM has also achieved promising results in text classification by using the conjunctive clauses to capture textual patterns [4]. By introducing clause weights, it has been demonstrated that the number of clauses can be reduced by up to 50×, without loss of accuracy [16]. Further, hyper-parameter search can be simplified with multi-granular clauses, eliminating the pattern specificity parameter [9]. By indexing the clauses on the features that falsify them, up to an order of magnitude faster inference and learning has been reported [8]. Additionally, regression TMs compare favorably with Regression Trees, Random Forest Regression, and Support Vector Regression [3]. In [1], stochastic searching on the line automata [15] learn integer clause weights, performing on-par or better than Random Forest, Gradient Boosting and Explainable Boosting Machines. While TMs are binary throughout, thresholding schemes open up for continuous input [2]. Finally, TMs have recently been shown to be fault-tolerant, completely masking stuck-at faults [17].

Paper Contributions. TMs rely heavily on energy-costly random number generation to stochastically guide a team of TAs to a Nash Equilibrium of the TM game. In this paper, we propose a novel finite state learning automaton that can replace the TAs of the TM, for increased determinism. The new automaton uses multi-step deterministic state jumps to reinforce sub-patterns. Simultaneously, flipping a coin to skip every d'th state update ensures diversification by randomization. The d-parameter thus allows the degree of randomization to be finely controlled. We further evaluate the scheme empirically on five datasets, demonstrating that the new d-parameter can be used to trade off accuracy against energy consumption.

Paper Organization: In Sect. 2, we introduce our new type of Learning Automaton (LA) – the multi-step variable-structure finite-state LA (MVF-LA). Replacing the TA with MVF-LA, we describe the Arbitrarily Deterministic TM (ADTM) in Sect. 3. Then, in Sect. 4, we evaluate ADTM empirically using five datasets. The performance of ADTM is investigated by varying the d-parameter, contrasting against the regular TM and five other state-of-the-art machine learning algorithms. Effect of determinism on energy consumption is discussed in Sect. 5. We conclude our work in Sect. 6.

2   A Multi-step Finite-State Learning Automaton

The origins of LA [13] can be traced back to the work of M.L. Tsetlin in the early 1960s [20]. The objective of an LA is to learn the optimal action through trial and error in a stochastic environment. Various types of LAs are available depending on the nature of the application [19]. Due to their computational simplicity, we here focus on two-action finite-state LA, which we extend by introducing a novel periodically changing structure (variable structure).

An LA interacts with its environment iteratively. In each iteration, the action that a finite-state LA performs next is decided by its present state (the memory). The environment, in turn, randomly produces a reward or a penalty according to an unknown probability distribution, responding to the action selected by the LA. If the finite-state LA receives a reward, it reinforces the action performed by moving to a "deeper" state. If the action results in a penalty, it instead changes state towards the middle state, to weaken the performed action, ultimately switching to the other action. In this manner, with a sufficient number of states, a finite-state LA converges to selecting the action with the highest probability of producing rewards – the optimal action – with probability arbitrarily close to 1.0   [13].

The transitions between states can be deterministic or stochastic. Deterministic transitions occur with probability 1.0, while stochastic transitions are randomly performed based on a preset probability. If the transition probabilities are changing, we have a variable structure automaton, otherwise, we have one with fixed structure. The pioneering TA, depicted in Fig. 1, is a deterministic fixed-structure finite-state automaton [20]. The state transition graph in the figure depicts a TA with $2N$ states. States 1 to N maps to Action 1 and states $N + 1$ to $2N$ maps to Action 2.

While the TA changes state in single steps, the deterministic Krinsky Automaton introduces multi-step state transitions [13]. The purpose is to reinforce an action more strongly when it is rewarded, and more weakly when penalized. The Krinsky Automaton behaves as a TA when the response from the environment is a penalty. However, when it is a reward, any state from 2 to N transitions to state 1, and any state from $N + 1$ to $2N - 1$ transitions to state $2N$. In effect, N consecutive penalties are needed to offset a single reward.

Another variant of LA is the Krylov Automaton. A Krylov Automaton makes both deterministic and stochastic single-step transitions [13]. The state transitions of the Krylov Automaton is identical to those of a TA for rewards. However, when it receives a penalty, it performs the corresponding TA state change randomly, with probability 0.5.

We now introduce our new type of LA, the multi-step variable-structure finite-state LA (MVF-LA), shown in Fig. 2. The MVF-LA has two kinds of feedback, strong and weak. As covered in the next section, strong feedback is required by the TM to strongly reinforce frequent sub-patterns, while weak feedback is required to make the TM forget infrequent ones. To achieve this, weak feedback only triggers one-step transitions. Strong feedback, on the other hand, triggers s-step transitions. Thus, a single strong feedback is offset by s instances

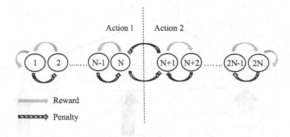

Fig. 1. Transition graph of a two-action Tsetlin Automaton with 2N memory states.

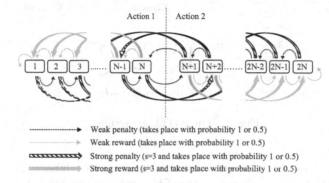

Fig. 2. Transition graph of the multi-step variable structure finite-state learning automaton.

of weak feedback. Further, MVF-LA has a variable structure that changes *periodically*. That is, the MVF-LA switches between two different transition graph structures, one deterministic and one stochastic. The deterministic structure is as shown in the figure, while the stochastic structure introduces a transition probability 0.5, for every transition. The switch between structure is performed so that every d'th transition is stochastic, while the remaining transitions are deterministic.

3   The Arbitrarily Deterministic TM (ADTM)

In this section, we introduce the details of the ADTM, shown in Fig. 3, where the TA is replaced by the MVF-LA. The purpose of the ADTM is to control stochasticity, thus allowing management of energy consumption.

3.1   ADTM Inference

Input Features. Like the TM, an ADTM takes a feature vector of o propositional variables as input, $\boldsymbol{X} = [x_1, x_2, x_3, \ldots, x_o]$, to be classified into one of two classes, $y = 0$ or $y = 1$. These features are extended with their negation, to produce a set of literals: $\mathbf{L} = [x_1, x_2, \ldots, x_o, \neg x_1, \neg x_2, \ldots, \neg x_o] = [l_1, l_2, \ldots, l_{2o}]$.

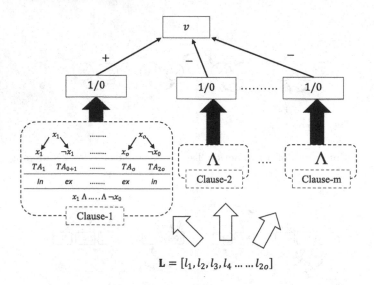

Fig. 3. The ADTM structure.

Clauses. Patterns are represented by m conjunctive clauses. As shown for Clause-1 in the figure, a clause in the TM comprises $2o$ MVF-LAs, each controlling the inclusion of a specific literal. Let the set I_j, $I_j \subseteq \{1, \ldots, 2o\}$ denote the indexes of the literals that are included in clause j. When evaluating clause j on input literals $\boldsymbol{L}$, the literals included in the clause are ANDed: $c_j = \bigwedge_{k \in I_j} l_k, j = 1, \ldots, m$. Note that the output of an empty clause, $I_j = \emptyset$, is 1 during learning and 0 during inference.

Classification. In order to identify the sub-patterns associated with both of the classes of a two-class ADTM, the clauses are grouped in two. The number of clauses employed is a user set parameter m. Half of the clauses are assigned positive polarity (c_j^+). The other half is assigned negative polarity (c_j^-). The clause outputs, in turn, are combined into a classification decision through summation and thresholding using the unit step function $u(v) = 1$ **if** $v \geq 0$ **else** 0:

$$\hat{y} = u\left(\sum_{j=1}^{m/2} c_j^+(X) - \sum_{j=1}^{m/2} c_j^-(X) \right). \tag{1}$$

That is, classification is based on a majority vote, with the positive clauses voting for $y = 0$ and the negative for $y = 1$.

3.2   The MVF-LA Game and Orchestration Scheme

The MVF-LAs in ADTM are updated by so-called Type I and Type II feedback. Depending on the class of the current training sample (X, y) and the polarity of the clause (positive or negative), the type of feedback is decided. Clauses with positive polarity receive Type I feedback when the target output is $y = 1$, and Type II feedback when the target output is $y = 0$. For clauses with negative polarity, Type I feedback replaces Type II, and vice versa. In the following, we focus only on clauses with positive polarity.

Type I Feedback: The number of clauses which receive Type I feedback is controlled by selecting them stochastically according to Eq. 2:

$$\frac{T - \max(-T, \min(T, v))}{2T}. \tag{2}$$

Above, $v = \sum_{j=1}^{m/2} c_j^+(X) - \sum_{j=1}^{m/2} c_j^-(X)$ is the aggregated clause output and T is a user set parameter that decides how many clauses should be involved in learning a particular sub-pattern. Increasing T proportionally with the number of clauses introduces an ensemble effect, for increased learning accuracy. Type I feedback consists of two kinds of sub-feedback: Type Ia and Type Ib. Type Ia feedback stimulates recognition of patterns by reinforcing the include action of MVF-LAs whose corresponding literal value is 1, however, only when the clause output also is 1. Note that an action is reinforced either by rewarding the action itself, or by penalizing the other action. Type Ia feedback is *strong*, with step size s (Fig. 2). Type Ib feedback, on the other hand, combats over-fitting by reinforcing the *exclude* actions of MVF-LAs when the corresponding literal is 0 or when the clause output is 0. Type Ib feedback is *weak* (Fig. 2) to facilitate learning of frequent patterns.

Type II Feedback: Clauses are also selected stochastically for receiving Type II feedback:

$$\frac{T + \max(-T, \min(T, v))}{2T}. \tag{3}$$

Type II feedback combats false positive clause output by seeking to alter clauses that output 1 so that they instead output 0. This is achieved simply by penalizing exclusion of literals of value 0. Thus, when the clause output is 1 and the corresponding literal value of an MVF-LA is 0, the exclude action of the MVF-LA is penalized. Type II feedback is *strong*, with step size s. Recall that in all of the above MVF-LA update steps, the parameter d decides the determinism of the updates.

4   Empirical Evaluation

We now study the performance of ADTM empirically using five real-world datasets.[1] The ADTM is compared against regular TMs to assess to what degree learning accuracy suffers from increased determinism. The ADTM is also compared against seven other state-of-the-are machine learning approaches: Artificial Neural Networks (ANNs), Support Vector Machines (SVMs), Decision Trees

---

[1] An implementation of ADTM can be found at https://github.com/cair/ Deterministic-Tsetlin-Machine.

(DTs), K-Nearest Neighbor (KNN), Random Forest (RF), Gradient Boosted Trees (XGBoost) [6], and Explainable Boosting Machines (EBMs) [14]. For comprehensiveness, three ANN architectures are used: ANN-1 – with one hidden layer of 5 neurons; ANN-2 – with two hidden layers of 20 and 50 neurons each, and ANN-3 – with three hidden layers and 20, 150, and 100 neurons. Performance of these predictive models are summarized in Table 6. We compute both F1-score (F1) and accuracy (Acc.) as performance measures. However, due to class imbalance, we emphasize F1-score when comparing the performance of the different predictive models.

Table 1. Performance of TM and ADTM with different d on Bankruptcy

	TM	ADTM					
		d = 1	d = 10	d = 100	d = 500	d = 1000	d = 5000
F1	0.998	1.000	1.000	1.000	0.999	0.999	0.988
Acc.	0.998	1.000	1.000	1.000	0.999	0.999	0.987

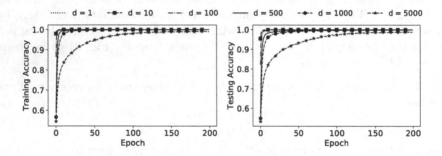

Fig. 4. Training and testing accuracy per epoch on Bankruptcy

4.1 Bankruptcy

The Bankruptcy dataset contains historical records of 250 companies[2]. The outcome, Bankruptcy or Non-bankruptcy, is characterized by six categorical features. We thus binarize the features using thresholding [2] before we feed them into the ADTM. We first tune the hyper-parameters of the TM and the best performance is reported in Table 1, for $m = 100$ (number of clauses), $s = 3$ (step size for MVF-LA), and $T = 10$ (summation target). Each MVF-LA contains 100 states per action. The impact of determinism is reported in Table 1, for varying levels of determinism. As seen, performance is indistinguishable for d-values 1, 10, and 100, and the ADTM achieves its highest classification accuracy. However, notice the slight decrease of F1-score and accuracy when determinism is further increased to 500, 1000, and 5000.

---

[2] Available from https://archive.ics.uci.edu/ml/datasets/qualitative_bankruptcy.

Figure 4 shows how training and testing accuracy evolve over the training epochs. Only high determinism seems to influence learning speed and accuracy significantly. The performance of the other considered machine learning models is compiled in Table 6. The best performance in terms of F1-score for the other models is obtained by ANN-3. However, ANN-3 is outperformed by the ADTM for all d-values except when $d = 5000$.

Table 2. Performance of TM and ADTM with different d on balance scale

	TM	ADTM					
		$d=1$	$d=10$	$d=100$	$d=500$	$d=1000$	$d=5000$
F1	0.945	0.982	0.983	0.982	0.968	0.951	0.911
Acc.	0.948	0.980	0.981	0.980	0.935	0.894	0.793

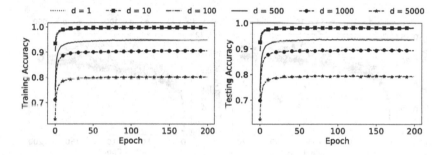

Fig. 5. Training and testing accuracy per epoch on the balance scale

4.2 Balance Scale

The Balance Scale dataset[3] contains three classes: balance scale tip to the right, tip to the left, or in balance. The class is decided by the size of the weight on both sides of the scale and the distance to each weight from the center. Hence the classes are characterized by four features. However, to make the output binary, we remove the "balanced" class ending up with 576 data samples. The ADTM is equipped with 100 clauses. Each MVF-LA is given 100 states per action. The remaining two parameters, i.e., s value and T are fixed at 3 and 10, respectively. Table 2 contains the results obtained with TM and ADTM. Even though ADTM uses the same number of clauses as the TM, the performance with regards to F1-score and accuracy is better with ADTM when all updates on MVF-LAs are stochastic. The performance of the ADTM remains

---

[3] Available from http://archive.ics.uci.edu/ml/datasets/balance+scale.

the same until the determinism-parameter surpasses 100. After that, performance degrades gradually.

Progress of training and testing accuracy per epoch can be found in Fig. 5. Each ADTM setup reaches its peak training and testing accuracy and becomes stable within a fewer number of training epochs. As can be seen, accuracy is maintained up to $d = 100$, thus reducing random number generation to 1% without accuracy loss. From the results listed in Table 6 for the other machine learning approaches, EBM achieves the highest F1-score and accuracy.

Table 3. Performance of TM and ADTM with different d on breast cancer

	TM	ADTM					
		$d=1$	$d=10$	$d=100$	$d=500$	$d=1000$	$d=5000$
F1	0.531	0.568	0.531	0.501	0.490	0.501	0.488
Acc.	0.703	0.702	0.698	0.691	0.690	0.690	0.693

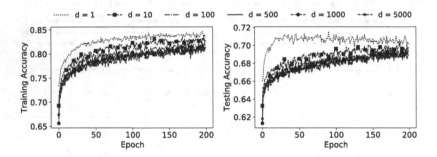

Fig. 6. Training and testing accuracy per epoch on breast cancer

4.3   Breast Cancer

The Breast Cancer dataset[4] contains 286 patients records related to the recurrence of breast cancer (201 with non-recurrence and 85 with recurrence). The recurrence of breast cancer is to be estimated using nine features: Age, Menopause, Tumor Size, Inv Nodes, Node Caps, Deg Malig, Side (left or right), the Position of the Breast, and Irradiation. However, some of the patient samples miss some of the feature values. These samples are removed from the dataset in the present experiment. The ADTM is arranged with the following parameter setup: $m = 100$, $s = 5$, $T = 10$, and the number of states in MVF-LA per action is 100. The classification accuracy of the TM and ADTM are summarized in Table 3. The performance of both TM and ADTM is here considerably lower than for the previous two datasets, and further decreases with increasing

---

[4] Available from https://archive.ics.uci.edu/ml/datasets/Breast+Cancer.

determinism. However, the F1 measures obtained by all the other considered machine learning models are also low, i.e., less than 0.500. The highest F1-score is obtained by ANN-1 and KNN. The training and testing accuracy progress per epoch is reported in Fig. 6, showing a clear degradation of performance with increasing determinism.

Table 4. Performance of TM and ADTM with different d on liver disorders

	TM	ADTM					
		$d=1$	$d=10$	$d=100$	$d=500$	$d=1000$	$d=5000$
F1	0.648	0.705	0.694	0.692	0.692	0.689	0.692
Acc.	0.533	0.610	0.610	0.612	0.612	0.610	0.611

Table 5. Performance of TM and ADTM with different d on heart disease

	TM	ADTM					
		$d=1$	$d=10$	$d=100$	$d=500$	$d=1000$	$d=5000$
F1	0.687	0.759	0.766	0.767	0.760	0.762	0.605
Acc	0.672	0.778	0.780	0.783	0.773	0.781	0.633

4.4 Liver Disorders

The Liver Disorders dataset[5] was created by BUPA Medical Research and Development Ltd. (hereafter "BMRDL") during the 1980s as part of a larger health-screening database. The dataset consists of 7 attributes. However, McDermott and Forsyth [12] claim that many researchers have used the dataset incorrectly, considering the Selector attribute as the class label. Based on the recommendation of McDermott and Forsythof, we here instead use the Number of Half-Pint Equivalents of Alcoholic Beverages as the dependent variable, binarized using the threshold ≥ 3. The Selector attribute is discarded. The remaining attributes represent the results of various blood tests, and we use them as features.

Here, ADTM is given 10 clauses per class, with $s = 3$ and $T = 10$. Each MVF-LA action possesses 100 states. The performance of ADTM for different levels of determinism is summarized in Table 4. For $d = 1$, the F1-score of ADTM is better than what is achieved with the standard TM. In contrast to the performance on previous datasets, the performance of ADTM on Liver Disorders dataset with respect to F1-score does not decrease significantly with d. Instead, it fluctuates around 0.690.

As shown in Fig. 7, unlike the other datasets, the ADTM with $d = 1$ requires more training rounds than with larger d-values, before it learns the final MVF-LA actions. It is also unable to reach the training accuracy obtained with higher

---

[5] Available from https://archive.ics.uci.edu/ml/datasets/Liver+Disorders.

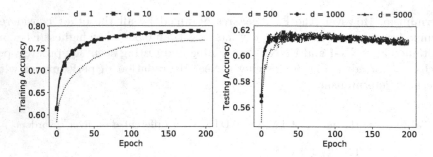

Fig. 7. Training and testing accuracy per epoch on liver disorders

d-values. Despite the diverse learning speed, testing accuracy becomes similar after roughly 50 training rounds. The other considered machine learning models obtain somewhat similar F1-scores, however, only DT, RF, and EBM surpass an F1-score of 0.700.

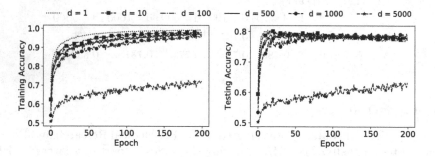

Fig. 8. Training and testing accuracy per epoch on heart disease

4.5   Heart Disease

The Heart Disease dataset[6] concerns prediction of heart disease. To this end, 13 features are available, selected among 75. Out of the 13 features, 6 are real-valued, 3 are binary, 3 are nominal, and one is ordered.

In this case, the ADTM is built on 100 clauses. The number of state transitions when the feedback is strong, s is equal to 3 while the target, T is equal to 10. The number of states per MVF-LA action in the ADTM is 100.

As one can see in Table 5, the ADTM provides better performance than TM in terms of F1-score and accuracy when $d = 1$. F1-score then increases with d and peaks at $d = 100$. After some fluctuation, it drops to a value of 0.605 when $d = 5000$.

---

[6] Available from https://archive.ics.uci.edu/ml/datasets/Statlog+%28Heart%29.

Figure 8 shows similar training and testing accuracy for all d-values, apart from the significantly lower accuracy of $d = 5000$.

Out of other machine learning algorithms, EBM provides the best F1-score, as summarized in Table 6. Even though ANN-1, ANN-2, DT, RF, and XGBoost obtain better F1-scores than TM, the F1 scores of ADTM when d equals to 1, 10, 100, 500, and 1000 are higher.

Table 6. Classification accuracy of selected machine learning models

	Bankruptcy		Balance scale		Breast cancer		Liver disorder		Heart disease	
	F1	Acc.	F1	Acc.	F1	Acc.	F1	Acc.	F1	Acc.
ANN-1	0.995	0.994	0.990	0.990	**0.458**	0.719	0.671	0.612	0.738	0.772
ANN-2	0.996	0.995	0.995	0.995	0.403	0.683	0.652	0.594	0.742	0.769
ANN-3	**0.997**	**0.997**	0.995	0.995	0.422	0.685	0.656	0.602	0.650	0.734
DT	0.993	0.993	0.986	0.986	0.276	0.706	0.728	0.596	0.729	0.781
SVM	0.994	0.994	0.887	0.887	0.384	0.678	0.622	0.571	0.679	0.710
KNN	0.995	0.994	0.953	0.953	**0.458**	**0.755**	0.638	0.566	0.641	0.714
RF	0.949	0.942	0.859	0.860	0.370	0.747	**0.729**	0.607	0.713	0.774
XGBoost	0.983	0.983	0.931	0.931	0.367	0.719	0.656	**0.635**	0.701	0.788
EBM	0.993	0.992	**1.000**	**1.000**	0.389	0.745	0.710	0.629	**0.783**	**0.824**

5   Effects of Determinism on Energy Consumption

In the hardware implementation of TM, power is consumed by the pseudorandom number generators (PRNGs) when generating a new random number [21]. This is referred to as *switching power*. In the TM, every TA update is randomized, and switching power is consumed by the PRNGs on every cycle. Additionally, power is also consumed by the PRNGs whilst idle. We term this *leakage power*. Leakage power is always consumed by the PRNGs whilst they are powered up, even when not generating new numbers.

In the ADTM with hybrid TA where the determinism parameter d is introduced, $d = 1$ would be equivalent to a TM where every TA update is randomized. $d = \infty$ means the ADTM is fully deterministic, and no random numbers are required from the PRNG. If a TA update is randomized only on the dth cycle, the PRNGs need only be actively switched (and therefore consume *switching power*) for $\frac{1}{d}$ portion of the entire training procedure. The switching power consumed by the PRNGs accounts for 7% of the total system power when using a traditional TA (equivalent to $d = 1$). With $d = 100$ this is reduced to 0.07% of the system power, and with $d = 5000$ this is reduced further to 0.001% of the same. It can be seen that as d increases in the ADTM, the switching power consumed by the PRNGs tends to zero.

In the special case of $d = \infty$ the PRNGs are no longer required for TA updates since the TAs are fully deterministic – we can omit these PRNGs from the design and prevent their *leakage power* from being consumed. The leakage power of the PRNGs accounts for 32% of the total system power. On top of the switching power savings this equates to 39% of system power, meaning large power and therefore energy savings can be made in the ADTM.

Table 7 shows comparative training power consumption per datapoint (i.e. all TAs being updated concurrently) for two different d values: $d = 1$ and $d = 5000$. Typically, the overall power is higher for bigger datasets as they require increased number of concurrent TAs as well as PRNGs. As can be seen, the increase in d value reduces the power consumption by 11 mW in the case of Heart Disease dataset. This saving is made by reducing the switching activity in the PRNGs as explained above. More savings are made by larger d values as the PRNG concurrent switching activities are reduced.

Table 7. Comparative power per datapoint with two different d values.

Dataset	Bankruptcy	Breast cancer	Balance scale	Liver disorder	Heart disease
Power ($d = 1$)	6.94 mW	15.8 mW	7.7 mW	12.6 mW	148.0 mW
Power ($d = 5000$)	6.45 mW	14.7 mW	7.2 mW	11.8 mW	137.6 mW

6   Conclusion

In this paper, we proposed a novel finite-state learning automaton (MFV-LA) that can replace the Tsetlin Automaton in TM learning, for increased determinism, and thus reduced energy usage. The new automaton uses multi-step deterministic state jumps to reinforce sub-patterns. Simultaneously, flipping a coin to skip every d'th state update ensures diversification by randomization. The new d-parameter thus allows the degree of randomization to be finely controlled. E.g., $d = 1$ makes every update random and $d = \infty$ makes the automaton fully deterministic. Our empirical results show that, overall, only substantial degrees of determinism reduces accuracy. Energy-wise, the pseudorandom number generator contributes to switching energy consumption within the TM, which can be completely eliminated with $d = \infty$. We can thus use the new d-parameter to trade off accuracy against energy consumption, to facilitate low-energy machine learning.

Acknowledgement. The authors gratefully acknowledge the contributions from Jonathan Edwards at Temporal Computing on strategies for deterministic Tsetlin Machine learning.

References

1. Abeyrathna, K.D., Granmo, O.C., Goodwin, M.: Extending the Tsetlin Machine with integer-weighted clauses for increased interpretability. arXiv preprint arXiv:2005.05131 (2020)

2. Abeyrathna, K.D., Granmo, O.-C., Zhang, X., Goodwin, M.: A scheme for continuous input to the Tsetlin Machine with applications to forecasting disease outbreaks. In: Wotawa, F., Friedrich, G., Pill, I., Koitz-Hristov, R., Ali, M. (eds.) IEA/AIE 2019. LNCS (LNAI), vol. 11606, pp. 564–578. Springer, Cham (2019). https://doi.org/10.1007/978-3-030-22999-3_49

3. Abeyrathna, K.D., Granmo, O.C., Zhang, X., Jiao, L., Goodwin, M.: The regression Tsetlin Machine - a novel approach to interpretable non-linear regression. Philos. Trans. R. Soc. A **378**, 20190165 (2019)

4. Berge, G.T., Granmo, O.C., Tveit, T.O., Goodwin, M., Jiao, L., Matheussen, B.V.: Using the Tsetlin Machine to learn human-interpretable rules for high-accuracy text categorization with medical applications. IEEE Access **7**, 115134–115146 (2019). https://doi.org/10.1109/ACCESS.2019.2935416

5. Chen, J., Ran, X.: Deep learning with edge computing: a review. Proc. IEEE **107**(8), 1655–1674 (2019)

6. Chen, T., Guestrin, C.: XGBoost: a scalable tree boosting system. In: Proceedings of the 22nd ACM SIGKDD International Conference on Knowledge Discovery and Data Mining, pp. 785–794 (2016)

7. García-Martín, E., Rodrigues, C.F., Riley, G., Grahn, H.: Estimation of energy consumption in machine learning. J. Parallel Distrib. Comput. **134**, 75–88 (2019). https://doi.org/10.1016/j.jpdc.2019.07.007

8. Rahimi Gorji, S., Granmo, O.-C., Glimsdal, S., Edwards, J., Goodwin, M.: Increasing the inference and learning speed of Tsetlin Machines with clause indexing. In: Fujita, H., Fournier-Viger, P., Ali, M., Sasaki, J. (eds.) IEA/AIE 2020. LNCS (LNAI), vol. 12144, pp. 695–708. Springer, Cham (2020). https://doi.org/10.1007/978-3-030-55789-8_60

9. Rahimi Gorji, S., Granmo, O.-C., Phoulady, A., Goodwin, M.: A Tsetlin Machine with multigranular clauses. In: Bramer, M., Petridis, M. (eds.) SGAI 2019. LNCS (LNAI), vol. 11927, pp. 146–151. Springer, Cham (2019). https://doi.org/10.1007/978-3-030-34885-4_11

10. Granmo, O.C.: The Tsetlin Machine - a game theoretic bandit driven approach to optimal pattern recognition with propositional logic. arXiv:1804.01508

11. Granmo, O.C., Glimsdal, S., Jiao, L., Goodwin, M., Omlin, C.W., Berge, G.T.: The convolutional Tsetlin Machine. arXiv preprint arXiv:1905.09688 (2019)

12. McDermott, J., Forsyth, R.S.: Diagnosing a disorder in a classification benchmark. Pattern Recogn. Lett. **73**, 41–43 (2016)

13. Narendra, K.S., Thathachar, M.A.: Learning Automata: An Introduction. Courier Corporation, North Chelmsford (2012)

14. Nori, H., Jenkins, S., Koch, P., Caruana, R.: InterpretML: a unified framework for machine learning interpretability. arXiv preprint arXiv:1909.09223 (2019)

15. Oommen, B.J.: Stochastic searching on the line and its applications to parameter learning in nonlinear optimization. IEEE Trans. Syst. Man Cybern. Part B (Cybern.) **27**(4), 733–739 (1997)

16. Phoulady, A., Granmo, O.C., Gorji, S.R., Phoulady, H.A.: The weighted Tsetlin Machine: compressed representations with clause weighting. In: Ninth International Workshop on Statistical Relational AI (StarAI 2020) (2020)

17. Shafik, R., Wheeldon, A., Yakovlev, A.: Explainability and dependability analysis of learning automata based AI hardware. In: IEEE 26th International Symposium on On-Line Testing and Robust System Design (IOLTS). IEEE (2020)

18. Strubell, E., Ganesh, A., McCallum, A.: Energy and policy considerations for deep learning in NLP. In: ACL (2019)

19. Thathachar, M.A.L., Sastry, P.S.: Networks of Learning Automata: Techniques for Online Stochastic Optimization. Kluwer Academic Publishers, Dordrecht (2004)
20. Tsetlin, M.L.: On behaviour of finite automata in random medium. Avtomat. i Telemekh **22**(10), 1345–1354 (1961)
21. Wheeldon, A., Shafik, R., Rahman, T., Lei, J., Yakovlev, A., Granmo, O.C.: Learning automata based energy-efficient AI hardware design for IoT. Philos. Trans. R. Soc. A **378**, 20190593 (2020)

Accelerating the Training of an LP-SVR Over Large Datasets

Pablo Rivas(✉) ⓘ

Computer Science, Baylor University, Waco, TX, USA
Pablo_Rivas@Baylor.edu

Abstract. This paper presents a learning speedup method based on the relationship between the support vectors and the within-class Mahalanobis distances among the training set. We explain how statistical properties of the data can be used to pre-rank the training set. Then we explain the relationship among the pre-ranked training set indices, convex hull indices, and the support vector indices. We also explain how this method has better efficiency than those approaches based on the convex hull, especially at large-scale problems. At the end of the paper we conclude by explaining the findings of the experimental results over the speedup alternative.

Keywords: Support vector machines for regression · Linear programming · Big data sets

1 Introduction

Support Vector Machines for Regression (SVRs) are popular option for learning to predict a real-valued target given some training data. Their most common applications include predicting the popularity of online videos [27], forecasting wind speed [25], energy consumption prediction [32], or forecasting rainfall [16]. SVRs can be posed in different ways motivated by different problems. For instance, $\epsilon - \text{SVR}$ was an attempt to provide flexibility to an inflexible SVR solution by allowing the SVR to make mistakes; any mistakes beyond ϵ would start being penalized [4]. This parameter needs to be set up experimentally by observing the data and determining what amount of error can be tolerated in proportion to the observed target data. However, the value of ϵ is very likely to vary from problem to problem, and its relationship with the support vectors is not intuitive; the $\nu - \text{SVR}$ was introduced to solve this problem [26]. Its parameter ν provides the necessary meaning with respect to the support vectors (SVs) and is consistent from problem to problem; the $\nu - \text{SVR}$ does not eliminate the parameter ϵ but removes the requirement of the user to provide it because it is introduced as part of the optimization problem and is calculated automatically. There are many other SVRs motivated by different issues. In this paper, we will focus on the formulation of our earlier work [24], which aims to address large-scale training of a linear programming SVR (LP-SVR) based on the solution of

© Springer Nature Switzerland AG 2020
M. Bramer and R. Ellis (Eds.): SGAI-AI 2020, LNAI 12498, pp. 123–136, 2020.
https://doi.org/10.1007/978-3-030-63799-6_9

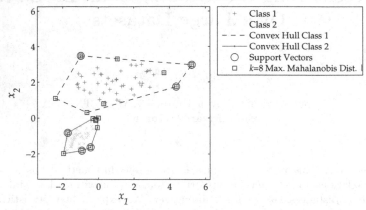

Fig. 1. Relationship between convex hull and maximum Mahalanobis distance for the two-class problem. Here it is shown the original separable two-class problem, class convex hull, support vectors, and $k = 8$ maximum Mahalanobis distance samples. Both SVs and Convex Hull match the $k = 8$ maximum Mahalanobis distance samples.

small LP problems. Our formerly proposed algorithm has been mathematically proven to converge, but the training process is still costly in proportion to the number of samples, N. This motivates the exploration of alternatives for speeding up the learning process. In this paper, we propose using a distance measure for ranking the training set and providing a sequence in which the data could be trained for speeding. To achieve the speed up, the data is ranked according to its distance to the class mean.

It is well known [1,9,11,13,19,28,29,33] that in classification tasks, those data points closer to the decision boundaries (*i.e.*, convex hull of the data class) are more likely to be support vectors, as illustrated in Fig. 1 with bold circles. Figure 1 depicts the relationship between convex hull and maximum Mahalanobis distance (MD) for an arbitrary two-class problem. The figure shows the convex hull of each class, the SVs that define the separating hyperplane, and the eight samples having the maximum MD from their class center. Note that both SVs and convex hull match the eight samples with maximum MD.

Vapnik [28] improved the speed of his learning method by considering only those variables on the boundaries of the feasible region instead of considering all the data, which allowed computational tractability of some problems. Then Joachims [9] defined a heuristic approach to identify variables at boundaries based on Lagrange multiplier estimates. Later, Bennett, *et al.* [1] posed the problem of finding the optimal separating hyperplane using the distance between class convex hulls. A similar concept was followed by Keerthi, *et al.* [11] in 2002, by Osuna, *et al.* [19] in 2003, and by Zhenbing, *et al.* [13] in 2010. In 2013, Wang *et al.* [29], describe an approach to calculate distances to the convex-hull to improve a particular kind of model known as online SVMs. Gu *et al.* in 2018

[8], proposed another convex-hull approach by directly calculating it and ranking data samples for naive versions of ℓ_1 and ℓ_2 SVMs. Most recently, in 2020, Chen *et al.* [3], provided an entire model based on Mahalanobis distances that are part of the learning process of a twin SVM formulation; such work has a similar motivation to our early work in 2011 [23]; however, they focus on an SVM model that incorporates sample selection into the learning process.

In this paper, we introduce an approach to accelerate the training of an LP-SVR, specifically, which uses a probabilistic argument and can be applied to other flavors of SVRs. It is unique in that it aims for a specific flavor of SVR and that it can easily be extended to other models with relative training speed improvements. This paper is organized as follows: Sect. 2 introduces the background information for an LP-SVR, convex hull, and Mahalanobis distances. Section 3 describes our experimental results, while Sect. 4 addresses some computational concerns of the proposed approach. Conclusions are drawn in Sect. 5.

2   Within-Class Distances for Learning Speed up

In the following discussion, we assume that our training data $\mathcal{T}_\phi = \{\mathbf{x}_i, d_i\}_{i=1}^N$ has been taken to the kernel-induced feature space; $\mathbf{x} = [x_1, x_2, \ldots, x_M]$ is a feature vector in $\mathbb{R}^M$, and $d \in \mathbb{R}$ is the target output.

2.1   LP-SVR

In this research we are training the following LP-SVR (see [24] for details):

$$\min_{\alpha^+, \alpha^-, b^+, b^-, \xi, \mathbf{u}} \sum_{i=1}^N \left(\alpha_i^+ + \alpha_i^- + 2C\xi_i \right) \tag{1}$$

$$\text{s.t.} \quad \begin{cases} -\sum_{i=1}^N (\alpha_i^+ - \alpha_i^-)k(\mathbf{x}_j, \mathbf{x}_i) \ldots \\ \qquad\qquad -b^+ + b^- - \xi_j + u_j = \epsilon - d_j \\ \sum_{i=1}^N (\alpha_i^+ - \alpha_i^-)k(\mathbf{x}_j, \mathbf{x}_i) \ldots \\ \qquad\qquad +b^+ - b^- - \xi_j + u_j = \epsilon + d_j \\ \alpha_j^+, \alpha_j^-, b^+, b^-, \xi_j, u_j \geq 0 \end{cases}$$

$$\text{for} \quad j = 1, 2, \ldots, N,$$

where the kernel mapping $k(\mathbf{x}_i, \mathbf{x}_j) : \mathcal{X}^{(N \times M) \times (M \times N)} \mapsto \mathcal{H}^{N \times N}$. Then, assume that the slack variables ξ_i, ξ_i^* can be expressed as simply $2\xi_i$ (e.g. $\xi_i \xi_i^* = 0$). Then, let us introduce a slack variable $\mathbf{u}$ to get rid of the inequalities in the original SVR formulation [24]. As a consequence of these assumptions,

Problem (1) can be posed as the linear programming problem in its canonical form. To do so, one can define the following equalities:

$$\mathbf{A} = \begin{pmatrix} -\mathbf{K} & \mathbf{K} & -\mathbf{1} & \mathbf{1} & -\mathbf{I}\,\mathbf{I} \\ \mathbf{K} & -\mathbf{K} & \mathbf{1} & -\mathbf{1} & -\mathbf{I}\,\mathbf{I} \end{pmatrix}, \tag{2a}$$

$$\mathbf{b} = \begin{pmatrix} \mathbf{1}\epsilon - \mathbf{d} \\ \mathbf{1}\epsilon + \mathbf{d} \end{pmatrix}, \tag{2b}$$

$$\mathbf{z} = \left(\boldsymbol{\alpha}^+ \ \boldsymbol{\alpha}^- \ b^+ \ b^- \ \boldsymbol{\xi} \ \mathbf{u} \right)^T, \tag{2c}$$

$$\mathbf{c} = \left(1 \ 1 \ 0 \ 0 \ 2\mathbf{C} \ \mathbf{0} \right)^T, \tag{2d}$$

where $\mathbf{A} \in \mathbb{R}^{(2N) \times (4N+2)}$, $\mathbf{b} \in \mathbb{R}^{2N}$, $\mathbf{z}, \mathbf{c} \in \mathbb{R}^{4N+2}$. If we use the above equalities, then problem (1) is identical to the canonical form, and we can claim that the problem has been posed as an LP problem.

We claim that problem (1) is an original formulation for LP-SVR. In comparison with the $\nu-$LPR formulation by Smola, *et al.* [26] problem (1) (i) uses the canonical formulation, (ii) computes b, and $\mathbf{u}$ implicitly, (iii) does not compute ϵ implicitly, (iv) does not require the parameter ν, (v) promotes efficiency in the sense of using only one ξ, and (vi) is a lower-dimensional problem.

In comparison with Mangasarian, *et al.* [14], problem (1) (i) uses the canonical formulation, (ii) computes b implicitly, (iii) does not compute ϵ implicitly, and (iv) does not require the parameter μ. By (iii) and (iv) we provide the experimenter with more control of the sparseness of the solution [31]. In this case, sparseness means fewer number of support vectors.

Similarly, Problem (1) in comparison to Lu, *et al.* [18] our LP-SVR formulation (1) (i) uses the canonical formulation and (ii) computes b implicitly. By (ii) the linear program (LP) size is reduced by a factor of $N^2 + N$.

In comparison with the ℓ_1-norm LP-SVR formulation by Zhang, *et al.* [31] problem (1) does not require parameter δ and is more efficient in several ways: (i) uses only one ξ, (ii) avoids penalization of b, (iii) reduces computational efforts by forcing positivity in $\mathbf{u}$ which reduces the LP problem size by $2N^2 + 2N$, and (iv) is a smaller problem.

Using equalities (2a)–(2d), we can obtain the dual problem of (1) as follows:

$$\max_{\boldsymbol{\lambda}} \quad \mathbf{b}^T \boldsymbol{\lambda} \tag{3}$$
$$\text{s.t.} \quad \begin{cases} \mathbf{A}^T \boldsymbol{\lambda} + \mathbf{s} = \mathbf{c} \\ \mathbf{s} \geq \mathbf{0}, \end{cases}$$

which is equivalent to the dual of a linear programming problem, where $\boldsymbol{\lambda}$ is a vector of dual variables defined over $\mathbb{R}^{2N}$, and $\mathbf{s}$ is a slack vector variable in $\mathbb{R}^{4N+2}$.

Similarly, for the primal (1) and dual (3), the KKT conditions are defined as follows:

$$\mathbf{A}^T \boldsymbol{\lambda} + \mathbf{s} = \mathbf{c}, \tag{4a}$$
$$\mathbf{A}\mathbf{z} = \mathbf{b}, \tag{4b}$$
$$z_i s_i = 0, \tag{4c}$$
$$(\mathbf{z}, \mathbf{s}) \geq \mathbf{0}, \tag{4d}$$
$$\text{for } i = 1, 2, \ldots, n,$$

where the equality $z_i s_i$ implies that one of both variables must be zero. This equality will be referred to as the *complementarity condition*. Note that the

KKT conditions depend on the variables $(\mathbf{z}, \boldsymbol{\lambda}, \mathbf{s})$, and if the set of solutions $(\mathbf{z}^*, \boldsymbol{\lambda}^*, \mathbf{s}^*)$ satisfy all the conditions, the problem is said to be solved. The set $(\mathbf{z}^*, \boldsymbol{\lambda}^*, \mathbf{s}^*)$ is known as a *primal-dual solution*.

2.2   Definitions

Definition 1 (Support Vectors). *Let* $\mathcal{T} = \{\mathbf{x}_i, d_i\}_{i=1}^N$ *be a training set; let* $\mathbf{z}$ *be a solution to problem (1); and let* $d_j \equiv f(\mathbf{x}_j) = \sum_{i=1}^N (\alpha_i^+ - \alpha_i^-)\, k(\mathbf{x}_i, \mathbf{x}_j) + (b^+ - b^-)$ *be the regression function for problem (1). Then,*

1. $\mathcal{V}_S = \{\mathbf{x}_i \; : \; d_i - \epsilon < f(\mathbf{x}_i) < d_i + \epsilon\}$ *defines the set of Saturated Support Vectors (SSVs).*
2. $\mathcal{V}_E = \{\mathbf{x}_i \; : \; f(\mathbf{x}_i) = d_i + \epsilon, \text{ or } f(\mathbf{x}_i) = d_i - \epsilon\}$ *defines the set of Exact Support Vectors (ESVs).*
3. $\mathcal{V}_N = \{\mathbf{x}_i \; : \; f(\mathbf{x}_i) < d_i + \epsilon, \text{ or } f(\mathbf{x}_i) > d_i - \epsilon\}$ *defines the set of Non-Support Vectors (NSVs).*
4. $\mathcal{V}_\alpha = \{\mathbf{x}_i \; : \; \alpha_i \neq 0\}$ *defines the set of Sparse Vectors (SPVs).*
5. $N = |\mathcal{V}_S| + |\mathcal{V}_E| + |\mathcal{V}_N|$.
6. $\mathcal{S} = \mathcal{V}_S \cup \mathcal{V}_E$, *means that the union of the SSVs and the ESVs is the set of Support Vectors (SVs).*
7. $\mathcal{A} = \{\alpha_i \; : \; \alpha_i \neq 0\}$ *denotes the set of Non-zero Coefficients of the decision function and of problem (1).*

2.3   Background

It is well known that SVR and support vector machines (SVM) formulations do not make assumptions about the probability distribution of the data. Nonetheless, each class ω_j, should have a conditional class distribution $p(\mathbf{x}|\omega_j)$, where $\mathbf{x} \in \mathcal{X} \subseteq \mathbb{R}^M$ is defined as an M-dimensional random variable which could be estimated if enough data points were available. Estimating a multidimensional probability density function (PDF) is difficult but we could make some basic assumptions. First, we could assume that the data has a uni-modal distribution which implies that data-samples would cluster around the class mean and the further a point is from its mean, the lower its probability and could be expected to be located on the convex hull of the data sample we are analyzing. A more strict assumption would be to consider that the $p(\mathbf{x}|\omega_j)$ are multivariate Gaussian distributed. Under this assumption, each $p(\mathbf{x}|\omega_j)$ could be modeled using only the sample mean $\boldsymbol{\mu}_{\mathbf{x}|\omega_j}$ and a covariance matrix $\boldsymbol{\Sigma}_{\mathbf{x}|\omega_j}$, that is $p(\mathbf{x}|\omega_j) \sim \mathcal{N}(\boldsymbol{\mu}_{\mathbf{x}|\omega_j}, \boldsymbol{\Sigma}_{\mathbf{x}|\omega_j})$. It is also well known that we can use the squared Mahalanobis distance (MD)

$$D(\mathbf{x}_i) = (\mathbf{x}_i - \boldsymbol{\mu}_{\mathbf{x}|\omega_j})^T \boldsymbol{\Sigma}_{\mathbf{x}|\omega_j}^{-1} (\mathbf{x}_i - \boldsymbol{\mu}_{\mathbf{x}|\omega_j}), \tag{5}$$

as a measure of the distance of a data point with respect to its mean.

Based on these assumptions, we propose a method for finding the SV candidates by computing the $D(\mathbf{x}_i)$ for all $i = \{1, 2, \ldots, N\}$. Once all training vectors are sorted by their MD to their respective mean, and saved into the sets $\mathcal{Z}_j$ for the j-th class, then we can form the initial working set $\mathcal{B}$ of size B_{ini} using the procedure described in Algorithm 1 (explained in the next section). We traverse elements of $\mathcal{Z}_{j,i}$ into to $\mathcal{B}$ until B_{ini} elements are added.

Algorithm 1. Mahalanobis Distance-Based Working-Set Selection for Large-Scale LP-SVR Training Speedup

---

Require: A training set $T_\phi = \{\mathbf{x}_i, d_i\}_{i=1}^N$.
Require: A desired number of samples per class v.
1: **for** $j = 1$ to $|D|$ **do**
2:     Estimate parameters $(\boldsymbol{\mu}_{\mathbf{x}|\omega_j}, \boldsymbol{\Sigma}_{\mathbf{x}|\omega_j})$.   ▷ Sample mean and variance.
3:     **for** $i = 1$ to N **do**
4:         Compute Mahalanobis distance $D(\mathbf{x}_i)_j$ with (5).
5:     **end for**
6:     Obtain indices $\mathcal{Z}_j$ corresponding to the sorted D_j.   ▷ Descending order.
7:     **for** $i = 1$ to v **do**
8:         $\mathcal{Z}_{j,i} = \mathcal{Z}(i)_j$.   ▷ In this case $B_{\text{ini}} = k \equiv v \times |\mathcal{D}|$.
9:     **end for**
10: **end for**
Ensure: Initial working set indices $\mathcal{B} \leftarrow \mathcal{Z}_{j,i}$.
Ensure: Initial fixed set indices $\mathcal{M} \leftarrow \{1, 2, \ldots, N\} \notin \mathcal{Z}_{j,i}$.

In this manner, the SVR could be trained faster if the first working-set $\mathcal{B}$ contains those k samples, thereby, speeding up the training process. A similar approach to ours is given by Zhou, *et al.* [33] in 2010; but again the authors approach is still based on class and subclass convex hulls, which makes it computationally expensive.

To explain the proposed approach, consider the following definitions: Let $\mathcal{D} = \{\omega_1, \omega_2, \ldots, \omega_j\}$ be the set of classes where j is the total number of classes. Let $\mathcal{C} = \{\mathcal{C}_1, \mathcal{C}_2, \ldots, \mathcal{C}_j\}$ denote a set of indices, where $\mathcal{C}_j$ contains the indices of all those samples associated with the j-th class, $\mathcal{C}_i \cap \mathcal{C}_j = \emptyset$ for all $i \neq j$, and $\mathcal{C} \equiv \{1, 2, \ldots, N\}$.

2.4   Within-Class Mahalanobis Distance and Class-Convex Hull

To explain the ideas behind the procedure shown in Algorithm 1, we will be considering the case of all the samples $\mathbf{x}_i$ belonging to the j-th class, that is, all $i \in \mathcal{C}_j$. The same principles will apply to all classes.

One of the first steps is to estimate the parameters $(\boldsymbol{\mu}_{\mathbf{x}|\omega_j}, \boldsymbol{\Sigma}_{\mathbf{x}|\omega_j})$, *i.e.*, from observed events. Then the within-class MD from the i-th feature vector $\mathbf{x}_i$ to the center of the j-th class $\boldsymbol{\mu}_{\mathbf{x}|\omega_j}$ is defined as $D(\mathbf{x}_i)$ from (5). Next, we define $\mathcal{Z}_j$ as the set of indices corresponding to the ordered Mahalanobis distance samples of the j−th class computed with (5). The indices in $\mathcal{Z}_j$ correspond to ordered values in descending form, as shown in Fig. 2.

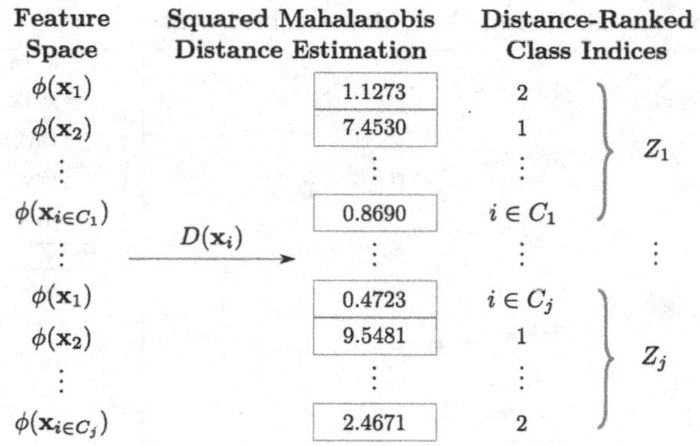

Feature Space	Squared Mahalanobis Distance Estimation	Distance-Ranked Class Indices	
$\phi(\mathbf{x}_1)$	1.1273	2	
$\phi(\mathbf{x}_2)$	7.4530	1	$\Big\} Z_1$
$\vdots$	$\vdots$	$\vdots$	
$\phi(\mathbf{x}_{i \in C_1})$	0.8690	$i \in C_1$	
$\vdots$	$\vdots$	$\vdots$	$\vdots$
$\phi(\mathbf{x}_1)$	0.4723	$i \in C_j$	
$\phi(\mathbf{x}_2)$	9.5481	1	$\Big\} Z_j$
$\vdots$	$\vdots$	$\vdots$	
$\phi(\mathbf{x}_{i \in C_j})$	2.4671	2	

with $D(\mathbf{x}_i)$ mapping between the Feature Space and Squared Mahalanobis Distance Estimation columns.

Fig. 2. Mahalanobis distance-ranking of class indices using feature vectors in either the input space or the kernel-induced feature space.

As mentioned before, we argument that the MD $D(\mathbf{x}_i)$ is related to the support vectors and the class convex hull (CCH), which is defined as follows:

$$\Theta(\omega_j) = \left\{ \sum_{i \in C_j} \beta_i \mathbf{x}_i \ : \ i \in C_j, \ \beta_i \in \mathbb{R}, \ \beta_i \geq 0, \ \sum_{i \in C_j} \beta_i = 1 \right\}, \tag{6}$$

where a number of $|C_j|$ points in the form of $\sum_{i \in C_j} \beta_i \mathbf{x}_i$ are the boundaries of the j-th class sample cloud. Then we can define the sets of indices corresponding to the convex hull of the j-th as $S = \Theta(\omega_j)$. The algorithm that obtains the convex hull has complexity of $\mathcal{O}(N^{\frac{M}{2}})$, where M is the dimensionality of the feature vector. The complexity of the method proposed here has a complexity of $\mathcal{O}(L)$, where $L = \max\left[N \log N, \binom{M}{2}\right]$. This demonstrates that our model has lower complexity than those based on convex hulls. Now, we define a relationship between Z, S, and SV in Proposition 1.

Proposition 1 (SVs and Within-Class Distances). *Assume classes in $\mathcal{D}$ are linearly separable. Let $Z_v = \{Z(1), Z(2), \ldots, Z(v)\}$ denote the v maximum Mahalanobis distance indices. Similarly, let $Z_{j,i} = \{Z_{1,v}, Z_{2,v}, \ldots, Z_{j,v}\}$ be the set of v maximum Mahalanobis distance indices of all classes. Then*

1. *the maximum Mahalanobis distance samples indices contain the convex hull indices: $Z_v \in S$,*
2. *the maximum Mahalanobis distance samples indices contain the support vector indices: $Z_{j,i} \in SV$,*

where v is an integer stating how many samples per class should be considered.

Proposition 1 states that the first v ranked MD indices Z_v contain the class convex hull indices S and, thus, contain the support vector indices. The integer v is bounded, $|\mathcal{D}| \leq v \leq |S|$, and SV is as in Definition 1. Therefore, if the initial

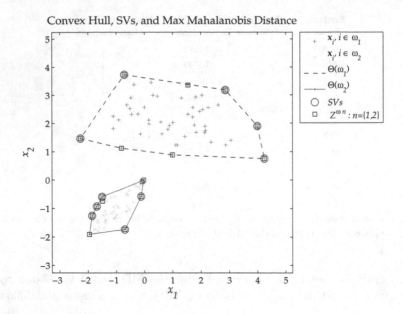

Fig. 3. Relationship between convex hull and maximum Mahalanobis distance for the two-class problem. Here it is shown the original separable two-class problem, class convex hull, support vectors, and k maximum Mahalanobis distance samples. Note that both SVs and Convex Hull match the k maximum Mahalanobis distance samples.

working-set is fixed to the indices in $\mathcal{Z}_{j,i}$, the training process will converge faster. This is mainly because if the support vectors are found at the very first iterations, the problem will be solved faster. Since $\mathcal{Z}_{j,i}$ is more likely (based on Mahalanobis distance information) to contain support vector indices, one can conclude that the training will be faster. We have found that a good value for v is the quotient between the initial working set size B_{ini} and the total number of classes: $v = \left\lceil \frac{B_{\text{ini}}}{|\mathcal{D}|} \right\rceil$. This choice of v was found empirically using the datasets discussed in the next section. This value v is used as input in Algorithm 1.

As an example, let us consider a case of a random variable $\mathbf{x} \in \mathbb{R}^2$. Then draw 50 samples that follows a multivariate normal distribution with parameters $\boldsymbol{\mu} = \begin{bmatrix} 1 & 2 \end{bmatrix}^T$ and $\boldsymbol{\Sigma} = \begin{bmatrix} 2 & 0 \,; 0 & \frac{1}{2} \end{bmatrix}$ and assign these to class ω_1; draw 50 more from a multivariate copula [6] distribution with parameter $\rho = 0.8$, and assign these to class ω_2. The problem is shown in Fig. 3 with the resulting convex hull. The associated support vectors are also shown in Fig. 3. Let us remark that the Mahalanobis distance is associated with the spreadness of the class sample cloud, such that the most uncertain samples have the highest Mahalanobis distance, as shown in Fig. 3. It is also important to remark that the highest Mahalanobis distance correspond to the lowest probability samples, which is also correlated to the support vectors as mentioned before. The next section addresses the speedup quantification and other numerical testing of Algorithm 1.

Table 1. Summary of the Dimensions and Properties of the Datasets.

Dataset	Classes	Features M	Training N	Reference
Ripley	2	2	250	[19]
Sonar	2	60	104	[7]
Wine	2	13	110	[12]
ADA	2	48	4, 147	[9, 21]
GINA	2	970	3, 153	[5, 21]
HIVA	2	1, 617	3, 845	[2]
NOVA	2	16, 969	1, 754	[2]
SYLVA	2	216	13, 086	[2, 5]
Iris	3	4	130	[15]
MODIS	4	4	374, 566	[22]
Power Load	$\mathbb{R}$	8	35, 064	[10]
Spiral	2	2	200	[30]
$f(x) =\mathrm{sinc}(x)$	$\mathbb{R}$	1	200	[20]
Synthetic S	3	2	3, 000, 000	–
Synthetic NS	3	2	3, 000, 000	–
$f(x) =\mathrm{sinc}(x) \times \pi$	$\mathbb{R}$	1	1 million	–

3   Experimental Results

To show the effectiveness and efficiency of the proposed algorithm, simulations were performed over different datasets. The summary of the properties of these datasets are shown in Table 1. Note that the simulations include classification in two and multiple classes, as well as regression problems. While the source of most of the datasets is referenced, the three synthetic datasets were generated as follows: "Synthetic S" is a non-linearly separable three-class problem whose classes are normally distributed; "Synthetic NS" is similar but the classes are non-separable; the "$f(x) = sinc(x) \times \pi$" consists of unevenly spaced points from the sinc function that are affected by multiplicative white Gaussian noise (WGN), making it very difficult to fit.

Here we analyze the speedup resulted of using the proposed sample selection algorithm using state of the art models and using benchmark datasets. The following paragraphs explain the results obtained.

3.1   Learning Speedup

Figure 4 depicts the behavior of the support vectors across iterations using the speedup strategy. The figure shows the number of support vectors, sparse support vectors, saturated support vectors, and exact support vectors. Note how the

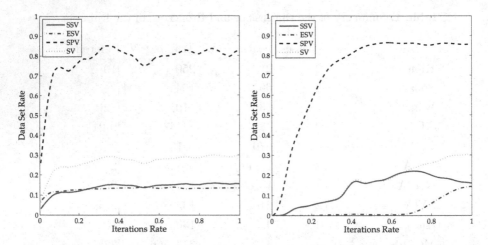

Fig. 4. Sample Selection. SVs as a Function of Iterations. SPV SSV ESV SV. (Left) With proposed sample selection. (Right) Without proposed sample selection.

Table 2. Total training time without speedup (sec)

Dataset	Classifiers					
	LS SVM	LP-SVR	IncSVM	LSSVM	D. Reg. Trees	FFNN [1, 20, 1]
Ripley	9	16	8	4	–	4
Wine	6	4	6	3	–	5
ADA	75	174	–	4412	–	63
GINA	50	116	–	1403	–	48
HIVA	73	161	–	–	–	–
NOVA	25	47	258	–	–	–
SYLVA	247	495	–	–	–	190
Iris	6	4	3	3	–	3
Spiral	10	10	14	8	–	10
$f(x) = \mathrm{sinc}(x)$	28	41	–	–	181	26
$f(x) = \mathrm{sinc}(x) \times \pi$	9376	806	–	–	6933	602
Synthetic S	9349	794	–	–	–	–
Synthetic NS	9180	817	–	–	–	–
Avg	2187	286	–	–	–	–

support vectors are found early in the learning process. If we compare Fig. 4 on the left to the analysis on the right, we notice that most of the support vectors are found in earlier iterates, which is the goal of the strategy. We determined experimentally that in the average case, most of the sparse support vectors (SPV) are found in around 40% of the total iterations. In the other hand, Fig. 4 tells that in around 20% of the total number of iterates.

Table 2 shows the total training time of the experiments without speedup. Compare to Table 3 that shows the total training time after using the speedup strategy. From these two tables, we can observe that if the strategy is used the

Table 3. Total training time with speedup (sec)

Dataset	Classifiers					
	LS SVM	LP-SVR	IncSVM	LSSVM	D. Reg. Trees	FFNN [1, 20, 1]
Ripley	8	9	7	4	–	4
Wine	1	2	4	3	–	5
ADA	71	74	–	3533	–	63
GINA	38	63	–	1191	–	48
HIVA	57	115	–	–	–	–
NOVA	17	19	234	–	–	–
SYLVA	246	230	–	–	–	190
Iris	2	2	2	2	–	3
Spiral	5	5	5	5	–	10
$f(x) = \text{sinc}(x)$	9	8	–	–	15	26
$f(x) = \text{sinc}(x) \times \pi$	5672	764	–	–	5597	602
Synthetic S	7038	467	–	–	–	–
Synthetic NS	8608	672	–	–	–	–
Avg	1674	187	–	–	–	–

total training time decreases, particularly as the problem size increases, as it was expected.

Besides a time reduction analysis, it is also important to observe if the total number of iterations is reduced when the speedup strategy is applied. Table 4 shows the total reduction of iterations, in percent, using the speedup strategy. Clearly, if the problem size is large, the reduction in number of iterations is also larger. A great benefit can be obtained of the speedup strategy, especially, if the class cloud is as close as possible to a multivariate Gaussian distribution within the kernel-induced feature space.

Another interesting thing to notice is that the percentage of iterations reduction seems to be superior in proportion to the learning time after speedup. This follows from noticing that, even if the support vectors are found at early iterations, still, the learning process has to perform several time-consuming decompositions and comparisons that might increment in size, specially, if the number of support vectors is large. However, since support vectors are found early at the learning process, there is no need to solve some of the subsequent sub-problems since the support vectors found will satisfy the KKT conditions of many of the sub-problems.

4   Computational Concerns

The primary concern of the speedup method is the computation of the covariance matrix $\Sigma_{x|\omega_j}$. In our implementation, the covariance matrix was estimated with the sample covariance matrix

$$\Sigma_{x|\omega_j} = \frac{1}{|\mathcal{C}_j| - 1} \sum_{i \in \mathcal{C}_j} (x_i - \mu_{x|\omega_j})(x_i - \mu_{x|\omega_j})^T \tag{7}$$

Table 4. Iterations reduction percentage after speedup.

Dataset	Classifiers					
	LS SVM	LP-SVR	IncSVM	LSSVM	D. Reg. Trees	FFNN [1, 20, 1]
Ripley	1	2	22	52	–	0
Wine	1	4	0	1	–	0
ADA	24	9	–	10	–	0
GINA	12	10	–	11	–	0
HIVA	39	9	–	–	–	–
NOVA	7	1	4	–	–	–
SYLVA	30	1	–	–	–	0
Iris	1	1	8	5	–	0
Spiral	15	12	4	7	–	0
$f(x) = \mathrm{sinc}(x)$	5	13	–	–	1	0
$f(x) = \mathrm{sinc}(x) \times \pi$	59	57	–	–	43	1
Synthetic S	23	51	–	–	–	–
Synthetic NS	27	37	–	–	–	–
Avg	18.7	15.7	–	–	–	–

where $\mathbf{x}_i \in \mathbb{R}^M$ is some random vector with $|\mathcal{C}_j|$ realizations, and $\boldsymbol{\mu}_{\mathbf{x}|\omega_j} \equiv \mathcal{E}[\mathbf{x}_i]$ for all $i \in \mathcal{C}_j$. Clearly, $\boldsymbol{\Sigma}_{\mathbf{x}|\omega_j} \in \mathbb{R}^{M \times M}$, thus, problems with a very large number of variables e.g., the NOVA dataset, cannot be resolved under current computational constraints. Therefore, some sort of feature reduction must be implemented to obtain the covariance matrix. In the case of the NOVA dataset, a large number of features are redundant or add no discriminant information and were eliminated without loss of generality.

Moreover, for the speedup process only, the kernel choice was also limited. The rule for selecting the kernel type is the following: If $N \geq 1000$ a polynomial kernel with degree $p = 1000$ is used, otherwise an RBF kernel is used. Since one of our goals is to deal with large-scale datasets most of the experiments used a polynomial kernel. The polynomial kernel is our second choice since it is known to be the second best after RBF kernels [17]. The degree of the polynomial kernel is directly related to the amount of data that can be efficiently handled for covariance matrix estimation purposes.

5   Conclusion

Within the context of kernel-induced feature space one can assume the data is (or is close to be) linearly separable and then compute the distances from each point to the center of the class cloud. This is done using the Mahalanobis distance. Since the support vectors (SVs) most likely lie on the class cloud boundaries or within the class convex hull, we can use the Mahalanobis distance to rank the training set, such that, the samples with the largest distances are used first as part of the working set. Experimental results suggest a reduction in the total training time, and a more dramatic decrease in the total iterations percentage. Results also suggest that, using the speedup strategy the support, the SVs are found early in the learning process. Furthermore, the speedup strategy was tested with other methods with similar results, suggesting that the proposed approach is not particular to LP-SVR but rather useful for other SV-based methods.

References

1. Bennett, K.P., Bredensteiner, E.J.: Duality and geometry in SVM classifiers. ICML **2000**, 57–64 (2000)
2. Cawley, G.C.: Leave-one-out cross-validation based model selection criteria for weighted LS-SVMs. In: The 2006 IEEE International Joint Conference on Neural Network Proceedings, pp. 1661–1668. IEEE (2006)
3. Chen, X., Xiao, Y.: Geometric projection twin support vector machine for pattern classification. Multimedia Tools Appl. **58**, 1–17 (2020)
4. Cherkassky, V., Ma, Y.: Practical selection of SVM parameters and noise estimation for SVM regression. Neural Netw. **17**(1), 113–126 (2004)
5. Collobert, R., Bengio, S.: Svmtorch: Support vector machines for large-scale regression problems. J. Mach. Learn. Res. **1**, 143–160 (2001)
6. Darsow, W.F., Nguyen, B., Olsen, E.T., et al.: Copulas and Markov processes. Ill. J. Math **36**(4), 600–642 (1992)
7. Gorman, R.P., Sejnowski, T.J.: Analysis of hidden units in a layered network trained to classify sonar targets. Neural Netw. **1**(1), 75–89 (1988)
8. Gu, X., Chung, F.l., Wang, S.: Fast convex-hull vector machine for training on large-scale ncRNA data classification tasks. Knowl. Based Syst. **151**, 149–164 (2018)
9. Joachims, T.: Making large-scale SVM learning practical. Technical Report (1998)
10. Karoas, A., Moshhadi, H.R., Miroolohi, M.M.: Market clearing price and load forecasting using cooperative co-evolutionary approach. Int. J. Electr. Power Energy Syst. **32**(5), 408–415 (2010)
11. Keerthi, S.S., Shevade, S.K., Bhattacharyya, C., Murthy, K.R.: A fast iterative nearest point algorithm for support vector machine classifier design. IEEE Trans. Neural Netw. **11**(1), 124–136 (2000)
12. Kinzett, D., Zhang, M., Johnston, M.: Using numerical simplification to control bloat in genetic programming. In: Li, X., et al. (eds.) SEAL 2008. LNCS, vol. 5361, pp. 493–502. Springer, Heidelberg (2008). https://doi.org/10.1007/978-3-540-89694-4_50
13. Liu, Z., Liu, J., Pan, C., Wang, G.: A novel geometric approach to binary classification based on scaled convex hulls. IEEE Trans. Neural Netw. **20**(7), 1215–1220 (2009)
14. Mangasarian, O.L., Musicant, D.R.: Large scale kernel regression via linear programming. Mach. Learn. **46**(1–3), 255–269 (2002)
15. McGarry, K.J., Wermter, S., MacIntyre, J.: Knowledge extraction from radial basis function networks and multilayer perceptrons. In: IJCNN'99, International Joint Conference on Neural Networks, Proceedings, vol. 4, pp. 2494–2497. IEEE (1999)
16. Mehr, A.D., Nourani, V., Khosrowshahi, V.K., Ghorbani, M.A.: A hybrid support vector regression-firefly model for monthly rainfall forecasting. Int. J. Environ. Sci. Technol. **16**(1), 335–346 (2019)
17. Mezghani, D.B.A., Boujelbene, S.Z., Ellouze, N.: Evaluation of SVM kernels and conventional machine learning algorithms for speaker identification. Int. J. Hybrid Inf. Technol. **3**(3), 23–34 (2010)

18. Niu, B., Jin, Y., Lu, W., Li, G.: Predicting toxic action mechanisms of phenols using adaboost learner. Chemom. Intell. Lab. Syst. **96**(1), 43–48 (2009)
19. Osuna, E., De Castro, O.: Convex hull in feature space for support vector machines. In: Garijo, F.J., Riquelme, J.C., Toro, M. (eds.) IBERAMIA 2002. LNCS (LNAI), vol. 2527, pp. 411–419. Springer, Heidelberg (2002). https://doi.org/10.1007/3-540-36131-6_42
20. Peng, X.: TSVR: An efficient twin support vector machine for regression. Neural Netw. **23**(3), 365–372 (2010)
21. Platt, J.C.: Using analytic QP and sparseness to speed training of support vector machines. In: Advances in Neural Information Processing Systems, pp. 557–563 (1999)
22. Rivas-Perea, P.: Southwestern us and northwestern mexico dust storm modeling trough moderate resolution imaging spectroradiometer data: a machine learning perspective. Technical report, NASA/UMBC/GEST GSSP (2009)
23. Rivas Perea, P.: Algorithms for training large-scale linear programming support vector regression and classification. The University of Texas at El Paso (2011)
24. Rivas-Perea, P., Cota-Ruiz, J.: An algorithm for training a large scale support vector machine for regression based on linear programming and decomposition methods. Pattern Recogn. Lett. **34**(4), 439–451 (2013)
25. Santamaría-Bonfil, G., Reyes-Ballesteros, A., Gershenson, C.: Wind speed forecasting for wind farms: A method based on support vector regression. Renew. Energy **85**, 790–809 (2016)
26. Smola, A., Scholkopf, B., Ratsch, G.: Linear programs for automatic accuracy control in regression. In: 1999 Ninth International Conference on Artificial Neural Networks ICANN 99, (Conf. Publ. No. 470), vol. 2, pp. 575–580. IET (1999)
27. Trzciński, T., Rokita, P.: Predicting popularity of online videos using support vector regression. IEEE Transactions on Multimedia **19**(11), 2561–2570 (2017)
28. Vapnik, V., Golowich, S., Smola, A.: Support vector method for function approximation, regression estimation, and signal processing. Adv. Neural Inf. Process. Syst. **9**, 281–287 (1997)
29. Wang, D., Qiao, H., Zhang, B., Wang, M.: Online support vector machine based on convex hull vertices selection. IEEE Trans. Neural Netw. Learn. Syst. **24**(4), 593–609 (2013)
30. Xu, Z., Huang, K., Zhu, J., King, I., Lyu, M.R.: A novel kernel-based maximum a posteriori classification method. Neural Netw. **22**(7), 977–987 (2009)
31. Zhang, L., Zhou, W.: On the sparseness of 1-norm support vector machines. Neural Netw. **23**(3), 373–385 (2010)
32. Zhong, H., Wang, J., Jia, H., Mu, Y., Lv, S.: Vector field-based SVR for building energy consumption prediction. Appl. Energy **242**, 403–414 (2019)
33. Zhou, X., Jiang, W., Tian, Y., Shi, Y.: Kernel subclass convex hull sample selection method for SVM on face recognition. Neurocomputing **73**(10–12), 2234–2246 (2010)

Short Technical Stream Papers

Learning Categories with Spiking Nets and Spike Timing Dependent Plasticity

Christian Huyck[✉]

Middlesex University, London NW4 4BT, UK
c.huyck@mdx.ac.uk

Abstract. An exploratory study of learning a neural network for categorisation shows that commonly used leaky integrate and fire neurons and Hebbian learning can be effective. The system learns with a standard spike timing dependent plasticity Hebbian learning rule. A two layer feed forward topology is used with a presentation mechanism of inputs followed by outputs a simulated ms. later to learn Iris flower and Breast Cancer Tumour Malignancy categorisers. An exploration of parameters indicates how this may be applied to other tasks.

Keywords: Spiking neural network · STDP · Categorisation

1 Introduction

AI is a critical technology with immense interest from governments, companies and society at large. Recent developments in machine learning and deep networks in particular have achieved success in a wide range of areas, such as face recognition [15] and games [13].

Deep Nets [8] are a diverse group of systems typically with large numbers of units between layers, and many layers that are well connected. These connectionist systems are typically inspired by the brain, and called neural networks.

Simulated biological neural networks, on the other hand, attempt to reproduce the behaviour of brains, or parts of brains [12]. These are based on models of biological neurons, models of biological learning, and biological topologies. The neural models are typically spiking neurons.

This paper describes a system that categorises data based on a neural network. The network has aspects of biological plausibility combined with a biologically unrealistic topology. The plausible aspects include learning via spike timing dependent plasticity, a Hebbian learning rule, and a widely used, though simple, biological neuron model. It is not clear that the presentation or testing mechanism is psychologically realistic.

2 Literature Review

There are many neural models including relatively simple point models that represent neurons by simple equations and elaborate compartmental models [9]

© Springer Nature Switzerland AG 2020
M. Bramer and R. Ellis (Eds.): SGAI-AI 2020, LNAI 12498, pp. 139–144, 2020.
https://doi.org/10.1007/978-3-030-63799-6_10

that break neurons into compartments and evaluate the conductance of these compartments. Leaky integrate and fire (LIF) neurons integrate activation from other neurons. The activation leaks away, but if enough accumulates, the neuron fires emitting a spike. The activation resets after it fires. In this paper, the LIF neural model is from Brette and Gerstner [4]. The model includes exponential current transmission, so that the current is transferred across the synapse (after the pre synaptic neuron fires) at an exponentially decaying rate.

In the brain, most if not all learning is Hebbian [7]. If the presynaptic neuron tends to cause the postsynaptic neuron to fire, the weight will tend to increase. There are many rules, but a great deal of biological evidence supports Spike Timing Dependent Plasticity (STDP) [3]. Bi and Poo [3] have perhaps the first published example that shows the performance of biological neurons. Song et al. [14] have developed an idealised curve that fits the biological data, though it is a curve fitting exercise. If the pre-synaptic neuron fires before the post, the weight is increased; if the post-synaptic neuron fires first, the weight is decreased. Note that the closer to precisely co-firing, the more the weight change. The simulations in the remainder of the paper use an STDP learning rule.

LIF neurons were used as the neural model. The system was developed using PyNN middleware [5], a python package to specify the topology and manage inputs. The backend was the NEST neuron simulation platform [6].[1]

3   Methods

Data was taken from the widely used University of California at Irvine (UCI) benchmark [1]. A commonly used task, categorisation of Iris flowers, is used initially. The data was split into two equal sized groups. The Iris data has 150 instances, 50 of each of three categories, so the data was split into two 75 item data sets with 25 of each category in each.

First the data is preprocessed by scaling the range of features to 0 to 100 with two digits of precision. Now all features are represented by an integer between 0 and 100 inclusive. The input to the system is represented by a neuron for each number. So, for the Iris data, there are four features, and thus 404 input neurons.

There is a neuron for each output category. For the Iris data, there are three categories, and thus three neurons. The input neurons are well connected to the output neurons using plastic synapses. The plasticity rule is a variant Hebbian STDP (consistent with Song et al. [14]).

During training, the input neurons are sent a spike, and the output neurons are sent a spike one ms. later. This uses the PyNN spike source, an impossible biological mechanism for learning. The input neurons consist of those with the input feature, and in a window of three. So, when the first training feature is 19, the neurons numbered 15 to 21 are stimulated as numbering is zero based. The neurons are stimulated so that they fire once.

One of the parameters that was explored in development was the number of training epochs. An epoch is the presentation of all the training examples; in

---

[1] The code can be found on http://www.cwa.mdx.ac.uk/NEAL/NEAL.html.

the case of irises, all 75 training items. There may be several epochs of training with all of the training items presented in sequence in each epoch.

The time between each example was another parameter that was explored. This time can affect the system for two main reasons. First, if the time is too small, an input example can continue to spike into the next example. Second, the STDP synaptic reduction window is effected by the prior example; if the prior example fires nearer to the time of the current example, the synaptic weight from the prior input neurons to the current category neurons may be reduced. During testing, the input neurons are stimulated, and the spikes of the output neurons are counted. The input is categorised based on the spiking behaviour with the neuron that spiked most winning.

It is possible to set the neural parameters for the model, but the default parameters were used, and varying them was not explored. Some important parameters are: the firing threshold, the higher the threshold, the more activation is required for a spike; the refractory period, after a neuron spikes, all input activation is ignored during the refractory period; and the leak rate, the higher the leak rate the faster activation leaks away making the neuron more difficult to fire over short periods of time. Another simulation parameter is the time step that sets how often are the neural and synaptic variables are updated. These simulations used a 1 ms time step.

The STDP learning rule is described by seven parameters. The first is the initial synaptic weight i, the second is the maximum weight m. The third is the minimum weight that has always been 0 in the simulations described in this paper; input features may have no influence on output categories, so the neurons that represent these values should have a 0 connection. There are many STDP rules, and a spike pair rule is used in the simulations in this paper. The weight is modified based on spike pairs alone. There are four parameters associated with this, two for increasing the weight and two for decreasing the weight. The increasing parameters are $A+$, for scaling how much the weight increases, and $\tau+$ for stretching the window of that the weight increases. The parallel decreasing parameters are $A-$ and $\tau-$. $\tau+$ and $tau-$ are in ms.

Parameters are explored to develop a system that categorises reasonably well. The data has been broken into a training and a test set. Parameters are explored using the training set, and the test set is used, largely, for reporting.

In the first example there are 5 training epochs; the time between examples is 30; the initial synaptic weight was 0; the maximum synaptic weight was 0.05; the synaptic increase parameters were $\tau+ = 20.0$ ms. and $A+ = 0.004$, and the decrease parameters were $\tau- = 20.0$ ms. and $A- = 0.003$. This is represented by the first line in Table 1.

4   Results

Exploration of parameters can include a change of topology, but some simple things to explore are the learning parameters, and presentation mechanism. In particular, the five learning parameters, the number of training epochs, and the length of a presentation are explored.

Exploration is done by training the system on the training set, and testing on the testing set. It is not a two fold cross validation. The system uses no randomness. Repeating a run will have the same results.

One large piece of information is how many test examples actually have neurons firing. The default categorisation works with no neurons firing but it shows that the system is not categorising. The parameters affect how many categorisation neurons fire in the test. Unsurprisingly, typically, the more training epochs, the more test firing; synaptic weights are initially zero and each presentation provides the opportunity to increase, and increased synaptic weight leads to further firing in future epochs, further increasing weights. This may not be the case if the initial weight is larger than zero.

Too much firing also has a problem in that the output becomes random. The neurons integrate input from a set of pre-synaptic neurons, all firing once at the same time. The neuron can get enough activation so that it fires multiple times. However, if two or three of the categorisation neurons get a great deal of input, they saturate and fire the same number of times. So, there is an ideal window of incoming synaptic strength to differentiate between the categories.

Perhaps the most powerful mechanism for increasing firing is to increase the maximum synaptic weight m. So, if the system with a particular parameter set had many tests with output neurons firing, m was increased. Similarly, the total output spikes can also be tabulated, and if this is very high, m can be reduced.

The synaptic weight increase and decrease constants $A+$ and $A-$ also influence output neuron firing. Increasing $A+$ or decreasing $A-$ leads to increased firing; decreasing $A+$ or increasing $A-$ leads to decreased firing.

The goal is to have a system that categorises well. So, the categorisation results also matter. By following the gradient so that all tests have categorisation neurons firing, but many with only one spike, parameters can be set to find a good result on the training set (e.g. the second row of Table 1).

Two other systems are shown for comparison. The first [10], in the third row is a spiking net using a compensatory Hebbian rule; the neurons have adaptation. As it uses randomness, the average results of a two fold test are shown. The second [16] uses a specialised feed forward neural topology and a variant of STDP that incorporates a learning signal; training and testing are separated in their evaluation, and in Table 1.

Wisconsin Breast Cancer Categorisation

A second task, the Wisconsin Breast Cancer Categorisation task, again from the UCI benchmark [1] is reported. An item refers to a patient and is represented by 9 relevant features, and the output is a binary value referring to whether the tumour was benign or malignant. There were 699 items, with 241 malignant category items. The data set was split into two with the training set having an extra item and an extra malignant item.

Each feature had a range from 1 to 10, one feature had missing values, and one feature had one value that was not represented. So, each input feature was represented by 10 neurons and the two output categories by one neuron each. When an item was presented, only one neuron was stimulated for each feature,

Table 1. Categorisation results: WBC refers to the Wisconsin breast cancer task.

Task	Epochs	Example time	Maximum weight m	$A+$	$\tau+$	$A-$	$\tau-$	Train result	Test result
Iris	5	30	0.005	0.004	20.0	0.003	20.0	86.67%	90.6%
Iris	6	50	0.003	0.005	20.0	0.002	20	92%	90.6%
Iris [10]									93.53%
Iris [16]								95.5%	95.3%
WBC	6	50	0.002	0.006	20.0	0.009	20	95.14%	95.7%
WBC [16]								96.2%	96.7%

and the missing feature was simply ignored; one of the benefits of this approach is that missing features are readily ignored.

A simple exploration of the parameter space began with the parameters from the Iris data set (line 2 of Table 1). This exhibited a great deal of firing during testing, so the Maximum Weight w was reduced. This left little firing, so $A+$ was increased. Somewhat surprisingly, increasing $\Lambda-$ also improved results leading to several training parameter sets that got 95.14%. One was chosen, and the results are displayed in the first WBC line of Table 1. Below that the results reported from another spiking system [16] are shown.

5 Discussion

This paper has shown an exploration of simple feed forward topology and a standard learning rule based on a standard biological LIF neuron, and a standard STDP rule. The presentation mechanism of turning on the input neurons one step before the output neurons is clearly biologically impossible. Similarly, the uniformity of the initial feed forward topology is also biologically implausible. While the results are below the state of the art, and the tasks are simple, the results are quite near the state of the art. This merely shows how powerful the strictly Hebbian STDP learning mechanism is.

STDP, with the topology and presentation mechanism used above, has a result that is a type of covariance rule. The synaptic weight from a neuron representing an input feature will increase if it is used as a member of the category. If it is also used for another category, it will decrease, so the weight roughly reflects the likelihood the feature discriminates between the categories. If it is involved in two categories, the weight will be lower, and if in three lower still. The feature breadth mechanism used in the Iris task supports learning from fewer examples, and generalisation to unpresented data.

STDP is strictly Hebbian, so is an entirely unsupervised mechanism. Reinforcement can be included by adding extra topology to encourage neurons to fire at appropriate times; this is a solution that has been included in spiking networks [2,16]. Adjusting synaptic weights to reflect desired outputs, as is done in supervised rules such as back propagation [11] does not seem to have a biological basis. This supervised learning is a powerful mechanism, particularly for feed forward networks. However, the brain is not feed forward but highly recurrent.

This paper has used a simple two layer feed forward approach. Learning here is based on particular inputs. Another approach would be to extend across layers with different times so that input could cascade through layers. Other precise timing mechanisms can be developed, but in the brain, most neurons fire more or less continuously at a low rate. Closely timed mechanisms will not work as models of actual biological processing.

References

1. Bache, K., Lichman, M.: UCI machine learning repository (2013). http://archive. ics.uci.edu/ml
2. Belavkin, R., Huyck, C.: Conflict resolution and learning probability matching in a neural cell-assembly architecture. Cogn. Syst. Res. **12**, 93–101 (2010)
3. Bi, G., Poo, M.: Synaptic modifications in cultured hippocampal neurons: dependence on spike timing, synaptic strength, and postsynaptic cell type. J. Neurosci. **18**(24), 10464–10472 (1998)
4. Brette, R., Gerstner, W.: Adaptive exponential integrate-and-fire model as an effective description of neuronal activity. J. Neurophysiol. **94**, 3637–3642 (2005)
5. Davison, A., Yger, P., Kremkow, J., Perrinet, L., Muller, E.: PyNN: towards a universal neural simulator API in python. BMC Neurosci. **8**(S2), P2 (2007)
6. Gewaltig, M., Diesmann, M.: NEST (NEural Simulation Tool). Scholarpedia **2**(4), 1430 (2007)
7. Hebb, D.: The Organization of Behavior: A Neuropsychological Theory. Wiley, New York (1949)
8. Hinton, G., Osindero, S., Teh, Y.: A fast learning algorithm for deep belief nets. Neural Comput. **18**(7), 1527–1554 (2006)
9. Hodgkin, A., Huxley, A.: A quantitative description of membrane current and its application to conduction and excitation in nerve. J. Physiol. **117**, 500–544 (1952)
10. Huyck, C.R., Mitchell, I.G.: Post and pre-compensatory Hebbian learning for categorisation. Cogn. Neurodyn. **8**(4), 299–311 (2014). https://doi.org/10.1007/ s11571-014-9282-4
11. Rumelhart, D., McClelland, J.: Parallel Distributed Processing. MIT Press, Cambridge (1986)
12. Sejnowski, T., Koch, C., Churchland, P.: Computataional neuroscience. Science **241**(4871), 1299–1306 (1988)
13. Silver, D., et al.: Mastering the game of go without human knowledge. Nature **550**, 354–59 (2017)
14. Song, S., Miller, K., Abbott, L.: Competitive Hebbian learning through spike-timing-dependent synaptic plasticity. Nat. Neurosci. **3**(9), 919–926 (2000)
15. Sun, Y., Liang, D., Wang, X., Tang, X.: DeepID3: face recognition with very deep neural networks. CoRR abs/1502.00873 (2015)
16. Wade, J., McDaid, L., Santos, J., Sayers, H.: SWAT: a spiking neural network training algorithm for classification problems. IEEE Trans. Neural Netw. **21**(11), 1817–1830 (2010)

Developing Ensemble Methods for Detecting Anomalies in Water Level Data

Thakolpat Khampuengson[1,2]($\boxtimes$), Anthony Bagnall[1]($\boxtimes$), and Wenjia Wang[1]($\boxtimes$)

[1] School of Computing Sciences, University of East Anglia, Norwich, UK
{T.Khampuengson,Anthony.Bagnall,Wenjia.Wang}@uea.ac.uk
[2] Hydro-Informatics Institute of Ministry of Higher Education, Science,
Research and Innovation, Bangkok, Thailand
thakolpat@hii.or.th

Abstract. Telemetry is an automatic system for monitoring environments in a remote or inaccessible area and transmitting data via various media. Data from telemetry stations can be used to produce early warning or decision supports in risky situations. However, sometimes a device in a telemetry system may not work properly and generates some errors in the data, which lead to false alarms or miss true alarms for disasters. We then developed two types of ensembles: (1) *simple* and (2) *complex* ensembles for automatically detecting the anomaly data. The ensembles were tested on the data collected from 9 telemetry water level stations and the results clearly show that the complex ensembles are the most accurate and also reliable in detecting anomalies.

Keywords: Ensemble methods · Water level telemetry monitoring · Anomaly detection

1 Introduction

The telemetry data can be analysed to produce early warnings and decision supports to the relevant government agencies for dealing with critical and risky situations. However, sometimes the devices in the telemetry system went wrong and generated various errors in data. Although, we can verify the data before dissemination, the process of detecting errors in the data requires experienced humans to investigate the data and make decisions. Moreover, it is time-consuming since there are the huge of the data that has to analyse, and also produces inconsistent decisions due to variations of human's experience. All these issues can cause considerable delay in detecting abnormal data at the right time and location, and issuing an early warning for a flood situation that may occur in real time. In this research, we aim to address these issues by developing some intelligent methods to automatic detecting anomalies in real-time telemetry water level data.

2 Related Works

The generated data from a water level monitoring station is time series data. There are several types of existing models to detect anomaly in time series data.

© Springer Nature Switzerland AG 2020
M. Bramer and R. Ellis (Eds.): SGAI-AI 2020, LNAI 12498, pp. 145–151, 2020.
https://doi.org/10.1007/978-3-030-63799-6_11

Most of their models have been computed based on a sliding window [3,5,6]. But it has two drawbacks: (1) the computed values limited to a specific window and (2) time-consuming. Some previous researches have shown that it is possible to combine various individually trained models to produce more accurate detections than any of the single models [7]. This combination of multiple models to work together is called ensemble method. It has been demonstrated to be effective in a widespread of real-life problems, such as weather forecasting [4], detecting anomalies in cellular networks [1], wireless sensor networks detection [2]. These successful studies motivated us to develop ensembles for our problem. Before describing our ensemble methods, we will introduce the data we used in this study.

3   Water Level Datasets

To demonstrate and compare the efficiency of each anomaly detection model that will be developed in this research, we chose the data collected from 9 telemetry stations of Hydro-Informatics Institute (HII) that installed in Yom Basin, Thailand. All the stations measured water level every 10 min during the years of 2013 to 2018. The data have been analysed by the experts at the HII to identified various anomalies to be used as ground-truth for the model's evaluation.

4   Anomaly Detection

4.1   Basic Anomaly Detection Model

Basic models were selected as the member candidates for building an ensemble, which are *Auto Regression (AR), Differenced Based (DB), Interquartile Range (IQR), Sigma rules of thumb (K-Sigma), and Z-Score.* In addition, we knew that anomaly data will have a slope angle close to $90°$, so we developed model Slope as an Angle (SA) which defined a point as an anomaly if there is angle slope more than $45°$. All of those models are simple and use no or few data for training. As a result, they take much shorter time to calculate, thus are suitable for detecting an anomaly in near real-time situations.

4.2   A Modified Sliding Window Algorithm

Every models, except SA, require to employ a *sliding window* algorithm to find the threshold $\theta(w_t)$ for the current window w_t and use it to decide if the value $x(t)$ is an anomaly or not. But it has a drawback, that is, when the window is moved forward to the next step, the detected anomaly data will be included in the window, it will add some bias to the threshold and then as a consequence it will affect the prediction of next possible anomaly value along the time series. We then modified this algorithm by remove the identified anomaly $x(t)$ and replace it with the values $x(t+i)$ when $i \in 1, 2, 3, ...n$, until values at $x(t+i)$ has been identified as normal, then let window moves forward as normal. So that the anomaly will not affect the threshold value of the next window, w_{t+1}. We named our modified algorithm as the *Only Normal Sliding Windows (ONSW)*.

4.3   Simple Ensemble

One of the co-authors has studied the fundamental issues of ensemble methods [8] and emphasised that a successful ensemble can be built with some appropriate models selected by using suitable criteria. Therefore, we devised a new scoring function (see below) to calculate the goodness score of a model, by using the values from the confusion matrix as criteria, and then use this score to determine if a model is good enough to be selected.

A simple ensemble operates in 2 main stages: *Model Selection* and *Decision Making*.

– *Model Selection*: It is done in three steps: (1) Evaluating the accuracies of models with TP, FP and FN, (2) Calculating ranking score R_j with those 3 measure by Eq. 1

$$S_{(m_i,R_j)} = \frac{N + 1 - r_{(m_i,R_j)}}{N}, \in [\frac{1}{N}, 1] \tag{1}$$

Where $S_{(m_i,R_j)}$ is score of model m_i in ranking R_j, $r_{(m_i,R_j)}$ is ranking position of m_i in R_j, N is number of models in a ranking, i is index of models: 1, 2, ..., N, and j is index of rankings: 1, 2, 3. Then we devised a new measure - *Total Score of Performance (TSP)*, that combines the three scores from each model (TSP_{m_i}) by the following equation.

$$TSP_{m_i} = 1/N \sum_{j=1}^{3} S_{(m_i,R_j)}, \in [\frac{1}{N}, 1] \tag{2}$$

Then all the models are ranked again by their TSP score in a descending order, (3) We chose 3, 5 and 7 models from top of each ranking to build simple ensembles respectively to avoid a tie-situation in decision making. In addition, we also used another pair of measures - *Sensitivity* and *Specificity* to select the same numbers of models to build ensembles for comparison.

– *Decision Making*: In this research we chose the simple majority voting approach for its simplicity and efficiency, which is particularly essential for our anomaly detection system to work fast enough in real-time with streaming data.

4.4   Complex Ensemble

A complex ensemble is built by using selected simple ensembles as its member models. It can simply be viewed as an ensemble of ensembles, so donated as *EoE*. An EoE still uses the majority voting among the selected simple ensembles to determine its final result. From the 13 simple ensembles built earlier, we can construct 5 complex ensembles by selecting top 3, 5, 7, 9 and 11 simple ensembles based on their TSP score, and another one with all the 13 simple ensembles. They are donated as EoE3, EoE5, EoE7, EoE9, EoE11 and EoE13, respectively.

5   Experiments and Results

The 7 classic anomaly detection methods have been trained by moving the windows over the entire data to find their decision threshold, and evaluate their accuracy with *Recall, Precision*, and *F*1 scores. Then these basic individual models were used to build simple ensembles and the simple ensembles were used to build complex ensembles. Their testing results are presented below separately.

The total and average TSP score from each model is presented in Table 1. The IQR model is the best individual model because it has not only the highest score in 7 stations but also the highest score of total and average. We evaluate the accuracy of IQR with other measurements as shown in Table 4. We can see that the IQR model performed well in terms of *Recall* score, but quite poor in *Precision* and *F*1. Moreover, from our experiment, it performed very poor on some stations with a high rate of false-alarm.

Table 1. Total and average TSP score of individual model

Station	AR	DB	IQR	KSigma	MAS	SA	ZScore
DIV002	0.43	0.43	**0.86**	0.43	0.76	0.43	0.76
DIV004	0.24	0.62	**0.81**	0.57	0.67	0.43	0.76
DIV006	0.52	0.52	**0.76**	0.33	0.67	0.43	**0.76**
VLGE13	0.43	0.48	**0.90**	0.48	0.81	0.52	0.76
YOM004	0.43	0.43	0.86	0.43	**1.00**	0.48	0.76
YOM005	0.52	0.48	**0.90**	0.48	0.52	0.52	0.76
YOM009	0.52	0.43	0.71	0.48	0.67	0.43	**0.76**
YOM010	0.33	0.62	**0.86**	0.48	0.62	0.43	0.67
YOM011	0.43	0.48	**0.81**	0.48	0.71	0.52	0.76
Total	3.86	4.48	**7.48**	4.14	6.43	4.19	6.76
Average	0.43	0.50	**0.83**	0.46	0.71	0.47	0.75
Std.	0.10	0.08	0.06	0.06	0.13	0.05	0.03

The testing results of 13 simple ensembles models are given in Table 2. They show that Top3TP, Top3FN, Top3Sen, and Top3TSP have the highest average scores of 0.75. But when we looked at them in more detail, we found that Top3TSP is the best model, it has the highest performance in 6 stations, meanwhile the others model have the highest score only 3 stations. Moreover, the average accuracy score of Top3TSP still remains at 99% for *Recall*, whilst the average *Precision* and *F*1 has been increased by 14% when compared with the best individual model as presented in Table 4.

Table 2. Total and average TSP scores of simple ensemble models.

Station	Ensem7	Top5TP	Top3TP	Top5FN	Top3FN	Top5FP	Top3FP	Top5Sen	Top3Sen	Top5Spec	Top3Spec	Top5TSP	Top3TSP
DIV002	0.49	0.59	**0.77**	0.59	**0.77**	0.59	0.44	0.59	**0.77**	0.59	0.44	0.67	**0.77**
DIV004	0.49	0.67	**0.77**	0.67	**0.77**	0.54	0.44	0.67	**0.77**	0.54	0.44	0.59	**0.77**
DIV006	0.54	0.67	0.69	0.67	0.69	0.54	0.44	0.67	0.69	0.54	0.44	0.28	**0.77**
VLGE13	**0.90**	0.85	0.77	0.85	0.77	0.49	0.44	0.85	0.77	0.49	0.44	0.87	0.77
YOM004	0.59	0.85	0.77	0.85	0.77	0.59	0.59	0.85	0.77	0.59	0.59	0.87	0.69
YOM005	0.49	0.62	0.74	0.62	0.74	0.49	0.44	0.62	0.74	0.49	0.44	0.51	**0.85**
YOM009	0.49	0.64	0.74	0.64	0.74	0.38	0.54	0.64	0.74	0.38	0.54	0.51	**0.77**
YOM010	0.49	0.64	**0.74**	0.64	**0.74**	0.49	0.44	0.64	**0.74**	0.49	0.44	0.51	0.62
YOM011	0.49	0.64	0.74	0.64	0.74	0.49	0.44	0.64	0.74	0.49	0.44	0.67	**0.77**
Total	4.95	6.15	6.74	6.15	6.74	4.59	4.18	6.15	6.74	4.59	4.18	5.49	**6.77**
Average	0.55	0.68	**0.75**	0.68	**0.75**	0.51	0.46	0.68	**0.75**	0.51	0.46	0.61	**0.75**
Std.	0.14	0.10	0.02	0.10	0.02	0.06	0.06	0.10	0.02	0.06	0.06	0.19	0.06

Table 3 shows the scores of complex ensembles. It is clear that EoE3 is the best with an overall average TSP score of 0.86. It is followed by EoE7 and EoE5 with the average TSP scores at 0.85 and 0.83. In addition, EoE3 has the best performance in 6 stations. Table 4 gives the average accuracy measures score for EoE3 and other best models from Individual and simple ensemble model. It shows that although the average *Recall* score of EoE3 decreased a bit, it has achieved the highest average *Precision* score, which is 5% more than the best simple ensemble Top3TSP and 20% more than the best individual model IQR. Especially, the number of False Positive predictions has reduced significantly.

Table 3. Total and average TSP scores of complex ensembles.

Station	EoE13	EoE11	EoE9	EoE7	EoE5	EoE3
DIV002	0.56	0.56	0.56	**0.83**	**0.83**	**0.83**
DIV004	**0.89**	**0.89**	0.67	0.72	**0.89**	**0.89**
DIV006	**1.00**	**1.00**	**1.00**	**1.00**	**1.00**	**1.00**
VLGE13	0.94	0.94	0.72	0.94	0.94	**1.00**
YOM004	0.72	**1.00**	0.44	**1.00**	0.83	0.83
YOM005	0.56	0.50	0.56	**0.83**	0.78	0.78
YOM009	0.61	**0.78**	0.67	0.72	**0.78**	**0.78**
YOM010	0.44	0.50	0.56	**0.83**	0.78	0.78
YOM011	0.67	0.61	0.78	0.78	0.61	**0.83**
Total	6.39	6.78	5.94	7.67	7.44	**7.72**
Average	0.71	0.75	0.66	0.85	0.83	**0.86**
Std	0.19	0.21	0.16	0.11	0.11	0.09

Table 4. Average accuracy measurement score for each models.

Model	Recall	Precision	F1
IQR	0.9877	0.3892	0.4787
Top3TSP	0.9862	0.5281	0.6196
EoE3	0.9601	0.5775	0.6626

6   Conclusions

The results show that IQR is the best individual model at detecting anomalies but poor for classifying normal data. In general simple ensembles are more accurate and consistent than individual models. The best simple ensemble, Top3TSP, outperformed IQR by achieving the same accuracy on detecting anomaly data and more accurate results for normal data. Further improvements were produced by our complex ensembles. It is clear that the complex ensemble EoE3, with only three member models, beats both the best individual model and the best simple ensemble with clear margins in detecting anomalies and also normal data. This is confirmed with the highest $F1$ score.

In conclusion, the developed ensemble methods can select some suitable basic individual models to build simple and complex ensembles to improve the accuracy of detecting anomalies in water level data. Our testing results demonstrated that our ensemble methods have a real potential to be further developed to help the related organisation to reduce their time in investigating the data and to improve the performance of early warning systems and decision support system. They can also be used for developing the firmware of telemetry station to be able to detect anomaly values by itself. In addition, we can apply the models to assist experts in labelling the data as ground-truth by comparing the results from our models.

References

1. Ciocarlie, G.F., Lindqvist, U., Nováczki, S., Sanneck, H.: Detecting anomalies in cellular networks using an ensemble method. In: Proceedings of the 9th International Conference on Network and Service Management (CNSM 2013), pp. 171–174. IEEE (2013)
2. Curiac, D.I., Volosencu, C.: Ensemble based sensing anomaly detection in wireless sensor networks. Expert Syst. Appl. **39**(10), 9087–9096 (2012)
3. Ding, Z., Fei, M.: An anomaly detection approach based on isolation forest algorithm for streaming data using sliding window. IFAC Proc. Vol. **46**(20), 12–17 (2013)
4. Gneiting, T., Raftery, A.E.: Weather forecasting with ensemble methods. Science **310**(5746), 248–249 (2005)
5. Golab, L.: Querying sliding windows over online data streams. In: Lindner, W., Mesiti, M., Türker, C., Tzitzikas, Y., Vakali, A.I. (eds.) EDBT 2004. LNCS, vol. 3268, pp. 1–11. Springer, Heidelberg (2004). https://doi.org/10.1007/978-3-540-30192-9_1

6. Jiang, D., Liu, J., Xu, Z., Qin, W.: Network traffic anomaly detection based on sliding window. In: 2011 International Conference on Electrical and Control Engineering, pp. 4830–4833. IEEE (2011)
7. Opitz, D., Maclin, R.: Popular ensemble methods: an empirical study. J. Artif. Intell. Res. **11**, 169–198 (1999)
8. Wang, W.: Some fundamental issues in ensemble methods. In: 2008 IEEE International Joint Conference on Neural Networks (IEEE World Congress on Computational Intelligence), pp. 2243–2250. IEEE (2008)

Detecting Node Behaviour Changes
in Subgraphs

Michael S. Gibson[✉][iD]

BT Applied Research, Adastral Park, Martlesham Heath, Ipswich IP5 3RE, UK
michael.s.gibson@bt.com

Abstract. Most interactions or relationships among objects or entities can be modelled as graphs. Some classes of entity relationships have their own name due to their popularity; *social graphs* look at people's relationships, *computer networks* show how computers (devices) communicate with each other and *molecules* represent the chemical bonds between atoms. Some graphs can also be dynamic in the sense that, over time, relationships change. Since the entities can, to a certain extent, manage their relationships, we say any changes in relationships reflect a change in entity *behaviour*. By comparing the relationships of an entity at different points in time, we can say there has been a *change in behaviour*. In this paper, we attempt to detect malicious devices in a network by showing a significant change in behaviour through analysing traffic data.

Keywords: Cybersecurity · Graph theory · Machine learning

1 Introduction

As users and devices become more connected, *cybersecurity* becomes more important to minimise malicious activity. Alongside the quantity of devices, the types of devices and topologies of networks have changed. Even how users interact with services has changed; moving away from client-side applications through the use of cloud computing [18] and relying on other users for information [6].

Detecting attacks, especially new types, is important for any cybersecurity system. It is also important for security analysists to quickly identify anomolous behaviour and have the resources to further investigate and determine if the anomaly is malicious. This is where *machine learning* (ML) can help by learning patterns from vast amounts of data and showing the results in a meaningful way.

We look at *node2vec* [7] to detect anomalies in networks. Whilst node2vec labels nodes, we extend it by measuring the difference of a node's context between graphs. Instead of just analysing traffic, using graph features such as degree and edge weights can provide more context into what is happening. For cybersecurity, this means identifying attacking nodes and seeing how they influence others.

In this paper, we show how we applied node2vec to *NetFlow* [9] in order to detect anomalies. In Sect. 2, we discuss relevant works and practices. Section 3 explains the process of creating comparable (sub)graphs to measure behaviour.

© Springer Nature Switzerland AG 2020
M. Bramer and R. Ellis (Eds.): SGAI-AI 2020, LNAI 12498, pp. 152–158, 2020.
https://doi.org/10.1007/978-3-030-63799-6_12

Section 4 details two experiments we carried out to showcase our approach. Finally, Sect. 5 summarises our work and details future work.

2   Background

Most networks employ some form of *intrusion detection system* to detect malicious traffic. This can be *signature* or *anomaly* based detection, where either the attack is known or identifying malicious intent from anomalies. As we assume no knowledge of potential attacks, we focus on anomaly-based detection. This relies on some form of heuristic analysis to show outliers and applications include financial fraud detection and medical analysis [13]. For networks, this can be detecting unusual patterns of connections, packets or other behaviours [5].

Machine learning is increasing being used in cybersecurity [3]. One approach is *supervised learning* using labelled NetFlow, where models use some network traffic with labels denoting normal and suspicious traffic and then evaluated [1]. Another approach is *unsupervised learning* which instead learns a representation of the data. An example of unsupervised learning on NetFlow is *ip2vec* [17] which determines the context of IP addresses from NetFlow. Botnets are determined by observing which clusters form and labelling IP addresses as botnets in outling clusters. This relies on *embeddings* which is a vector-space generated from contexts in linear structures. Embeddings were popularised by *word2vec* [15] which analyses sentences to see how words relate to each other.

Graphs have proved to be useful in cybersecurity [2]. Metrics such as centrality and PageRank have been used to model attackers [10,14]. These focus on one graph at a time and comparing subgraphs is not trivial; these metrics do not fully capture context. Node2vec can capture the context (neighbourhood) of a node and the resulting vector used for measuring behaviour. Extensions have been made to work on complex graphs. For example, *dynnode2vec* works on dynamic graphs [12], but it does not cater for seasonality at different observations.

3   Methodology

We use NetFlow to create the graphs for node2vec. Each flow record represents communication between devices; the source and destination IP addresses as nodes and the row itself a directed edge. Edge weights are needed for node2vec's walking algorithm. This can be an aggregation of attributes, but as we are looking for botnets which attempt multiple connections, we use this count as weights. Node2vec also has parameters for walk length and probability to stay close to neighbours during walks. As we are interested in how botnets affect local nodes, we kept the walk length to 3 and set probability to stay close to neighbours.

Algorithm 1 shows how node score are computed. The inputs are a set of graphs over periods of NetFlow: a *baseline* G_0 and *observations* $G_1, \ldots, G_t$ with time periods T. Each graph consists of nodes V, edges E and edge weights W. The value r is for removing random variation from node2vec; this is explained

---

Algorithm 1: Generate node behaviour scores

Input   : Graphs $\{G_0, \ldots, G_t\}$ where $G = \{V, E, W\}$, Time periods
              $T = \{0, \ldots, t\}$, Representation accuracy r
Output: Node scores over time M
$G_0' \leftarrow$ ReverseEdges($|G_0|$)
for $i \leftarrow 1$ **to** r **do** $P_i \leftarrow$ Node2Vec(G_0')
$\Pi^0 \leftarrow$ Procrustes(P)
for $j \leftarrow 1$ **to** t **do**
   $\quad G_j' \leftarrow$ ReverseEdges($|G_0 \cup G_j|$)
   $\quad$ **for** $k \leftarrow 1$ **to** r **do** $Q_k \leftarrow$ Node2Vec(G_j')
   $\quad \Pi^j \leftarrow$ Procrustes(Q)
   $\quad$ **for** $v \in V_0 \cap V_j$ **do** $M_{j,v} \leftarrow$ CosineSimilarity(Π_v^0, Π_v^j)
end

---

later but we found a value of 5 suitable in most cases. The output is a matrix where each row is a time period and each column for the score of a node.

The baseline represents average activity. This means it should cover a large period of time to include seasonal changes. To compare it with observed graphs, its edge weights are normalised (averaged to fit a period t) to produce $|G_0|$.

For botnets, we are looking for nodes which send out more messages than normal. This means botnet edges tend to be outgoing. Node2vec's walking algorithm works by walking from one node to another along directed edges and recording the nodes visited. Therefore a set of walks will rarely contain botnets as most nodes will not have high-weighted directed edges towards them. To solve this, the edge directions are reversed. Now during walks, there's a higher chance of reaching botnets, thus making them more prominent in the embedding.

Node2vec is then used to create an embedding. Since it uses random walks, the embedding will not be a definite representation of the graph [8]. A definite embedding is required when comparing a node from different embeddings; the difference in vectors must only be a result from the contexts and not randomness. We solve this by creating a *representational embedding* which is formed by performing an *orthogonal Procrustes problem* on a set of embeddings. This was inspired by Muromägi [16] who combined word embeddings of different languages to create an ensemble to improve training. We produce a set of embeddings P which are processed by a *linear optimisation* of Procrustes to find the baseline representational embedding Π_0. This process is simplified in the algorithm by saying Π is the optimum embedding from a set of r embeddings; a higher r means a more accurate representational embedding but requiring more iterations.

For each observation G_j, it is normalised with the baseline. Since an observation is a fraction of the NetFlow, its seasonalities will have to be removed. This is done by merging with the baseline and normalising the edge weights, $|G_0 \cup G_j|$. It then has its edges reversed to prioritise botnets. Once a representational embedding of G_j is made, Π_j, the same nodes appearing in Π_0 and Π_j are compared using *cosine similarity*. This takes two vectors, a node's behaviour during baseline and observation, and calculates the cosine of the angle between them. This is used to determine the difference in behaviour; if it's low, this shows anomalous behaviour from baseline to observation, indicating a botnet. The cosines (scores) of each node across all observations are stored in M.

Table 1. Los Alamos similarity scores

(a) Normal

Device	C11264		C14926		C10920		C5618	C17693	
Similarity	0.79	...	0.90	...	0.95	...	0.99	0.99	...

(b) Attack

Device	C5618	C17693		C10920		C11264	C14926
Similarity	0.58	0.62	...	0.90	...	0.99	0.99

4   Experiments

We performed two experiments to show how this technique can detect botnets. The first shows the behaviours of computers at different times and the second measures the behaviours of known botnets over time. The aim of the first experiment is to show how the behaviours of some computers may influence others and to highlight the largest changes. The second aims to show how known botnets change behaviour over time. This can be used to define thresholds of when a computer's behaviour should be investigated. The purpose of both experiments is not about how accurate this technique is, but how it can be used to highlight anomalies. Further investigations would determine the cause of the anomaly.

The first experiment uses the Los Alamos dataset [11] which contains Net-Flow from Los Alamos' internal computer network. A timeline shows when malicious activities were performed, so we split the NetFlow into three sets: a baseline covering ten hours including benign botnet activity, an hour of normal activity and another hour containing known attacks. The resulting normal and attack embeddings are compared to show how a node's behaviour changes from baseline. Table 1 shows the scores of some devices at both periods. Since there are over 7600 devices with activity at these times, only significant computers are shown: the lowest scoring, where they start to score 0.90 (over 99% score 0.90 or above during both periods) and a known botnet labelled C17693 which has been highlighted. Although the Los Alamos dataset mentions multiple computers acting maliciously, we only focus on C17693 as it behaves like a botnet. In Table 1a, the scores show the change of behaviour from the baseline to the normal observation. Since the lowest score is 0.79, we can assume that any score equal or above this will be classed as normal behaviour. This threshold should be at a point between registering the computer to be a botnet and allowing uncommon but tolerable spikes in activity; for example C10920 with a file transfer. Table 1b shows computers during the attack, including the botnet. Whilst C17693 has the second lowest score, other computers have low scores. Not only does the attacker's score drop, but also potential victims, in this case C5618. Looking at the NetFlow do we see that C17693 communicates with C5618 during the attack.

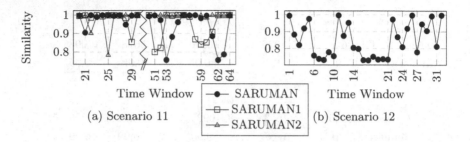

Fig. 1. CTU-13 botnet behaviours over time

The second experiment uses the CTU-13 dataset [4] which contains 13 scenarios, each varying type and quantity of botnets. We used scenarios 11 and 12 as these contain three botnets performing a DDoS attack at different times. Instead of observing all computers at one point in time, we look at the botnets over the whole capture. The captures were split into baselines and observations: scenario 11 had a baseline length of 300 s and observation lengths of 10 s, resulting in 67 observations, whereas scenario 12 had a baseline length of 600 s and the same observation lengths, resulting in 66 observations. Each observation was normalised and compared with the baseline to show behaviours over time. Figure 1 shows the similarity scores of three botnets: SARUMAN (s), SARUMAN1 ($s1$) and SARUMAN2 ($s2$). One point to make is the missing $s1$ and $s2$ results in scenario 12 as shown in Fig. 1b. When the baseline was created for scenario 12, it only included s; $s1$ and $s2$ were deployed after the baseline period. Also some regions have been trimmed as they showed scores above 0.98. In Fig. 1a, there are two regions of interest: time windows 21 to 29 and 51 to 62. The first region shows low scores; this correlates with the report saying they are being initialised and infected. Also, the second region shows s and $s1$ having much lower scores than during the infection period. This coincides with the report stating that an attack starts with $s1$ first and then s. Although $s2$ was infected, there is no data to suggest it attacked. In Fig. 1b, the attacks from s started earlier and were more frequent. Up to time window 6, s was started and infected. Between time windows 6 and 10 and between 14 and 21, multiple connections were attempted from s. During these times s was able to retrieve data and since its score dropped, this would be an indicator for investigation.

5   Conclusion

In this paper, we have shown how a graph embedding algorithm can be used to compare the behaviours of nodes from different graphs. Whilst node2vec was designed to compare the similarity of nodes within a graph, we extended it to allow cross-graph comparisons through the use of representational embeddings. By creating representational embeddings from network traffic, the context of connections were able to be compared. This was shown by comparing behaviours at set times as well as analysing the behaviour of known botnets over time.

We kept close to the original specifications of node2vec. This meant having to handle non-definite embeddings because of random walks. Representational embeddings helped solve this by merging multiple embeddings through Procrustes. Because this is a computationally expensive operation, it would be difficult to use in live systems, especially in cybersecurity where it is important to detect threats quickly. Relying on a baseline embedding for comparisons would also need improving; networks are dynamic where nodes can connect and disconnect. To improve this, another walk algorithm should be investigated. It should not rely on randomisation and prioritise on important edges as well as use other NetFlow attributes. This will produce more definite embeddings and eliminate the need for representational embeddings.

References

1. Das, R., Morris, T.H.: Machine learning and cyber security. In: 2017 ICCECE, pp. 1–7. IEEE (2017)
2. Dawood, H.A.: Graph theory and cyber security. In: 3rd International Conference on ACSAT, pp. 90–96. IEEE (2014)
3. Ford, V., Siraj, A.: Applications of machine learning in cyber security. In: Proceedings of the 27th International Conference on CAINE-2014 (2014)
4. Garcia, S., Grill, M., Stiborek, J., Zunino, A.: An empirical comparison of botnet detection methods. Comput. Secur. **45**, 100–123 (2014)
5. Garcia-Teodoro, P., Diaz-Verdejo, J., Maciá-Fernández, G., Vázquez, E.: Anomaly-based network intrusion detection: techniques, systems and challenges. Comput. Secur. **28**(1–2), 18–28 (2009)
6. Gibson, M.S., Vasconcelos, W.W.: A knowledge-based approach to multiplayer games in peer-to-peer networks. Knowl. Inf. Syst. **61**(2), 1091–1121 (2018). https://doi.org/10.1007/s10115-018-1295-6
7. Grover, A., Leskovec, J.: node2vec: scalable feature learning for networks. In: Proceedings of the 22nd ACM SIGKDD International Conference on KDD, pp. 855–864 (2016)
8. Heimann, M., Koutra, D.: On generalizing neural node embedding methods to multi-network problems. In: KDD MLG Workshop (2017)
9. Hofstede, R., et al.: Flow monitoring explained: from packet capture to data analysis with NetFlow and IPFIX. IEEE Commun. Surv. Tutor. **16**(4), 2037–2064 (2014)
10. Holme, P., Kim, B.J., Yoon, C.N., Han, S.K.: Attack vulnerability of complex networks. Phys. Rev. E **65**(5), 056109 (2002)

11. Kent, A.D.: Cyber security data sources for dynamic network research. In: Dynamic Networks and Cyber-Security, pp. 37–65. World Scientific (2016)
12. Mahdavi, S., Khoshraftar, S., An, A.: dynnode2vec: scalable dynamic network embedding. In: IEEE International Conference on Big Data, pp. 3762–3765. IEEE (2018)
13. Mehrotra, K.G., Mohan, C.K., Huang, H.M.: Anomaly Detection Principles and Algorithms. TSC. Springer, Cham (2017). https://doi.org/10.1007/978-3-319-67526-8
14. Mehta, V., Bartzis, C., Zhu, H., Clarke, E., Wing, J.: Ranking attack graphs. In: Zamboni, D., Kruegel, C. (eds.) RAID 2006. LNCS, vol. 4219, pp. 127–144. Springer, Heidelberg (2006). https://doi.org/10.1007/11856214_7
15. Mikolov, T., Chen, K., Corrado, G., Dean, J.: Efficient estimation of word representations in vector space. In: Proceedings of Workshop at ICLR (2013)
16. Muromägi, A., Sirts, K., Laur, S.: Linear ensembles of word embedding models. In: Proceedings of the 21st Nordic Conference on Computational Linguistics, pp. 96–104. Association for Computational Linguistics (2017)
17. Ring, M., et al.: IP2Vec: learning similarities between IP addresses. In: 2017 IEEE ICDMW, pp. 657–666. IEEE (2017)
18. Singh, P., Student, M.T., Jain, A.: Survey paper on cloud computing. IJIET **3**, 84–89 (2014)

ReLEx: Regularisation for Linear Extrapolation in Neural Networks with Rectified Linear Units

Enrico Lopedoto[✉] and Tillman Weyde

Department of Computer Science, University of London, Northampton Square,
London, UK
{enrico.lopedoto,t.e.weyde}@city.ac.uk

Abstract. Despite the great success of neural networks in recent years, they are not providing useful extrapolation. In regression tasks, the popular Rectified Linear Units do enable unbounded linear extrapolation by neural networks, but their extrapolation behaviour varies widely and is largely independent of the training data. Our goal is instead to continue the local linear trend at the margin of the training data. Here we introduce ReLEx, a regularising method composed of a set of loss terms design to achieve this goal and reduce the variance of the extrapolation. We present a ReLEx implementation for single input, single output, and single hidden layer feed-forward networks. Our results demonstrate that ReLEx has little cost in terms of standard learning, i.e. interpolation, but enables controlled univariate linear extrapolation with ReLU neural networks.

Keywords: Neural networks · Regression · Regularisation · Extrapolation

1 Introduction

Neural Networks (NN) are very successful for many applications in artificial intelligence and the rectified linear function used in rectified linear units (ReLU) has become the most popular activation function. However, neural networks with ReLUs produce widely varying extrapolation behaviour that is determined more by the random initialisation of the network weights than by the training data.

Our goal in this study is to improve the extrapolation behaviour of NNs with ReLUs for regression tasks in three ways:

1. the extrapolation should be mainly defined by the data and not the random initialisation of the NN;
2. the extrapolation should continue the local linear trend with more influence from training data points closer to the margin;
3. the non-linearities should not be outside the training data range.

© Springer Nature Switzerland AG 2020
M. Bramer and R. Ellis (Eds.): SGAI-AI 2020, LNAI 12498, pp. 159–165, 2020.
https://doi.org/10.1007/978-3-030-63799-6_13

To realise these goals we develop, implement and evaluate ReLEx, a regularisation method to control extrapolation. In this study, we focus specifically on univariate regression with a single input and output and a single hidden layer, and do not address multi-dimensional settings.

2   Related Work

Neural Networks (NN) are universal function approximators [1,5] on a compact interval. While it has often been observed that neural networks interpolate very effectively between data points, it has been found in many studies that neural networks do not extrapolate well, where extrapolation is generally understood as the application of the trained model to data that is in some sense outside the range of the training data [6,8]. This can even affect very simple functions like the identity, which NNs do not generalise well to unseen data [11]. Linguistic structures are an example that recently attracted attention. It has been shown that NN do not generalise between different words [3]. This problem is being addressed in current research with more complex NN architectures [4].

For numeric extrapolation, there have recently been several studies that aim at learning functions that are more akin to those used physics by including multiplication, linear and periodic functions as activation functions [7,10]. These networks can produce good extrapolation if they can express the true function and the training finds suitable weights. However, this is not the case in general so that the extrapolation behaviour is unpredictable.

In this study, we choose a simpler approach, which uses a standard network architecture and activation function, but aims to control a linear extrapolation such that it matches the data. Linear extrapolations are often a simplification, but they are often useful, e.g. in LIME (Local Interpretable Model-Agnostic Explanations), which is widely used for explaining the behaviour of complex models [9].

3   Model

We use a simple fully connected feed-forward network that has a single hidden layer of N ReLUs, a single input neuron and a single linear output neuron. The network output for an input x_i is $\hat{y}_i = b_o + \sum_{n=1}^{N} w_{on} \cdot ReLU(x_i \cdot w_n + b_n)$, where b_o is the bias of the output neuron and w_{on} and w_n are the outgoing and incoming weights, respectively, of the nth hidden neuron and b_n is its bias. We use stochastic gradient descent to train the network.

The neurons are rectified linear units, that use a rectified linear function as the activation function: $ReLU(x) = x$ if $x > 0$, 0 otherwise. In the constant part $(x < 0)$ the gradient of the activation is always 0. If the activation of the ReLU is in the constant part for all inputs, the ReLU does not contribute to the output of the network and this is called a 'dying ReLU' [2].

We are particularly interested in the *0-Points*, where the non-linearities of the hidden neurons are: the input values x_{k0} that lead to input 0 for the activation function of hidden neuron k: $0 = w_k \cdot x_{k0} + b_k$, such that $x_{k0} = -b_k/w_k$.

4 ReLEx Loss Definitions

We control the extrapolation behaviour of the neural network with additional loss terms that achieve our design goals in the learning process. The losses are Centripetal (CP), Mutually Repellent (MR), Weight Orientation (WO) and Weight Sign (WS) and are defined below in more details. The final loss to be minimised, including the sum of squared errors, is therefore:

$$\mathcal{L} = \sum (\hat{y} - y)^2 + \theta_{CP}\, \mathcal{L}_{CP} + \theta_{MR} \mathcal{L}_{MR} + \theta_{WO}\, \mathcal{L}_{WO} + \theta_{WS}\, \mathcal{L}_{WS}, \qquad (1)$$

with $\theta_{\mathcal{X}}$ being the weighting factors for each additional loss term $\mathcal{L}_{\mathcal{X}}$.

Centripetal Loss. $\mathcal{L}_{CP}$, aims to move the 0-points inside the training range to fulfil design goals 1 and 3. It is defined as the sum of the squared distances between the 0-points and the data points:

$$\mathcal{L}_{CP} = \sum_k^N \sum_i^K (x_{k0} - x_i)^2, \qquad (2)$$

where N is the number of hidden neurons and K is the number of data points.

Mutual Repellent Loss. $\mathcal{L}_{MR}$, is designed to fulfil design goal 2 by avoiding the concentration of 0-points around the data mean, which can be the effect of $\mathcal{L}_{CP}$. This loss term aims to equally distribute the 0-points by penalising pairs of 0-points with a small distance. $\mathcal{L}_{MR}$ is the sum of the inverted pairwise distances between the positions of the 0-points with a small constant ε added to avoid division by zero:

$$\mathcal{L}_{MR} = \sum_{i=1}^N \sum_{j>i}^N \frac{1}{(x_{i0} - x_{j0})^2 + \varepsilon} \qquad (3)$$

Weight Orientation Loss. $\mathcal{L}_{WO}$ also relates to design goal 2. The data points that are closer to the margin of the data range should influence the extrapolation beyond that margin more strongly. This can be achieved by the linear parts of the ReLUs covering more of the data points that are close to the margin. Intuitively speaking, we encourage the linear part of the ReLU to point outwards by penalising when a linear part of a ReLU covers more than half the data range:

$$\mathcal{L}_{WO} = -\sum_{i=1}^N ReLU((x_{k0} - \bar{x}) \cdot w_i + \varepsilon), \qquad (4)$$

where $\bar{x}$ is the data mean and ε is a small amount of linear part beyond the data mean that we do not penalise.

Weight Sign Loss. L_{WS} prevents a degenerate condition and encourages an equal distribution of weight signs so that linear parts of ReLUs are pointing to both directions of extrapolation:

$$L_{WS} = \left(\sum_{i=1}^{N} w_i \right)^2. \tag{5}$$

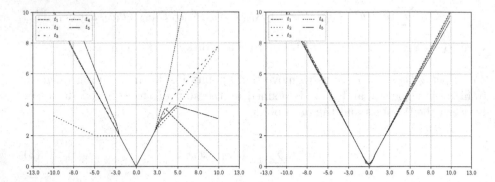

Fig. 1. Comparison of extrapolation after standard (left) and ReLEx training (right) with 5 models each. Input on x axis, output on y axis.

5   Experiments

5.1   Settings and Metrics

We use five functions to generate data: identity, absolute, scaled squared, sigmoid and sine $(x, |x|, x^2/5, 1/(1 + e^{-x}), sin(x))$. We sample on 200 equidistant points for the training data-set and another 200 points at random for the interpolation test set from the range $[-2, 2]$. The extrapolation data range is $[-10, 10]$ with another 200 points. To measure extrapolation performance, we propose several metrics as there is no natural target when we are not assuming a true underlying linear function:

MSE_{int} measures the interpolation error on test data that was randomly sampled from the training data range.

σ_{ES} measures the consistency of the extrapolation as the standard deviation of the slope of the extrapolations as determined by a linear regression over the NN predictions on the test set on ranges $x \in [-10, -2]$ and $[2, 10]$.

MSE_{ex-tan} measures extrapolation accuracy as the MSE relative to the tangent of the generating function at the margins of the training data range.

MSE_{ex-wlr} measures accuracy against a more realistic extrapolation reference: a linear regression on the training data with higher weights on the data points closer to the margin of the data range. We use this function for weighting $w_{x,\tau} = x^{(\tau-1)}(1 - x)^{(\tau-1)}$, where x is the position of the data point in the data range and τ is a free parameter.

5.2   Results

Preliminary experiments confirmed that the $\mathcal{L}_{CP}$ is effective at concentrating the 0-points. θ_{CP} was set to 0.03 throughout, which was determined as an effective values in most contexts. One issue that we observed was that for high θ_{CP}, values all 0-points would cluster around the data mean. This prevented a good fit and extrapolation in some cases, which is the reason for introducing $\mathcal{L}_{MR}$. By choosing a suitable ratio between θ_{MR} and θ_{CP}, we can adjust the 0-point spread to the data range.

Table 1. The effect of applying all ReLEx losses (CP, MR, WO and WS).

Method	$f(\cdot)$	MSE_{int}	MSE_{ex-tan}	MSE_{ex-wlr}	σ_{ES}
Std	x	0.00	18.41	18.45	1.18
ReLEx	x	0.03	0.02	0.02	0.02
Std	$\|x\|$	0.00	6.32	7.13	1.31
ReLEx	$\|x\|$	0.18	0.01	0.45	1.00
Std	$x^2/5$	0.02	14.63	14.06	12.92
ReLEx	$x^2/5$	0.03	0.07	0.04	10.50
Std	$1/(1+e^{-x})$	0.01	4.55	3.97	7.83
ReLEx	$1/(1+e^{-x})$	0.03	0.11	0.02	2.48
Std	$\sin(x)$	12.65	41.71	53.14	1.36
ReLEx	$\sin(x)$	0.43	1.82	34.78	0.02

Figure 1 show results from standard NN and ReLEx networks and makes clear how ReLEx reduces extrapolation variability and leads to a good continuation of the local linear trend at the margins. When comparing to the weighted linear extrapolation in the MSE_{ex-wlr} loss, we found that τ values above 0.5, indicating higher weights for points close to the margin, gave better results. We used a final τ value of 0.8, which generally leads to a good fit.

Table 1 shows the metrics for ReLEx in comparison with standard network training. We can see that the MSE_{int} is in most cases not affected much by ReLEx, except for an increase for the $|x|$ function and a decrease for the $\sin(x)$. The extrapolation error against the tangents (MSE_{ex-tan}) is in all cases greatly reduced, as is the error against the WLR extrapolation (MSE_{ex-wlr}). Both extrapolation error measures are higher for the $\sin(x)$ function compared to other functions, while the standard deviation of the slope (σ_{ES}) is low, indicating that for the $\sin(x)$ function the ReLEx NN extrapolation behaves differently than for the other functions. In terms of standard deviation of the extrapolation slope, the quadratic function ($x^2/5$) shows much higher spread, even with ReLEx.

$\mathcal{L}_{WO}$ and $\mathcal{L}_{WS}$ can efficiently be calculated in $O(N)$ time. However, the computational complexity of calculating $\mathcal{L}_{CP}$ and $\mathcal{L}_{MR}$ is $O(N \cdot K)$ and $O(N^2)$, respectively. These may be computationally too expensive for large models and data-sets. There are alternative variants with $O(N)$ complexity, such as replacing both with a small penalty on distance to the mean, or fixed boundaries for the 0-points, but they require an extra pass through the data before training.

6   Conclusions

The ReLU function offers the possibility of performing linear extrapolation, which standard bounded activation functions do not. However, they show high variability and little correlation with the data when trained, as standard, by minimising just the error against the data. We proposed ReLEx, a set of loss terms that provide regularisation for the behaviour of a ReLU network, such that it produces linear extrapolations beyond the range of the training data that are consistent and continue the local linear trend of the data at the margins.

The accuracy of the extrapolation has no single definition as there is no pre-defined target, but measured against the tangent and a weighted linear regression, ReLEx shows large improvements over a standard network. The ReLEx loss terms can be directly integrated into a standard neural network framework, as we have done with our implementation in PyTorch.[1]

The computational complexity of the loss functions can become relevant for large networks and large data-sets, but had little impact in our experiments. Future work will include the exploration of more efficient ReLEx variants, the generalisation to multi-dimensional inputs and outputs and multiple layers, as well as experiments with noisy and real-world data.

References

1. Cybenko, G.: Approximation by superpositions of a sigmoidal function. Math. Control, Signals Syst. **2**(4), 303–314 (1989)
2. Douglas, S.C., Yu, J.: Why ReLU units sometimes die: analysis of single-unit error backpropagation in neural networks. In: 52nd Asilomar Conference on Signals, Systems, and Computers, pp. 864–868. IEEE (2018)
3. Lake, B., Baroni, M.: Generalization without systematicity: on the compositional skills of sequence-to-sequence recurrent networks. PMLR. **80**, 2873–2882 (2018)
4. Lake, B.M.: Compositional generalization through meta sequence-to-sequence learning. In: NeurIPS, pp. 9791–9801 (2019)
5. Leshno, M., Lin, V.Y., Pinkus, A., Schocken, S.: Multilayer feedforward networks with a nonpolynomial activation function can approximate any function. Neural Netw. **6**(6), 861–867 (1993)
6. Marcus, G.: Deep learning: a critical appraisal. CoRR abs/1801.00631 (2018)
7. Martius, G., Lampert, C.H.: Extrapolation and learning equations. In: ICLR, Workshop Track Proceedings (2017)
8. Mitchell, J., Minervini, P., Stenetorp, P., Riedel, S.: Extrapolation in NLP. In: Proceedings of the Workshop on Generalization in the Age of Deep Learning (2018)

---

[1] The source code and more supporting material can be found at https://github.com/ EnricoLope/PhD_ReLEx.

9. Ribeiro, M.T., Singh, S., Guestrin, C.: "Why Should I Trust You?": explaining the predictions of any classifier. In: ACM KDD, pp. 1135–1144 (2016)

10. Trask, A., Hill, F., Reed, S.E., Rae, J., Dyer, C., Blunsom, P.: Neural arithmetic logic units. In: NeurIPS, pp. 8035–8044 (2018)

11. Weyde, T., Kopparti, R.M.: Feed-forward neural networks need inductive bias to learn equality relations. In: NeurIPS Workshop on Relational Representation Learning (2018)

Application Papers

Partial-ACO Mutation Strategies to Scale-Up Fleet Optimisation and Improve Air Quality (Best Application Paper)

Darren M. Chitty[✉]

Aston Lab for Intelligent Collectives Engineering (ALICE), Aston University,
Birmingham B4 7ET, UK
darrenchitty@googlemail.com

Abstract. Fleet optimisation can significantly reduce the time vehicles spend traversing road networks leading to lower costs and increased capacity. Moreover, reduced road use leads to lower emissions and improved air quality. Heuristic approaches such as Ant Colony Optimisation (ACO) are effective at solving fleet optimisation but scale poorly when dealing with larger fleets. The Partial-ACO technique has substantially improved ACO's capacity to optimise large scale vehicle fleets but there is still much scope for improvement. A method to achieve this could be to integrate simple mutation with Partial-ACO as used by other heuristic methods. This paper explores a range of mutation strategies for Partial-ACO to both improve solution quality and reduce computational costs. It is found that *substituting* a majority of ant simulations with simple mutation operations instead improves both the accuracy and efficiency of Partial-ACO. For real-world fleet optimisation problems of up to 45 vehicles and 437 jobs reductions in fleet traversal of approximately 50% are achieved with much less computational cost enabling larger scale problems to be tackled. Moreover, CO_2 and NO_x emissions are cut by 3.75 Kg and 1.71 g per vehicle a day respectively improving urban air quality.

Keywords: ACO · MDVRP · Partial-ACO · Mutation · Air quality

1 Introduction

Fleet optimisation is an increasingly important issue and many organisations can benefit from optimising their fleets ranging from service companies such as builders or gas engineers to any company delivering products or even courier firms. These companies have a set of customers over a geographical area to deliver to or service and a set of vehicles to assign each customer to. Therefore, the problem is which customers to assign to each vehicle and the order they must be visited such that the traversal time of the fleet of vehicles is minimised.

© Springer Nature Switzerland AG 2020
M. Bramer and R. Ellis (Eds.): SGAI-AI 2020, LNAI 12498, pp. 169–184, 2020.
https://doi.org/10.1007/978-3-030-63799-6_14

The main benefits from fleet optimisation are reduced costs in terms of fuel and labour and increased task capacity due to reduced time spent traversing roads.

A further important benefit in reducing vehicular fleet traversal is the reduction of emissions leading to improved air quality in towns and cities. Diesel vehicles are especially polluting in terms of emissions and the World Health Organisation (WHO) reports the levels of nitrogen oxides in the air of major cities are increasing markedly[1]. These can cause breathing problems and have been linked to increased cardiovascular disease rates [14]. Many cities have limits on permissible pollution and clean air policies are being pursued, such as the London congestion charge or Clean Air Zone (CAZ) being considered by Birmingham City Council and fleet optimisation can assist with clean air policies.

Optimising fleets of vehicles though is NP-hard in nature and even techniques such as heuristics applied to the problem fail to scale well. Ant Colony Optimisation (ACO) [6] is a popular meta-heuristic for routing problems and a recent advance known as Partial-ACO [2] has made ACO much more scalable when applied to large fleet optimisation problems [3,4]. However, further improvement is required for application to larger fleet optimisation problems. Many meta-heuristics can become trapped in local optima and hence use *random mutation* to escape. Moreover, mutation can be a simple fast operation and therefore could improve the scalability of Partial-ACO when applied to fleet optimisation.

Consequently, this paper will investigate a range of mutation strategies for integration with Partial-ACO when applied to fleet optimisation and analyse the results both in terms of solution quality and execution time. The paper is laid out as follows: Sect. 2 describes the fleet optimisation problem, prior heuristic approaches and mutation combined with heuristics. Section 3 profiles ACO, the Partial-ACO approach, application to fleet optimisation and the integration of mutation operators. The results from applying Partial-ACO to real-world fleet optimisation problems with increasing complexity will be demonstrated in Sect. 4 using a set of mutation strategies. Finally, Sect. 5 sums up the benefits of Partial-ACO for fleet optimisation when integrating mutation.

2   Background and Related Work

The problem of fleet optimisation is to assign and schedule jobs at geographical positions to a set or fleet of vehicles such that the time or distance traversed by the fleet of vehicles is minimised. Associated constraints include vehicle weight capacities and time windows. This type of problem is applicable to many areas such as companies providing services i.e. gas fitters whereby a large company needs to optimally organise jobs to vehicles. Others include businesses needing to deliver products optimally or courier type companies. The advantages are reduced fuel costs and increased capacity whilst also reducing emissions.

---

[1] Air pollution levels rising in many of the worlds poorest cities. https://www.who.int/mediacentre/news/releases/2016/air-pollution-rising/en.

This type of problem is related to the Travelling Salesman Problem (TSP) and can be described as the Multi Depot Vehicle Routing Problem (MDVRP) formulated in 1959 by Dantzig and Ramser [5]. The MDVRP can be formally defined as a complete graph $G = (V, E)$, whereby V is the vertex set and E is the set of all edges between vertices in V. The vertex set V is further partitioned into two sets, $V_c = V_1, ..., V_n$ representing customers and $V_d = V_{n+1}, ...V_{n+p}$ representing depots or vehicles whereby n is the number of customers and p is the number of vehicles. Each customer $v_i \in V_c$ has an associated service time and each vehicle $v_i \in V_d$ has an associated capacity defining the ability to fulfil customer service. Each edge in the set E has an associated cost of traversing it represented by the matrix c_{ij}. The problem is to find the set of vehicle routes such that customers are serviced once, vehicles start and finish from the same depot, do not exceed their capacity and the cost of the combined routes is minimised.

The MDVRP is recognised as an NP-hard problem and hence difficult to solve using exact mathematical approaches. Indeed, for symmetric cases and a single vehicle, exact methods do not scale beyond 50 customers and only up to a few hundred for asymmetric cases [9]. Better suited are heuristic approaches, rule of thumb methods, not guaranteed to find the optimal solution but solutions close to optimal in significantly less computational time. For example, a sweep heuristic assigned customers to their nearest depot and the depot polar angle calculated [19]. Customers are sorted in ascending order of angle and iteratively assigned to routes with least additional distance. A "multi-level composite" heuristic identifies good solutions at a fraction of the computational cost and improves them with an insertion heuristic to minimise routing cost [15].

However, meta heuristic approaches see greater use being search based and problem independent. Early use involved tabu search exploring the search space by potentially moving to neighbouring solutions even with a quality degradation [8]. Solutions recently examined are declared *tabu* for a time so that cycling is avoided. A common meta-heuristic approach to solving MDVRPs is a Genetic Algorithm (GA) [11], a population based approach which uses Darwinian evolutionary principles of natural selection, genetic crossover and *mutation*. The first use of a GA to solve the MDVRP was proposed by Filipec *et al.* for non-fixed destinations [7]. Skok *et al.* used a GA and compared six differing crossover operators [17] later applying them to a real-world problem with 248 customers and three depots [18]. A survey of GAs for solving MDVRPs can be found in [12].

The key alternative meta-heuristic is based on the foraging behaviours of ants, Ant Colony Optimisation (ACO) [6]. Ants deposit pheromone on the paths they take when finding food and taking it back to their nest. Pheromone levels build up on edges leading to food enabling further ants to discover the food source. This approach is particularly well suited to solving graph based problems such as TSP or MDVRP problems. Calvete *et al.* contrasted two ACO approaches, one using a single *super depot* and the other a GA-ACO approach whereby customers are assigned to depots using a GA and then the routing solved by ACO for problems of up to 288 customers and 6 depots [1]. Yao *et al.* used a single depot approach to solve a real-world MDVRP finding multiple routes from this central depot and assigning the individual routes to depots [22].

A key issue with ACO is that it can get trapped in local optima as a result of pheromone building up. Meta-heuristics such as a GA have a *mutation* operator which with low probability make random changes to solutions to escape local optima. Hence, it was recognised that ACO could benefit from mutation. Yang *et al.* used ACO with simple swap mutation and local search to avoid ACO being stuck in local optima to solve generalised TSP instances [21]. Zhao *et al.* use simple mutation and ACO to solve TSP instances noting that there is no extra computational cost [24]. Shokouhifar and Sabet use ACO with dynamic pheromone and mutation to solve TSPs of up to 200 cities [16]. Some of the ants generate solutions normally whilst others mutate the best found solutions. Regards the MDVRP, Yu *et al.* used a parallel ACO algorithm whereby a virtual depot is used with mutation operators applied to problems with up to 360 customers and 6 depots [23]. Yalian implemented a version of ACO which combined a scanning algorithm to initially assign jobs to nearest depots and then combined with GA inspired mutation operators and local search [20]. However, strategies for integrating mutation with Partial-ACO are yet to be investigated.

3   Partial-ACO

Ant Colony Optimisation (ACO) [6] is a heuristic technique that has been applied to routing problems such as TSP and MDVRP type problems with relative success. This algorithm is based on the study of how ants forage for food, ants deposit pheromone on the paths they take when searching for food and when bringing it back to their nest. Pheromone levels will build up on the paths leading to food enabling further ants from the colony to navigate to the food source.

ACO simulates ants moving through a graph G probabilistically visiting vertices and depositing pheromone. The degree of pheromone an ant deposits on the edges E of graph G is defined by the quality of the solution the ant has generated. Ants probabilistically decide which vertex to visit next using these pheromone levels on the edges of G plus local heuristic information such as distance to travel. An *evaporation* effect prevents pheromone levels building up too much and reaching a state of local optima. Therefore, ACO consists of two stages, the first *solution construction*, simulating ants, the second stage *pheromone update*. The solution construction stage involves m ants constructing complete solutions to problems. Ants start from a random vertex and iteratively make probabilistic choices using the *random proportional rule* as to which vertex to visit next. The probability of ant k at point i visiting point $j \in N^k$ is defined as:

$$p_{ij}^k = \frac{[\tau_{ij}]^\alpha [\eta_{ij}]^\beta}{\sum_{l \in N^k} [\tau_{il}]^\alpha [\eta_{il}]^\beta} \tag{1}$$

where $[\tau_{il}]$ is the pheromone deposited on the edge leading from vertex i to vertex l; $[\eta_{il}]$ is the heuristic information of this edge; α and β are tuning parameters controlling the influence of the pheromone $[\tau_{il}]$ and heuristic information $[\eta_{il}]$.

Once all ants have completed the solution construction stage, pheromone levels on the edges E of graph G are updated. First, evaporation of pheromone levels upon every edge of graph G occurs whereby the level is reduced by a value ρ relative to the pheromone upon that edge:

$$\tau_{ij} \leftarrow (1 - \rho)\tau_{ij} \tag{2}$$

where ρ is the *evaporation rate* typically set between 0 and 1. Once this evaporation is completed each ant k will then deposit pheromone on the edges it has traversed based on the quality of the solution found:

$$\tau_{ij} \leftarrow \tau_{ij} + \sum_{k=1}^{m} \Delta\tau_{ij}^k \tag{3}$$

where the pheromone ant k deposits, $\Delta\tau_{ij}^k$ is defined by:

$$\Delta\tau_{ij}^k = \begin{cases} 1/C^k, & \text{if edge } (i,j) \text{ belongs to } T^k \\ 0, & \text{otherwise} \end{cases} \tag{4}$$

where $1/C^k$ is the quality of ant k's solution T^k ensuring that better quality solutions found by ants results in greater levels of pheromone being deposited.

However, ACO is memory intensive requiring an n by n pheromone matrix. Secondly, ACO is computationally expensive. Consider that at each ant decision point pheromone levels need to be compared for every unvisited edge. For a five customer TSP instance, at the first step four comparisons are needed and the next step three and so forth. In total, nine comparisons are required to construct a complete solution similar to the triangular number sequence described as $(n(n-1)/2)$. Thus, for a 100,000 customer problem, nearly five billion pheromone edge comparisons are required to construct one complete solution.

Consequently, an improved ACO algorithm has been developed to address these issues known as Partial-ACO [2] which has several fundamental differences. Firstly, to avoid using a pheromone matrix requiring significant memory, Partial-ACO uses a population based approach (P-ACO) [10] whereby pheromone levels are calculated for edges of graph G based on a population of ant solutions. Similar to a GA, a population of ants is maintained and operate in a steady state manner in that each keeps a *local memory* of their best found solution. Pheromone deposit also operates differently as pheromone cannot *build up* on the edges of graph G. Instead, the pheromone deposit of ant k on an edge E of graph G is related to the quality of the solution l_{best}^k in comparison to the best solution found, g_{best}. Hence, the pheromone ant k deposits, $\Delta\tau_{ij}^k$ is defined by:

$$\Delta\tau_{ij}^k = \begin{cases} (g_{best}/l_{best}^k)^\alpha, & \text{if edge } (i,j) \text{ belongs to } T^k \\ 0, & \text{otherwise} \end{cases} \tag{5}$$

where (g_{best}/l_{best}^k) is the quality of ant k's locally best found solution in relation to the globally best found solution and α is a parameter controlling the influence of pheromone. An ant k when building a solution has to reconstruct the pheromone levels on the edges from its current location to all unvisited locations. This involves iterating through all the l_{best} solutions of the ant population and finding the edges taken from the current location and depositing pheromone if that location is yet to be visited.

Secondly, Partial-ACO significantly reduces computational costs by ants only *partially* modifying their best found solution held in their local l_{best} memory in the same probabilistic manner as previously. This is similar to crossover in a GA. First, a random point is selected in the l_{best} tour. Second, a random length of the tour to be retained is decided and this section is copied into the new solution. The remaining part of the solution is then constructed as normal. To highlight the computational advantage of this technique, consider retaining 50% of a solution for a 100,000 job problem. Now, only 50,000 probabilistic decisions need to be made and only 1.25 billion pheromone comparisons are required, a 75% reduction and quadratic computational cost saving. An overview of the Partial-ACO technique is described in Algorithm 1.

Algorithm 1. Partial-ACO

1: **for** each ant **do**
2:     Generate an initial l_{best}^k solution probabilistically
3: **end for**
4: **for** number of iterations **do**
5:     **for** each ant k **do**
6:         Select uniform random start point from l_{best}^k solution
7:         Select uniform random length of l_{best}^k to preserve
8:         Copy l_{best}^k points from start for specified length
9:         Complete remaining aspect probabilistically
10:         If new solution better than l_{best}^k then update l_{best}^k
11:     **end for**
12: **end for**
13: Output best l_{best} solution (the g_{best} solution)

3.1   Partial-ACO Applied to Fleet Optimisation

Fleet optimisation is in effect the MDVRP problem whereby there are a range of vehicles operating from a number of depots that need to be assigned jobs to complete such that all jobs are completed and the total traversal time of the fleet of vehicles is minimised. To represent this problem a solution will consist of a set of vehicles and a list of jobs for each to be completed in the order they need to be completed. This representation is observed in Fig. 1 whereby V relates to a vehicle and J relates to a job. Ants build a solution in a similar manner to a TSP instance in that the number of locations to visit equates to the number of jobs and the number of vehicles. Ants probabilistically move to unfulfilled jobs or another vehicle at which point the current vehicle returns to its depot and the next sequence of jobs to be assigned to this new vehicle commences.

To retain part of an ant's locally best found solution an improvement to Partial-ACO is used specific to the MDVRP whereby by a random number of

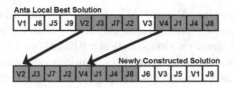

Fig. 1. Illustration of Partial-ACO methodology with two vehicle schedules preserved.

vehicle schedules will be preserved [3]. Essentially, if 50% of an l_{best} tour is to be preserved this means 50% of the vehicles and their associated schedules will be maintained. Figure 1 demonstrates Partial-ACO retaining two vehicle schedules and then probabilistically determining the remaining schedules as previously described. This enhancement to Partial-ACO enables better quality results to be achieved by retaining up to 90% of an ant's locally best solution reducing execution time by 75% and scales significantly better than ACO [3].

Once a new solution has been generated by Partial-ACO its quality is measured using two objectives, the first of which is to maximise the number of jobs correctly performed within their given time window, missed jobs are assigned a penalty related to their predicted duration. The second objective is to minimise the total traversal time of the fleet of vehicles. Reducing the number of missed jobs is considered the primary objective.

Pheromone deposit is calculated using the two objectives to be optimised, the number of customers serviced and the length of the traversal time between customers. A penalty based function will be utilised for the first objective whereby any customers that have not been serviced due to capacity limitations or missing the time window will be penalised by the predicted job time. The secondary objective is to minimise the time the fleet of vehicles spend traversing the road network between jobs thus the quality of a tour can be described as:

$$C^k = (S - s^k + 1) * L^k \tag{6}$$

where S is the total time of jobs to be serviced, s^k is the amount of job service time achieved by ant k and L^k is the total fleet traversal time of ant k's solution. If all customer demand S is fulfilled then C^k is simply the total traversal time of the vehicle fleet which needs to be minimised.

3.2 Partial-ACO with Mutation for Fleet Optimisation

As profiled in Sect. 2, mutation has often been used to improve the results of a range of meta-heuristic algorithms. A key reason is that without mutation many of these meta-heuristic algorithms can be become trapped in local optima. Mutation is a way for the technique to *break out* of these local optima or consider improbable changes. With regards to ACO and Partial-ACO, if the pheromone levels on sub-optimal edges becomes too high compared to other edges then it is difficult for other edges to be traversed which could be an optimal edge.

Integrating mutation into Partial-ACO is simple. Once an ant has constructed a new potential solution by partially modifying its best found solution a simple mutation can be performed on this solution with a given probability. If a mutation is to be performed then one of three random operations specific to fleet optimisation or routing solutions can be performed with uniform probability:

- **Insertion Mutation:** Takes a scheduled job from one part of a solution and inserts it elsewhere enabling moving jobs from one vehicle to another;
- **Swap Mutation:** Randomly takes two scheduled jobs in a solution and swaps them around enabling trading of two vehicle's assigned jobs;
- **3-Opt Mutation:** Based upon the 3-opt technique used for solving TSP problems [13], three edges are disconnected creating three sub-tours which are reconnected in a differing manner. The 3-opt heuristic tries every combination of edges and manner of reconnecting until no improvement. This is computationally expensive so instead one random 3-opt mutation is made;

4   Results

To test the effect of mutation combined with Partial-ACO for solving MDVRP problems, a real-world problem will be considered. This takes data from a Birmingham maintenance company with multiple vehicles and customers requiring periodic maintenance of properties. Each vehicle starts from a depot and returns to this depot when finished servicing customers. Each customer is defined by a latitude and longitude, a predicted job duration and occasionally, a time window for the job. A working day is defined as between 08:00 and 19:00 h.

Table 1. Real-world problem scenarios supplied by a Birmingham maintenance company with the total fleet travel time using the company's current scheduling.

Problem	Number of Jobs	Job Servicing Time (hh:mm)	Fleet Traversal Time (hh:mm)
16 Vehicle Scenario A	156	95:33	54:01
24 Vehicle Scenario A	237	144:06	73:55
24 Vehicle Scenario B	221	151:49	68:38
32 Vehicle Scenario A	298	198:58	99:50
32 Vehicle Scenario B	313	190:26	96:28
45 Vehicle Scenario A	437	267:47	142:46

The data supplied by the company is split into a number of differing scenarios with increasing fleet sizes and customer jobs. For each scenario, the company has supplied the actual division of jobs between vehicles used and the order that the jobs were conducted. This facilitates a *ground truth* to be established of vehicle usage for the company and consequently real-world reductions can be ascertained. The company divided jobs between vehicles geographically and then derived the route for each vehicle to complete its assigned tasks by directing it to do the job furthest from its depot and then work its way back towards its depot only deviating if there are jobs with time windows. The details of each of the individual scenarios supplied by the company are shown in Table 1.

Table 2. Parameters used with the Partial-ACO algorithm

Number of Ants – 32	Max Iterations – 2,000,000
α – 3.0	Solution Retention – 90%
β – 1.0	Initial Pheromone – 0.01

Experiments were conducted using an AMD Ryzen 2700 processor using 16 parallel threads of execution to utilise all the available cores of the processor whereby ant simulation and solution evaluation are conducted in a parallel asynchronous manner. The algorithms were compiled using Microsoft C++. Experiments are averaged over 25 execution runs for each problem with differing random seeds. The parameters used with Partial-ACO are shown in Table 2. A high α and low β reduces emphasis on edge distances for fleet optimisation.

4.1   Initial Results

To begin with the Partial-ACO algorithm will be tested on each scenario and each time after an ant has constructed a new solution, like a GA, a mutation will be performed with a given random probability. A range of probabilities will be tested ranging from 10% to 90%. A 0% probability will also be tested to provide a comparison to Partial-ACO without mutation. When mutation occurs one of the three previously defined mutation operators are randomly selected.

The results from these initial experiments are shown in Fig. 2 whereby the first observation that can be made is that in five scenarios an improvement in the reductions in fleet traversal over the company's *ground truth* have been made by adding mutation to the Partial-ACO algorithm. However, other than the simplest scenario these improvements are only minor. Secondly, as the probability of mutation being performed increases Partial-ACO becomes less effective. This is especially visible for the larger problems. A potential reason could be that an ant makes at least one poor choice in the tour construction phase and added mutation will further weaken the solution. A final observation is that the execution time plotted on the same graphs in Fig. 2 only varies by a few seconds. Therefore, it can be ascertained that performing a mutation has little computational cost when compared to simulating an ant and evaluating the resulting solution.

4.2   Simulating an Ant or Performing a Random Mutation

The previous results demonstrated that mutation had in most cases a small beneficial effect on Partial-ACO and this had little if any extra computation

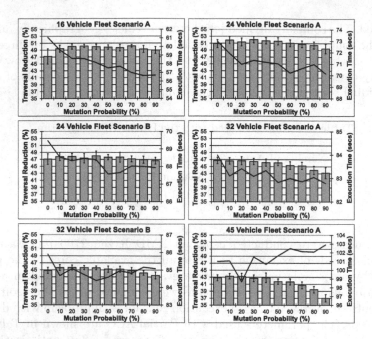

Fig. 2. Reductions in fleet traversal time and run-times for each scenario and a range of mutation probabilities whereby mutation occurs after Partial-ACO ant simulation.

cost. Furthermore, the greater the probability of mutation the less effective the approach became. Consequently, two things can be ascertained, firstly mutation is very fast to perform and likely much faster than simulating an ant. Secondly, performing mutation on top of ant simulation generally reduces solution quality.

Therefore, a second mutation strategy is proposed whereby mutation only is performed *instead* of generating a solution by simulating an ant and then performing mutation. This is achieved by performing the mutation on an ant's locally held best found solution l_{best}. Recall that each ant operates in a steady state manner keeping track of its own individually best found solution.

Mutation *instead* of ant simulation occurs with a given uniform probability and a range of probabilities will be tested on the fleet optimisation scenarios as previously. These results are shown in Fig. 3 and contrasting these results to those in Fig. 2 two observations can be made. Firstly, improvements in reductions in fleet traversal are achieved of several percent when choosing to mutate *instead* of simulate an ant particularly for the largest scenario of 45 vehicles. This reinforces the hypothesis that mutation on top of ant simulation can in effect *double* the error. The second observation is that execution time reduces significantly as the probability of mutation *instead* of ant simulation increases. Indeed, using a 90% probability of mutation, execution time is a quarter of that of Partial-ACO with no mutation. This reinforces the hypothesis that simulating ants is much more computationally expensive than simple mutation operators.

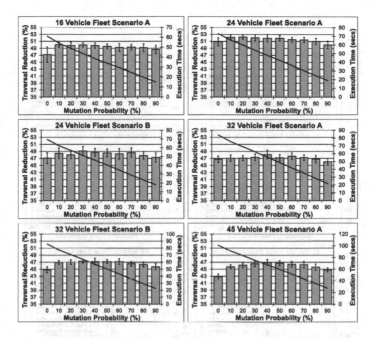

Fig. 3. Reductions in fleet traversal and run-times for each scenario and a range of mutation probabilities whereby mutation occurs *instead* of Partial-ACO ant simulation.

It can also be observed that in general, higher probability of performing mutation leads to a slight degradation in quality but with much reduced execution times. Indeed, even with very high levels of mutation, better solutions than standard Partial-ACO are derived. Given this performance the convergence rates for differing degrees of mutation should be analysed. These are shown in Fig. 4 whereby it can be observed that the convergence rate over time is slowest in all cases bar the simplest scenario when using only 10% probability of mutation instead of ant simulation. The mutation rate which combines a fast convergence rate with good final results is a rate of 70% meaning that simple mutation is performed more often than ant simulation. The combination of mainly fast mutations with some ant simulation which enables information from other ants to be integrated enables good solutions to be found quickly. The fastest Partial-ACO approach with the greatest mutation rate makes fast initial gains but plateaus.

Given that using a mutation rate of 70% provides good results in less than half the time of Partial-ACO using no mutation it can be considered appropriate to execute for a similar amount of time. In fact, all the rates of mutation should be executed for the same degree of time by increasing iterations. Thus, if using a mutation rate results in an execution time one quarter of standard Partial-ACO then a fourfold increase in iterations to eight million should be allowed. These results can be considered to be *normalised* for time and are shown in Fig. 5.

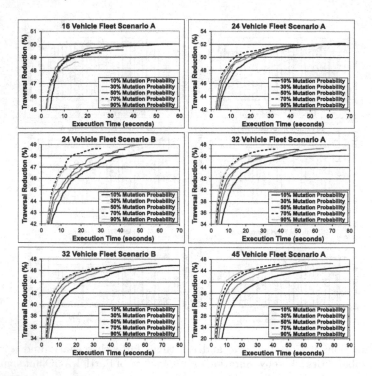

Fig. 4. Convergence rates over time from the results shown in Fig. 3

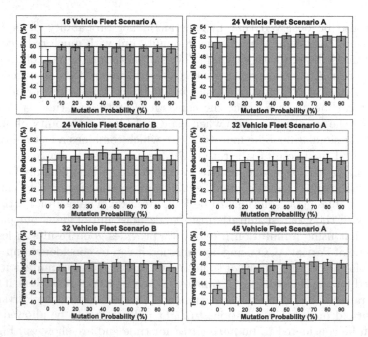

Fig. 5. Reductions in fleet traversal per scenario and range of mutation probabilities for mutation *instead* of ant simulation run for same time as standard Partial-ACO.

From these results it can be observed that when compared to not using any mutation significant improvements in fleet traversal reduction are achieved by exploiting the speed advantage. In fact, for the largest scale problem, optimising for 45 vehicle schedules, an improvement of over 5% in fleet traversal reduction is achieved when using a rate of 70% probability of mutation over ant simulation. A second observation is that when normalising for time results are very similar aside from the highest degree of mutation, 90%. Therefore, mutation is beneficial when integrated with Partial-ACO but there is a limit to how much mutation over ant simulation is beneficial. A final observation is that variation exists between scenarios in terms of which mutation rate provides the best results but it can be determined that a minimum of 40% is required to get the best solutions.

4.3 Decoupling Mutation and Ant Simulation

A final aspect to consider with integrating mutation with Partial-ACO is to decouple the construction of solutions by ants and mutation. Recall the hypothesis that ant simulation followed by mutation can compound one error on another. This is borne out by the results observed in Fig. 2. Therefore it could be feasible to separate mutation from ant simulation as mutation has little computational cost. One method could be to perform an ant simulation using Partial-ACO and evaluate the solution. If better than an ant's local best then this is updated. The ant's local best is then mutated and evaluated and the ant's local best updated if required. This strategy gives an ant effectively two attempts to improve its l_{best} and can be referred to as *TwoAttempts*. An alternative strategy would be to only perform mutation on a newly constructed solution if this is not an improvement on the ant's l_{best} solution. This strategy can be referred to as *TwoStage*. These strategies enable mutation of 100% probability but *decoupled* from ant simulation although more solution evaluations are required.

Table 3. Reductions in fleet traversal and run-times per scenario for *TwoAttempts* and *TwoStage* Partial-ACO mutation strategies.

Problem	*TwoAttempts*		*TwoStage*	
	Traversal Reduction (%)	Execution Time (s)	Traversal Reduction (%)	Execution Time (s)
16 Vehicle Scenario A	49.90 ± 0.58	65.48 ± 1.09	49.94 ± 0.63	66.55 ± 1.25
24 Vehicle Scenario A	52.66 ± 0.46	81.15 ± 1.61	52.52 ± 0.52	82.54 ± 1.19
24 Vehicle Scenario B	49.53 ± 0.99	77.14 ± 1.29	49.26 ± 1.35	78.84 ± 1.51
32 Vehicle Scenario A	48.72 ± 0.89	94.41 ± 1.74	48.63 ± 1.11	96.03 ± 1.57
32 Vehicle Scenario B	47.69 ± 0.53	97.73 ± 1.80	48.13 ± 0.58	98.53 ± 1.69
45 Vehicle Scenario A	48.40 ± 0.80	116.53 ± 2.12	48.16 ± 0.67	117.64 ± 1.93

The results from these two mutation strategies are shown in Table 3 whereby it can be observed that the *TwoAttempts* mutation strategy has a minor performance advantage over the *TwoStage* strategy. However, it should be noted these results are only a slight improvement on those shown in Fig. 5. Moreover, the execution time of these two strategies is greater than standard Partial-ACO as a result of increased solution evaluations. It is likely that with further iterations to match these run-times the results from Fig. 5 would further improve.

5 Conclusions

This paper has investigated improving the ability to solve effectively large-scale fleet optimisation problems using ACO. Specifically, the use of the novel Partial-ACO approach, a population based ACO approach which only partially reconstructs solutions making it more scalable than standard ACO. However, further scalability is required and to achieve this the integration of simple mutation operations were considered with a number of strategies tested.

These experiments found that whilst performing mutations after an ant has constructed a potential solution had some benefit, better performance is achieved by choosing to *either* simulate an ant or *instead* perform a mutation of an ant's best found solution. This proved to be both more effective regards solution quality and considerably faster due to the low computational cost of simple mutation. Moreover, with this strategy the best results were observed when using a high probability of mutation over ant simulation of at least 40% or higher.

Indeed, this mutation strategy resulted in reducing a company's fleet routing by several percent more than standard Partial-ACO in faster timescales. This enables optimisation of larger fleets of vehicles to be undertaken. For large fleets of up to 45 vehicles a reduction in routing of up to 50% over the company approach can be achieved in just a minute of computational time. This reduced their fuel costs by an equivalent amount. Moreover, using EU van emission limits of $175\,g/Km\ CO_2$ and $0.08\,g/Km\ NO_x$, each company vehicle produces on average $3.75\,Kg$ less CO_2 and $1.71\,g\ NO_x$ per day improving air quality. Further work will consider more advanced mutation operators and investigate dynamic approaches for choosing to simulate ants to construct solutions or to perform mutations.

References

1. Calvete, H.I., Galé, C., Oliveros, M.J.: Evolutive and ACO strategies for solving the multi-depot vehicle routing problem. In: IJCCI (ECTA-FCTA), pp. 73–79 (2011)
2. Chitty, D.M.: Applying ACO to large scale TSP instances. In: Chao, F., Schockaert, S., Zhang, Q. (eds.) UKCI 2017. AISC, vol. 650, pp. 104–118. Springer, Cham (2018). https://doi.org/10.1007/978-3-319-66939-7_9
3. Chitty, D.M., Wanner, E., Parmar, R., Lewis, P.R.: Can bio-inspired swarm algorithms scale to modern societal problems? In: Artificial Life Conference Proceedings, pp. 13–20. MIT Press (2019)
4. Chitty, D.M., Wanner, E., Parmar, R., Lewis, P.R.: Scaling ACO to large-scale vehicle fleet optimisation via Partial-ACO. In: Proceedings of the Genetic and Evolutionary Computation Conference Companion, pp. 97–98 (2019)

5. Dantzig, G.B., Ramser, J.H.: The truck dispatching problem. Manage. Sci. **6**(1), 80–91 (1959)
6. Dorigo, M., Gambardella, L.M.: Ant colony system: a cooperative learning approach to the traveling salesman problem. IEEE Trans. Evol. Comput. **1**(1), 53–66 (1997)
7. Filipec, M., Skrlec, D., Krajcar, S.: Darwin meets computers: new approach to multiple depot capacitated vehicle routing problem. In: 1997 IEEE International Conference on Systems, Man, and Cybernetics, 1997. Computational Cybernetics and Simulation, vol. 1, pp. 421–426. IEEE (1997)
8. Gendreau, M., Hertz, A., Laporte, G.: A tabu search heuristic for the vehicle routing problem. Manage. Sci. **40**(10), 1276–1290 (1994)
9. Gilbert, L.: The vehicle routing problem: an overview of exact and approximate algorithms. Euro. J. Oper. Res. **59**(3), 345–358 (1992)
10. Guntsch, M., Middendorf, M.: A population based approach for ACO. In: Cagnoni, S., Gottlieb, J., Hart, E., Middendorf, M., Raidl, G.R. (eds.) EvoWorkshops 2002. LNCS, vol. 2279, pp. 72–81. Springer, Heidelberg (2002). https://doi.org/10.1007/3-540-46004-7_8
11. Holland, J.H.: Adaptation in natural and artificial systems: an introductory analysis with applications to biology, control, and artificial intelligence. U Michigan Press (1975)
12. Karakatič, S., Podgorelec, V.: A survey of genetic algorithms for solving multi depot vehicle routing problem. Appl. Soft Comput. **27**, 519–532 (2015)
13. Lin, S.: Computer solutions of the traveling salesman problem. Bell Syst. Techn. J. **44**(10), 2245–2269 (1965)
14. Requia, W.J., Adams, M.D., Arain, A., Papatheodorou, S., Koutrakis, P., Mahmoud, M.: Global association of air pollution and cardiorespiratory diseases: a systematic review, meta analysis, and investigation of modifier variables. Am J Public Health **108**(S2), S123–S130 (2018)
15. Salhi, S., Nagy, G.: A cluster insertion heuristic for single and multiple depot vehicle routing problems with backhauling. J. Oper. Res. Soc. **50**(10), 1034–1042 (1999)
16. Shokouhifar, M., Sabet, S.: PMACO: a pheromone-mutation based ant colony optimization for traveling salesman problem. In: 2012 International Symposium on Innovations in Intelligent Systems and Applications, pp. 1–5. IEEE (2012)
17. Skok, M., Skrlec, D., Krajcar, S.: The non-fixed destination multiple depot capacitated vehicle routing problem and genetic algorithms. In: Proceedings of the 22nd International Conference on Information Technology Interfaces, 2000. ITI 2000, pp. 403–408. IEEE (2000)
18. Skok, M., Skrlec, D., Krajcar, S.: The genetic algorithm scheduling of vehicles from multiple depots to a number of delivery points. Arfit. Intell. **349** 56 (2001)
19. Wren, A., Holliday, A.: Computer scheduling of vehicles from one or more depots to a number of delivery points. J. Oper. Res. Soc. **23**(3), 333–344 (1972)
20. Yalian, T.: An improved ant colony optimization for multi-depot vehicle routing problem. Int. J. Eng. Technol. **8**(5), 385–388 (2016)
21. Yang, J., Shi, X., Marchese, M., Liang, Y.: An ant colony optimization method for generalized TSP problem. Prog. Nat. Sci. **18**(11), 1417–1422 (2008)
22. Yao, B., Hu, P., Zhang, M., Tian, X.: Improved ant colony optimization for seafood product delivery routing problem. PROMET-Traffic&Transport. **26**(1), 1–10 (2014)

23. Yu, B., Yang, Z., Xie, J.: A parallel improved ant colony optimization for multi-depot vehicle routing problem. J. Oper. Res. Soc. **62**(1), 183–188 (2011)
24. Zhao, N., Wu, Z., Zhao, Y., Quan, T.: Ant colony optimization algorithm with mutation mechanism and its applications. Expert Syst. Appl. **37**(7), 4805–4810 (2010)

Industrial Applications

A Metaheuristic Search Technique for Solving the Warehouse Stock Management Problem and the Routing Problem in a Real Company

Christian Perez$^{(\boxtimes)}$, Miguel A. Salido, and David Gurrea

Universitat Politecnica de Valencia, Valencia, Spain
cripeber@doctor.upv.es, msalido@dsic.upv.es, davidgurreaher@gmail.com

Abstract. In many transport companies, one of the main objectives is to optimize the travel cost of their fleet. Other objectives are related to delivery time, fuel savings, etc. However warehouse stock management is not properly considered. Warehouse stock control is based on the correct allocation of resources to each order. In this paper, we combine the warehouse stock management problem and the routing problem to be applied in a real company that allows negative stock in their warehouses. The proposed multi-objective problem is modeled and solved by the greedy randomized adaptive search (GRASP) algorithm. The results shows that the proposed algorithm outperforms the current search technique used by the company mainly in stock balancing, improving the negative average stock by up to 82%.

Keywords: Warehouse stock control · Metaheuristic · GRASP

1 Introduction

Nowadays, transport companies focus on obtaining automatic forecasts and order planning within a given time frame. Many different techniques can be found in the literature to solve this kind of problem. There is a set of problems that brings together many of the cases of graphics-related problems in the context of transport design. The multi-objective transportation network design provides a framework that lists all types of transportation problems together. In this context, a first level taxonomy is developed in which methods and techniques are grouped by mathematical structure or the purpose of the problem formulation [4]. The Multi-objective Transportation Network Design (MTND) is set of definitions that try to address all different cases in transportation problems. In this paper, we focus on two types of problems, the vehicle routing problems (VRP) and the assignment problems (AP).

VRPs can be represented as theoretical problems in graphs. Given a complete network $G = \{V, A\}$ in which V is a list of vertices and A is a list of arcs, most problems represent the zero vertex as the starting point and the rest of

© Springer Nature Switzerland AG 2020
M. Bramer and R. Ellis (Eds.): SGAI-AI 2020, LNAI 12498, pp. 187–201, 2020.
https://doi.org/10.1007/978-3-030-63799-6_15

the vertices as customers to be passed through to deliver an order. The list of arcs is made up of i, j pairs that connect two vertices. These arcs have a cost associated with going from the i vertex to the j vertex [5]. From this point on, the wide development of solutions for diverse problems has generated an extensive amount literature. VRP problems are mainly multi-target problems in which there are certain features that combine with each other to deal with other types of problems. However, there is a more specific set of real-life problems that traditional VRP approaches cannot solve, such as: the Open VRP, the Dynamic VRP, the Time-Dependent VRP problems.

In the Open VRP (OVRP) problems, the main feature that interests us is that the vehicles are not forced to return to the starting point, so problems of this type seek to minimize the number of vehicles used and the total distance traveled (e.g., [3,11]). Some real life problems can be modelled as OVRP [8,10].

Taking into account the rapid evolution of technologies, we can obtain a large amount of data in real time, including not only the status of the vehicle or the order but also the time of delivery to the customer, the status of the route that will be use oby the vehicle, etc. That is why the development of Dynamic VRP (DVRP) is so important; it allows us to assume changes in the solutions obtained and modify them with the updated data, generating optimal solutions until the last moment [1,9].

Another problem affecting VRPs is that the travel time between one vertex and another is deterministic; However in real life, the travel time between vertices is not deterministic since there are many variables that can affect it. These problems are defined as Time-dependent VRP, in which it is assumed that the trip is not deterministic and does not have constant times in the trips between vertices [6].

The Assignment problems (AP) deal with the question of how to assign n items (vehicles, machines, agents, etc.) to m different tasks or procedures. However, it is normal to take into account some limitations that allow the algorithm to focus on a specific case and make it more specific [2]. One of the most commonly used assignment problems is called The Quadratic Assignment Problem (QAP). This kind of AP does not require all objective functions to be linear, focusing on assigning a set of n elements in m locations. The cost of QAP is composed of a series of smaller costs that are minimized to find the minimum cost.

Taking into account the existing QAP, this paper focus specifically on the storage assignment location problem (SLAP). SLAP involves a group of problems that refers to the allocation of products in a storage space and the optimization of material handling costs, among others. The SLAP problem usually depends on parameters such as the distance between the source and the destination with respect to the items and the warehouses, the availability of stock, the physical characteristics of the items, the stock refill price, etc. The main optimization approaches are related to storage space usage and the cycle time of order-picking operations, taking into account constraints such as available storage capacity, order picking resource capacities, and dispatch policies [12].

In this paper, we focus on a logistic problem provided by a company that focuses its activity on the rental of a wide variety of reusable packaging for the storage and transport of a wide variety of food products. The main priority of this company is to provide containers to allocate fruits, vegetables, fish, etc., in supermarkets that need a wide distribution throughout the country.

The containers are manufactured to simplify the process of transporting, storing, and linearly arranging consumer goods. Today the company has multiple containers that are manufactured under the idea of eco-design which complies with the rule of the three Rs: reduction, reuse and recycling. The company's business model proposes a reduction in the environmental cost of processes through the optimization and responsible use of materials and waste (see Fig. 1).

Fig. 1. Different containers used by the company

Currently the company has 13 warehouses that are strategically distributed throughout the country to facilitate the attention to their clients. In all of the warehouses, there are a number of containers/items of different types. These containers can be available to be used in a warehouse, they can be stacked to be repaired in the same warehouse, or they can be sent to a recycling center to make new ones. Each warehouse has a limited number of containers available for each type. However, if a large number of containers is needed, the company has the capacity to acquire more in order to cover the demand.

The main goal of the company is to transport the containers from warehouses to supermarkets. Currently, the company must optimize the planning of 2000 trips weekly. To this end, the company must develop an efficient search algorithm to plan the weekly allocation of a fleet of trucks in the different warehouses that are spread throughout the country. Due to physical and temporal constraints, the company aims to minimize the cost of transport generated by the trucks and the cost of stock in each of the warehouses. Since the amount of stock in the warehouses may be negative, the demand for items is greater than the stock available and the company must acquire them, therefore the stock cost is directly associated with the price of the items with negative stock.

This paper proposes a new SLAP proposal for balancing stocks. This proposal takes into account that the problem can be modelled as a VRP (more specifically as an OVRP) where the vehicle that transports the order does not return to its point of origin. To do this we propose a metaheuristic search algorithm is proposed the greedy randomized adaptive search (GRASP) [7]. It searches for the first solution by applying a series of heuristics. Later, the local search is performed by applying a series of multi-target heuristics to filter the different solutions and choose the most optimized one.

2 Problem Specification

This section presents, the problem specification posed by the company in order to provide a better understanding of the proposed algorithm, highlighting the most relevant aspects. The main objective is to assign each trip to a warehouse, taking into account all of the characteristics of each trip and each warehouse. To do this, we seek to minimize the transport cost and the stock cost. Minimizing transport cost is relatively simple by obtaining the trip with the minimum transport value. However, the stock cost poses a challenge due to the fact that the stock of each container type must be balanced. To solve this, a multi-objective function must be determined by assigning weights to the transport cost and the stock cost in order to determine the fitness function. This function must keep the transport cost stable while the stock in the warehouses is distributed homogeneously. Thus, the most important variables involved in the problem must be taken into account.

- **Transport cost** (TC): this is the cost associated with an order. This cost is based on the distance between the starting point and the warehouse, which is proportional to the distance. This is taken into account when calculating the final cost in the fitness function.
- **Stock cost** (SC): If an order composed of N items to be delivered is loaded at a warehouse where the current stock is less than the one required, the remaining negative stock quantity must be replaced. Therefore, the cost of the stock will be proportional to the negative stock multiplied by the cost of replacing each of the items.
- **Delay of delivery** (DD): Each of the possible warehouses associated with an order are located at a certain distance from the origin. Therefore, depending on the warehouse chosen for loading the order, a different delay will be assigned. This delay affects the amount of stock that is reduced from the warehouse from the planned date to the real delivery date.
- **Single load point** (SLP): Each order has a number of locations to which it can be loaded. Each of these locations has a number of important decision features. An order can only be loaded at one location, with the constraint that all of the items needed in the order must be loaded at the same location. Therefore, it is not allowed to load at different locations.

The problem is composed of a dataset (DS) that is based on the combination of three main elements it contains all of the information necessary to represent a problem instance (see Eq. 1). Thus, each problem instance is composed of a set of orders (O) each of which represent a trip to transport items, a set of available warehouses (W) to load the items, and a set of prices (P) for each item.

$$DS = \{O, W, P\} \tag{1}$$

The set $O = \{o_1, o_2, \ldots, o_N\}$ contains all of the information about the orders, where N is the number of orders. Each order $o_i \in O$ is composed of three parameters $o_i = [D_{o_i}, Ir_{o_i}, W_{o_i}]$:

– D_{o_i} is the delivery date of o_i.
– Ir_{o_i} contains the set of items to be loaded (see Eq. 2). Each element $ir_{o_i j} \in Ir_{o_i}$ represents the number of items to be loaded.

$$Ir_{o_i} = \{ir_{o_i 1}, ir_{o_i 2} \ldots, ir_{o_i P}\} \tag{2}$$

– W_{o_i} is a set of possible warehouses where order o_i can load all of the required items (see Eq. 3).

$$Ware_{o_i} = \{Ware_{o_i 1}, Ware_{o_i 1}, \ldots Ware_{o_i Q}\} \tag{3}$$

Each element $W_{o_i j}$ is composed of by three values:
- $ava_{o_i j}$ represents the availability of platform j to load all of the items of order o_i. Thus, $ava_{o_i j} = 1$ means the warehouse is available, and $ava_{o_i j} = 0$ means that is not available.
- $pr_{o_i j}$ contains the transport cost of order o_i from platform j. If $ava_{o_i j} = 0$, this value is null.
- $dl_{o_i j}$ is the delay to load the order o_i from platform j. If $ava_{o_i j} = 0$, this value is null.

To control the amount of stock at the beginning of each week, the company provides a three-dimensional matrix with the current status of each warehouse W (see Eq. 4).

$$W = \{w_1, w_2, w_3, \ldots w_P\} \tag{4}$$

where each $wst_i \in W$ is composed of a bidirectional matrix (item x week days). The model of the company, allows negative stock to be generated in the warehouses associated to an order $wst_{ijk} \in \mathbb{N}$. This is allowed because each of the logistic centers (warehouses) can replace the lack of containers by shipping them.

Finally, P is the set of unitary price for each items (see Eq. 5).

$$P = \{p_1, p_2, p_3, \ldots, p_i, \ldots p_P\} \tag{5}$$

3   Solving Techniques

This section explains the current algorithm being used by the company, pointing out the structure and specifications of the implemented greedy algorithm as well as the characteristics that make it up. The proposed GRASP algorithm, local search, and several improvements are detailed below.

3.1   The Greedy Algorithm

Today, the objective of the company is the planning of weekly orders based on the demand of customers taking into account the available stock expected for each day of the week. The company has developed its own algorithm to obtain an optimized solution based on a greedy technique with a post-processing phase. The stock available in each item model in each day of week is obtained from a weekly load plan. This stock is obtained from the sum of the remaining containers from the previous week, the containers that have been successfully refilled and those obtained by shipments, etc. The greedy algorithm has additional constraints imposed by the perspective of the customer, warehouses, and geographical areas, as well as to other factors:

– A certain number of clients only allow loading in a certain warehouse due to distance and convenience factors.
– The zone of influence or geographical area has a higher priority in the assignment of orders by each warehouse.
– The loading of an order is restricted to the type of items it contains, so there are certain warehouses that do not serve a particular item.
– The warehouses or loading centers have independent delays for each product at different times of the year because the quantity of products (fruit, vegetables, fishes) is not constant throughout the year.

These constraints make the generated search tree too large to be addressed in one go. Therefore, the current algorithm developed by the company is split into several layers, which are put together in a post-processing step.

First, the algorithm performs an ordering according to priorities. It uses a heuristic called closeness centrality that is applied to network theory. This measure allows us to obtain a measure of centrality of a transport network by adding the length of the paths between the different nodes, obtaining the central nodes as those that are closer to the other nodes. Later, the orders are classified according to the item with the greater portion of the order, assigning all if the available stock of the nearest warehouses by this article model.

In the second layer, there are orders that are unassigned to a warehouse because they have failed to meet any of the restrictions of the first layer. These remaining orders are reordered using the centrality closeness heuristics to assign them to less central warehouses with larger stock. The orders that have not been assigned can be renegotiated using the customers in order to improve the response of the warehouse system or to make up for the lack of stock by manufacturing the containers needed to meet the customers' needs. However, after this second layer, there may be unassigned orders which are assigned to the most optimal warehouse in a post processing. These are marked so that an expert human can review them, looking for combinations that improve the cost of global transport without increasing the stock cost to manufacture containers. The constraints that are joined in the greedy algorithm by layers only take into account the cost generated by the transport and the requests of the clients. This makes it necessary for an expert to review all of the trips to be able in order to obtain a better solution for the company.

3.2 GRASP

Taking into account the structure of the above greedy method and its drawbacks in to obtaining a good solution, a GRASP algorithm has been developed to obtain a balanced solution in terms of travel cost and stock balance. To do this, we focus on obtaining an efficient solution and keeping the stock as balanced as possible among the warehouses.

Algorithm 1. GRASP

1: *input:* All orders O, All stock matrix W, Item price vector P, Size of LCR list n
2: *output:* Optimized solution s^*
3: $i \longleftarrow 0$
4: $t \longleftarrow [1, 2, 3, \ldots, |O|]$
5: **while** empty(t) **do:**
6:     **if** sort-criterion(i) **then:**
7:         swap$(\, o_{i-1} \,,\, o_i \,)$
8:         $t \longleftarrow t \setminus i$
9:         $i \longleftarrow i + 1$
10:    **end if**
11: **end while**
12:
13: $s \longleftarrow [\;\;]$
14: $LCR \longleftarrow [o_1, \ldots, o_n]$
15: **while** $|s| \neq |LCR|$ **do:**
16:    $j \longleftarrow 0$
17:    $lcr \longleftarrow [\;\;]$
18:    **while** $j < |LCR|$ **do:**
19:        $lcr \longleftarrow lcr \cup \mathbf{LocalSearch}(LCR_j, \alpha, |LCR|)$
20:        $j \longleftarrow j + 1$
21:    **end while**
22:    $s \longleftarrow s \cup lcr*$
23:    $LCR \longleftarrow LCR \setminus lcr*$
24:    $LCR \longleftarrow LCR \cup o_{n+1}$
25: **end while**

The proposed Algorithm 1 is based on two steps. First, the list of orders is sorted to improve the response of the algorithm (from lines 5 to 11). This assumption is based on the idea of constrainedness, analyzing the most restrictive orders first in order to give the algorithm more decision power in the final iterations. Second, the iterative part of GRASP (from line 15 to 20) obtains a list that a fraction of the size of the list of requests (called LCR). This list contains the algorithm's candidates to assign a warehouse. Then, a local search is generated in which the best warehouse is obtained. Once we have the best warehouses for all of the trips, we select the warehouse with the lowest cost, eliminating the order from the LCR list and adding the next one from the sorting list.

LRC Ordering: The sorting of the LCR list is carried out to give more flexibility and to test the behavior of the algorithm with different inputs. This preprocessing auto-allocates all of the trips that have only one available warehouse due to availability or customer restrictions.

This type of ordering is modular for easier testing. For this purpose, a sorting algorithm has been developed based on a criterion (see Line 6). Once all of the values an the list are correctly sorted, a list with these values is returned.

– **Sort by number of warehouses:** The list is ordered by the number of possible warehouses, that is, the first order an the list will have fewer warehouses, allowing the algorithm to assign them with fewer of decisions to make (constrainedness).
  - **Sort by number of warehouses and items:** The trips ordered by warehouses and with the same value are ordered by the lowest number of items required for the trip.
  - **Sort by number of warehouses and delay:** The trips ordered by warehouse are ordered according to the number of days of delay for that order. This is because the more days of delay there are, the more blocked stock remains during the week.
– **Sort by Delay and Items:** In this case, orders are classified by the sum of the delays of all their warehouses and by the amount of items required for the trip.
– **Sort by warehouses plus standardized delay and items:** This sorting is carried out by mixing the three criteria previously defined. To do this, we add the standardization of the delay and the number of warehouses and then order by the number of items.
– **Sort by number of weight warehouses and delay:** This sorting is based on the previous one by adding a beta weight to the delay. Then, the sorting is done by the number of items.

After carrying out some tests to verify the viability of all sorting types, it was found that sorting by the number of warehouses() more specifically, sorting by number of warehouses and items) gave the best results without negatively affecting time or computer costs.

3.3   Local Search

Once the order list is sorted, we iterate it to execute a local search on each order in order to obtain the best assignation. This local search is based on obtaining the objective function for each of the possible warehouses in a trip, by generating a list of values for each warehouse. Once this list is obtained, we obtain the minimum value on the list and the selected warehouse is assigned to the trip.

Algorithm 2. Local Search

1: *input:* A order o, List of item price P, Alpha value for objective function α, Length of LCR list $nLCR$
2: *output:* Index of warehouse chosen j, Minimum cost of warehouse chosen $Q*$
3: $Q \longleftarrow [\ ]$
4: $I \longleftarrow Ir_o$
5: $M \longleftarrow W_o$
6: **For** j in $\{0, \ldots, |M|\}$:
7:    $Cs \longleftarrow []$
8:    $Ct \longleftarrow \textbf{getTransportCost}(M_j)$
9:    **For** i in $\{0, \ldots, |I|\}$:
10:      $Cs_i \longleftarrow P_i * \sum_{k=D_o}^{|wst_{ij}|} wst_{ijk} \mid wst_{ijk} < 0$
11:      $Cs \longleftarrow Cs \cup Cs_i$
12:    **end for**
13:    $Q_j \longleftarrow \alpha * Ct + (1-\alpha) * \sum Cs$
14:    $Q \longleftarrow Q \cup Q_j$
15:    $F_\alpha \longleftarrow (1-\alpha)/nLCR$
16:    **if** $\sum Cs < 0$ **then:**
17:      $\alpha \longleftarrow \alpha + F_\alpha$
18:    **else:**
19:      $\alpha \longleftarrow \alpha - F_\alpha$
20:    **end if**
21: **end for**

In each iteration, one of the orders an the LCR list is analyzed, and the objective function is calculated with all the items that compose the order and the possible warehouses in order to obtain the best one. The objective function is based on calculating the transport cost and the stock cost and weighting them with an alpha value in order to give more weight to the transport cost which generates more costs (see Line 15). The transportation cost of a trip is obtained by adding the price of traveling to a warehouse for each order (see Line 8). The stock cost is obtained by subtracting the quantity of an item required in a warehouse an a certain day, multiplying it by the price of manufacturing the item in the case that the stock is negative. If the stock remains positive the stock cost will be zero (see Line 11). Finally, the warehouse assignments for each trip are saved.

3.4   Improvements

During the development of the algorithm, several problems appear that negatively affect the optimization of the solution. To overcome these problems, parts of the main code have been improved:

– **LCR sorting:** As mentioned above, the ordering of the LCR list improves the allocation of the order with the most restrictive characteristics, leaving those with a larger set of solutions for the end.

– **Shuffle:** In each one of the iterations of the GRASP algorithm, it is observed that the LCR list sorting generates the same order of the orders. A shuffle method has been developed that randomizes the LCR list from the criteria used in LCR sorting. This method allows us to generate in each of the iterations of the algorithm a different LCR list from the others in order to avoid identical solutions.

– **Scheduler:** The objective function seeks to minimize both the transport cost and the stock cost. To do this, an alpha value is applied to each of the variables to be minimized in order to find the optimal point. During the execution of the tests, it is observed that to greater amount of items with negative stock in the warehouses the objective function is polarized losing the optimal value. This is because of a fixed alpha value that reduces the dynamism of the function and, therefore, worsens the results. For this purpose, a *scheduler* that modifies the alpha value in each of the iterations has been developed. This scheduler increases or decreases the alpha variable regardless of whether or not the assigned order is in a warehouse with negative stock. The factor that is used in the *scheduler* is calculated by dividing the rest of alpha minus 1 by the number of trips that remain to be assigned. This allows the *scheduler* to minimize the stock cost more easily.

4   Evaluation

This section presents the results of each of the proposed improvements, as well as the results of the comparison of the greedy algorithm and the GRASP algorithm with all of the implemented improvements.

The first part of the algorithm to be improved is the sorting of the list of possible candidates. This is done by obtaining the different costs for each of the models explained (see Fig. 2).

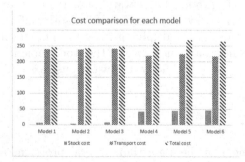

Fig. 2. Cost comparison for each model.

These results indicate that in models where delay is prioritized over warehouses or items, transport cost improves but stock cost worsens. To contrast in those models where the number of available warehouses is prioritized and the models are combined with other parameters, a stable transport cost and a significantly lower stock cost are obtained. In order to check these results, a series of metrics is obtained that allows a deeper evaluation of the stock balance in the warehouses by comparing these metrics in the greedy algorithm and the proposed one. To do this, we first obtain the average negative stock of all platforms (see Fig. 3a).

The average number of items with negative stock reinforces our hypothesis that the number of warehouses available per trip is a determining factor. In order to decide which model to use for the LCR list, we obtain the number of items where the stock is negative (see Fig. 3b).

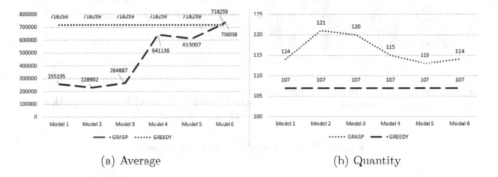

(a) Average   (b) Quantity

Fig. 3. Metrics of items with negative stock for each model.

Finally, we decided to use the ordering model based on quantity of available warehouses and amount of items in the order. We selected this model because it is the one that generates the least number of items with negative stock and the lowest average of negative stock, and it keeps the cost of transport constant.

The set of improvements optimize the scheduling of the algorithm and maintain balanced stock. These improvements are evaluated by measuring metrics that are similar to those used previously. Each one of these improvements implements the previous one, because they depend on each other. In all of the improvements applied to the algorithm, they are implemented with a LCR ordering model 2. Basically, we obtain the different transport and stock costs and compare them in order to have a general view of the impact of the improvement on the solution of the algorithm (see Fig. 4).

As shown, the test results do not show significant differences in costs; only the implementation of all of the improvements slightly reduces the total cost. To ensure that the improvements used optimize the solution, we obtain metrics based on stock balancing (see Fig. 5).

The results obtained from the metrics for the evaluation of the balance of the stock show us that the average stock of the items in the warehouses remains stable with a difference of between 67% and 71%, while the number of items with

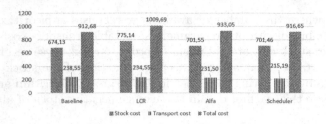

Fig. 4. Different costs for each improvements.

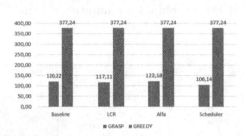

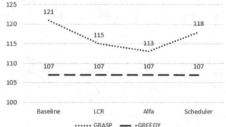

(a) Average number of items with negative stock for each improvement.

(b) Amount of items with negative stock for each improvement

Fig. 5. Metrics based on stock balancing

negative stock increases with respect to the algorithm already implemented. This is a good result. If we compare the average and the amount negative stock of items at warehouses, we determine that there are more items with negative stock but the value of these is much lower. Therefore, the negative stock is balanced with the new improvements. Finally, the two algorithms are compared completely, using the cost and stock balancing metrics used previously. First, the total cost is evaluated for the first two weeks of July 2020 (see Fig. 6b). The results indicate that the algorithm improves the results of the first week but worsens the second week. This is because GRASP was developed to improve the balance at the expense of the transport cost. Second, the stock metrics are evaluated to determine whether or not the algorithm balances the stocks correctly.

First, a metric is shown that calculates the average negative stock amount for all of the warehouses (see Fig. 6a). This metric is very important because it allows us to see how the stock is distributed in the warehouses. The improvement provided by the GRASP in the average negative stock quantity is between 60% and 81%. On the other hand the number of items with negative stock (see Fig. 7a) is also a metric that helps us to measure the dispersion of stock among the warehouses. In this case, you can see an improvement by the GRASP of between 41% and 60% based on data from the greedy algorithm. Finally, the costs of the two weeks are obtained to evaluate them jointly (see Fig. 7b)

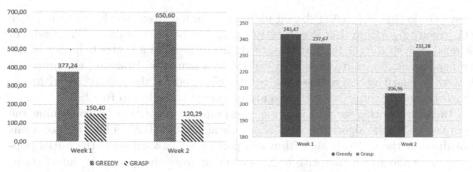

(a) Average number of negative stock items.

(b) Total cost comparison.

Fig. 6. Metrics in the first half of July 2020.

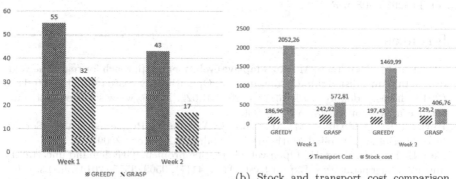

(a) Quantity of negative stock items in the first half of July 2020

(b) Stock and transport cost comparison between the greedy algorithm and GRASP

Fig. 7. Metrics in the first half of July 2020.

The results show a large difference in the ock cost between the different algorithms for the two weeks shown. It can also be observed that even through the transport cost is higher in GRASP. The penalty is relatively low compared to the improvement in the stock cost. The stock cost improves by about 72% and the transport cost worsens by between 13% and 21%. The computational time taken by the greedy algorithm is about 20 to 30 min, while GRASP takes between 0.45 and 1.5 min.

5 Conclusions and Future Work

Transport companies need to optimize their logistics infrastructures and strategies in order to be more efficient in a more competitive world. This work tries to merge two different problems, the warehouse stock management problem and the routing problem in order to minimize both the negative stock and the transport cost. To do this, a GRASP-based metaheuristic has been developed to improve the greedy algorithm that is currently being used by the company. The results in several case studies show that the greedy algorithm had a better behavior in the transport cost, since it is specially guided by a heuristic. However, the proposed GRASP algorithm overcomes the results obtained by the greedy algorithm in stock balancing, improving the negative average stock by up to 82%.

In future works, we will improve the proposed algorithm by combining the proposed GRASP algorithm with a genetic algorithm (GA). Thus, the solutions obtained by the GRASP algorithm will participate as a subset of the initial population for the genetic algorithm. This could improve the quality of the solutions due to the high capability of the GA to combine previous solutions and avoid blockage in the local optimal.

Acknowledgement. The paper has been partially funded by the Spanish research project TIN2016-80856-R.

References

1. Barkaoui, M., Gendreau, M.: An adaptive evolutionary approach for real-time vehicle routing and dispatching. Computers & Operations Research **40**(7), 1766–1776 (2013). https://doi.org/10.1016/j.cor.2013.01.022, http://www.sciencedirect.com/science/article/pii/S0305054813000300
2. Burkard, R., Dell'Amico, M., Martello, S.: Assignment Problems. SIAM - Society of Industrial and Applied Mathematics, 1 edn., 382 Seiten (2009)
3. Cao, E., Lai, M., Yang, H.: Open vehicle routing problem with demand uncertainty and its robust strategies. Expert Syst. Appl. **41**(7), 3569–3575 (2014). https://doi.org/10.1016/j.eswa.2013.11.004, http://www.sciencedirect.com/science/article/pii/S0957417413009044
4. Current, J., Marsh, M.: Multiobjective transportation network design and routing problems: taxonomy and annotation. Euro. J. Oper. Res. **65**(1), 4–19 (1993). https://doi.org/10.1016/0377-2217(93)90140-I, http://www.sciencedirect.com/science/article/pii/037722179390140I
5. Eksioglu, B., Vural, A.V., Reisman, A.: The vehicle routing problem: a taxonomic review. Comput. Ind. Eng. **57**(4), 1472–1483 (2009). https://doi.org/10.1016/j.cie.2009.05.009, http://dx.doi.org/10.1016/j.cie.2009.05.009
6. Li, X., Leung, S.C.H., Tian, P.: A multistart adaptive memory-based tabu search algorithm for the heterogeneous fixed fleet open vehicle routing problem. Expert Syst. Appl. **39**(1), 365–374 (2012). https://doi.org/10.1016/j.eswa.2011.07.025, http://www.sciencedirect.com/science/article/pii/S0957417411009870
7. Li, Y., Pardalos, P.M., Resende, M.G.C.: A Greedy Randomized Adaptive Search Procedure for the Quadratic Assignment Problem **0000**, 1–21 (1991)
8. López-Sánchez, A.D., Hernández-Díaz, A.G., Vigo, D., Caballero, R., Molina, J.: A multi-start algorithm for a balanced real-world Open Vehicle Routing Problem. Euro. J. Oper. Res. **238**(1), 104–113 (2014). https://doi.org/10.1016/j.ejor.2014.04.008, http://www.sciencedirect.com/science/article/pii/S0377221714003178
9. Pillac, V., Gendreau, M., Guéret, C., Medaglia, A.L.: A review of dynamic vehicle routing problems. European J. Oper. Res. **225**(1), 1–11 (2013). https://doi.org/10.1016/j.ejor.2012.08.015, http://www.sciencedirect.com/science/article/pii/S0377221712006388

10. Salari, M., Toth, P., Tramontani, A.: An ILP improvement procedure for the open vehicle routing problem. Comput. Oper. Res. **37**(12), 2106–2120 (2010). https://doi.org/10.1016/j.cor.2010.02.010, http://www.sciencedirect.com/science/article/pii/S0305054810000547
11. Subramanian, A., Uchoa, E., Ochi, L.S.: A hybrid algorithm for a class of vehicle routing problems. Comput. Oper. Res. **40**(10), 2519–2531 (2013). https://doi.org/10.1016/j.cor.2013.01.013, http://www.sciencedirect.com/science/article/pii/S030505481300021X
12. Syed-abdullah, S.S., Abdul-rahman, S., Mauziah, A.: Solving Quadratic Assignment Problem with Fixed Assignment (QAPFA) using Branch and Bound Approach Solving Quadratic Assignment Problem with Fixed Assignment (QAPFA) using Branch and Bound Approach (2018). https://doi.org/10.1088/1757-899X/300/1/012002

Investigating the Use of Machine Learning for South African Edible Garnish Yield Prediction

Yolandi Le Roux[1,2] and Jacomine Grobler[1,2(✉)] ⓘ

[1] Department of Industrial and Systems Engineering, University of Pretoria, Pretoria, South Africa
jacomine.grobler@gmail.com
[2] Department of Industrial Engineering, Stellenbosch University, Stellenbosch, South Africa

Abstract. This paper focuses on the specific scenario of capturing data in the South African agricultural industry; an industry where it can be difficult, expensive and time consuming to gather information, yet the need for information is critical. The aim is to conduct an introductory study into determining which aspects: location, irrigation, fertilizer application, temperature, or type of growing medium, has the most significant impact on the yield of edible garnish and then to predict the yield of a specific plant. A dataset collected over a three year period and supplemented with empirical knowledge and expert opinion, is analysed and a number of classifiers are applied to select the best strategy for predicting future yield of edible garnish. A random forest classifier showed the most promise and location on the farm was shown to have the largest influence on yield.

Keywords: Machine learning · Agriculture · Yield prediction

1   Introduction

Company XYZ is a South African agricultural company that cultivates edible garnishes. Their products are sold locally and internationally to high end retailers, wholesalers, and the restaurant industry. They cultivate more than a 100 different product lines, mostly in greenhouses and some in open fields. Each crop has a different set of requirements, such as water, fertilizer, sunlight, temperature and growing medium (soil). Furthermore, the products all differ in terms of their growing method, lifespan, and harvesting season.

In the last five years the company expanded rapidly. Due to this growth, XYZ needs to evaluate how they capture data, and how this data is analysed for them to make more informed decisions. Before the growth spurt, managerial decisions at XYZ was based on experience and intuition. However, the company has expanded so rapidly, that it is essential that data is converted into information that is timely and relevant to their specific needs.

M. Bramer and R. Ellis (Eds.): SGAI-AI 2020, LNAI 12498, pp. 202–214, 2020.
https://doi.org/10.1007/978-3-030-63799-6_16

One challenge is that many agricultural operations in South Africa are still "old school". Farmers are reluctant to invest in information technology, especially if the system might cost more than the value of the data it supplies. In addition, the labour is for the most part unschooled, so resistance to change, especially to a new technology based system, is real. Workers fear the new technology would replace them, or that they would not be able to understand or operate the new technology and as a result, lose their employment.

Another challenge to consider is that XYZ operates on expensive land located in an urban area, making expansion very difficult. The need to optimise the available space is crucial to "schedule" the cultivation activities in such a way that space in the greenhouses is not taken up by crops which could either be grown outside, or which is not sufficiently profitable to justify growing inside greenhouses. Determining in advance what set of specific circumstances would be the best for a certain crop, will allow management to schedule production in such a way as to ensure the production space is always optimally utilised.

Most agricultural companies focus on a few large crops, like maize or corn, for example. In such a scenario some of the attributes of the crop are the same. There are still many variables such as temperature, rainfall and different locations to consider, but other aspects, such as growing method, pesticides, seasonality, water requirements, harvesting method, transport and storage requirements, for the most part, stay the same. XYZ cultivates more than a 100 different crops, each with a different set of requirements. Since the data is still highly limited and there are not yet standardized data collection processes or infrastructure in place, it is important to gather as much data as possible, without wasting precious resources such as time and skilled labour to acquire irrelevent data. This paper thus aims to analyse XYZ's data to determine which factors have the most significant impact on the yield of specific crops and then to utilize the information to predict the future yield of that crop.

The paper describes the collection, construction, and preliminary analysis of a dataset containing information with regard to the location, rainfall, temperature, fertilizer application, growing medium, and yield of an edible garnish crop. A number of classification algorithms are tested to determine which algorithm provides the best prediction of yield based on the abovementioned features. Twenty seven algorithms are compared and a random forest algorithm was identified as the most promising candidate, able to predict crop yield with an accuracy of 94.17%.

This paper is significant because to the best of the authors' knowledge, it describes the first application of machine learning in an edible garnish environment.

The rest of this paper is organised as follows: Sect. 2 provides an overview of the relevant literature and Sect. 3 describes the case study environment. Section 4 describes the dataset in more detail. Section 5 describes the experimental setup and results of the empirical evaluation of the different classifiers. Section 6 considers the validity of the solutions and variable importance in more detail. Finally, Sect. 7 concludes the paper.

2   Machine Learning in Agriculture

Liakos et al. [10] categorises agricultural machine intelligence research into crop management, livestock management, water management, and soil management applications. In the field of crop management, a number of examples can be found where authors used machine learning to predict yield. A number of articles focused on using digital images as input to predict yield. Some examples include:

- Ramos et al. [12] used a support vector machine on digital images to automatically count the number of coffee fruits on a coffee branch.
- Amatya et al. [1] also analysed digital images depicting leaves, branches and cherry fruits to detect cherry branches with full foilage. They used a gaussian naive bayes algorithm.
- Sengupta and Lee [13] identified immature green citrus fruit through a similar approach and used a support vector machine.

More relevant to this paper is the work by Su et al. [15] who used agricultural, surface weather, and soil physico-chemical data to predict the development stage of rice paddies by means of a support vector machine. Pantazi et al. [11] used a combination of satellite imagery, crop growth characteristics and soil data to predict the yield of wheat fields by means of a neural network. Kung et al. [9] used relative humidity, precipitation, planting area, air temperature, cost of production, and market trading price to predict the total harvest of Taiwanese crops by means of an ensemble neural network. No literature was found that focused on the application of machine learning in an edible garnish environment.

Finally, various authors [4,7,14], have highlighted the enormous amount of data currently available to make decisions and have emphasized that it is important to identify the most critical data elements when resources are limited. The idea of the cost of data collection versus the value the data has, however, not yet been investigated in an edible garnish context.

3   Details of the Case Study

Collecting data in the agricultural industry can be very difficult since, the importance of the accuracy of the data is not always understood by the persons responsible for capturing the data. For this paper, one of the edible garnish crops was chosen for analysis purposes. Even though there is limited IT infrastructure at XYZ, data such as rainfall and temperature are still recorded manually each day. The main advantage is that this is an inexpensive way to gather the information; the disadvantage is the data is incomplete. To fill in the gaps, observations and empirical knowledge were used to generate a full dataset with the help of experts in the field of agriculture as well as publicly available knowledge.

The dataset consisted of a number of features that are explained in more detail below:

– Location: To ensure year round production, most of the crops need to be grown in highly specialised greenhouses, under controlled circumstances. Inside these greenhouses, factors such as temperature, humidity, water and even daylight can be manipulated. Maintaining the optimal conditions for the crop extends the lifespan of the plant and improves the quality of the harvest. The downside of these greenhouses are that they are expensive to build and maintain. It is important that only the products that cannot grow outside, or is of the highest value, is grown inside. At XYZ there are five different locations where the products can be planted:

- **Outside beds** are used for the toughest crops or crops of low value. These beds are considered bonus high risk production space. When it rains, for example, produce cannot be harvested from the outside beds, as the produce rots if packed while wet, and bruises if dried manually. On the plus side, the outside beds are the least expensive areas on the farm. Almost no capital investments are required and no additional electricity to power extractor fans is required. Inside the greenhouses crops are grown in plastic containers or trays. These are expensive, and are not used for outside production.

- Of all the fixed structures at XYZ, the **shade nets** are the least expensive (but more expensive than the outside beds). In summer the advantage is that the nets reduces the impact of the sun by keeping the direct sunlight off the crops, and in winter the nets keep the frost off the crops. The structure also lends support for irrigation infrastructure (sprinklers are suspended from the overhead structure). The disadvantage is that there is no control over factors such as humidity, and the shade net only cools the produce off to a certain extent. Sensitive crops are still damaged during extremely cold or hot days and during harsh winters or very hot summers the crops suffer.

- **Rain shades** are sturdy open structures with plastic roofs, similar to greenhouses. Rain shades have no side panels and do not require extractor fans. The advantage is that they are less expensive than closed greenhouses. Rain shades are excellent at keeping the rain and frost off the crops and they form a buffer between the crops and the harsh sun. The structure lends support to all the irrigation requirements. An extra overhead curtain can be closed to reduce the impact of the sun during the middle of the day or be opened to let in more light on a cloudy day or at dusk and dawn. The high roof and the openings therein allows for excellent ventilation at the slightest breeze. The disadvantage is that the temperature cannot be controlled as precisely as in the greenhouses and no control over humidity is possible.

- **Large greenhouses**: Greenhouses are classified as large or small, depending on the length of the north-south axis. The greenhouses at XYZ are impressive, but expensive, structures. They are smart houses and can be programmed to control factors such as irrigation, fertiliser, daylight intensity, humidity levels and temperature. This control is achieved by pad walls and large extractor fans. Water runs down the pad walls and the extractor fans force air through the pad walls, lowering temperature and increasing humidity, as required. The longer the North-South Axis, the less the previously mentioned factors can be controlled, making the larger greenhouses slightly less effective than the smaller greenhouses.

- **Small greenhouse**: The small greenhouses are more expensive as their building cost is the same as the large greenhouses but they cover a smaller surface area. The plus side is that temperature and humidity can be controlled more rigorously over the shorter north-south axis, resulting in the best yield.

- The **growing medium** (soil) influences the life span of the plants and the quality of the harvest. Soil that is brought in from external suppliers, who take great care to comply with strict regulations to ensure the soil contains the necessary nutrients, give the plants the nutrition they require, therefore increasing the yield. XYZ uses four types of soil:

  - Rough medium: purchased; mostly pine bark; excellent drainage; but expensive.
  - Fine medium: purchased; high in nutrients; perfect for containers and pots; but expensive.
  - Outside red: naturally occurring soil; can be purchased if required; good levels of nutrients; high in iron; excellent for outside beds; and affordable.
  - Outside grey: naturally occurring soil; very low in nutrients; not ideal for cultivation; but inexpensive.

  Inside the greenhouses only purchased mediums are used. Under the shade net, rain shade and for the outside beds, the natural occurring soil is mostly relied on, but purchased soil is sometimes added.

- Different types of **fertiliser** can be applied. Adding the fertiliser to the water tanks and applying it through the sprinklers in the greenhouses every day at a low dosage (fertigation), is a way to keep the plants sustained for longer and increase the yield. Fertiliser is applied manually to the outside beds. "Basic" fertiliser application means the plant was given the standard treatment, whereas "complete" refers to a more extensive fertiliser regiment.

- **Temperature** plays a significant role in the lifespan of a crop and the quality of the harvest. Unsuitable temperatures stresses the plants and reduces both the yield and the lifespan of the plants. Continuous exposure to unsuitable temperatures could lead to serious crop damage. Temperature is measured in degrees Celsius and the maximum daily temperature was used for this feature.

- **Rainfall**: No crop can survive without water. Too much water on the other hand can lead to root rot. In the greenhouses irrigation is controlled, but the outside beds are directly influenced by the rainfall. When it rains, produce cannot be harvested from the outside beds, since produce that is packed while wet rots. Another factor to consider is that the irrigation for the outside beds are not as effective as in the greenhouses (more evaporation, wind etc.) and during periods of drought the outside beds are the first to suffer. Long term drought can impact even the inside crops since the boreholes eventually dry up and the greenhouses are watered with borehole water.

- **Yield** refers to the product collected from a specific plant in a specific instance. For the purpose of this paper, yield is expressed on a scale from 0 to 10, where 0 refers to no suitable produce available and 10 refers to a large harvest of excellent quality.

4   Exploratory Data Analysis

Historical data over a period of three years as well as empiricial knowledge and expert opinion, was used to construct the dataset. This dataset consists of a measurement of each of the discussed features recorded for the edible garnish crops for each day. The final dataset consisted of 1095 instances. Figure 1 shows a sample of the first couple of observations of this dataset.

Location	Max Temp (°C)	Rainfall (mm)	Fertiliser	Medium (Soil Type)	Yield
Outside	21	8	Complete	OutsideRed	0
Outside	27	2	Complete	OutsideGrey	3
LargeGreenhouse	27	1	Complete	Fine	6
LargeGreenhouse	27	5	Basic	Fine	6
Outside	19	0	Basic	OutsideRed	6
Rainshade	18	3	Basic	Fine	7
SmallGreenhouse	15	0	Complete	Rough	5
Outside	10	0	Complete	OutsideRed	1
Outside	10	2	Complete	Rough	1
SmallGreenhouse	28	6	Basic	Fine	4
LargeGreenhouse	23	2	Complete	Rough	8
SmallGreenhouse	22	0	Basic	Rough	5
Rainshade	24	1	Basic	Rough	6
LargeGreenhouse	27	7	Complete	Rough	7
Outside	27	0	Complete	OutsideGrey	3
Outside	20	2	Basic	OutsideRed	5

Fig. 1. Sample of the XYZ edible garnish dataset.

As part of an exploratory data analysis, the graphs in Figs. 2, 3 and 4 were generated. A number of interesting observations became apparent from the exploratory data analysis:

- It appeared that location had a significant impact on yield. Most of the instances that resulted in a zero to low yield, occured in the outside beds, whereas most of the instances that generated a larger yield occurred in the large and small greenhouses. The shade net and rain shade had more or less the same effect, resulting in an average yield. These results indicate that it may be justified for XYZ to cultivate the edible garnish in the expensive greenhouses, as a better yield is achieved in the greenhouses when compared to the outside beds.

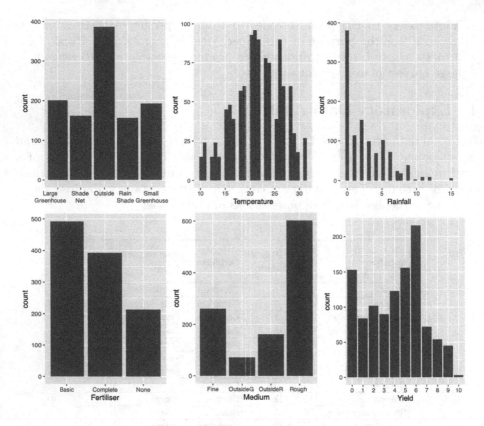

Fig. 2. Visualisation of features.

- The largest yields were obtained between the temperatures of 18 °C to 25 °C, confirming that edible garnish, is sensitive to extreme temperatures.. However, the graphs also show that temperature alone does not always generate a high yield, the other factors need to be considered as well.
- The rainfall did not have a direct influence on the closed structures (greenhouses and rain shade). When it rains, the exposed locations, such as the outside beds and even the shade nets cannot be harvested.
- The outside soil which is of lower nutritional value, clearly resulted in a lower yield, than the purchased soil which contains the nutrients required by the plants. An inappropriate soil medium can thus have a significant impact on crops.
- Incorrect fertiliser application results in fewer instances with a higher yield. Other factors are also, however, at play.

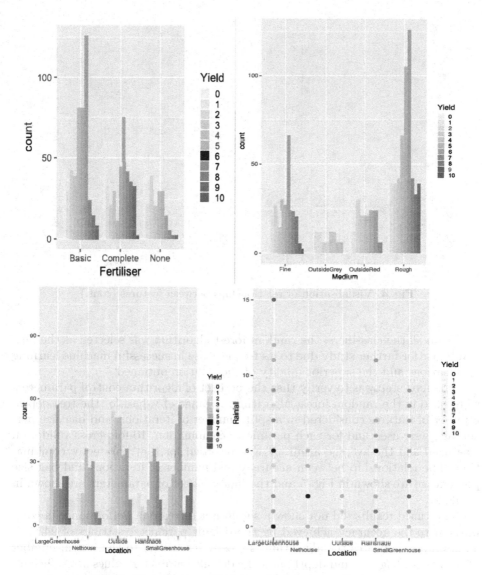

Fig. 3. Visualisation of relationships between features.

5   Empirical Evaluation of the Classifiers

Twenty seven classifiers were tested to predict the target variable yield based on all the other attributes described previously. These classifiers included different types of algorithms such as naive bayes [6], logistic regression [8], and decision trees [2,3]. Weka [5] was used for the evaluation and the results are shown in Table 1. The default algorithm control parameter settings were used and 10-fold cross validation was used to obtain the average accuracy.

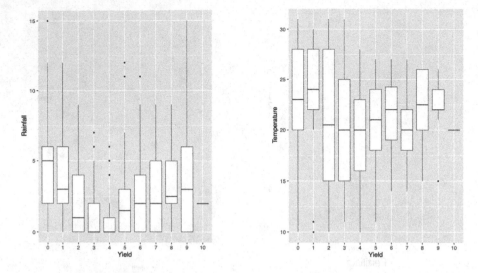

Fig. 4. Visualisation of relationships between features (cont.).

From all the classifiers, the random forest algorithm was selected as the best candidate for further study due to its frequent use in successful machine learning applications and the superior quality of the solution obtained.

The next step was to verify that the best set of algorithm control parameters were used in the random forest algorithm. A range of values for the tree depth, number of features considered in a split, number of iterations, and bag size percentage were used and for each parameter combination, 10-fold cross validation was used and the average accuracy was recorded for that parameter combination. The relationship between accuracy and number of iterations and bag size percentage are shown in Fig. 5 and the final best set of parameters are shown in Table 2.

The tuned results did not show a significant increase in performance in comparison to the accuracy achieved by the default parameter settings of 94.17%. This finding indicates the algorithm is mostly insensitive to changes in number of iterations, bag size and depth, and the default parameter values are sufficient.

6   Validation of Variable Importance

To further validate the importance of the different variables, the J48 decision tree is visualised in Figure 6. The complete tree is much more complex. For illustration and discussion purposes, only the first three levels are shown.

The decision tree clearly indicates that location is the most important aspect for XYZ to consider. The greenhouses result in the highest yield, followed by the rain shades, the shade nets and lastly, the outside beds.

Table 1. Results of the classifier evaluation.

Classifier type	Algorithm	Accuracy
Bayesian	Bayesian network classifier	40.89%
	Naive bayes	36.89%
Functions	Logistic regression	35.15%
	Multi layer perceptron	55.92%
	Simple logistic regression	33.79%
	Support vector machine	38.34%
Lazy	K-nearest neighbour	93.90%
	K-star	90.16%
	Locally weighted learning	30.51%
Meta	Attribute selected classifier	81.79%
	Bagging	73.59%
	Classification via regression	74.59%
	Filtered classifier	61.11%
	Iterative classifier optimiser	44.72%
	ILogit boost	44.72%
	Multi class classifier	34.15%
	Random committee classifier	94.17%
	Randomizable filtered classifier	94.17%
	Random sub space classifier	68.49%
Rules	Decision table	63.48%
	JRip	68.76%
	Part	88.25%
Trees	Hoeffding tree	36.16%
	J48	87.7%
	Random forest	94.17%
	Random tree	93.9%
	Fast decision tree learner	63.39%

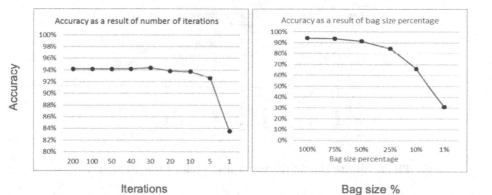

Fig. 5. Relationship between accuracy and iterations and bag size percentage.

The second most important factor varies, based on location. The only locations directly impacted by rainfall are the outside beds and the shade nets. The greenhouses and rain shade is not impacted directly because of their plastic roofs. The outside beds are impacted most severely by rain, since wet crop cannot be harvested and even 2 mm has a negative impact on yield. The shade net is impacted by rain as well, but it takes more than 5 mm to reach the crop. In the greenhouses, the next factor to consider is temperature.

Table 2. Best random forest parameters.

Parameter	Value
Tree depth	Infinite
Number of features considered in split	1
Number of iterations	30
Bag size percentage	100%
Accuracy	94.35%

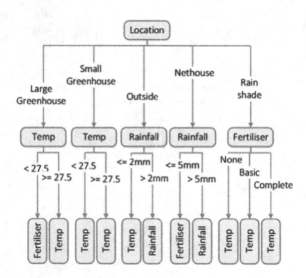

Fig. 6. Illustration of the first three levels of the decision tree.

The threshold temperature for edible garnish is 27.5 °C and higher temperatures than 27.5 °C result in a lower yield. This result implies that management must carefully monitor the temperatures inside the greenhouses. Under the rain shade, the next factor to consider is the fertiliser application for the plants. Management must ensure the fertiliser program is executed thoroughly, even more so when the crop is planted in soil with a lower nutrient content.

7 Conclusion

This paper aimed to determine which aspects: location, irrigation, fertilizer application, temperature, or type of growing medium, has the most significant impact on the yield of the crops of XYZ and to develop a mechanism to predict the yield of a specific crop. The data was analysed and patterns in the data were discussed and illustrated graphically. The graphs indicated that location, rainfall and temperature are the factors which impacts the yield of the crop most severely. A number of classifiers were tested to predict the yield of edible garnish. The random forest algorithm, a decision tree classifier, resulted in the highest accuracy of 94.17%.

Future research can focus on a more in-depth analysis of the other good performing algorithms, the impact of algorithm control parameters on algorithm performance, and utilising time series data over growing time and the additional associated features such as average rainfall and temperature. The analysis can also be extended to different types of products cultivated by XYZ. Different products would have significantly different inputs to that of edible garnish, and would most likely generate different results.

References

1. Amatya, S., Karkee, M., Gongal, A., Zhang, Q., Whiting, M.D.: Detection of cherry tree branches with full foliage in planar architecture for automated sweet-cherry harvesting. Biosyst. Eng. **146**, 3–15 (2016)
2. Breiman, L.: Random forests. Mach. Learn. **45**(1), 5–32 (2001)
3. Breiman, L., Friedman, J., Stone, C.J., Olshen, R.A.: Classification and Regression Trees. CRC Press, Livermore (1984)
4. Goodhue, D.L., Wybo, M.D., Kirsch, L.J.: The impact of data integration on the costs and benefits of information systems. MIS Q. **16**, 293–311 (1992)
5. Hall, M., Frank, E., Holmes, G., Pfahringer, B., Reutemann, P., Witten, I.H.: The weka data mining software: an update. ACM SIGKDD Explor. Newsl. **11**(1), 10–18 (2009)
6. Hand, D.J., Yu, K.: Idiot's bayes–not so stupid after all? Int. Stat. Rev. **69**(3), 385–398 (2001)
7. Hazen, B.T., Boone, C.A., Ezell, J.D., Jones-Farmer, L.A.: Data quality for data science, predictive analytics, and big data in supply chain management: an introduction to the problem and suggestions for research and applications. Int. J. Prod. Econ. **154**, 72–80 (2014)
8. Hosmer Jr., D.W., Lemeshow, S., Sturdivant, R.X.: Applied Logistic Regression, vol. 398. Wiley, Hoboken (2013)
9. Kung, H.Y., Kuo, T.H., Chen, C.H., Tsai, P.Y.: Accuracy analysis mechanism for agriculture data using the ensemble neural network method. Sustainability **8**(8), 735 (2016)

10. Liakos, K.G., Busato, P., Moshou, D., Pearson, S., Bochtis, D.: Machine learning in agriculture: a review. Sensors **18**(8), 2674 (2018)
11. Pantazi, X.E., Moshou, D., Alexandridis, T., Whetton, R.L., Mouazen, A.M.: Wheat yield prediction using machine learning and advanced sensing techniques. Comput. Electron. Agric. **121**, 57–65 (2016)
12. Ramos, P., Prieto, F.A., Montoya, E., Oliveros, C.E.: Automatic fruit count on coffee branches using computer vision. Comput. Electron. Agric. **137**, 9–22 (2017)
13. Sengupta, S., Lee, W.S.: Identification and determination of the number of immature green citrus fruit in a canopy under different ambient light conditions. Biosyst. Eng. **117**, 51–61 (2014)
14. Shmueli, G., Koppius, O.R.: Predictive analytics in information systems research. MIS Q. **35**, 553–572 (2011)
15. Su, Y.X., Xu, H., Yan, L.J.: Support vector machine-based open crop model (SBOCM): Case of rice production in china. Saudi J. Biol. Sci. **24**(3), 537–547 (2017)

Semantic Technologies Towards Accountable Artificial Intelligence: A Poultry Chain Management Use Case

Iker Esnaola-Gonzalez[✉][ID]

TEKNIKER, Basque Research and Technology Alliance (BRTA), Iñaki Goenaga 5, 20600 Eibar, Spain
iker.esnaola@tekniker.es

Abstract. Even though the Artificial Intelligence (AI) has overtaken many decision-making responsibilities in recent years, there still exists legitimate concerns of relying on AI due to their potentially incorrect, unjustified or even unfair results. Consequently, in order to overcome these issues, additional approaches are needed to make AI systems accountable, governable, and in general, trustworthy. In this article, Semantic Technologies are suggested towards making AI systems accountable. The proposed approach enables a fine-grained traceability of the predictions generated by the AI system. Summarising, the presented proposal is expected to make an initial step in the use of Semantic Technologies for addressing different aspects that may contribute to the trustworthiness of AI systems.

Keywords: Artificial Intelligence · Semantic Technologies · Accountability

1 Introduction

Although historically many important decisions were strictly made by humans, the rise of Artificial Intelligence (AI) in recent years has overtaken these responsibilities. AI systems not only can make these decisions more quickly, but also in a more efficient and effective manner. However, there are still legitimate concerns of relying on the decisions made by AI systems due to their unintentional negative consequences in the form of potentially incorrect, unjustified or even unfair results [3]. Since humans are reluctant to adopt systems that are not directly interpretable or tractable [32], additional approaches are needed to overcome these concerns and make AI systems accountable, governable, and in general, trustworthy [20].

The Explainable AI (XAI) proposes the creation of a suite of Machine Learning techniques which, on the one hand, produce more explainable models without neglecting their performance, and on the other, enable human users to understand, trust, and manage the emerging generation of AI systems [16]. As a matter of fact, it can be considered that the XAI addresses the 'right to explanation' debated in the latest revision of the European Union's General Data

M. Bramer and R. Ellis (Eds.): SGAI-AI 2020, LNAI 12498, pp. 215–226, 2020.
https://doi.org/10.1007/978-3-030-63799-6_17

Protection Regulation (GDPR) [14]. This regulation provides the right to be given an explanation about the existence, logic and foreseen consequences of automated decision-making systems, as well as the right not to depend on automated decision-making processes[1]. In a similar way, the European Commission's High-Level Expert Group on AI presented the Ethic Guidelines for Trustworthy Artificial Intelligence[2] to tackle the aforementioned human mistrust in AI systems.

Although there has been an increasing trend for black-box models (e.g. deep neural networks) due to their high performance, that is, predictive models that cannot explain their predictions in a way that humans can understand, there are still white-box algorithms which clearly explain how they behave, how they produce predictions and what the influencing variables are. However, the transparency or explainability of white-box based AI systems is necessary but far from sufficient for understanding them and hold them accountable [11,20]. Furthermore, it is common that deployed models' performance degrade over time due to a change in the environment that violates the model's assumptions, that is, due to a concept drift [30]. The most common method to deal with concept drifting is the retraining of the model, which consists in re-running the process that generated the previous model on the new set of data available. Therefore, in order to make the AI systems trustworthy, not only should they be explainable, but also accountable.

The accountability can be defined as the ability to determine whether a decision was made in accordance with procedural and substantive standards and to hold someone responsible if those standards are not met [20]. This means that with an accountable AI system, the causes that derived a given decision can be discovered, even if its underlying model's details are not fully known or must be kept secret. Therefore, accountability should not be dependent on the algorithm's transparency.

In this article, the accountability of an AI system for poultry chain management is addressed. The accountability of this AI system is faced leveraging Semantic Technologies to enable a fine-grained traceability of the outcomes generated. The presented proposal is expected to make an initial step in the use of Semantic Technologies for addressing different aspects that may contribute to the trustworthiness of AI systems.

The rest of the article is structured as follows. Section 2 outlines the existing work in the field. Section 3 introduces the AI system for poultry chain management and the proposed approach. Finally, in Sect. 4 outcomes of the article are discussed and future work is considered.

---

[1] http://data.europa.eu/eli/reg/2016/679/oj.

[2] https://ec.europa.eu/digital-single-market/en/news/ethics-guidelines-trustworthy-ai.

2   Related Work

Although in many situations data analysts may accept the outcome of an AI system by default, having a detailed explanation of such outcome seems necessary to ensure trustworthiness and enable the evaluation of the legal norms, ethical and moral standards of AI systems [28].

Decisions made by machines are meant to be fair, as they should lack of any racial, gender or other type of prejudges. However, the unwitting biases included in the training data sets definitely affect AI systems and they derive in the predilection or antipathy and penalisation of certain results or social groups. In the healthcare domain, imbalanced data sets may be rebalanced, causing the AI system to over-diagnose rare health problems [22]. For example, an AI system which predicts impending acute kidney injuries became less accurate over time, as disease patterns changed and tend to over-predict false positives [7]. But the threat of unfair AI systems spans other domains too such as the security. AI systems are increasingly being used as a tool to predict the risk of recidivism for criminal defendants and to consider that assessment at sentencing [19], although skewed penalisation toward minorities have been reported. Another example of a biased AI system is a facial recognition system which disproportionately labelled minority students and faculty members of an American university as criminals[3].

Similar to other domains, the technological advancements in the various fields of the AI are not used only for good, and they may face several threats. One of those threats are adversarial attacks, which attempt to induce the trained models to produce erroneous outputs by subtly altering their inputs [21]. Many machine learning methods have been proven to be vulnerable to these type of attacks [13,27], ranging from Deep Neural Networks [25] to SVM (Support Vector Machine) models [2]. In addition, many different applications have been targeted by these adversarial attacks. In the automatic speech recognition field, speech-to-text transcription systems have been fooled to transcribe any desired target phrase by adding small perturbations [4]. In Optical Character Recognition, systems can be induced by adding subtle variations pretending to be watermark or printing defects, thus remaining hidden from human eyes [5]. Autonomous Vehicles have also been targeted by adversarial attacks, specially by misleading traffic sign classification systems in real vehicles [23]. Other AI-based applications targeted by adversarial attacks include face recognition systems [15], object detectors [6] and autonomous robotic systems [1].

All these evidences reinforce the need for holding AI systems accountable.

3   Accountability of a Predictive Model for a Real-World Poultry Chain

Maintaining the health and welfare status of animals at optimal levels has traditionally been one of the main concern of farmers, and, more recently, of consumers [18]. Therefore, it is necessary to ensure the comfort of livestock, from

---

[3] https://spectrum.ieee.org/tech-talk/computing/software/do-you-have-the-right-complexion-for-facial-recognition.

their breeding in farms until their arrival to slaughterhouses. The monitoring of these comfort parameters throughout the whole production chain may not only contribute to determining the quality of each phase, but also to supporting the implementation of timely actions towards avoiding and solving potentially harmful situations for animals. In the IoF2020 H2020 project[4], the PCM (Poultry Chain Management) platform was developed to collect data throughout the different phases of the whole poultry production chain [10]. Then, the tool named PUMA (PoUltry Management Advisor) exploits this data for the holistic improvement of the production chain.

PUMA is an AI system inspired by the inherent requirements for improvement of the whole poultry production chain. Namely, it is a Decision Support System for poultry chain managers which is based on analytic models to extract knowledge from the data collected by the PCM platform and suggest timely corrective actions. The machine learning algorithm used is the Classification and Regression Tree (CART), which is a supervised learning method that uses a tree structure to go from features of an item (represented as branches) to conclusions about the item's final value (represented as leaves). The CART algorithm is implemented using R's Recursive Partitioning And Regression Tree (RPART) package[5]. The functionality of PUMA which this article focuses is the prediction of the meat quality of a given flock once such flock arrives at the slaughterhouse. The meat quality may take two categorical values depending on the quality of the final product: A if the majority of the final meat is of a high-level, and B otherwise.

The predictive model which PUMA is based on, is a white-box type of algorithm, but this fact does not make the whole AI system trustworthy. Under normal circumstances, forecasting models' performance degrade over time due to a change in the environment that violates model assumptions [30]. This fact is known as concept drift and the most common way to deal with this performance degradation is the retraining of the model. Therefore, as more data is available, PUMA automatically retrains such predictive model. Once the retraining process is executed, the resulting predictive model is deployed and replaces the previous one. Consequently, different versions of the model may be used to make the predictions of different flocks, as it can be seen in Fig. 1. Therefore, there is no accountability, that is, it is not possible to know which predictive model was responsible for predicting the meat quality of a given flock. Even more, as the old predictive model is replaced by the newest one, there is no way to keep track where the meat quality predictions come from, that is, their underlying rationale. As a matter of fact, this is something that increases the mistrust of poultry chain managers in the AI system, hindering its adoption.

In this article, the lack of PUMA's accountability is addressed using the Semantic Technologies. This is expected to lower this AI system's adoption barriers.

---

[4] https://www.iof2020.eu.

[5] https://www.rdocumentation.org/packages/rpart/versions/4.1-15.

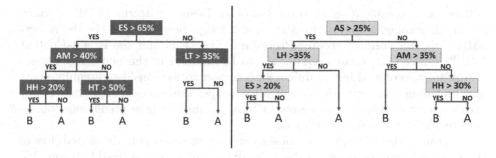

Fig. 1. The graphic representation of two different predictive models based on decision trees. (ES = Emergency Situation; AM = Abrupt Movements; HH = High Humidity; HT = High Temperature; LT = Low Temperature; AS = Alert Situation, LH = Low Humidity)

3.1 Semantic Technologies for Accountability

Semantic Technologies enable the management of data semantics, data interrelationships and knowledge representation among others. An important element of these technologies are ontologies, which appear as a way to describe and represent the concepts and relationships of a certain domain, and can be defined as "a formal, explicit specification of a shared conceptualization" [24]. Linking or mapping all the relevant data involved to appropriate ontological terms, allows structuring it and representing formal types, relations, properties and restrictions that hold among them. In the context of this article, ontologies contribute to formally represent the predicted meat quality of a given flock as well as the process that lead to such prediction. In combination with ontology-driven data access that enables poultry chain managers discovering the rationale behind those predictions, this is expected to make the PUMA AI system accountable.

After considering different ontologies and resources available in catalogues such as LOV[6] (Linked Open Vocabularies) [29], the PFEEPSA (Poultry Farm Energy Efficiency Prediction Semantic Assistant) ontology[7] was selected to represent the relevant elements and processes of the problem at hand [9]. This ontology was developed as part of the IoF2020 project with the aim of capturing all the necessary knowledge to support data analysts in the development of a system that warns farmers about potential future situations which may be uncomfortable or even harmful for the animals. Although not being specifically designed for the challenge tackled in this article, the PFEEPSA ontology can also be used to satisfy such challenge's requirements. The details of how the PFEEPSA provides assistance to data analysts are out of scope of this article.

The PFEEPSA ontology's development process was based on the well-known NeOn Methodology [26] and with views to being compliant with the FAIR (Findable, Accessible, Interoperable and Reusable) principles [31]. Its core is

---

[6] https://lov.linkeddata.es.
[7] https://w3id.org/pfeepsa.

defined as a combination of three Ontology Design Patterns (ODPs), which are small ontologies that address recurrent design problems [12,17]: the AffectedBy[8], the Execution-Executor-Procedure (EEP[9]) [8] and the Result-Context (RC[10]) ODPs. These three ODPs try to be minimal in the number of classes and properties offered but complete with respect to the considered requirements and including ontology axioms that allow proper inferences. Furthermore, they provide a set of concepts to represent basic scenarios where predictions, observations and actuations are involved.

On top of these ODPs, a set of six ontology modules were developed: five of them specialising knowledge in the scope of the stub classes defined in the ODPs, and one of them containing relevant expert knowledge in the domain at hand. More specifically, these ontology modules are FoI4PFEEPSA[11] for representing building, building spaces and animal husbandry equipment; Q4PFEEPSA[12] for representing qualities of these spaces; EXR4PFEEPSA[13] for representing executors such as sensors and actuators that may be installed in farms; P4EEPSA[14] for representing specific plans or methods; and EXN4PFEEPSA[15] for representing executions such as observations, actuations and predictions. The sixth ontology module EK4PFEEPSA[16] does not specialise any stub class and it is designed to contain expert knowledge representing different types of spaces within farms and the variables affecting their indoor conditions. The adequate integration of these six modules forms the PFEEPSA ontology which is shown in Fig. 2.

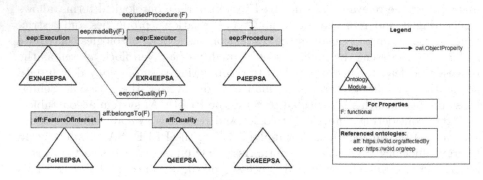

Fig. 2. The PFEEPSA ontology.

---

[8] https://w3id.org/affectedBy.
[9] https://w3id.org/eep.
[10] https://w3id.org/rc.
[11] https://w3id.org/pfeepsa/foi4pfeepsa.
[12] https://w3id.org/pfeepsa/q4pfeepsa.
[13] https://w3id.org/pfeepsa/exr4pfeepsa.
[14] https://w3id.org/eepsa/p4eepsa.
[15] https://w3id.org/pfeepsa/exn4pfeepsa.
[16] https://w3id.org/pfeepsa/ek4pfeepsa.

It is worth mentioning that, since the PFEEPSA ontology is aimed to be reusable and applicable for similar problems in other domains, fostering its usability has been a prime requisite. It has a careful documentation, adequate metadata and it is aligned with related domain ontologies like AGROVOC[17]. Furthermore, it is published in public catalogues like LOV and LOV4IoT (within the Agriculture section).

3.2 An Implementation in a Real-World Use Case

In order to showcase the use of Semantic Technologies for making PUMA accountable, a real-world poultry chain production scenario is considered. In this scenario, a poultry flock of 33,000 animals raised in a farm on 2019-04-30 is involved. On 2019-07-01, a group of 5,000 poultry of this flock were transported to the slaughterhouse. The AI system PUMA predicted that the meat quality of such group of 5,000 poultry was A (i.e. high-quality).

In order to make PUMA accountable, a Java service has been developed. First of all, this service semantically annotates the relevant elements and processes involved in this scenario using the appropriate PFEEPSA ontology terms. This semantic annotation is performed with the JENA framework[18], and the resulting triples are stored in a RDF Store, namely in a Virtuoso Open Source version 07.20.3217 Server[19]. As it was mentioned before, the two main elements that are semantically annotated are PUMA's prediction (e.g. a meat quality of value A) and the predictive model that led to such a prediction (e.g. a model based on a decision tree). A fragment of the semantic representation of the prediction for the flock in the presented scenario is as follows.

```
:prediction_3579  rdf:type  eep:Execution ;
    rc:hasGenerationTime  "2020−05−04T11:00:00"
        ^^xsd:dateTimeStamp ;
    rc:hasResult  :meatQualityA ;
    eep:madeBy  :system_PUMA ;
    eep:usedProcedure  :model_CART_A4J09 ;
    eep:onQuality  :flock_3579_MeatQuality .

:system_PUMA  rdf:type  eep:Executor .
:model_CART_A4J09  rdf:type  eep:Procedure .

:flock_3579_MeatQuality  rdf:type  aff:Quality ;
    aff:belongsTo  :flock_3579 .

:flock_3579  rdf:type  aff:FeatureOfInterest ;
    dc:identifier  "3579"^^xsd:String .
```

---

[17] http://aims.fao.org/en/agrovoc.
[18] http://jena.apache.org/.
[19] https://virtuoso.openlinksw.com/.

The other element that needs to be represented in order to make PUMA accountable is the predictive model that lead to the prediction of the flock's meat quality. In this case, the predictive model is based on a white-box algorithms from which a data analyst may infer which are the influencing variables and which is the criteria used to reach the final prediction. The underlying functioning of the predictive model is obtained from the R environment with the *rpart.rules* function[20], which retrieves the predictive model as a set of rules. For example, the following rules mean that when the value of variable ES (corresponding to 'Emergency Situation' state occurring during the transport phase) was lower than 65%, the meat quality was predicted to be A, and B otherwise[21].

```
A [1.00  0.00] when ES < 65
B [0.00  1.00] when ES >= 65
```

However, poultry chain managers' lack of expertise in predictive analytics definitely hinder their ability to reach the predictive model's underlying functioning and rules, therefore, they have no straightforward way to understand the process that lead to the final meat quality prediction. Therefore, first of all these rules are translated to natural language with a Java-based service. The previous two mentioned could be translated as follows:

```
A MEAT QUALITY is obtained when
    EMERGENCY SITUATION DURING TRANSPORT PHASE occurs
    LESS THAN 65% of the total time.
B MEAT QUALITY is obtained when
    EMERGENCY SITUATION DURING TRANSPORT PHASE occurs
    MORE THAN OR EQUAL TO 65% of the total time.
```

After transforming the corresponding rules in the form of natural language, which are far more intuitive for poultry chain managers, they are semantically annotated along with the *p4pfeepsa : hasRule* data property. This semantic annotation is performed with the JENA framework. A fragment of the semantic representation of the prediction for the flock in the presented scenario is as follows:

```
:model_CART_A4J09  rdf:type  eep:Procedure;
    p4pfeepsa:hasRule "A MEAT QUALITY is obtained when
        EMERGENCY SITUATION DURING TRANSPORT PHASE occurs
        LESS THAN 65% of the total time."^^xsd:String;
    p4pfeepsa:hasRule "B MEAT QUALITY is obtained when
        EMERGENCY SITUATION DURING TRANSPORT PHASE occurs
        MORE THAN OR EQUAL TO 65% of the total time."
        ^^xsd:String.
```

Likewise the triples of the prediction, this information is stored in the Virtuoso triplestore, where it remains accessible via SPARQL queries. Therefore,

---

[20] https://www.rdocumentation.org/packages/rpart.plot/versions/3.0.8/topics/rpart.rules.

[21] These rules are a simplification of an actual predictive model.

a user can retrieve the value of the prediction made to a given flock, and it may know the rationale of such a prediction, by looking at the rules that guide the predictive model. For example, if a user wants to know which was the predicted meat quality for a given poultry flock, the following SPARQL query can be executed:

```
SELECT ?meatQuality
WHERE {
    ?prediction eep:onQuality ?flockMeatQuality;
        rc:hasResult ?meatQuality.
    ?flockMeatQuality aff:belongsTo ?flock.
    ?flock dc:identifier $FLOCK_ID
}
```

Additionally, if a user wants to know the rules that led to the prediction of a given flock, this SPARQL query can be executed:

```
SELECT ?rule
WHERE {
    ?prediction eep:onQUality ?flockMeatQuality;
        eep:usedProcedure ?predictiveModel.
    ?predictiveModel p4pfeepsa:hasRule ?rule.
    ?flockMeatQuality aff:belongsTo ?flock.
    ?flock dc:identifier $FLOCK_ID
}
```

In both cases, the wild card $FLOCK_ID needs be replaced with the identifier of the flock the user is targeting.

Poultry chain managers, which are the ones who may check the accountability of a predictive model, may not necessarily be familiar with the Semantic Technologies. Therefore, the execution of the proposed SPARQL queries should be managed by a graphic interface that isolates users from the underlying language.

4 Discussion and Future Work

In this article, the accountability of an AI system for the management of poultry chains has been addressed. Using the Semantic Technologies not only is it possible to know which predictive model was responsible for predicting the meat quality of a given flock, but also, to understand where such predictions come from, that is, which is their underlying rationale.

Although some contributions are made in this article, it should be considered as a first step and therefore, many aspects need to be further researched.

Currently the rules that conform the decision tree are represented in the form of strings by means of the *p4pfeepsa : hasRule* data property. These rules' underlying semantics could be exploited if, instead of strings, they were represented with appropriate ontological concepts. Therefore, the PFEEPSA should be extended to contribute in this regard.

Furthermore, the translation from the original rules (which the predictive model is based on) to the natural language could be enhanced. As a matter of fact, this is a future direction where NLP (Natural Language Processing) techniques could contribute to ease poultry chain managers' understanding, thus lowering the PUMA AI system's adoption.

Additionally, the current approach duplicates the storage of the PUMA predictions. As a matter of fact, they are stored in the relational database where PUMA stores all its predictions, and the Virtuoso triplestore. This duplication of data should be studied and solved.

Acknowledgements. This research was partly supported by the Internet of Food 2020 (IOF2020) project which has received funding from the European Union Horizon 2020 research and innovation programme under grant agreement number 731884, as well as the project 3KIA (KK-2020/00049), funded by the SPRI-Basque Government through the ELKARTEK program.

References

1. Bezzo, N., Weimer, J., Pajic, M., Sokolsky, O., Pappas, G.J., Lee, I.: Attack resilient state estimation for autonomous robotic systems. In: 2014 IEEE/RSJ International Conference on Intelligent Robots and Systems, pp. 3692–3698. IEEE (2014)
2. Biggio, B., Nelson, B., Laskov, P.: Poisoning attacks against support vector machines. arXiv preprint arXiv:1206.6389 (2012)
3. Bostrom, N.: Ethical Issues in advanced artificial intelligence. In: Science Fiction and Philosophy: From Time Travel to Super Intelligence, pp. 277–284 (2003)
4. Carlini, N., and Wagner, D. Audio adversarial examples: targeted attacks on speech-to-text. In 2018 IEEE Security and Privacy Workshops (SPW), pp. 1–7. IEEE (2018)
5. Chen, L., Xu, W.: Attacking optical character recognition (OCR) systems with adversarial watermarks. arXiv preprint arXiv:2002.03095 (2020)
6. Chen, S.-T., Cornelius, C., Martin, J., Chau, D.H.P.: ShapeShifter: robust physical adversarial attack on faster R-CNN object detector. In: Berlingerio, M., Bonchi, F., Gärtner, T., Hurley, N., Ifrim, G. (eds.) ECML PKDD 2018. LNCS (LNAI), vol. 11051, pp. 52–68. Springer, Cham (2019). https://doi.org/10.1007/978-3-030-10925-7_4
7. Davis, S.E., Lasko, T.A., Chen, G., Siew, E.D., Matheny, M.E.: Calibration drift in regression and machine learning models for acute kidney injury. J. Am. Med. Inform. Assoc. **24**(6), 1052–1061 (2017)
8. Esnaola-Gonzalez, I., Bermúdez, J., Fernandez, I., and Arnaiz, A.: Two ontology design patterns toward energy efficiency in buildings. In: Proceedings of the 9th Workshop on Ontology Design and Patterns (WOP 2018) co-located with 17th International Semantic Web Conference (ISWC 2018) (2018), vol. 2195, CEUR, pp. 14–28
9. Esnaola-Gonzalez, I., et al.: Towards animal welfare in poultry farms through semantic technologies. In: IoT Connected World & Semantic Interoperability Workshop (IoT-CWSI) 2019 (2019)

10. Esnaola-Gonzalez, I., Gómez-Omella, M., Ferreiro, S., Fernandez, I., Lázaro, I., García, E.: An IoT platform towards the enhancement of poultry production chains. Sensors **20**(6), 1549 (2020)
11. Fox, J.: The uncertain relationship between transparency and accountability. Dev. Pract. **17**(4–5), 663–671 (2007)
12. Gangemi, A., Presutti, V.: Ontology design patterns. In: Staab, S., Studer, R. (eds.) Handbook on Ontologies. IHIS, pp. 221–243. Springer, Heidelberg (2009). https://doi.org/10.1007/978-3-540-92673-3_10
13. Goodfellow, I.J., Shlens, J., Szegedy, C.: Explaining and harnessing adversarial examples. arXiv preprint arXiv:1412.6572 (2014)
14. Goodman, B., Flaxman, S.: European union regulations on algorithmic decision-making and a "right to explanation". AI Mag. **38**(3), 50–57 (2017)
15. Goswami, G., Ratha, N., Agarwal, A., Singh, R., Vatsa, M.: Unravelling robustness of deep learning based face recognition against adversarial attacks. In: Thirty-Second AAAI Conference on Artificial Intelligence (2018)
16. Gunning, D.: Explainable artificial intelligence (XAI). Defense Advanced Research Projects Agency (DARPA), nd Web 2 (2017)
17. Hitzler, P., Gangemi, A., Janowicz, K.: Ontology Engineering with Ontology Design Patterns: Foundations and Applications, vol. 25. IOS Press (2016)
18. Ingenbleek, P.T., Immink, V.M.: Consumer decision-making for animal-friendly products: synthesis and implications. Anim Welf. **20**(1), 11–19 (2011)
19. Kehl, D.L., Guo, P., Kessler, S.A.: Algorithms in the Criminal Justice System: Assessing the Use of Risk Assessments in Sentencing. Responsive Communities Initiative, Berkman Klein Center for Internet & Society, Harvard Law School (2017)
20. Kroll, J.A., Barocas, S., Felten, E.W., Reidenberg, J.R., Robinson, D.G., Yu, H.: Accountable algorithms. U. Pa. L. Rev. **165**, 633–705 (2016)
21. Papernot, N., McDaniel, P., Goodfellow, I.: Transferability in machine learning: from phenomena to black-box attacks using adversarial samples. arXiv:1605.07277 (2016)
22. Quiñonero-Candela, J., Sugiyama, M., Schwaighofer, A., Lawrence, N.D.: When training and test sets are different: characterizing learning transfer. In: Dataset Shift in Machine Learning, pp. 3–28. MIT Press, (2009)
23. Sitawarin, C., Bhagoji, A. N., Mosenia, A., Mittal, P., Chiang, M.: Rogue signs: deceiving traffic sign recognition with malicious ads and logos. arXiv preprint arXiv:1801.02780 (2018)
24. Studer, R., Benjamins, V.R., Fensel, D.: Knowledge engineering: principles and methods. Data Knowl. Eng. **25**(1), 161–198 (1998)
25. Su, J., Vargas, D.V., Sakurai, K.: One pixel attack for fooling deep neural networks. IEEE Trans. Evol. Comput. **23**(5), 828–841 (2019)
26. Suárez-Figueroa, M.C., Gómez-Pérez, A., Fernández-López, M.: The NeOn methodology for ontology engineering. In: Suárez-Figueroa, M.C., Gómez-Pérez, A., Motta, E., Gangemi, A. (eds.) Ontology Engineering in a Networked World, pp. 9–34. Springer, Heidelberg (2012). https://doi.org/10.1007/978-3-642-24794-1_2
27. Szegedy, C., et al.: Intriguing properties of neural networks. arXiv preprint arXiv:1312.6199 (2013)
28. Tom Yeh, M., et al.: Designing a moral compass for the future of computer vision using speculative analysis. In: Proceedings of the IEEE Conference on Computer Vision and Pattern Recognition Workshops, pp. 64–73 (2017)

29. Vandenbussche, P.-Y., Atemezing, G.A., Poveda-Villalón, M., Vatant, B.: Linked open vocabularies (LOV): a gateway to reusable semantic vocabularies on the web. Semant. Web **8**(3), 437–452 (2017)

30. Widmer, G., Kubat, M.: Learning in the presence of concept drift and hidden contexts. Mach. Learn. **23**(1), 69–101 (1996)

31. Wilkinson, M.D., et al.: The fair guiding principles for scientific data management and stewardship. Sci. Data **3** (2016)

32. Zhu, J., Liapis, A., Risi, S., Bidarra, R., Youngblood, G.M.: Explainable AI for designers: a human-centered perspective on mixed-initiative co-creation. In: 2018 IEEE Conference on Computational Intelligence and Games (CIG), pp. 1–8. IEEE (2018)

Short-Term Forecasting Methodology for Energy Demand in Residential Buildings and the Impact of the COVID-19 Pandemic on Forecasts

Meritxell Gomez-Omella[1,2]([✉]) [iD], Iker Esnaola-Gonzalez[1] [iD],
and Susana Ferreiro[1]

[1] TEKNIKER, Basque Research and Technology Alliance (BRTA),
Iñaki Goenaga 5, 20600 Eibar, Spain
{meritxell.gomez,iker.esnaola,susana.ferreiro}@tekniker.es
[2] Faculty of Informatics, University on the Basque Country (UPV/EHU),
Paseo Manuel Lardizabal, 1, 20018 Donostia-San Sebastian, Spain

Abstract. Demand Response (DR) can contribute towards the energy efficiency in buildings, which is one of the major concerns among governments, scientists, and researchers. DR programs rely on the anticipation to electric demand peaks, for which the development of short-term electric demand forecasting models may be valuable. This article presents two different variants of the KNN algorithm to predict short-term electric demand for apartments located in Madrid (Spain). On the one hand, the use of an approach based on the estimation of a Machine Learning model (KNFTS) is studied. In this method, time-related and date-related features are used as exploratory variables. On the other hand, a method based on the recognition of similar patterns in the time series (KNPTS) is analysed. The Edit Distance for Real Sequences (EDR), Root Mean Square Error (RMSE) and Dynamic Time Warping (DTW) are used to measure the accuracy of forecasts for both approaches. The experiments demonstrate that the KNPTS has a higher accuracy over the KNFTS when predicting the short-term electric demand. Furthermore, the models' adaptation to unusual situations is showcased in this article. The impact of the COVID-19 pandemic derived in a worldwide electric demand drop due to the lockdown and other confinement measures, and the retraining method proposed for the KNPTS model has been demonstrated to be valid, as it improves the forecasting accuracy.

Keywords: Time series forecasting · K-nearest neighbours · COVID-19 · Demand Response

1 Introduction

The energy consumed by buildings has dramatically increased over the last decade due to diverse causes including the population growth, an increase in

© Springer Nature Switzerland AG 2020
M. Bramer and R. Ellis (Eds.): SGAI-AI 2020, LNAI 12498, pp. 227–240, 2020.
https://doi.org/10.1007/978-3-030-63799-6_18

the time spent indoors or the rise of demand for building functions and indoor quality [1]. As a matter of fact, ensuring the energy efficiency of the built environment is one of the major concerns among governments, scientists and researchers since the building sector consumes more than 35% of the global energy [2].

Apart from the total energy consumed, another challenge is the management of peak energy demands. The energy during these periods is supplied by the Peaking Power Plants, which are carbon-intense generation plants with a negative impact on energy grid capital, operational cost and environmental aspects. In this regard, DSM (Demand Side Management) actions such as load curtailment (i.e. a reduction of electricity usage) or reallocation (i.e. a shift of energy usage to other off-peak periods) have the potential to minimise the undesirable peak periods, and consequently, to reduce the use of the Peaking Power Plants. In combination with DSM activities, the Demand Response (DR) can influence customer's use of electricity in ways that will produce desired changes in the utility's load shape, that is, changes in the time pattern and magnitude of a utility's load [3]. DR can be understood as the set of technologies or programs that concentrate on shifting energy use [4], and although traditionally the DR programs' implementation has been limited to industrial buildings due to their high energy demand, residential buildings are specially promising due to their potential to reduce demand peaks [5]. The RESPOND H2020 project[1] aims to bring DR programs to the residential sector in order to reduce these undesirable energy demand peaks. To do so, it is necessary to identify these demand peaks ahead of time. This is why, the RESPOND Energy Demand Forecasting service is developed, which allows the forecasting of electric demand for houses participating in the project.

In this article, the development of the forecasting models that are the main base of the Energy Demand Forecasting service is addressed. And subsequently, the degradation of the models during the COVID-19 pandemic in Spain is analysed and an approach to mitigate this situation is proposed.

The rest of the article is organised as follows. Section 2 presents two different methods to multi-step ahead forecasting in time series. All the steps are described including the forecasting strategies, the forecasting methods, and the performance measurement metrics. Next, Sect. 3 describes the context in which this study is carried out. The data set is presented, and the implementation and deployment of the methodology are explained. As a result, in Sect. 4 the results are discussed, and it is shown how to forecast electric demand during the COVID-19 crisis. Finally, Sect. 5 introduces the conclusions and future work.

2   Short-Term Forecasting Methodology for Time Series

A Time Series is a collection of values $Y = \{y_t\}$ obtained over time, often at regular intervals, where $t = 1, ..., T$ represents the time elapsed. A discrete time series is the one that the index set contains discrete points of time. The

---

[1] http://project-respond.eu/.

consecutive observations can usually be recorded at equally spaced time intervals such as hourly, daily, weekly, monthly or yearly time separations [6].

The interest in the analysis of time series lies in the estimation of the behaviour of the historical data to forecast future values. Time series forecasting is a method to estimate future values in a temporal sequence. Given a univariate time series $\{y_t\}$ where $t = 1, .., T$ the interest of this work is focused on the forecasting of future values $\{y_{T+h}\}$ with $h \in \mathbb{N}$. A single-step ahead forecasting is made when $h = 1$ and only the next value in the series is estimated. Multi-step ahead forecasting is used to forecast more than one value, that is $h > 1$.

2.1 Strategies for Multi-Step Ahead Time Series Forecasting

A multi-step ahead time series forecasting consists of estimating the next h values $\{y_{T+1}, ..., y_{T+h}\}$ using the previous values $\{y_1, ..., y_T\}$. In order to forecast more than one value $h > 1$ in time series using Machine Learning (ML) algorithms, five strategies can be chosen called *Recursive, Direct, DirRec, MIMO* and *DIRMO* strategies. This work is focused on *Multi-Input Multi-Output (MIMO) Strategy*. The remaining strategies are left out of this section and a detailed explanation of them can be found at [7].

The *MIMO* strategy executes one prediction after learning a single multiple-output model. It consists of a target vector of length equal to the number of points to be forecast h and a feature vector containing the previous values. The same model is used for all the horizons so the computational time needed is less than necessary for strategies that include the *Direct* approach (*Direct, DirRec* and *DIRMO* strategies). In addition, the accumulation of errors that is obtained using the recursive strategy does not happen. The forecasts are returned in one-step by a multiple-output model.

2.2 KNN Algorithm

The methodology presented in this work is based on the KNN algorithm, which is a non-parametric method used for classification and regression problems in ML. The general idea is to examine the distance between the independent variables, then choose the K nearest observations and finally use a combination of their response values to estimate the next value of the output variable. In order to forecast future values using a ML algorithm, some decisions have to be made including the multi-step ahead strategy and the selection of input variables. Particularly for the KNN, other decisions are made: the distance function to evaluate the similarity between instances, the value of K nearest neighbours and the way output points are combined [8]. Different distance functions can be used to define the similarity between instances, although the most commonly used is the Euclidean distance [9]. A cross-validation can be implemented to evaluate different values of K, looking for the one that minimises the error. This error is a metric chosen to measure the difference between the estimated and actual values. Once the best parameter K is chosen, the future value is estimated as a combination of the target values of each K nearest neighbours. The most common combination is the arithmetic mean, which assigns the same weight to all values. Alternatively, the distance weighted average can be used, where some data points contribute more than others to the estimated value. Assuming that d_k is the distance between the pattern and the k-th nearest neighbour, $\omega_k = 1/d_k^2$ is defined to be its weight. In order that the neighbors' weights add up to 1, they are each divided by the sum of all the weights.

In this article, two ways of making time series forecasting based on the KNN algorithm are proposed. On the one hand, an approach based on the estimation of a ML model where the features extracted from the time variable are used as exploratory variables. On the other hand, a method based on the recognition of similar patterns in the time series.

K-Nearest Features for Time Series (KNFTS). An important step prior to training any ML model is the choice of n exploratory variables of T values X_t^i, $i = 1, ..., n$, $t = 1, ..., T$. These variables are introduced as input into the model and serve as an aid to estimate the value of the response variable Y. Input variables are also called features in the field of ML, and feature engineering is the task of creating and using them to improve the performance of ML algorithms [10].

Exploratory variables X_t^i are extracted from the time variable when the data is a univariate time series. So the input variables X_t^i are date and time related features. Below is a description of some features X_t^i than are used to calculate the distances between observations.

- Date-related features are numerical values having information about day, month and year.
- Time-related features are extracted for the time stamp and are numerical variables like hour, minute and second.
- Weekday is a variable that takes values between 0 and 6 providing information of the day of the week from Monday to Sunday.

The nearest neighbours are obtained by comparing the Euclidean distance between X_t^i variables in each observation. Some of these variables have a cyclical meaning that is not reflected in the calculation of distances. For example, the Euclidean distance between January and December (represented by 0 and 11 respectively) is 11 but they are two consecutive months. To avoid this fact, a trigonometric transformation v is done in this kind of variables[2]. First, the periodicity of the variable is found (in this case $P = 12$). Then, the Eq. 1 is applied to each value X_t^i, $t = 1, ..., T$. Two variables are obtained from each of the transformations made (one from the sine and the other from the cosine).

$$v : [0, P] \longrightarrow [-1, 1]$$

$$X_t^i \rightarrow v(X_t^i) = \left(\sin\left(\frac{2\pi X_t^i}{P}\right), \cos\left(\frac{2\pi X_t^i}{P}\right) \right) \tag{1}$$

---

[2] https://www.avanwyk.com/encoding-cyclical-features-for-deep-learning/.

The Euclidean distance between $(X_{T+1}^1, ..., X_{T+1}^n)$ and $(X_t^1, ..., X_t^n)$, for all $t = 1, ..., T$ is calculated to choose the K nearest neighbours. The next value Y_{T+1} is obtained as a weighted combination of the target values of the K nearest neighbour.

$$Y_{T+1} = \frac{\sum_{k=1}^K \omega_k Y^k}{\sum_{k=1}^K \omega_k} \tag{2}$$

where Y^k is the value of the target variable corresponding on the k nearest neighbour. This argument applies to all h horizon values to be forecast. The general idea of this method is that in two similar moments of time in terms of date and time, the value of the response variable should be similar.

K-Nearest Patterns in Time Series (KNPTS). The nearest neighbours are defined as the most similar subsets of data in the time series using this KNN approach. Given the window size $m \in \mathbb{N}$, a reference pattern consisting of the last values of the output variable $(y_{T-m}, ..., y_T)$ is used in the training process. This pattern is compared with all the other subsets of length m in the series, that is, $Y^j = (y_j, ..., y_{j+m})$, for all $j = 1, ..., T - m - h$ by calculating the Euclidean distance. Therefore, it is determined that the K subsets with the lowest Euclidean distance are the K nearest neighbours [11].

Figure 1 represents an example of nearest-neighbour multiple-step forecasting using MIMO strategy. It represents a simple case in which $m = 5$ previous values are used to find the $K = 1$ nearest neighbour. Then, the most similar subset is used to forecast the $h = 3$ future values of the time series.

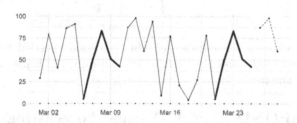

Fig. 1. Nearest-neighbour three-step-ahead forecasts. A window of length five is selected and one neighbour is used to estimate the next three values.

The next value Y_{T+1} is calculated by the weighted average of the next values of each k nearest neighbour.

$$Y_{T+1} = \frac{\sum_{k=1}^K \omega_k Y_{k+m+1}^k}{\sum_{k=1}^K \omega_k} \tag{3}$$

This argument applies to all h horizon values to be forecast. The general idea of this method is that, in two different periods of time with similar values, the following value should be similar as well.

2.3   Evaluation

In the context of this article, the following three metrics have been considered to assess the accuracy of the forecasting models, as they are representative for measure the similarity between time series: Root Mean Square Error (RMSE), Dynamic Time Warping (DTW) and Edit Distance for Real Sequences (EDR) [12].

(i) **Root Mean Square Error (RMSE)** The RMSE measures the error by calculating the difference between the current and predicted values and it has been widely used for the evaluation of the goodness of fit in regression models. The RMSE value is always non-negative and the lower the RMSE, the more similar the time series are.

(ii) **Dynamic Time Warping (DTW)** The DTW algorithm is used to compare the similarity or calculate the distance between two time series and minimises the effects of shifting and distortion in time [?]. A dynamic programming approach is used to align the series and allows to compare series of different length [13]. The lower the DTW value, the more similar the time series are.

(iii) **Edit Distance for Real Sequences** Edit Distance (ED) was initially used to calculate the similarity between two strings. It quantifies the basic edit operations (insert, delete and replace) needed to transform one string into the other. In order to define matching between numerical series, different adaptations are proposed in [14]. Given a positive threshold ϵ, the distance between two points is reduced to 0 or 1 as below.

$$d_\epsilon(\hat{y}_t, y_t) = \begin{cases} 0, & d(\hat{y}_t, y_t) \leq \epsilon \\ 1, & d(\hat{y}_t, y_t) > \epsilon \end{cases} \tag{4}$$

The EDR metric is the number of edit operations needed to transform a numerical series into an other, taking into account the Eq. 4. The lower the EDR value, the more similar the time series are.

3   The RESPOND Energy Demand Forecasting Service

The RESPOND project aims to bring DR programs to neighbourhoods across Europe, and in particular, to dispatch real-time optimal DR strategies to dwellers towards the achievement of demand peak reduction. RESPOND has developed an Artificial Intelligence (AI) system to detect potential energy conservation opportunities while ensuring the occupants' required comfort levels [15]. One of the components of this AI system is the RESPOND Energy Demand Forecasting service, which allows the short-term forecasting (i.e. hourly for the upcoming 24 h) of electric demand for the houses participating in the project. In total, over 40 houses are participating in the RESPOND project, including participants from Aarhus (Denmark), the Aran Islands (Ireland) and Madrid (Spain).

Unlike the regularity within commercial buildings, electric consumption in the residential sector may vary significantly from house to house. As a matter of fact, this high electricity usage variance derives from the users' lifestyle, occupancy behaviour, building characteristics and calendar information [16]. Figure 2 shows the differences in the data distributions in some apartments in Madrid.

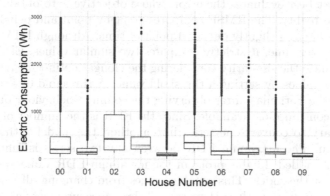

Fig. 2. The electric consumption data distribution in Madrid apartments.

3.1   The Methodology Implementation

In this section, the methodology explained in Sect. 2 is implemented. The rationale behind choosing the KNN algorithm over other methods is based on the results of a previous experimentation, which is out of scope of this article.

The strategy chosen for the multi-step ahead time series forecasting was *MIMO*, based on the comparison made in the article [7].

The *hour*, *day* and *month* are used as features for the KNFTS model training process. Four new features are created from the *hour* and *month* (called *sin.Hour*, *cos.Hour*, *sin.Month* and *cos.Month*), by calculating the sine and cosine (trigonometric transformations explained in the Sect. 2.2), to have more discriminatory power than in the original space. And apart from these, new features are added (*Season* and *Workingday*) taking into account the behaviour of electric consumption data. A snippet of this data can be seen in Table 1.

Table 1. A snippet of the electric consumption data set for a participant house.

Timestamp	EC	sin.Hour	cos.Hour	Day	sin.Month	cos.Month	Season	Weekday	Workingday
2019-10-10 15:00:00	114.8796	−0.7071	−0.7071	10	−0.8660	0.5000	Fall	Thursday	Yes
2019-10-10 16:00:00	156.0299	−0.8660	−0.5	10	−0.8660	0.5	Fall	Thursday	Yes
2019-10-10 17:00:00	350.0857	−0.9659	−0.2588	10	−0.8660	0.5	Fall	Thursday	Yes
...	...	...	...	...	...	...	...	...	...
2019-10-12 00:00:00	98.7279	0	1	12	−0.8660	0.5000	Fall	Saturday	No

In the training process, to calculate good estimates of the error rate of the models, a 10-fold cross validation is applied and repeated 5 times. For both methods, the K value is tested from 1 to 10 to find the optimal value. And finally, EDR, RMSE and DTW error measures are calculated. The EDR is considered the metric that best evaluates the error, whose objective is to obtain a forecast that adapts to reality. The RMSE compares point by point and penalises a prediction of a value at a slightly deviated point of time. Although DTW considers the deviation over time, it strictly compares two similar values. EDR, instead, allows to evaluate the similarity considering the elongation in time and the similarity of close values by setting a threshold value. A threshold of $\epsilon = 30$ Wh is stablished in the Formula 4 after observing the common behaviour of the series of electricity consumption available. Since the EDR is the number of edit operations necessary to convert one series into another, the model with the lowest EDR is chosen. The maximum EDR between any two series is infinity unless restrictions are added. In this problem the maximum EDR value is considered as the length of the series. This number comes from changing all values in one series to values from the other. However, all three measurements are calculated in this study. The model with the lower EDR is chosen as the one that provides the more accurate forecasts. If there is more than one model with the same EDR result, the DTW and RMSE values are compared. RMSE and DTW values are obtained from the calculation of distances between consumption values and are not useful to compare between houses since, as previously mentioned, each one presents a different variability in the data. For this reason, the scale on which it is measured is important. In order to compare more efficiently the values obtained from the different apartments, these two error measures are normalised by the average as follows.

$$NRMSE = \frac{RMSE}{\bar{y}} \qquad NDTW = \frac{DTW}{\bar{y}} \qquad (5)$$

where $\bar{y}$ is the average of the historical consumption $\{y_1, ..., y_T\}$.

3.2   The Service Deployment

Based on the proposed methodology, two models (based on KNFTS and KNPTS methods) has been developed for each of the 40 houses participating in RESPOND project. In total, 80 models that forecast the hourly electric consumption for the upcoming 24 h. These models have been developed in R programming language. The KNFTS models have been developed with the functions within the caret package[3]. However, the functions used to develop the KNPTS have been implemented by the authors for this work. As for the functions to evaluate the similarity between estimated and actual values in terms of DTW and EDR, they have been taken from the TSdist package [12].

The developed predictive models have been exported in the form of .rds files and deployed in an R Server, where they are currently automatically executed

---

[3] http://topepo.github.io/caret/index.html.

using periodical tasks executed by a *cron daemon* process. Furthermore, both the predictions made by the models and the actual values, subsequently obtained, are stored in a database for further exploitation (data visualisation and data analysis purposes).

4 Evaluation and Results Discussion

In this section, the accuracy of both forecasting methods proposed in Sect. 2 to estimate a day ahead forecast are evaluated and discussed. The results collected below are focused on the houses located in Madrid. Table 2 shows the average of the performance measures evaluated on ten different random days. The data prior to those dates is used to train the model and then, a 24 h ahead forecasting is done.

As explained above, the performance measure that provides more information in our case is the EDR. The value of the EDR is lower for the KNPTS rather than for the KNFTS method in all the houses, and the same happens with the NRMSE and NDTW for most of the houses.

Table 2. Comparative results of forecast accuracy with KNFTS and KNPTS

	EDR		NRMSE		NDTW	
	KNFTS	KNPTS	KNFTS	KNPTS	KNFTS	KNPTS
House 00	19.3	**18**	**0.8812**	1.0010	**12.4415**	15.0408
House 01	14.8	**14.3**	0.8772	**0.7343**	13.0310	**9.6848**
House 02	19	**17.6**	**0.6403**	0.6533	9.8858	**9.2594**
House 03	16.6	**14.4**	0.5109	**0.3383**	7.3718	**5.7123**
House 04	10.1	**9.1**	**0.5983**	0.5995	7.7291	**7.6235**
House 05	18.4	**17.1**	0.7383	**0.6793**	8.8291	**8.3404**
House 06	18.3	**15.6**	1.0956	**0.9926**	17.7200	**14.9810**
House 07	12.6	**12.4**	0.6840	**0.6762**	9.5653	**9.3508**
House 08	15.2	**13.5**	0.6915	**0.6643**	10.3706	**8.6867**
House 09	10.6	**8.5**	0.7408	**0.7057**	9.2065	**8.3519**

In House 02, the NRMSE value is 0.013 higher for the KNPTS. The average electric consumption in that house is 634.92 Wh, which means that a mean deviation of 8.25 Wh happens in each of the predicted points. This value is not considered high enough to conclude that the forecaster's accuracy overall is worse in the KNPTS compared with the KNFTS. Furthermore, the RMSE is a performance measurement that compares a point by point performance, that is, it compares each real consumption value with its corresponding forecast at the same instant. For this reasons, the KNPTS method is identified as better approach considering the best results in EDR and NDTW. A similar situation happened in House 04, where the KNPTS has a higher NRMSE, but it is too low (0.001, which means a deviation of 0.13 Wh in each point) to consider that it has a worse performance than the KNFTS.

As for House 00, the NRMSE and NDTW values are higher in the KNPTS compared with the KNFTS. The variation of 0.1198 in the NRMSE represents a mean deviation of 47.58 Wh. The difference in NDTW is 2.5993, equivalent to 1032 Wh of total distance between forecasts in 24 h (43.02 Wh per hour on average). The average of the electric consumption in House 00 is 397.20 Wh and the standard deviation is 507.8 Wh so, the mentioned mean deviation is not considered high enough either.

In the rest of the houses, the KNPTS obtains a considerable improvement for the three performance measures. In particular, House 06 gets an average improvement of 2.7 edition changes in EDR. Given two series of 24 points each, the maximum value for the EDR metric is 24 (the number of values to be forecast). An improvement of 2.7 changes represents an increase in EDR of 11.25%. Figure 3a shows a 24 h ahead forecast in House 06 and Fig. 3b shows the comparison of the three error measures for this forecast. This evaluation demonstrated

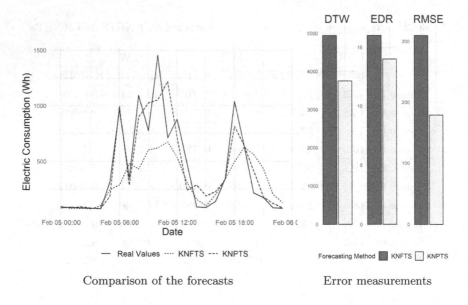

Comparison of the forecasts   Error measurements

Fig. 3. Evaluation of one-day ahead forecasting with KNFTS and KNPTS.

that the forecasts and the real values are more similar in the results obtained with the KNPTS method. This suggests that KNPTS method is more accurate to forecast the electrical consumption of the Madrid apartments. Then, KNPTS method is implemented for the future models of the RESPOND Electric Demand Forecasting service.

4.1   COVID-19 Impact on Electric Demand Forecasting

According to the International Energy Agency's latest report[4], the impact of the COVID-19 pandemic derived in a worldwide electric demand drop due to the lockdowns and other confinement measures, although this demand is steadily recovering now that measures are softened. In the case of Spain, according to Cornwall Insight during the first four weeks of the state of alarm, power demand fell by 16.7%. However, this fall is attributable mainly to industry and commerce, since according to the Spanish Consumer and User Organisation, there has been an increase of 28% in household bills in Spain[5].

The average daily consumption in the Madrid apartments participating in RESPOND has stabilised around a lower value since the beginning of the lockdown. Thus, as of March 14, the electric consumption data distribution changed and the data variability has decreased. This fact is evidence of the change in the distribution of the data in such a way that the electric consumption among days is more similar, without ceasing to appear the characteristic peaks of electricity consumption. This is definitely an indicator that the obligation to remain confined due to the state of alarm has altered users' daily habits. Therefore, forecasting models trained on normal human behaviour data are finding that the normality has changed and they are no longer working as expected. And the RESPOND Energy Demand Forecasting service is no exception.

Under normal conditions, forecasting models' performance degrade over time due to a change in the environment that violates the models assumptions [17]. This fact is known as concept drift, and the most common method to deal with it is the retraining of the model, which consists in re-running the process that generated the previous model on the new set of data available. However, the unusual change of daily habits derived by the COVID-19 pandemic, the typical retraining strategies are not sufficient.

The correlations between the features and their distributions are commonly examined to identify the concept drift. In the case of the KNPTS, there are no features, but the change in the accuracy of the predictions is given by a change in the output variable. Furthermore, the reason for this change is known (i.e. the confinement measures) and therefore, action can be taken to control it. The data preprocessing task prior to the training of any forecasting model includes the selection of the appropriate data and features to improve the precision of the estimation. Understanding the importance of the distance between instances in the KNN methodology, a necessary step before training the forecast model for estimating electric consumption during the lockdown days, is the selection of the data generated during the lockdown. This way, the model is more effective since it finds the nearest neighbours within a data set where the variability is less. This restriction prevents estimates to be based on the data from the previous year, as it is known that the behaviour of the electric consumption is not the same.

---

[4] https://www.iea.org/reports/covid-19-impact-on-electricity.
[5] https://www.ocu.org/vivienda-y-energia/gas-luz/noticias/aumento-consumo-electrico-confinamiento.

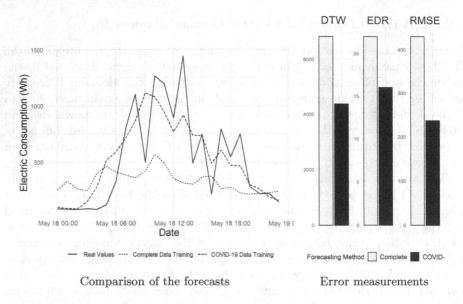

Comparison of the forecasts   Error measurements

Fig. 4. Improving the accuracy of electric consumption forecasting in the COVID crisis.

The model trained using only lockdown data gives better results than using all the data available. Figure 4 shows an example of the comparison of the one-day ahead forecast using the complete historical data available and using only the lockdown data after March 14. These results were obtained for House 06.

An improvement of the estimation of the peak values is observed when only the lockdown data is used. The model trained with complete data gets a EDR value of 22, while the model developed for estimating the electric consumption of days prior to March 14 got a EDR value of 16. In order to reduce the EDR value for forecasts after March 14, the model is trained only with lockdown data. This new model gets an EDR value of 16, which represents an improvement of 25%. A decrease of 193.53 Wh per hour on average in RMSE and a decrease of 2466.38 Wh in total distance between both forecasts in DTW (102.77 Wh per hour) can be observed.

The improvement derived from the retraining approach followed for the COVID-19 can be observed in all the houses in Madrid during the lockdown period. The average EDR reduction is 6.67%.

5   Conclusions

In order to dispatch real-time optimal DR strategies, a reliable and accurate forecast of short-term electricity demand is needed. In this work, two different methods based on the KNN algorithm have been developed and validated: the KNFTS based on the similarity of time-related and date-related features, and the KNPTS based on the similarity of the sequences of the response variable. Both approaches are identified as adequate for the problem of forecasting electricity consumption after previous experimentation with other ML algorithms (beyond the scope of this article). The extraction of date and time-related features and the use of past values of the output variable to forecast future consumption values was satisfactory. It suitably considers the relation between instances in the time series.

The accuracy of the forecast has been tested in 10 different apartments located in Madrid, and their performance has been evaluated based on the EDR, NDTW and NRMSE error measures. The EDR value has been the most effective measure to assess the accuracy of multi-step ahead forecasting in time series, although it is not commonly used in previous works. It provides a more realistic measure of the number of changes to be made and therefore, it does not penalize error in time. The results have showed that the predictions are more accurate using KNPTS model. The EDR metric gets lower values for all the cases. The average obtained is 1.44 edit operation and it represents an improvement of the 6%. As for the NDTW, it improved on the 90% of the houses, and the NRMSE in the 70%.

The COVID-19 pandemic changed users' electricity consumption habits, which let to the degradation of the performance of forecast models. This is understood as the concept drift problem and the models had to be retrained. The results have showed that the retraining of the models using only data from the lockdown period, provides an average improvement of 6.67% in terms of EDR.

5.1 Future Work

The improvement in the prediction of peak values has been observed using KNPTS method instead of KNFTS. However, the accuracy to predict these values remains a challenge for time series forecasting models. A pattern classification model in the series could be useful in dealing with sharp peaks. It consist of a step prior to prediction and allow the choice of trained models with similar data. Another solution that might be appropriate would be the combination of both models, assigning more weight to the delayed values of the output variable.

Acknowledgments. This work is partly supported by the RESPOND (integrated demand REsponse Solution towards energy POsitive NeighbourhooDs) and the REACT (Renewable Energy for self-sustAinable island CommuniTies) projects, which have received funding from the European Union's Horizon 2020 research and innovation programme under grant agreement no. 768619 and no. 824395 respectively.

References

1. Cao, X., Dai, X., Liu, J.: Building energy-consumption status worldwide and the state-of-the-art technologies for zero-energy buildings during the past decade. Energy Build. **128**, 198–213 (2016)

2. Global Alliance for Buildings and Construction, International Energy Agency and the United Nations Environment Programme. 2019 global status report for buildings and construction: Towards a zero-emission, efficient and resilient buildings and construction sector. Technical report (2019)
3. Contreras, J., Asensio, M., de Quevedo, P.M., Muñoz-Delgado, G., Montoya-Bueno, S.: Demand response modeling (chap. 4). In: Contreras, J., Asensio, M., de Quevedo, P.M., Muñoz-Delgado, G., Montoya-Bueno, S. (eds.) Joint RES and Distribution Network Expansion Planning Under a Demand Response Framework, pp. 33–40. Academic Press (2016)
4. Warren, P.: A review of demand-side management policy in the UK. Renew. Sustain. Energy Rev. **29**, 941–951 (2014)
5. Bartusch, C., Alvehag, K.: Further exploring the potential of residential demand response programs in electricity distribution. Appl. Energy **125**, 39–59 (2014)
6. Adhikari, R., Agrawal, R.K.: An introductory study on time series modeling and forecasting. Ph.D. thesis (2013)
7. Ben Taieb, S., Bontempi, G., Atiya, A.F., Sorjamaa, A.: A review and comparison of strategies for multi-step ahead time series forecasting based on the NN5 forecasting competition. Expert Syst. Appl. **39**, 7067–7083 (2012)
8. Martínez, F., Frías, M.P., Pérez, M.D., Rivera, A.J.: A methodology for applying k-nearest neighbor to time series forecasting. Artif. Intell. Rev. **52**, 2019–2037 (2019). https://doi.org/10.1007/s10462-017-9593-z
9. Abu Alfeilat, H.A., et al.: Effects of distance measure choice on k-nearest neighbor classifier performance: a review. Big Data **7**, 221–248 (2019)
10. Zheng, A., Casari, A.: Feature Engineering for Machine Learning. O'Reilly Media, Inc., Sebastopol (2018)
11. Bontempi, G., Ben Taieb, S., Le Borgne, Y.-A.: Machine learning strategies for time series forecasting. In: Aufaure, M.-A., Zimányi, E. (eds.) eBISS 2012. LNBIP, vol. 138, pp. 62–77. Springer, Heidelberg (2013). https://doi.org/10.1007/978-3-642-36318-4_3
12. Mori, U., Mendiburu, A., Lozano, J.A.: Distance measures for time series in R: the TSdist package. R J. **8**, 451 (2016)
13. Berndt, D., Clifford, J.: Using dynamic time warping to find patterns in time series. In: Workshop on Knowledge Knowledge Discovery in Databases (1994)
14. Chen, L., Özsu, M.T., Oria, V.: Robust and fast similarity search for moving object trajectories. In: Proceedings of the ACM SIGMOD International Conference on Management of Data (2005)
15. Esnaola-Gonzalez, I., Diez, F.J., Pujic, D., Jelic, M., Tomasevic, N.: An artificial intelligent system for demand response in neighbourhoods. In: AIPES - The Workshop on Artificial Intelligence in Power and Energy Systems (Accepted, to be published)
16. Lusis, P., Khalilpour, K.R., Andrew, L., Liebman, A.: Short-term residential load forecasting: impact of calendar effects and forecast granularity. Appl. Energy **205**, 654–669 (2017)
17. Widmer, G., Kubat, M.: Learning in the presence of concept drift and hidden contexts. Mach. Learn. **23**(1), 69–101 (1996). https://doi.org/10.1023/A:1018046501280

Weather Downtime Prediction in a South African Port Environment

Nyiko Cecil Musisinyani[1], Jacomine Grobler[2]⊙, and Mardé Helbig[3](✉)

[1] Department of Industrial and Systems Engineering,
University of Pretoria, Pretoria, South Africa
nyiko.cecil@gmail.com
[2] Department of Industrial Engineering,
Stellenbosch University, Stellenbosch, South Africa
jacomine.grobler@gmail.com
[3] School of Information and Communication Technology,
Griffith University, Southport, Australia
m.helbig@griffith.edu.au

Abstract. Sea ports act as a gateway for a country's imports and exports. Delays of vessels at the anchorage due to adverse weather events are becoming increasingly problematic. This paper investigates using weather data to accurately predict delays experienced by ships at the port anchorage by means of both regression (delay duration) and classification (delay impact). The data sets consist of five years of weather information and vessel weather delay data obtained for a South African port. The weather information consist of three data sources, including rainfall, wind and wave data. An artificial neural network was found to perform the best in the prediction of vessel weather delay duration for both three day and weekly data sets and a random forest performed the best in predicting likelihood of weekly vessel weather delays.

Keywords: Machine learning · Downtime prediction · Port environment

1 Introduction

The World Economic Forum (WEF) Global Risk Report of 2018 ranked extreme weather events (sea level rise, strong winds, storms, floods, extreme heat, extreme cold, and drought) and climate change related risks among the top global risks in the world in terms of likelihood and consequence over the next ten year horizon [8]. These changes in climate are expected to manifest in increased frequency and severity of extreme weather events [26]. Southern African regions are expected to become drier and hotter in future [26]. It is important to quantify the impact of extreme weather conditions to preempt the impact of the extremes and to plan effectively [26]. The ability to predict weather delays in the port environment will have both direct and indirect benefits to the sea port. The direct benefits include improved planning activities, such as better allocation of berth slots and resources

© Springer Nature Switzerland AG 2020
M. Bramer and R. Ellis (Eds.): SGAI-AI 2020, LNAI 12498, pp. 241–255, 2020.
https://doi.org/10.1007/978-3-030-63799-6_19

due to reduced uncertainties, and the indirect benefit will be the increased competitive edge that can be realized by providing more reliable services to the carriers.

Many studies have been conducted for estimated time of arrival (ETA) from one port to another, however, there are limited studies on vessel delays in the port due to adverse weather. From the literature, wave height and wind speed are the most common weather data for sea port and terminal research. However, other weather variables such as precipitation, sea level pressure, visibility and temperature have also been used. Various simulation, optimisation, and machine learning techniques have been used for prediction of ETA for rail, road, air, and maritime research. Classification of weather related incidents has been used extensively for flight delays, but there is limited research for the port environment.

The main objective of the paper is to use weather and time or seasonality data to accurately predict weather delays of ships in the port environment. Both a regression problem (predicting delay duration) and a classification problem is solved using machine learning algorithms. Another objective includes exploration and clustering of the data variables using self-organizing maps (SOM).

The classification problem is formulated to predict weekly vessel weather delays using yes (delays) or no (no delays) classes, while a regression problem is formulated to predict weekly or 3 day vessels weather delay duration. Seven machine learning algorithms are evaluated for predicting weekly or 3 day vessel weather delay duration and eight machine learning algorithms were evaluated for predicting the likelihood that vessels would be delayed in any given week.

This paper is significant because to the best of the authors' knowledge, it describes the first investigation of machine learning techniques to predict weather delays in a South African port environment.

The rest of this paper is organised as follows: Sect. 2 provides an overview of the relevant literature. Section 3 describes the research methodology and exploratory data analysis, and data preparation. Section 4 presents the results of the regression problem analysis and Sect. 5 presents the results of the classification problem analysis. Finally, Sect. 6 concludes the paper.

2 Related Literature

Table 1 shows a summary of articles focusing on transport delays in maritime, sea port, and land transportation. It is clear from Table 1 that weather data has rarely been incorporated in related marine and port research, and little research has focused on prediction of vessels' estimated time of arrival using machine learning. In addition, there is a gap in research into the prediction of vessels' waiting times or delay duration at port anchorage or port environment due to weather. The use of hybrid methods combining clustering and supervised machine learning techniques in marine and aviation research is also notable.

3 Data Description and Data Preparation

Section 3.1 describes the data sets used for this study and the results of an exploratory data analysis are described in Sect. 3.2. A clustering analysis based on a SOM is presented in Sect. 3.3.

Table 1. Summary of techniques used in port or maritime, land transport, and other sectors.

Author (s)	Domain	Problem	Classification/ regression?	Weather data?	Methods used?
Parolas [21]	Port or maritime	ETA	Regression	Yes	ANN and SVM
Malekipirbazari et al. [14]	Port or maritime	Anchorage duration	Classification	No	Decision tree, K-Nearest Neighbor (KNN), & Naïve Bayes
Pani et al. [19]	Port or maritime	ETA	Regression	No	CART
Mestl and Dausendschön [16]	Port or maritime	ETA	NA	No	ETA for liners and ETA for tramps
Kim et al. [13]	Port or maritime	ETA	Regression	No	CBR
Meijer [15]	Port or maritime	ETA	Regression	No	MLR, a decision tree, SVM, ANN, KNN
Fancello et al. [7]	Port or maritime	ETA and resources allocation	Regression	No	ANN for ETA and ILP for optimisation
Pani et al. [20]	Port or maritime	ETA	Classification	Yes	Logistic regression, CART, and random forest
Yu et al. [29]	Port or maritime	ETA and resource & optimisation	Classification	No	Random forest, CART, ANN and GA
Asperen et al. [2]	Port or maritime	Ships arrival process & optimisation	NA	No	Discrete event simulation
Shahpanah et al. [23]	Port or maritime	Ships waiting time & resource optimisation	NA	NA	ANN-GA
Stanivuk and Tokić [24]	Port or maritime	Resource optimisation	NA	Yes	Monte-carlo simulation
Yaakob and Chau [27]	Port or maritime	Effects of extreme weather & on fish operations	NA	Yes	Diagnostic or descriptive statistics
Daranda [6]	Port or maritime	Vessels traffic	Classification	No	DBSCAN and ANN
Heij and Knapp [10]	Port or maritime	Ships incidents	Classification	No	Logistic regression
Oneto et al. [18]	Railway	Train delay	Regression	No	SELM and DELM
Grabbel and Banavar [9]	Aviation	Flight delays	Classification	Yes	LMT and EM clustering
Satyakrishna and Sagar [22]	Railway	Train delay	Regression	Yes	SELM and DELM
Valenti et al. [25]	Road	Road incident duration	Regression	Yes	MLR, decision trees, ANN, RVM, KNN
Zong et al. [30]	Road	Road incident duration & and severity	Both	Yes	SVM, Ordered probit and hazard survival models
Rebollo and Balakrishnan [3]	Aviation	Flight delay	Both	No	K-means clustering and SVM
Yaghini et al. [28]	Railway	Train delay	Classification	No	ANN, decision tree, multinomial logistic regression
Kalliguddi and Leboulluec [12]	Aviation	Flight delays	Regression	No	MLR, decision trees, and Random forest
Joseph [11]	Health	Waiting times	Regression	No	MLR, SVM, decision trees, and Random forest
Prabakaran and Kannadasan [17]	Aviation	Flight delays	Regression	No	Polynomial regression and linear regression
Belcastro et al. [4]	Aviation	Flight delays	Classification	Yes	Random forest
Simmons [1]	Aviation	Flight delays	Classification	Yes	LDA and Naïve Bayes

3.1 Data Description

The data sets used in this study consist of weather information and vessels' weather delay data. Weather information consists of three data sources, namely rainfall, wind and wave data. Wind and wave data were obtained from port control weather stations near the port used for this case study. Rainfall data at the weather station closest to the sea port is provided by the South African Weather Services (SAWS). Vessels' weather delay data consist of vessels' movement delays impacted by extreme weather events and is supplied by the port authority. The data sets were acquired for a large South African port for daily events in a five year period between 2013 and 2017. The variables, data types, and variable descriptions of the data used in this paper are described in Table 2.

3.2 Exploratory Data Analysis

This section focuses on deriving the relationship between weather and vessel weather delay using exploratory data analysis. Each of the features were first analysed individually and then the relationships between features were explored. The highlights of this analysis is presented throughout the rest of this section.

Vessels' Weather Delay Data: Figure 1 indicates the number of incidents per move type, per time of the day, per season, and per weather event for 2013 to 2017. From Fig. 1 (c), it is evident that the majority of incidents occurred in spring, followed by winter. It is evident in Fig. 1 (a) that most incidents occurred via incoming ships, followed by departure vessels, over the years. In Fig. 1 (b), most incidents occur during the morning hours and the evening hours. From Fig. 1 (d) can be seen that the types of weather delays require a more accurate classification.

Figure 2 indicates delay hours by (a) time of the day, (b) per season, (c) per season and ship type, and (d) per month or year for 2013 to 2017. In Fig. 2, similar trends to Fig. 1 are evident. In Fig. 2 (d), it is evident that substantial delay hours occur during spring followed by winter across the years, with the highest delay hours in October, followed by November and September.

Wind Data: From Fig. 3, it is clear that a high wind speed maximum and wind speed average occur in spring, followed by summer. An extreme wind speed maximum of above 40 m/s and wind speed average of above 25 m/s were recorded during spring in 2017.

Wave Data: From Fig. 4, it is clear that high Hs occurred in spring, followed by winter.

Integrated Weather Data: Figure 5 presents graphs of delay hours and weather variables for four seasons per year that were created to gain insight into the relationship between delay hours and weather conditions. The weather variables are split into minimum, maximum and average measurements.

Figure 5 indicates that the highest Hmax_ave is approximately 4.65 m in spring in 2014 aligning with the spike in delay hours. The lowest Hmax_ave was

Table 2. Variables, data types and variable descriptions

Daily vessels' weather delay data for 2013 to 2017, consisting of 1523 instances.

Variable name	Data type	Description
Vessel	Character	Vessel names
Move type	Category	Three types of ship movements that include incoming ships (INC), shifting ships (SFT), and ships at departure (DEP).
Ship type	Character	The ship types include general cargo, container, tanker, car carriers and unknown ships.
Berth	Character	Name of berth or ships' allocation place.
Requested	Character	Date and time of requested service for berthing in the format ddmmyy hh:mm
Served	Character	Date and time the vessel served, ddmmyy hh:mm
Reason	Character	Extreme weather event that resulted in a vessel delay. The reasons include ADVERSE WEATHER, PORT CLOSED, PORT MEETING, and WIND DELAY.

Twenty minute daily wind data for 2013 to 2017, consisting of 123 069 instances.

Variable name	Data type	Description
Date	Character	mmddyy for month, day and year of recording.
Hour	Character	hh, for hour of recording.
Minute	Character	mm, for minute of recording.
Wind dir (deg TN)	Numeric	Wind direction (wd) measured in degree TN.
Wind spd av (m/s)	Numeric	Wind speed average (ws) measured in meters per second.
Wind spd max (m/s)	Numeric	Wind speed maximum (wsm) measured in metres per second.
Time of wind spd max	Numeric	Time of wind speed maximum (wsmxt).

Thirty minute daily wave information for 2013 to 2017, consisting of 84 902 instances.

Variable name	Data type	Description
Date	Character	mmddyy, for day, month and year of recording
Time	Character	mmhh, for minute and hour of recording.
Hmo	Numeric	Significant wave height (hm0) measured in meters.
H1	Numeric	Extreme wave height (h1) measured in meters and defined as the sum of the highest peak and the deepest trough.
Tp	Numeric	Spectral peak wave period measured in seconds.
Tz	Numeric	Average zero down-crossing wave period measured in seconds.
Tc	Numeric	Spectral crest period (tm24) measured in seconds.
Directn	Numeric	Peak direction measured in degree TN.
SpreadF	Numeric	Peak spreading factor measured in degrees.
Hs	Numeric	Average height of highest 1/3 of all waves measured in meters.
Hmax	Numeric	Maximum wave height measured in meters.
Tb	Numeric	Average spectral period (tm01) measured in seconds.

Daily hourly rainfall data for 2013 to 2017. The data set consists of 1826 instances.

Variable name	Data type	Description
Day	Numeric	Day of recording.
Month	Character	Month of recording.
Year	Numeric	Year of recording.
Hourly rainfall	Numeric	Hourly rainfall recorded per day, measured in millimeters.
Total rainfall	Numeric	Total daily rainfall measured in millimeters.

experienced in summer in 2013 at approximately 2.8 m. The average Hmax_ave over the five year period is approximately 2.65 m. The highest Hmax_max was recorded in summer in 2014 at 12.9 m and the lowest Hmax_max was recorded in 2015 in summer at 5.27 m. The average Hmax_max is approximately 5.1 m over the five year period. The average Tp and average Tz is approximately 9.8 s and 5.75 s, respectively.

Figure 6 indicates a longer wave period during autumn and winter, and shorter wave periods during spring and summer. The average ws_ave is approximately 6.4 m/s and the maximum ws is 26.6 m/s over the five year period. Figure 7 indicates that the highest ws_ave was recorded in spring in 2014 at approximately 11.4 m/s and the lowest ws_ave was experienced in 2016 in autumn at approximately 6.4 m/s. The average wsm_max is approximately 19.8 m/s over the five year period. The highest wsm_max was recorded in 2017 in spring at 43.4 m/s and the lowest wsm_max was recorded in 2016 in the winter at 19.4 m/s.

When comparing wind and wave variables with delay hours, as illustrated in Fig. 8, there appears to be a relationship between wave variables and delay hours. The average Hs_ave is approximately 1.69 m over the five year period. The largest average Hs_ave was experienced in spring in 2014 at approximately 1.90 m and the smallest average Hs_ave in autumn at approximately 1.55 m. Figure 9 indicates that the largest Hs_max was recorded in autumn in 2017 at 5.45 m and the smallest Hs_max in summer in 2013 at 2.73 m. The largest Hs_ave was recorded in spring in 2014 at 2.9 m and the smallest Hs_ave in summer at 1.8 m.

Correlation coefficients showed a stronger correlation between delay hours and wave variables compared to delay hours and wind variables. A strong positive correlation was found between maximum wave height and extreme wave height, thus the maximum wave height feature was removed. A strong negative relationship between delay hours and total rainfall in 2014 was found and a stronger relationship between delay hours and total rainfall in other years.

3.3 SOM Cluster Analysis

The purpose of the SOM cluster analysis is to identify similar groups based on weather patterns and vessel weather delays. Clustering was performed on the SOM nodes or codes, and the number of clusters, namely 4, were selected using the k-means elbow method within cluster sum of squares (WCSS). Partitioning

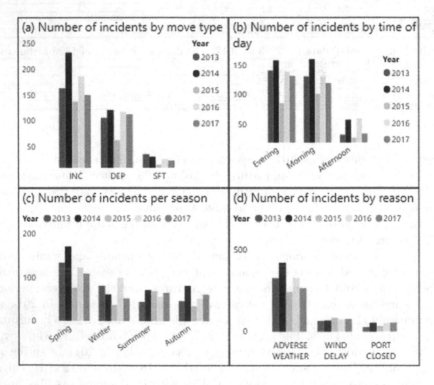

Fig. 1. Number of incidents per (a) move type, (b) per time of the day, (c) per season, and (d) per weather event for 2013 to 2017.

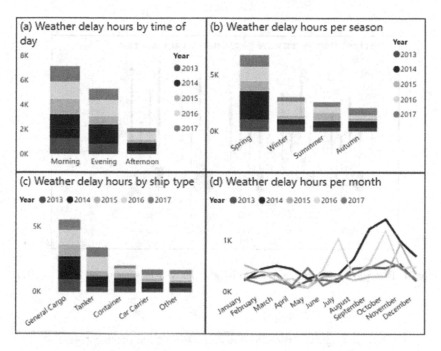

Fig. 2. Delay hours by (a) time of the day, (b) per season, (c) ship type and season, and (d) per month or year for 2013 to 2017.

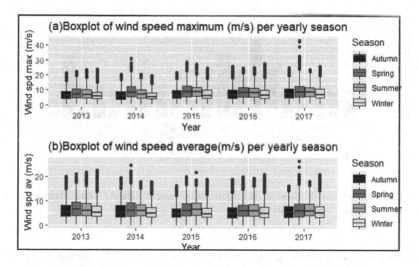

Fig. 3. Box plots of wind speed per season for 2013 to 2017.

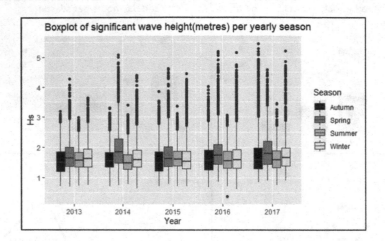

Fig. 4. Box plots of significant wave height per yearly season for 2013 to 2017.

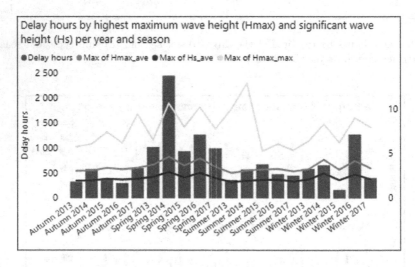

Fig. 5. Delay hours by highest maximum wave height (Hmax) and significant wave height (Hs) per year and season.

was performed using hierarchical clustering. As per Fig. 10, Cluster 1 accounted for approximately 61% (141 observations), Cluster 2 for 33.3% (77 of observations), Cluster 3 for 3% (7 observations) and Cluster 4 for 2.6% (6 observations).

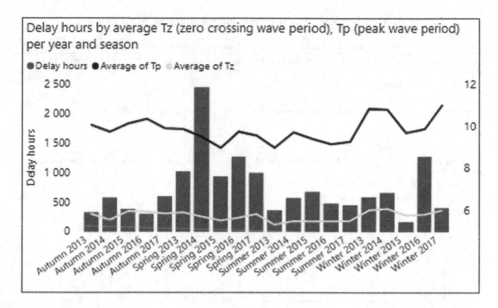

Fig. 6. Delay hours by average Tz (zero crossing wave period), Tp (peak wave period) per year and season.

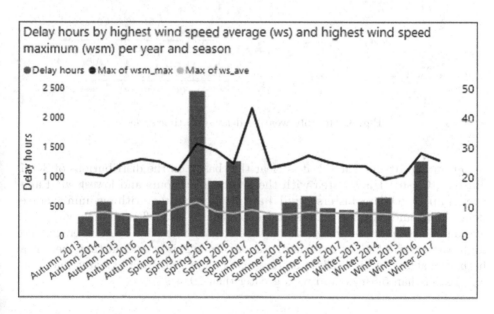

Fig. 7. Delay hours by highest wind speed average (ws) and highest wind speed maximum (wsm) per year and season.

Table 3. Weather and season thresholds for different SOM clusters.

Delays	Hs, Tp, Tz	Hmax	Season	ws	wsm
High average delays (3%):	$2.1 \leq Hs < 2.8$	$6.2 \leq Hmax < 10.3$	Spring and winter	$5.8 \leq ws < 1.7$	$19 \leq wsm < 29.1$
Cluster 3	$8.5 \leq Tp < 12.5$				
	$5.4 \leq Tz < 7.6$				
Low average delays (61%):	$1.05 \leq Hs < 2.1$	$2.8 \leq Hmax < 6.8$	All	$1.6 \leq ws < 7.94$	$2.5 \leq wsm < 24$
Cluster 1	$6.6 \leq Tp < 14.2$				
	$4.6 \leq Tz < 7.5$				
Medium average delays (36.4%):	$1.35 \leq Hs < 2.4$	$4.2 \leq Hmax < 13$	All	$4.8 \leq ws < 9.9$	$12.9 \leq wsm < 43.5$
Clusters 2 and 4	$7.1 \leq Tp < 13.8$				
	$4.9 \leq Tz < 7.65$				

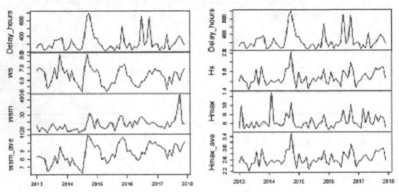

Fig. 8. Monthly weather delay data time series.

From Fig. 10 and Table 3, it is clear that based on the distributions of SOM clusters, Cluster 1 is an area with the lowest delay hours and lowest wind and wave impact, whilst Clusters 2 and 4 are medium clusters with medium average delay hours and extreme wind speed maximum. Cluster 3 is an area with high average delay hours, high significant wave height, high wind speed average, and high average wind speed maximum. As per Table 2, it is evident that there is a high probability of high delays at Hs greater than 2 m, Hmax greater than 6m, ws greater than 5.8 m/s, and wsm greater than 19 m/s.

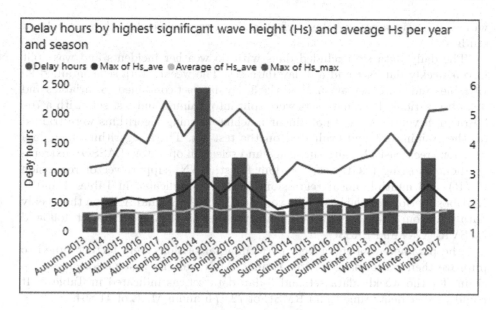

Fig. 9. Delay hours by highest significant wave height (Hs) and average Hs per year and season.

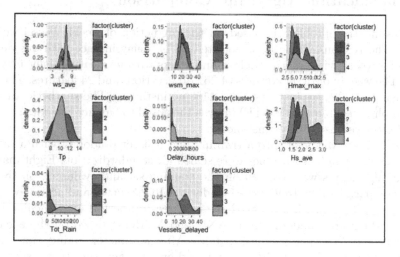

Fig. 10. Distribution of SOM clusters.

4   Regression Algorithm Comparison

In formulating the weather delay prediction problem as a regression problem, delay hours was used as a target variable and was transformed using a log transformation to treat outliers and skewed data. Seven linear and non-linear machine learning algorithms were evaluated using mean absolute error (MAE) and the root mean squared error (RMSE) in hours. RMSE and MAE metrics have been widely using in assessing the performance of regression algorithms in related studies.

The daily data set excluded days with no weather incidents and was split into a weekly data set and a 3-day data set. The weekly data set contained 29 variables and 261 observations, and the 3-day data set contained 28 variables and 392 observations. Both data sets were split into training and test sets with a 70–30 ratio. Seven linear and non-linear machine learning algorithms were trained on the training set and evaluated on the test set. These algorithms include a decision tree, least absolute shrinkage and selection operator (LASSO), extreme gradient boosting (XGBoost), random forest, ANN, support vector regression (SVR), and multiple linear regression (MLR). As indicated in Tables 4 and 5, XGBoost performed the best, followed by MLR, LASSO and ANN on the weekly data set. From Table 5, MLR performed the best for the 3-day data set, followed by SVR, ANN and LASSO.

The parameters of the 4 best performing algorithms were further tuned to improve their performance. After tuning, ANN was the best performing algorithm for the weekly data set and 3-day data set, as indicated in Table 5. It could predict delay time to an RMSE of 72.27 h and a MAE of 41.86 h.

5   Classification Algorithm Comparison

The classification problem is based on the prediction of weekly vessel weather delays. The response variable is selected to be delay_impact with yes and no classes for weeks with weather delays and weeks with no weather delays, respectively. The weekly data set consists of 261 observations and 24 features. The data set consists of 89% yes instances and 11% no instances. The synthetic minority oversampling technique (SMOTE) [5] was thus used to balance the data set (40% no instances versus 60% yes instances).

The data set was split into a training and test set randomly with a ratio of 70–30. All independent variables were scaled for standardization. Eight machine learning algorithms were trained on the training set and evaluated on the test set by comparing AUC ROC (Area under the ROC curve) and accuracy.

As per Table 5(a), it is clear that the three top performing machine learning algorithms are: random forest, ANN and XGBoost based on the accuracy, specificity and AUC performance metrics. After parameter tuning, random forest outperformed ANN and XGBoost based on accuracy, sensitivity, specificity, and AUC performance metrics as per Table 5(b). The random forest algorithm could predict a weather related delay with an accuracy of 90%.

Table 4. Algorithm evaluation for 3 day and weekly data set comparing RMSE and MAE.

Machine Learning Algorithm	Weekly data set		3-day data set	
	RMSE(hours)	MAE(hours)	RMSE(hours)	MAE(hours)
Decision Tree	85.69836	54.04277	55.35788	30.68653
LASSO	73.9948	43.05751	50.07435	27.27436
XGBoost	72.26689	44.53248	52.7452	27.57089
Random Forest	75.69254	45.68761	51.09041	27.48626
ANN	74.07982	43.12758	49.17486	30.1705
SVR	74.90556	44.53427	48.38665	27.59284
MLR	73.88061	42.59953	48.21344	26.83878

Prediction errors after parameter tuning for weekly and 3 day data sets.

Algorithm	Weekly data set			3-day data set		
	Optimal parameters	RMSE (hours)	MAE (hours)	Optimal parameters	RMSE (hours)	MAE (hours)
XGBoost	nrounds=10	72.26689	44.53248			
ANN	hidden=(4,4) epochs=200	72.09263	41.86229	epochs=200 hidden=(3,3) Rectifier activation function	44.09281	25.51541
MLR	N/A	73.88061	42.59953	N/A	48.21344	26.83878
LASSO	λ= 0.07559103	72.50292	42.81334	λ= 0.05224589	49.44594	27.15527
SVR Linear				C = 0.05018317	48.38665	27.59284

Table 5. Results of machine learning algorithms

(a) Performance evaluation of machine learning algorithms.

Algorithm	ConfusionMatrix Results	AUC
SVM	Accuracy: 0.8444 Sensitivity : 0.8889 Specificity : 0.8148	AUC: 0.8766
Naïve Bayes	Accuracy: 0.7667 Sensitivity : 0.8889 Specificity : 0.6852	AUC: 0.8102
Decision Tree	Accuracy: 0.7667 Sensitivity : 0.8056 Specificity : 0.7407	AUC: 0.7894
Random Forest	Accuracy: 0.8889 Sensitivity : 0.9167 Specificity : 0.8704	AUC: 0.9396
ANN	Accuracy: 0.8556 Sensitivity : 0.8611 Specificity : 0.8519	AUC: 0.9362
XGBoost	Accuracy: 0.9 Sensitivity : 0.9167 Specificity : 0.8889	AUC: 0.9254
LDA	Accuracy: 0.6222 Sensitivity : 0.6667 Specificity : 0.5926	AUC: 0.6698
LASSO	Accuracy: 0.6889 Sensitivity : 0.6667 Specificity : 0.7037	AUC: 0.7762

(b) Results after classification algorithm parameter tuning.

Algorithm	Optimal parameters	ConfusionMatrix Results	AUC
Random Forest	mtry=3	Accuracy:0.9 Sensitivity : 0.9167 Specificity : 0.8889	AUC:0.9447
ANN	hidden=(7,7) epochs=100	Accuracy: 0.8556 Sensitivity : 0.8611 Specificity : 0.8519	AUC: 0.9362
XGBoost	nrounds=10	Accuracy: 0.9 Sensitivity : 0.9167 Specificity : 0.8889	AUC: 0.9254

6   Conclusion

The main objective of this study was to use machine learning algorithms to predict weather downtime in a port environment using time and weather data. A classification problem was formulated to predict weekly vessel weather delays using yes or no instances, while a regression problem was formulated to predict weekly or 3 day vessels weather delay duration. Seven machine learning algorithms were evaluated for predicting weekly or 3 day vessel weather delay duration and eight machine learning algorithms were evaluated for predicting the likelihood that vessels would be delayed weekly. ANN was found to perform better in the prediction of weather delay duration for both 3 day and weekly data sets. Random Forest was found to perform the best in predicting the likelihood of weekly vessel weather delays. Furthermore, Hs_ave was found to be the most important variable for both the regression and the classification problem.

Future research opportunities lie in expanding this study to do a comparative analysis between multiple ports, the evaluation of other feature selection techniques, and incorporating additional data elements into the analysis.

References

1. Arteche Simmons, A.: Flight delay forecast due to weather using data mining (2015)
2. van Asperen, E., Dekker, R., Polman, M., de Swaan Arons, H.: Waterway, shipping, and ports: modeling ship arrivals in ports. In: Proceedings of the 35th Conference on Winter Simulation: Driving Innovation, Winter Simulation Conference, pp. 1737–1744 (2003)
3. Rebollo de la Bandera, J.J.: Characterization and prediction of air traffic delays. Ph.D. thesis, Massachusetts Institute of Technology (2012)
4. Belcastro, L., Marozzo, F., Talia, D., Trunfio, P.: Using scalable data mining for predicting flight delays. ACM Trans. Intell. Syst. Technol. (TIST) **8**(1), 5 (2016)
5. Chawla, N.V., Bowyer, K.W., Hall, L.O., Kegelmeyer, W.P.: SMOTE: synthetic minority over-sampling technique. J. Artif. Intell. Res. **16**, 321–357 (2002)
6. Daranda, A.: Neural network approach to predict marine traffic. Trans. Balt. J. Mod. Comput. **4**(3), 483 (2016)
7. Fancello, G., Pani, C., Pisano, M., Serra, P., Zuddas, P., Fadda, P.: Prediction of arrival times and human resources allocation for container terminal. Marit. Econ. Logist. **13**(2), 142–173 (2011). https://doi.org/10.1057/mel.2011.3
8. Forum, W.E.: The global risks report 2018 (2018)
9. Grabbe, S.R., Sridhar, B., Mukherjee, A.: Clustering days with similar airport weather conditions. In: 14th AIAA Aviation Technology, Integration, and Operations Conference, p. 2712 (2014)
10. Heij, C., Knapp, S.: Effects of wind strength and wave height on ship incident risk: regional trends and seasonality. Transp. Res. Part D: Transp. Environ. **37**, 29–39 (2015)
11. Joseph, A., Hijal, T., Kildea, J., Hendren, L., Herrera, D.: Predicting waiting times in radiation oncology using machine learning. In: 2017 16th IEEE International Conference on Machine Learning and Applications (ICMLA), pp. 1024–1029. IEEE (2017)
12. Kalliguddi, A.M., Leboulluec, A.K.: Predictive modeling of aircraft flight delay (2017)
13. Kim, S., Kim, H., Park, Y.: Early detection of vessel delays using combined historical and real-time information. J. Oper. Res. Soc. **68**(2), 182–191 (2017). https://doi.org/10.1057/s41274-016-0104-4

14. Malekipirbazari, M., Aksakalli, V., Aydogdu, Y.V.: Predicting anchorage duration of commercial vessels. Int. J. Mach. Learn. Comput. **6**(1), 62 (2016)
15. Meijer, R : Predicting the ETA of a container vessel based on route identification using AIS data. Master's thesis, Delft University of Technology (2017). https://repository.tudelft.nl/islandora/object/uuid%3Acba0ef59-dd23-49aa-91d5-bed239e27395
16. Mestl, T., Dausendschön, K.: Port ETA prediction based on AIS data. In: 15th International Conference on Computer and it Applications in the Maritime Industries (2017)
17. Prabakaran, N., Kannadasan, R.: Airline delay predictions using supervised machine learning. Int. J. Pure Appl. Math. **119**, 329–337 (2018)
18. Oneto, L., et al.: Train delay prediction systems: a big data analytics perspective. Big Data Res. **11**, 54–64 (2018)
19. Pani, C., Fadda, P., Fancello, G., Frigau, L., Mola, F.: A data mining approach to forecast late arrivals in a transhipment container terminal. Transport **29**(2), 175–184 (2014)
20. Pani, C., Vanelslander, T., Fancello, G., Cannas, M.: Prediction of late/early arrivals in container terminals-a qualitative approach. Eur. J. Transp. Infrastruct. Res. **15**(4), 536–550 (2015)
21. Parolas, I.: ETA prediction for containerships at the port of Rotterdam using machine learning techniques (2016)
22. Satyakrishna, J., Sagar, R.: Train delay prediction systems using big data analytics (2018)
23. Shahpanah, A., Poursafary, S., Shariatmadari, S., Gholamkhasi, A., Zahraee, S.: Optimization waiting time at berthing area of port container terminal with hybrid genetic algorithm (GA) and artificial neural network (ANN). In: Advanced Materials Research, vol. 902 (2014)
24. Stanivuk, T., Tokić, T.: Impact of weather conditions on the construction of the terminal-Monte Carlo simulation. Int. J. Traffic Transp. Eng. **3**(1), 431 (2013)
25. Valenti, G., Lelli, M, Cucina, D.: A comparative study of models for the incident duration prediction. Eur. Transp. Res. Rev. **2**(2), 103–111 (2010). https://doi.org/10.1007/s12544-010-0031-4
26. Winsemius, H., et al.: The potential value of seasonal forecasts in a changing climate in Southern Africa. Hydrol. Earth Syst. Sci. **18**(4), 1525–1538 (2014)
27. Yaakob, O., Chau, Q.P.: Weather downtime and its effect on fishing operation in Peninsular Malaysia. Jurnal Teknologi **42**(A), 13–26 (2005)
28. Yaghini, M., Khoshraftar, M.M., Seyedabadi, M.: Railway passenger train delay prediction via neural network model. J. Adv. Transp. **47**(3), 355–368 (2013)
29. Yu, J., et al.: Ship arrival prediction and its value on daily container terminal operation. Ocean Eng. **157**, 73–86 (2018)
30. Zong, F., Zhang, H., Xu, H., Zhu, X., Wang, L.: Predicting severity and duration of road traffic accident. Math. Probl. Eng. **2013**, 9 (2013)

Advances in Applied AI

Software Fault Localisation via Probabilistic Modelling

Colin G. Johnson$^{(\boxtimes)}$ (iD)

School of Computer Science, University of Nottingham, Jubilee Campus,
Nottingham, UK
Colin.Johnson@nottingham.ac.uk

Abstract. Software development is a complex activity requiring intelligent action. This paper explores the use of an AI technique for one step in software development, *viz.* detecting the location of a fault in a program. A measure of program progress is proposed, which uses a Naïve Bayes model to measure how useful the information that has been produced by the program to the task that the program is tackling. Then, deviations in that measure are used to find the location of faults in the code. Experiments are carried out to test the effectiveness of this measure.

Keywords: Software development · Bug finding · Naïve Bayes

1 Introduction

Software development is a task requiring substantial intelligence. In recent years, a number of AI based approaches have been taken to software development tasks [8], both in terms of actually writing code, and in the wide variety of tasks that surround this, such as decomposition of tasks [17], fault finding and fixing [15,16], building and improving test suites [3], etc.

This paper is concerned with applying an AI technique to fault localization—that is, is the problem of identifying which component of a faulty system is causing the fault [23]. For a software system, fault localization can be used at a number of scales, from identifying which component of a large multi-component system is causing the fault, through to identifying which line of code is the cause of a fault in a single function.

In this paper, we are concerned with the smallest scale of fault localization, finding the location of a fault in a single unit of faulty code: a function/method consisting of a number lines of code. The problem is as follows. Take the source code for a function f, and a test set consisting of sample inputs f and the expected output for each sample input. A fault in f means that the input-output behaviour of the function on the inputs in the test set do not match with the input-output pairs in the test set; for some inputs, the output from f is different to the output in the test set. The localization problem is to identify the line(s) of code that give rise to this fault.

© Springer Nature Switzerland AG 2020
M. Bramer and R. Ellis (Eds.): SGAI-AI 2020, LNAI 12498, pp. 259–272, 2020.
https://doi.org/10.1007/978-3-030-63799-6_20

This problem is commonly tackled using a *spectrum*-based approach. This is where a spectrum matrix, indexed by test set inputs × lines of code in f is created, with the entry being *True* if that line of code was executed during that test case, and *False* otherwise. Fault localization is then carried out using one of many *suspiciousness metrics* [21], which assign a numerical value to each line of code, with the idea that the lines most likely to get a high suspiciousness value are those that are the causes of the fault. Typically, suspiciousness metrics are based on the difference between program paths taken when the correct output is obtained and when a wrong output is obtained; lines which occur most frequently in traces that give incorrect outputs are treated as most suspicious.

However, sometimes the cause of the fault is to do with the *values taken* during that execution, not the different paths taken. Indeed, in some applications—signal processing, image and audio transformation, numerical computation, etc.—there many be few conditional statements to facilitate the creation of usefully different traces to calculate suspiciousness metrics from. The focus of this paper is on testing such programs, consisting of a succession of calculations.

To tackle these problems, we introduce two concepts. The first is that of a *rich spectrum*. A conventional program spectrum consists of a two dimensional array of size (*numberOfTestCases, numberOfLines*) with entries in the set *True, False*). The entries indicate, for each test case, whether the program executed that particular line whilst running that test case. A rich spectrum is a three dimensional array, of size (*numberOfTestCases, numberOfLines, numberOfVariables*). In the examples in this paper, the values in this spectrum are integer or floating point numbers, but they could be any variable type. The entries in the rich spectrum represent the values computed by the various lines of the code. The aim of this is to capture a richer set of data about the program's execution, to which AI and data mining algorithms can be applied.

The second concept is the idea of probabilistic accumulation of evidence as a program executes. The key concept here is that we can quantify an approximation to the progress of a program towards solving its task. In this paper the model used is a Naïve Bayes model, which is recalculated as each line is executed. A record is kept of the accuracy of each of these models. The key idea is that, if a program is successful at its task, the accuracy of this model will increase line-by-line, because the data encoded in the variables at the end of each line is more informative, therefore the probability of being able to predict the output based on that information will increase. Conversely, if there is a fault, then a piece of irrelevant, distracting information will be created, which will mean that there will be a dip in that probability.

The paper is structured as follows. Section 2 explains previous approaches to the problem, Sect. 3 explains the new model of measuring program execution, and then Sect. 4 explains how that model is used to detect faults. Two experiments are described in Sect. 5, then there is a discussion in Sect. 7 of the limitations and threats to validity of the model. Finally, Sect. 8 summarises the ideas in the paper and presents ideas for further developments.

2   Background

A number of approaches to software fault localisation have been investigated in the literature (see e.g. [22] for a survey). Some of these are driven by human programmer's understanding of the program—e.g. printing out variable values and looking for patterns in light of the fault, comparing program activities with asserted properties, inserting breakpoints to review machine state at certain points, or examining the run time or execution frequencies of parts of the program and comparing it to an expected profile.

There are a number of approaches to automating or semi-automating the fault location detection process. One of these is based around *slicing* the program, that is, finding which subset of the code precede the point where the fault has been detected. A related idea is that of *spectral* testing [11], where an array is constructed to map out which statements are executed when there is a fault, and when there isn't. Then, a *suspiciousness statistic* is calculated, which predicts which line is most likely to be the cause of the fault—the basic idea being that lines that are often executed when a fault occurs, but not when it doesn't, are more likely to be the cause of the fault. We will take this idea further in this paper, both extending the idea of the spectrum, and using a different kind of statistical model to detect faults.

Another approach concentrates on detecting or constructing test examples that cause faults, so that the programmer can look for patterns in these test examples. For example, delta debugging [6] focuses on trimming down failure-causing inputs until some minimal failure-causing cases are found.

A number of approaches to the localisation problem have been grounded in AI and machine learning methods. For example [24] have used neural networks to discover the association between test case failures and code coverage, whilst another paper [4] has used decision trees to group together test cases that cause similar kinds of faults. Machine learning has also been used to improve existing techniques—for example, the spectral based approach to fault localisation has been improved by using genetic programming to discover suspiciousness formulae that are more effective than the traditional formulae [10] written by people [25]

There are a number of problems that contemporary fault localization methods struggle to address. Some of these are concerned with multiple faults in the same program—a fault can be obstructed by a later fault, and sometimes a later fault can mask or even undo earlier one. In this paper we address this problem by constructing a set of models that take a certain number of lines of the code and build a probabilistic model for the remainder of the computation, thus meaning that the rest of the code after the initial fault is not executed. Secondly, most approaches rely on differences between different execution paths in code. This means that localisation cannot be done in blocks of code without any conditional branching. By contrast, in this paper, we focus on the information calculated by each step in the code, meaning that faults can be localised within a non-branching piece of code.

3   Modelling Program Execution with Naïve Bayes Models

Programs are written to carry out a task. This task can be described in a number of ways: by a formal specification, by a set of input-output examples, and/or by a natural language description. As a program executes, it makes progress on the task. A key idea of this approach is that we can quantify this progress. For a correct program without any computations that are irrelevant to the task, we expect each line to calculate some information that is relevant to the task. After each line of the program has been executed, the computer's memory contains more information relevant to the task then it did before.

For the purposes of this paper we will focus on imperative programs that have no loops or conditionals (apart from single-line conditions and folds). There is no fundamental reason why these ideas cannot be developed for such programs, or for other programming paradigms, but for a first attempt at these approaches, this provides a starting point. Furthermore, it emphasises an aspect of code that has been neglected by previous approaches to fault localisation. In many previous approaches, such as the spectral approaches discussed above, the branching execution of the program is key to discovering the fault, and the location of faults in parts of code without branches cannot be found.

3.1   Progress Modelling

This section explains how we quantify the progress of a program towards its task. Before the program is executed, no memory is allocated to the program. Therefore, there is no information to tell us whether the program has made any progress towards the solution. As each statement is executed, the state of the computer's memory contains more information that is relevant to the task. To measure this progress, we execute the program on a large number of test cases, accumulating the variable states after each statement has been executed.

There is then a gap between these variable values for the partially-executed program and the test case outputs—what Androutsopoulos et al. [1] call a "ghost" program. We then build a probabilistic model of the relationship between these variable values and the set of outputs in the test cases. The measure of progress is the accuracy of that model on a reserved test set of examples of variable values and test case outputs. Repeating this process for each line of the program in turn gives a vector of numbers, each corresponding to a line in the code. This process is illustrated in Fig. 1.

This program progress measure should increase monotonically where a program is correct (and doesn't contain any irrelevant or redundant lines), because each execution step will provide some useful information towards solving the test cases, thus reducing the complexity of model needed to bridge the gap to the target output. Contrastingly, many kinds of error will break this monotonicity: by executing an error-causing step, either an irrelevant or distracting piece of information will be created, or a piece of information needed to solve the test

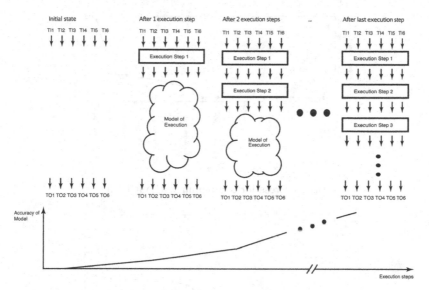

Fig. 1. Measuring the progress of a program towards its task, by building a model of the remaining computation at the end of each line in the program.

cases will be deleted, thus making the learned model *more* complex. By looking for these "spikes" in the model complexity/execution time graph, suspicious statements in the code can be identified for future examination by the programmer. This is illustrated by the example in Fig. 2, which shows the difference in progress curves (calculated by the process described below) for a correct and faulty program.

Importantly, this process can also be run on *incomplete* code. The system will only need to execute the actual code up to the current step of interest, the learned model substituting for the remainder of the processing. This is valuable because it can be used to test code which is actually incomplete, or where the latter part of the code is uncompilable. This also means that bug localisation can begin before a particular unit is finished. Furthermore, the common problem of masking [5], where bugs later in a program make it difficult to find the location of a bug, is not an issue for this approach because the portion of the code that would cause the masking is not executed, but modelled by the machine learning model.

3.2 Building the Rich Spectrum

We implement this in the following way. The inputs to the process are a piece of program code (the final line of which calculates a single integer value that is the output from the code), and a set of test cases that are in the form of input-output pairs.

Firstly, we scan the program for variable names, and make a list of these. We remove any variable names that represent libraries etc. For the purposes

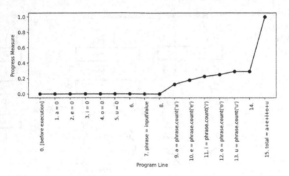

(a) Progress for a program without fault

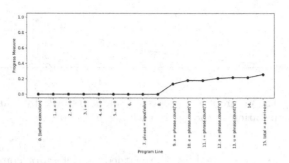

(b) Progress for a program with a typo (line 11)

Fig. 2. Progress measures for a program without a fault and with a small typographical error.

of this paper, these variables will all be integers, but extensions to other data types are readily possible. We then create a three dimensional array $S(t, l, v)$, indexed by the test cases, the lines of code in the program, and the variable names discovered in that initial pass. Let us call S the *execution trace spectrum* of the program with regard to that test case set.

We then fill values into S in the following way. For each test case, we run the following process. Create a sequence of program texts, the first one with the first line of the program, the second one with the first two lines of the program, and so on until the final sequence contains the whole program. For each of the programs in this sequence, we run them on the current test case, and calculate any variable value that has changed due to the execution of that line.

We call the output of this the rich spectrum because it is calculated in the same way as a program spectrum in traditional spectral testing [21], but each line contains a richer set of information. A related idea is the execution trace spectrum by Harrold et al. [9], but that is focused on tracking the text of the lines of code visited rather than the values computed by those lines.

Algorithm 1. Construct the Rich Spectrum

1: **procedure** CONSTRUCTEXECUTIONTRACESPECTRUM(P, T)
$\quad\quad\quad\quad\quad\quad\quad\quad\quad\quad\quad\quad\quad$ ▷ P is the program text, T the set of test-case pairs
2: $\quad$ **let** V be the set of variable names in P
3: $\quad$ **let** $n_t \leftarrow |T|$
4: $\quad$ **let** $n_v \leftarrow |V|$
5: $\quad$ **let** $n_p \leftarrow$ number of lines in P
6: $\quad$ **create** 3-d array S with dimensions (n_t, n_p, n_v)
7: $\quad$ **for** $t \in T$ **do**
8: $\quad\quad$ **for** $\ell \in [1, n_p]$ **do**
9: $\quad\quad\quad$ **let** $v_n \leftarrow$ NULL
10: $\quad\quad\quad$ **let** $P_\ell \leftarrow$ first ℓ lines in P
11: $\quad\quad\quad$ **execute** P_ℓ with input from t
12: $\quad\quad\quad$ **if** the last line of P_ℓ sets a variable value **then**
13: $\quad\quad\quad\quad$ **let** v_n be the variable name that is set in the last line of P_ℓ
14: $\quad\quad\quad\quad$ **let** v_c be the variable value that is set in the last line of P_ℓ
15: $\quad\quad\quad\quad$ **let** $S(t, \ell, v_n) \leftarrow v_c$
16: $\quad\quad\quad$ **end if**
17: $\quad\quad\quad$ **for** $v \in V$ **do** (**except** when $\ell == 0$)
18: $\quad\quad\quad\quad$ **if** $v \neq v_n$ **then**
19: $\quad\quad\quad\quad\quad$ **let** $S(t, \ell, v) \leftarrow S(t, \ell - 1, v_n)$
20: $\quad\quad\quad\quad$ **end if**
21: $\quad\quad\quad$ **end for**
22: $\quad\quad$ **end for**
23: $\quad$ **end for**
24: $\quad$ **return** S
25: **end procedure**

We now use this to calculate a vector of numbers, the *progress measure*, with one number in the interval $[0.0, 1.0]$ for each line in the code. As discussed above (and illustrated in Fig. 1), the key idea is to take the rich spectrum as computed above, and for each line to take the variable values for each test case, and the test case outputs, and build a probabilistic model of the dependencies between them. In this case, the model is the Naïve Bayes classification model; for each line in the code, a Naïve Bayes model is produced that takes the current variable values, and tries to predict the output. The progress measure associated with each line is the accuracy of its Naïve Bayes model on a reserved test set. Pseudocode for this is given in Algorithm 2.

4 Applying This Model to Fault Localisation

We now have a notion of identifying a *progress model* with a piece of code and associated test case set. For a correct program, we would expect this progress model to output a monotonically increasing vector of values of the progress metric—each line executed produces task-relevant information, and so the accuracy of the mode will increase because it has more task-relevant information.

Algorithm 2. Construct the Progress Vector

1: **procedure** CONSTRUCTPROGRESSVECTOR(P, T)

                                    ▷ P is the program text, T is the set of test cases

2:     let $S \leftarrow$ ConstructExecutionTraceSpectrum(P, T)

3:     let $X_{\text{train}} \leftarrow []$ ▷ empty list

4:     let $y_{\text{train}} \leftarrow []$

5:     let $X_{\text{test}} \leftarrow []$

6:     let $y_{\text{test}} \leftarrow []$

7:     let V $\leftarrow []$

8:     for $t \in T$ do

9:         let $t_0 \leftarrow$ output value of t

10:       if random() > 0.1 then

11:          let $X_{\text{train}} \leftarrow S(t, \ell, *)$ ▷ slice of the spectrum for line ℓ

12:          let $y_{\text{train}} \leftarrow$ output value of t

13:       else

14:          let $X_{\text{test}} \leftarrow S(t, \ell, *)$

15:          let $y_{\text{test}} \leftarrow$ output value of t

16:       end if

17:       let $c \leftarrow$ **run** Naïve Bayes classifier on $X_{\text{train}}, y_{\text{train}}$

18:       **append** accuracy(c) **to** V

19:     end for

20:     for $\ell \in [2, |P|]$ do

21:       if $P[\ell]$ is a comment, a blank line, or a library import **then**

22:          let $V[\ell] \leftarrow V[\ell - 1]$

                 ▷ if the line makes no substantive computation, copy value from previous line

23:       end if

24:     end for

25:     return V

26: **end procedure**

In this section of the paper, we look at how this can then be used to find the location of faults. The kind of faults we are interested in here are the minor typographic faults that are commonly made by programmers—typing the wrong variable name, typing the wrong operator value, mixing up 0 and o or 1 and i or l, or copying-and-pasting and then failing to make the required changes. These are the kinds of faults that the competent programmer hypothesis [7] predicts will be common—most of the time, a competent programmer will not make egregious errors of logic or language syntax, but minor typographical errors and "brainos" will remain regardless of high-level competence.

Our approach looks for two kinds of departures from monotonicity in the progress vectors. The first approach finds the earliest (large) downtick in the progress vector. The second approach finds the largest downtick. In the results, we present both of these.

Algorithm 3. Find the Fault Location

1: **procedure** FINDFAULTLOCATION(P, T, m, n_r)
   ▷ P is the program text, T is the set of test cases, m is the method used, n_r the number of runs
2:     let $F \leftarrow [0, 0, \ldots, 0]$ of length $|P|$
3:     **for** $r \in [1, n_r]$ **do**
4:         let $V \leftarrow$ ConstructProgressVector(P, T)
5:         **append** 0.0 to start of V
6:         **if** $m ==$ "first substantive downtick" **then**
7:             **for** $v \in V[2 : |V|]$ **do**
8:                 **if** $V[v] - V[v - 1] < -0.025$ **then**
                    ▷ is decreasing, and not by a trivial amount
9:                     let $F[v] \leftarrow F[v] + 1$
10:                    let $a \leftarrow$ *True*
11:                    **break**
12:                **end if**
13:            **end for**
14:        **end if**
15:        **if** $m ==$ "largest downtick" **then**
16:            let $d \leftarrow \infty$
17:            let $\arg_d \leftarrow$ *NULL*
18:            **for** $v \in V[2 : |V|]$ **do**
19:                **if** $V[v] - V[v - 1] < d$ **then**
                   ▷ is decreasing by more than previous lines
20:                    let $d \leftarrow V[v] - V[v - 1]$
21:                    let $a \leftarrow$ *True*
22:                    let $\arg_d \leftarrow v$
23:                **end if**
24:            **end for**
25:            let $F[\arg_d] \leftarrow F[\arg_d] + 1$
26:        **end if**
27:    **end for**
28:    **return** $a, \text{argmax}(F)$
              ▷ return both whether a solution has been found, and the solution
29: **end procedure**

---

5 Experiments

Two experiments have been carried out to test the above ideas and algorithms. The first of these examines whether the program progress model accurately captures the progress of the example programs, and the second measures whether that same measure can be used to detect the location of faults.

Two python programs will be used in both experiments. These are given in Fig. 3. These are designed to represent the kinds of simple data-transformation functions that are often written as units of a larger piece of code. The first counts the vowels in a piece of text, the second adds a vector of eight numbers together. For each program, 50000 random test cases are generated.

```
a = 0                                  a0 = inputValue[0]+inputValue[1]
e = 0                                  a1 = inputValue[2]+inputValue[3]
i = 0                                  a2 = inputValue[4]+inputValue[5]
o = 0                                  a3 = inputValue[6]+inputValue[7]
u = 0
                                       b0 = a0+a1
phrase = inputValue                    b1 = a2+a3

a = phrase.count('a')                  c0 = b0+b1
e = phrase.count('e')
i = phrase.count('i')
o = phrase.count('o')
u = phrase.count('u')


total = a+e+i+o+u
```

Fig. 3. The programs used in the experiments: `VowelCounter.py` and `AddingNumbers.py`.

5.1 Experiment 1: Does the Program Progress Measure Actually Measure Progress?

In this experiment we run the *ConstructProgressVector* algorithm (described above as Algorithm 2 on the four sample programs. We then measure whether the progress measure is monotonically increasing. Because there are occasionally minor fluctuations in the measure because of the Naïve Bayes process detecting random coincidences in otherwise uncorrelated data, we discount small downturns, where the downward difference between successive entries is less than 0.01. So, we refer to this behaviour as "near monotonic". The results for this experiment are presented in Table 1; the results show that the progress measure is capturing progress in the program.

Table 1. Measure of whether the progress measure is near monotonic (for 100 runs of the algorithm per program)

Program Name	Number of Near-monotonic Vectors
VowelCounter.py	100/100
AddingNumbers.py	100/100

6 Experiment 2: Can the Program Progress Measure Detect Faults?

In this experiment we run the *FindFaultLocation* algorithm (described above as Algorithm 3) on several erroneous versions of the programs from Fig. 3. The details of the errors introduced, and the results of the experiments, are detailed in Table 2. Overall, the results are positive; in the majority of cases, the most common line identified as erroneous was the genuine erroneous line, and when it is not, in all but one case the erroneous line was the second most common line identified.

Table 2. Error detection experiment (for 100 runs per error). The rank of the erroneous line (ranked by how many times out of 100 that line was chosen as the error) is also indicated.

Program	Change made	Method	Error found	Number of Correct Pred's	Rank of best pred
VowelCounter.py	i = phrase.count('i') → i = phrase.count('1')	first	yes	39/100	1/15
VowelCounter.py	i = phrase.count('i') → i = phrase.count('1')	largest	yes	44/100	1/15
VowelCounter.py	i = phrase.count('i') → i = phrase.count('e')	first	yes	65/100	1/15
VowelCounter.py	i = phrase.count('i') → i = phrase.count('e')	largest	yes	93/100	1/15
VowelCounter.py	i = phrase.count('i') → e = phrase.count('e')	first	yes	9/100	1/15
VowelCounter.py	i = phrase.count('i') → e = phrase.count('e')	largest	no		2/15
VowelCounter.py	total = a+e+i+o+u → total = a-e+i+o+u	first	yes	42/100	1/15
VowelCounter.py	total = a+e+i+o+u → total = a-e+i+o+u	largest	yes	87/100	1/15
AddingNumbers.py	b1 = a2+a3 → b1 = a2+a1	first	yes	94/100	1/9
AddingNumbers.py	b1 = a2+a3 → b1 = a2+a1	largest	no		2/9
AddingNumbers.py	b1 = a2+a3 → b1 = a2-a3	first	no		2/9
AddingNumbers.py	b1 = a2+a3 → b1 = a2-a3	largest	no		2/9
AddingNumbers.py	a2 = inputValue[4]+inputValue[5] → a2 = inputValue[2]+inputValue[5]	first	no		2/9
AddingNumbers.py	a2 = inputValue[4]+inputValue[5] → a2 = inputValue[2]+inputValue[5]	largest	no		4/9

7   Limitations and Threats to Validity

One limitation of the current work is that the programs are fairly small and simple, and that they lack substantial use of loops and conditionals. However, there is no principled reason why these ideas cannot be applied to these more complex programs, and techniques such as that of Silva et al. [20] show how the execution traces can be aligned between programs of different lengths of execution.

One threat to the wider applicability of these techniques is their reliance on a large number of test cases. For example, in the above experiments, 50000 test cases were used for each program. Initially, this would seem to render the approach useless (the so-called *test oracle* problem [2])—you need a program to correctly carry out the tasks in order to debug the program that is doing the task. In some cases, this might not be a problem, for example there might be a program in another language to generate the test problems, or some kind of dataset or physical phenomenon to provide the examples. But, it is more likely that an alternative approach to generating the test cases will be needed—for some problems, it is possible to calculate a set of inputs back from a target output, and in others it is possible to use generate-and-test methods or machine learning driven by an oracle that can say whether a particular example is a valid [18].

One limitation of the current approach is that each test case set has a small number of possible outputs, which renders possible the use of a classification algorithm as our model for program progress. For more complex cases, the output might be continuous, multi-dimensional, or be of a complex data type. In such cases, other modelling approaches will be needed, for example replacing the classification model with a regression model.

8   Conclusions and Future Work

The probabilistic model used in this work is somewhat simplistic. By using the naïve Bayes model, we are assuming that all values calculated are equally and independently contributing towards the prediction of the output. This provides a first approximation for this, but in future it would be interesting to explore how the program progress measures proposed in this paper could be combined with more sophisticated models of program execution, such as probabilistic graphical models (as explored by Yu et al. [26]).

This paper has focused on providing candidate bug locations to human programmers. However, this work could also, in the future, support the growing research effort into automated bug *fixing* [15,16], for example using genetic programming approaches. These automated bug-fixing systems rely heavily on automated methods for finding the location of bugs as their starting point, so methods such as the ones on this paper can feed directly into this important new direction in automated software development.

A related idea would be to use these progress measures to achieve program synthesis from scratch. Rather than beginning the program synthesis process from random code as is done in methods such as genetic programming [19], instead the system would synthesise a number of putative first lines, then use the program progress measure to ascertain which of those lines was making the strongest contribution to the problem as defined by the test cases. This line would then be fixed, and the system would move onto the next line, and so on with the aim of finding a monotonically increasing sequence of lines with the last one computing the output.

There are more general implications here for building AI systems. Usually, we build a machine learning model such as a classifier so that we can apply it to new data, and use the results of the classification. Here, we are using the success of the model as a proxy for some more complex task. This echoes the arguments recently made by Krawiec, Swan and O'Reilly [12–14], who use the complexity of a machine-learned model as a proxy for the difficulty of computing a given task.

Source code for the experiments can be found at http://www.colinjohnson. me.uk/researchSoftware.php.

References

1. Androutsopoulos, K., Clark, D., Dan, H., Hierons, R., Harman, M.: An analysis of the relationship between conditional entropy and failed error propagation in software testing. In: Proceedings of the 36th International Conference on Software Engineering (ICSE) (2014)
2. Barr, E., Harman, M., McMinn, P., Shahbaz, M., Yoo, S.: The oracle problem in software testing: a survey. IEEE Trans. Software Eng. **41**(5), 507–525 (2015)
3. Briand, L.C., Labiche, Y., Bawar, Z.: Using machine learning to refine black-box test specifications and test suites. In: 2008 The Eighth International Conference on Quality Software, pp. 135–144 (2008)
4. Briand, L.C., Labiche, Y., Liu, X.: Using machine learning to support debugging with Tarantula. In: The 18th IEEE International Symposium on Software Reliability (ISSRE 2007), pp. 137–146 (2007)
5. Clark, D., Hierons, R.M.: Squeeziness: an information theoretic measure for avoiding fault masking. Inf. Process. Lett. **112**(8–9), 335–340 (2012)
6. Cleve, H., Zeller, A.: Locating causes of program failures. In: Proceedings of the 27th International Conference on Software Engineering, New York, NY, USA, pp. 342–351. Association for Computing Machinery (2005). https://doi.org/10.1145/1062455.1062522
7. DeMillo, R.A., Lipton, R.J., Sayward, F.G.: Hints on test data selection: Help for the practicing programmer. IEEE Comput. **11**(4), 34–41 (1978)
8. Harman, M., Mansouri, S.A., Zhang, Y.: Search-based software engineering: trends, techniques and applications. ACM Comput. Surv. **45**(1) (2012). https://doi.org/10.1145/2379776.2379787
9. Harrold, M.J., Rothermel, G., Sayre, K., Wu, R., Yi, L.: An empirical investigation of the relationship between spectra differences and regression faults. Software Test. Verification Reliabil. **10**(3), 171–194 (2000). https://doi.org/10.1002/1099-1689(200009)10:3⟨171::AID-STVR209⟩3.0.CO;2-J
10. Jones, J., Harrold, M.: Empirical evaluation of the Tarantula automatic fault-localization technique. In: Proceedings of the 20th IEEE/ACM International Conference on Automated Software Engineering, pp. 273–282 (2005)
11. Keller, F., Grunske, L., Heiden, S., Filieri, A., van Hoorn, A., Lo, D.: A critical evaluation of spectrum-based fault localization techniques on a large-scale software system. In: 2017 IEEE International Conference on Software Quality, Reliability and Security (QRS), pp. 114–125 (2017)

12. Krawiec, K., O'Reilly, U.M.: Behavioral programming: a broader and more detailed take on semantic GP. In: Proceeding of the Sixteenth Annual Conference on Genetic and Evolutionary Computation Conference, New York, NY, USA. ACM (2014)

13. Krawiec, K., Swan, J.: Pattern-guided genetic programming. In: Proceedings of the 15th Annual Conference on Genetic and Evolutionary Computation, GECCO 2013, New York, NY, USA, pp. 949–956. ACM (2013). https://doi.org/10.1145/2463372.2463496

14. Krawiec, K., Swan, J., O'Reilly, U.-M.: Behavioral program synthesis: insights and prospects. In: Riolo, R., Worzel, B., Kotanchek, M., Kordon, A. (eds.) Genetic Programming Theory and Practice XIII. GEC, pp. 169–183. Springer, Cham (2016). https://doi.org/10.1007/978-3-319-34223-8_10

15. Le Goues, C., Dewey-Vogt, M., Forrest, S., Weimer, W.: A systematic study of automated program repair: fixing 55 out of 105 bugs for $8 each. In: Glinz, M., Murphy, G.C., Pezzè, M. (eds.) International Conference on Software Engineering, pp. 3–13. IEEE (2012)

16. Le Goues, C., Nguyen, T., Forrest, S., Weimer, W.: Genprog: a generic method for automatic software repair. IEEE Trans. Software Eng. **38**, 54–72 (2012)

17. Lutz, R.: Evolving good hierarchical decompositions of complex systems. J. Syst. Architect. **47**(7), 613–634 (2001). https://doi.org/10.1016/S1383-7621(01)00019-4. evolutionary computing

18. McMinn, P.: Search-based software test data generation: a survey. Software Test. Verification Reliabil. **14**(2), 105–156 (2004). https://doi.org/10.1002/stvr.294

19. Poli, R., Langdon, W.B., McPhee, N.F.: A Field Guide to Genetic Programming. Published via `http://lulu.com` and freely (2008). http://www.gp-field-guide.org.uk, (With contributions by J. R. Koza)

20. Silva, L., Paixão, K., de Amo, S., de Almeida Maia, M.: Software evolution aided by execution trace alignment. In: 2010 Brazilian Symposium on Software Engineering, pp. 158–167 (2010)

21. de Souza, H.A., Chaim, M.L., Kon, F.: Spectrum-based software fault localization: a survey of techniques, advances, and challenges (2016)

22. Wong, W.E., Gao, R., Li, Y., Abreu, R., Wotawa, F.: A survey on software fault localization. IEEE Trans. Software Eng. **42**(8), 707–740 (2016)

23. Wong, W.E., Debroy, V.: A survey of software fault localization, university of Texas at Dallas, Department of Computer Science, Technical report UTDCS-45-09 (2009)

24. Wong, W.E., Qi, Y.: BP neural network effective fault localization. Int. J. Software Eng. Knowl. Eng. **19**(04), 573–597 (2009). https://doi.org/10.1142/S021819400900426X

25. Xie, X., Kuo, F.C., Chen, T.Y., Yoo, S., Harman, M.: Provably optimal and human-competitive results in SBSE for spectrum based fault localisation. In: Ruhe, G., Zhang, Y. (eds.) Search Based Software Engineering. Lecture Notes in Computer Science, vol. 8084, pp. 224–238. Springer, Berlin Heidelberg (2013)

26. Yu, X., Liu, J., Yang, Z., Liu, X.: The Bayesian network based program dependence graph and its application to fault localization. J. Syst. Softw. **134**, 44–53 (2017). https://doi.org/10.1016/j.jss.2017.08.025

Candidates Reduction and Enhanced Sub-Sequence-Based Dynamic Time Warping: A Hybrid Approach

Mohammed Alshehri[1,2]([✉]), Frans Coenen[1]([✉]), and Keith Dures[1]([✉])

[1] Department of Computer Science, University of Liverpool, Liverpool, UK
{M.A.Alshehri,Coenen,K.Dures}@liverpool.ac.uk
[2] Department of Computer Science, King Khalid University, Abha, Saudi Arabia

Abstract. Dynamic Time Warping (DTW) coupled with k Nearest Neighbour classification, where $k = 1$, is the most common classification algorithm in time series analysis. The fact that the complexity of DTW is quadratic, and therefore computationally expensive, is a disadvantage; although DTW has been shown to be more accurate than other distance measures such as Euclidean distance. This paper presents a hybrid, Euclidean and DTW time series analysis similarity metric approach to improve the performance of DTW coupled with a candidate reduction mechanism. The proposed approach results in better performance than alternative enhanced Sub-Sequence-Based DTW approaches, and the standard DTW algorithm, in terms of runtime, accuracy and F1 score.

Keywords: Time series analysis · Dynamic time warping · K-Nearest Neighbour Classification · Sub-Sequence-Based DTW · Candidate reduction

1 Introduction

A time series is a collection of sequentially recorded numeric values. Example application domains include stock market analysis [8] and meteorological forecasting [12]. A typical category of application is time series classification. Many techniques have been used for time series classification, examples include: Decision Trees [6], Support Vector Machines (SVM) [10] and Artificial Neural Networks [7]. However, the most frequently used classification mechanism is the k Nearest Neighbour (kNN) mechanism [11,16,17]. The most frequently used value for k is $k = 1$ because it has been shown to work well [14], and because it avoids the need for a conflict resolution mechanism (required when $k > 1$).

Whatever classification mechanism ends up being used, both the building of the classification model and the eventual utilisation of the model entail a significant amount of time series similarity checking. This is especially the case given long time series. Selection of an appropriate similarity checking mechanism

© Springer Nature Switzerland AG 2020
M. Bramer and R. Ellis (Eds.): SGAI-AI 2020, LNAI 12498, pp. 273–285, 2020.
https://doi.org/10.1007/978-3-030-63799-6_21

is, therefore, an important part of the classification process [14]. Frequently sited similarity checking mechanisms include: Euclidean Distance (ED) and Dynamic Time Warping (DTW). DTW, it can be argued, is more accurate and does not require time series to be of the same length. ED, in turn, tends to be faster; this is particularly the case given very long time series. A hybrid approach, therefore, seems like a credible alternative.

In [2] the Sub-Sequence-Based DTW mechanism was proposed, a mechanism designed to speed up the DTW process without adversely affecting effectiveness. The fundamental idea was to divide the time series to be compared into sets of equal-sized subsequences of length ℓ, and then to first compute DTW values for corresponding individual subsequences in a pair of given time series, before deriving an overall DTW similarity measure. This produced some good results, outperforming standard DTW. In [1] it was hypothesised that the equal-sized approach advocated in [2] was not the most appropriate approach and that a certain amount of "fuzziness" should be introduced into the process. More specifically it was proposed that the "cut point" should be wherever the two time series converged, although limited to a range of points defined by a tail parameter t measured backwards from ℓ. However, in [2], the values for ℓ and t were predefined. Building on the work presented in [2] and [1], this paper proposes a variation of the Sub-Sequence-Based DTW mechanism that includes: (i) a novel mechanism for reducing the KNN search space by first applying the computationally less expensive ED measure and then applying DTW to r retained time series (in other words a hybrid ED-DTW approach), and (ii) optimisation of the parameter t, ℓ and r. The proposed mechanism is fully described and evaluated using 15 time series datasets taken from the UEA and UCR (University of East Anglia and University of California Riverside) Time Series Classification Repository [4].

The remainder of this paper is organised as follows. Some background and a review of related work are presented in Sect. 2. The operation of the proposed hybrid Sub-Sequence-Based DTW mechanism is then presented in Sect. 3. The theoretical computational complexity of the proposed approach is presented in Sect. 4. The evaluation of the proposed mechanism is then presented in Sect. 5, together with a discussion of the results obtained. The paper is concluded in Sect. 6. For convenience, a symbol table is given in Table 1 listing the symbols frequently used throughout this paper.

2   Background and Previous Work

As noted in the introduction to this paper, the most common similarity measures used in time series analysis are Euclidean Distance (ED) and Dynamic Time Warping (DTW). Euclidean distance has been widely used in time series analysis applications to measure the similarity between time series in terms of the distance between corresponding points within pairs of time series. Given two time series $S = [p_1, p_2, \ldots, p_x]$ and $S = [q_1, q_2, \ldots p_x]$, both of length x, ED similarity d_E is measured as shown in Eq. 1, the square root of the sum of the

Table 1. Symbol Table

Symbol	Description
p or q	A point in a time series described by a single value
S	A time series such that $S = [p_1, p_2, \ldots]$ $(S = [q_1, q_2, \ldots])$, $S \in D$
x or y	The length of a given time series
M	A distance matrix measuring $x \times y$
$m_{i,j}$	The distance value at location i, j in M
WP	A warping path $[w_1, w_2, \ldots]$ where $w_i \in M$
wd	A warping distance derived from WP
ℓ	The number of points in a subsequence
s	A number of sub-sequences into which a given time series is to be split
C	A set of class labels $C = \{c_1, c_2, \ldots\}$
D	A collection of time series $\{S_1, S_2, \ldots, S_r\}$
r	The number of time series in in a dataset D
t	The tail measured backwards from ℓ within which the cut is to be applied; thus given $S = [p_0, \ldots, p_\ell]$ the cut will fall between p_ℓ and $p_{\ell-t}$
w	A time series subsequence $\{p_i, p_{i+1}, \ldots\}$, such that $w \in S$
W	A set of s time series subsequences, $\{w_1, w_2, \ldots w_s\}$ contained in a given time series S
$\mathfrak{r}$	The number of candidates selected from a dataset
$\mathfrak{t}$	A new previously unseen time series

squares of the differences between corresponding points in the two time series [11]. ED similarity calculation offers the advantage, over DTW, that it is fast; its weakness is in terms of classification accuracy. Moreover, it only works with time series of the same length [14].

$$d_E = \sqrt{\sum_{i=1}^{n} (x_i - y_i)^2} \tag{1}$$

DTW was originally directed at speech recognition applications [15]. The idea was to find the minimum warping distance (wd) between two time series in non-linear alignment. The process of DTW can be described as follows. Given two time series $S_1 = [p_1, p_2, \ldots, p_x]$ and $S_2 = [q_1, q_2, \ldots, q_y]$ a distance matrix M of size $x \times y$ will be constructed such that the value held at each cell $m_{i,j}$ is the distance calculated using Eq. 1, between the corresponding points [1]. In other words, the distance value assigned to $m_{i,j}$ is the summation of $d_{i,j}$ and the minimum cumulative distance value held at one of the three "previous" cells to $m_{i,j}$ [13]. At the end of the process, the minimum warping distance (wd) will be held at $m_{x,y}$. Even though DTW has quadratic time complexity, it tends to perform better than ED in term of accuracy; and offers the additional advantage that it works with time series of different length. Figure 1 gives examples of both similarity measurements (taken from [14]).

$$m_{i,j} = d_{i,j} + min\{m_{i-1,j}, m_{i,j-1}, m_{i-1,j-1}\} \tag{2}$$

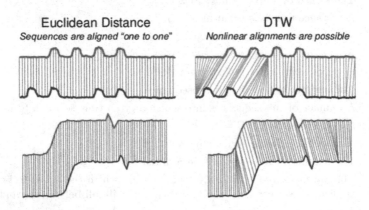

Fig. 1. Example of Euclidean Distance (left) and Dynamic Time Warping (right) [14].

Given the time complexity of DTW, a number of mechanisms have been proposed to address this complexity. This work can be categorised as either being directed at limiting the number of values to be calculated to construct the matrix M, or at limiting the number of comparisons to be considered. Examples of the first can be found in [9,13,15,16], examples of the second can be found in [5,14,18]. In [11] an investigation was reported that considered a number of different distance measures (Euclidean distance, Normalised Euclidean distance, Manhatten distance and Canberra distance) for calculating the values to be held in M. Experiments were done for each distance measure using ten datasets and k-Nearest Neighbour Classification. The results demonstrated that Euclidean distance was the most appropriate distance measure to be used to build DTW distance matrices.

The Sub-Sequence-Based DTW idea, first proposed in [2], took a different approach that did not fit well with the above categorisation. As noted in the introduction to this paper, the main idea was to segment each time series into a predefined set of s sub-sequence and apply the DTW process to corresponding pairs of sub-sequences before deriving an overall DTW similarity value. Thus, given two time series S_1 and S_2, these would be divided into s sub-sequences so that we have $S_1 = [U_{1_1}, U_{1_2}, \ldots U_{1_s}]$ and $S_1 = [U_{2_1}, U_{2_2}, \ldots U_{2_s}]$. DTW is then applied to each sub-sequence paring U_{1_i}, U_{2_j} where $i = j$. The final minimum warping distance arrived at will then be the accumulated warping distance for each sub-sequence of s applications of DTW. This mechanism was shown to improve the DTW calculation runtime significantly compared to alternative approaches, especially given very long time series. However, the fixed sub-sequence size advocated in [2] was conjectured to be a disadvantage with respect to the accuracy of the approach. An enhanced Sub-Sequence-Based DTW mechanism was therefore proposed in [1]. The fundamental idea of the improved mechanism was to find the most appropriate size for s by utilising two parameters: the maximum length of a sub-sequences ℓ and a tail t, measured backwards from ℓ, within which the cut was to be applied. Thus given $S = [p_0, \ldots, p_\ell]$ the cut will fall between p_ℓ and $p_{\ell-t}$. Consideration was also given to whether the split point should be included in the first sub-sequence only, in both subsequences or the second subsequences only, Split Point Allocation Options (SPAO) A, B and C respectively as illustrated in Fig. 2. Option C provided the best performance and was therefore used with respect to the evaluation presented later in this paper.

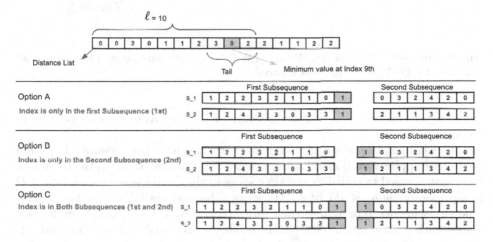

Fig. 2. Segmentation examples given two time series S_1 and S_2, and SPAO options A, B or C [1].

3   Enhanced Sub-Sequence-Based DTW

A block-diagram outlining the proposed Sub-Sequence-Based DTW process is presented in Fig. 3. The process commences with a Database D of r time series $D = \{S_1, S_2, \ldots, S_r\}$. The first stage is to identify the most appropriate values for the parameters ℓ, t and $\mathfrak{r}$; rather than adopting the parameter pre-specification approach advocated in [2] and [1]. We thus have a three-dimensional search space $|I| \times |T| \times |R|$ where $I = \{\ell_1, \ldots, \ell_{|I|}\}$, $T = \{t_1, \ldots, t_{|T|}\}$ and $R = \{\mathfrak{r}_1, \ldots, \mathfrak{r}_{|R|}\}$. Preliminary experiments indicated that, typically, there was no global "peak" in this space, but instead many local maxima with, again typically, one that was better than the rest. This precluded any form of "hill-climbing" strategy. An exhaustive search strategy was therefore adopted. For the

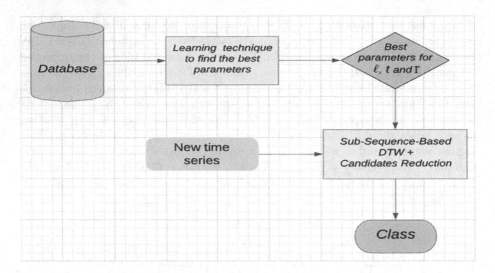

Fig. 3. Proposed Sub-Sequence-Based DTW Process with parameter optimisation and a hybrid ED-DTW similarity mechanism

evaluation discussed in the following section, F1 score was used as the parameter to be maximised.

Once the most appropriate parameters settings have been identified, given a particular application domain as represented by the time series in the database, these can be used to translate the time series in the database so that each $S_i \in D$ is represented as a set W_i of s time series subsequences $W_i = \{w_1, w_2, \ldots w_s\}$. The sub-sequence represented time series then form a kNN "bank", each associated with a class label, with which to label a previously unseen time series t. Note that t is first recast, using the learnt parameter values ℓ and t, so that it also comprises a set of subsequences. However, instead of comparing t to every set of subsequences in the kNN bank the idea is to first reduce the search space by applying a "candidate reduction" process founded on ED similarity measurement. The motivation here is that ED outperforms DTW in terms of runtime. Using this approach r candidates were retained to which DTW was applied, because it had been shown to be more accurate than ED.

4   Time Complexity

In this section, the time complexity of the proposed mechanism is presented. In time series classification, when using standard DTW, the complexity of the comparison between two time series, S_1 and S_2 is dependent on the size of the distance matrix M. The time complex thus is given by $O(x \times y)$ where x and y are the lengths of S_1 and S_2 respectively [1]. For the experiments reported in the evaluation section below, each evaluation data set featured time series of the same length, the calculation of standard DTW complexity, $DTW_{compStand}$, thus simplifies to:

$$DTW_{compStand} = O\left(x^2\right) \tag{3}$$

When using ED the complexity, in terms of the number of similarity calculations, will be:

$$ED_{compStand} = O\left(x\right) \tag{4}$$

When using the Enhanced Sub-Sequence-Based DTW, proposed in this paper, the DTW time complexity reduces to:

$$DTW_{compSplit} = O\left(\frac{x^2}{x \div \ell}\right) \tag{5}$$

As note earlier, kNN classification was used with respect to the evaluation reported below, with $k = 1$ because this is the most commonly used value for k for time series classification [2,3], the new unseen time series t needs to be compared with all records r in the dataset D in order to be classified. The time complexity for comparing a single record using 1NN will be:

$$O\left(r \times complexity\right) \tag{6}$$

where complexity can be measured using: (i) $DTW_{compStand}$ (ii) $ED_{compStand}$ or (iii) $DTW_{compSplit}$.

If there are $|t|$ new time series to be classified ($|t| > 1$) the complexity will become:

$$O\left(r \times complexity \times |t|\right) \tag{7}$$

When using the proposed, Candidate Reduction, the time complexity is given by:

$$O\left(|t| \times \left((\mathsf{r} \times DTW_{compSplit}) + ((r - \mathsf{r}) \times ED_{compStand})\right)\right) \tag{8}$$

where r is the number of time series retained after candidate reduction.

5   Evaluation

In this section, the evaluation of the proposed mechanism is presented. Experiments were conducted using: (i) Standard DTW (the benchmark), (ii) Enhanced Sub-Sequence-Based DTW as described in [1] and using $\ell = 40$ and $t = 2$ and Option C (the parameters that produced the best results), (iii) Enhanced Sub-Sequence-Based DTW with parameter learning but without candidate reduction and (iv) Enhanced Sub-sequence-Based DTW with parameter learning and candidate reduction (the proposed mechanism). As noted earlier, the evaluation was performed using the kNN classification algorithm. Fifteen datasets from the

UEA and UCR Time Series Classification repository [4] were used. Further detail regarding the datasets used is given in Subsect. 5.1. The evaluation objectives were:

1. To review the operation of the proposed Enhanced Sub-sequence-Based DTW with parameter learning and candidate reduction in terms of the parameters used
2. To evaluate the run-time of the proposed approach in comparison with the other approaches considered.
3. To evaluate the accuracy of the proposed approach in comparison with the other approaches considered.

Each is considered in turn in the following three sub-sections, Subsect. 5.1 to Subsect. 5.3.

For the experiments, a desktop computer with a 3.5 GHz Intel Core i5 processor and 16 GB, 2400 MHz, DDR4 of primary memory was used. The reported values are Ten Cross Validation (TCV) average values.

5.1 Parameter Settings

This section presents an overview of the data sets used and the learnt parameter settings. A total of fifteen datasets were taken form the UEA and UCR repository [4]. The datasets were chosen so that a range of datasets of different sizes, in terms of the number of records and time series lengths, were considered and different numbers of classes. The lengths varied between 8 and 2000 points; the number of records varied between 60 to 10992. An overview of the fifteen datasets, ordered according to ascending order of time series length (x), is given in Table 2. Column 3, x, gives the time series length (number of points) for each dataset. The number of records r for each dataset is given in Column 4, and the number of classes in Column 5. The parameter values learnt using the proposed Sub-Sequence-Based DTW approach, for ℓ, t and $\mathfrak{r}$, are given in Columns 6, 7 and 8 respectively. The runtime to learn the parameters is given in Column 9. From the table, it can be seen that each dataset has its own values for the parameters; although it should be noted that $\ell = 40$ is the best length for almost 50% of the datasets used in the experiments. For runtime, as expected, the size of the dataset ($x \times r$) plays an important role to determine the required time for learning the parameters.

5.2 Run Time Performance

In this sub-section, the runtime performance with respect to the labelling of a single previously unseen time series is presented. The runtime results are presented in Table 3; again, the data sets are ordered according to ascending order of time series length. The columns equate to the four alternatives considered in the evaluation as listed earlier. From the table, it can be seen that using the proposed approach, with parameter learning and candidate reduction, significant

Table 2. Evaluation Time Series Datasets Used and Learnt Parameters ℓ, t and r.

ID No.	Dataset Name	Length (x)	Num. records (r)	Num. Classes	Parameters			Runtime (sec)
					ℓ	t	r	
1.	PenDigits	8	10992	10	5	2	1	8867
2.	SmoothSubspace	15	300	3	7	3	20	236
3.	ItalyPowerDemand	24	1096	2	10	4	5	1131
4.	Libras	45	360	15	10	2	5	886
5.	SyntheticControl	60	600	10	30	2	32	2187
6.	GunPoint	150	200	2	40	2	8	1630
7.	OliveOil	570	60	4	40	9	4	1854
8.	Trace	275	200	4	80	2	10	2449
9.	ToeSegment2	343	166	2	40	9	20	2558
10.	Car	577	120	4	60	6	13	3018
11.	Lightning2	637	121	2	80	4	10	3564
12.	ShapeletSim	500	200	2	40	2	22	6032
13.	DiatomSizeRed	345	322	4	40	2	1	6198
14.	Adiac	176	781	37	40	8	13	9213
15.	HouseTwenty	2000	159	2	40	5	12	11098

efficiency gains are earned. The runtimes recorded using the proposed approach are almost the same. The same results are plotted in Fig. 4, where the x-axis represents the dataset names, see Table 2, and the y-axis represents the runtime in seconds. From the figure, it can again be seen that the runtime using the proposed mechanism (red line) is almost constant regardless of the nature of the data set used. Also, the runtime for the Enhanced Sub-Sequence-Based DTW and Enhance parameter Learning are almost identical.

Table 3. Runtime (sec) Results for a Single Record.

ID No.	Data set	Standard DTW (B'mark)	Enhanced Sub-Seq. Based DTW	Enhanced Param. Learning	Enhanced Param. Learn Cand. Reduct.
1.	PenDigits	19.00	4.40	4.50	0.27
2.	SmoothSubspace	1.33	0.45	0.45	0.26
3.	ItalyPowerDemand	2.20	0.70	0.75	0.26
4.	Libras	1.40	0.45	0.50	0.26
5.	SyntheticControl	1.65	0.60	0.55	0.25
6.	GunPoint	1.20	0.40	0.35	0.25
7.	OliveOil	1.30	0.36	0.40	0.25
8.	Trace	1.40	0.52	0.52	0.26
9.	ToeSegment2	1.55	0.54	0.60	0.25
10.	Car	1.90	0.51	0.52	0.26
11.	Lightning2	1.85	0.50	0.55	0.26
12.	ShapeletSim	2.11	0.65	0.72	0.28
13.	DiatomSizeRed	2.39	0.79	0.85	0.26
14.	Adiac	2.30	1.10	1.22	0.25
15.	HouseTwenty	17.01	1. 43	1.70	0.28

5.3 Accuracy of Performance

In term of the effectiveness of the proposed technique comparisons were conducted using accuracy and F1 score. The results are presented in Table 4, standard deviation values are given in parenthesis. The presented are average values derived using Ten Cross Validation (TCV). From the table, it can be seen that the accuracy and F1 score are either improved or remain unchanged using the proposed mechanism (and with runtime gains). In some datasets, such as SmoothSubspace, Libras, GunPoint, Car, and ShapeletSim have improved significantly in comparison with the fundamental DTW. Whilst the Enhanced Sub-Sequence-Based DTW and Enhanced Parameters Learning has similar performance in term of accuracy and F1 score.

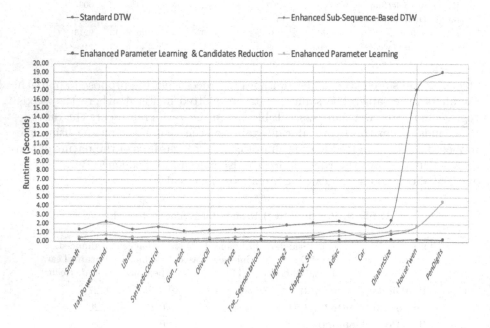

Fig. 4. Average TCV runtime results (seconds) to classify a single record. (Color figure online)

Table 4. Best accuracy and F1 results, overall best accuracies and F1 values highlighted in bold font.

ID #	Data set	Bencmark Standard DTW		Enhanced Sub-Sequenc Based DTW		Enhanced Param. Learning		Sub-Sequence B0.98ased DTW and Cand. Reduct.	
		Acc	F1	Acc	F1	Acc	F1	Acc	F1
1	PenDigits	85.50 (0.01)	0.85 (0.01)	88.48 (0.01)	0.88 (0.01)	88.48 (0.01)	0.88 (0.01)	**89.28** (0.01)	**0.89** (0.01)
2	Smooth Subspace	91.00 (0.04)	0.91 (0.04)	98.33 (0.03)	**0.99** (0.03)	98.33 (0.03)	**0.99** (0.03)	**98.67** (0.01)	0.99 (0.01)
3	ItalyPower Demand	95.70 (0.02)	**0.96** (0.02)	96.34 (0.01)	**0.96** (0.01)	96.34 (0.02)	**0.96** (0.02)	**96.62** (0.01)	0.96 (0.01)
4	Libras	62.59 (0.10)	0.60 (0.11)	66.51 (0.14)	0.64 (0.15)	67.22 (0.12)	0.65 (0.12)	**68.00** (0.11)	**0.66** (0.11)
5	Synthetic Control	98.00 (0.01)	**0.98** (0.01)	98.33 (0.01)	**0.98** (0.01)	98.33 (0.01)	0.98 (0.01)	**98.50** (0.01)	0.98 (0.01)
6	GunPoint	93.97 (0.04)	0.94 (0.05)	99.00 (0.02)	**0.99** (0.02)	99.00 (0.02)	**0.99** (0.02)	**99.50** (0.01)	0.99 (0.01)
7	Oil~Oil	89.52 (0.15)	0.88 (0.16)	90.12 (0.10)	0.89 (0.12)	90.12 (0.10)	0.89 (0.12)	**91.54** (0.11)	**0.91** (0.11)
8	Trace	99.00 (0.03)	**0.99** (0.03)	96.50 (0.04)	0.97 (0.04)	99.00 (0.03)	**0.99** (0.03)	**99.50** (0.01)	0.99 (0.01)
9	Toe Segmentation2	89.07 (0.09)	0.88 (0.10)	92.26 (0.03)	0.92 (0.04)	90.56 (0.06)	0.90 (0.07)	**92.30** (0.04)	**0.92** (0.04)
10	Car	80.83 (0.07)	0.80 (0.09)	82.50 (0.10)	0.81 (0.11)	81.67 (0.11)	0.80 (0.12)	**88.33** (0.08)	**0.88** (0.09)
11	Lightin2	87.74 (0.09)	0.87 (0.08)	87.40 (0.08)	0.87 (0.09)	89.26 (0.06)	0.89 (0.07)	**91.00** (0.09)	**0.91** (0.09)
12	DiatomSize Reduction	99.36 (0.01)	0.99 (0.01)	**100.00** (0.00)	**1.00** (0.00)	**100.00** (0.00)	**1.00** (0.00)	**100.00** (0.00)	**1.00** (0.00)
13	ShapleletSim	82.37 (0.09)	0.81 (0.11)	**93.00** (0.04)	**0.93** (0.04)	92.00 (0.06)	0.92 (0.06)	**93.00** (0.04)	**0.93** (0.04)
14	Adiac	64.63 (0.03)	0.62 (0.04)	64.98 (0.03)	0.62 (0.04)	65.43 (0.02)	0.63 (0.03)	**66.70** (0.02)	**0.66** (0.03)
15	HouseTwenty	**93.75** (0.04)	**0.94** (0.04)	91.17 (0.07)	0.91 (0.07)	91.17 (0.07)	0.91 (0.07)	**93.75** (0.04)	**0.94** (0.04)

6 Conclusion

In this paper, an enhanced Sub-Sequence-Based DTW approach, the Enhanced Sub-sequence-Based DTW with parameter learning and candidate reduction mechanism, has been presented. The operation of the proposed approach was compared with Standard DTW, Enhanced Sub-Sequence-Based DTW and Enhanced Sub-Sequence-Based DTW with parameter learning but no candidate reduction. For the experiments the k-Nearest Neighbour classification algorithm, with $k = 1$, was used, coupled with the Ten Cross Validation (TCV) technique, with respect to 15 datasets taken from the UEA and UCR (University of East Anglia and University of California Riverside) Time Series Classification Repository [4]. A comparison was conducted in terms of runtime, and accuracy and F1 score. The runtimes recorded for the four mechanisms were presented, these demonstrated that the proposed approach outperformed the other models significantly. In addition, as the number of records, or time series length, was increased, the runtime advantage becomes more evident. With respect to the recored accuracy and F1 scores, the results demonstrated that the proposed mechanism, incorporating candidate reduction, produced better performance compared to other mechanisms considered.

References

1. Alshehri, M., Coenen, F., Dures, K.: Effective sub-sequence-based dynamic time warping. In: Bramer, M., Petridis, M. (eds.) SGAI 2019. LNCS (LNAI), vol. 11927, pp. 293–305. Springer, Cham (2019). https://doi.org/10.1007/978-3-030-34885-4_23
2. Alshehri, M., Coenen, F., Dures, K.: Sub-sequence-based dynamic time warping. In: KDIR, pp. 274–281 (2019)
3. Bagnall, A., Lines, J.: An experimental evaluation of nearest neighbour time series classification. arXiv preprint arXiv:1406.4757 (2014)
4. Bagnall, A., Lines, J., Bostrom, A., Large, J., Keogh, E.: The great time series classification bake off: a review and experimental evaluation of recent algorithmic advances. Data Min. Knowl. Disc. **31**(3), 606–660 (2017). https://doi.org/10.1007/s10618-016-0483-9
5. Bringmann, K., Künnemann, M.: Quadratic conditional lower bounds for string problems and dynamic time warping. In: 2015 IEEE 56th Annual Symposium on Foundations of Computer Science, pp. 79–97. IEEE (2015)
6. Brunello, A., Marzano, E., Montanari, A., Sciavicco, G.: A novel decision tree approach for the handling of time series. In: Groza, A., Prasath, R. (eds.) MIKE 2018. LNCS (LNAI), vol. 11308, pp. 351–368. Springer, Cham (2018). https://doi.org/10.1007/978-3-030-05918-7_32
7. Gamboa, J.C.B.: Deep learning for time-series analysis. arXiv preprint arXiv:1701.01887 (2017)
8. Huang, S.F., Guo, M., Chen, M.R.: Stock market trend prediction using a functional time series approach. Quant. Financ. **20**(1), 69–79 (2020)
9. Itakura, F.: Minimum prediction residual principle applied to speech recognition. IEEE Trans. Acoust. Speech Signal Process. **23**(1), 67–72 (1975)

10. Kocian, A., Chessa, S.: Auto regressive integrated moving average modeling and support vector machine classification of financial time series. In: Bucciarelli, E., Chen, S.-H., Corchado, J.M. (eds.) DCAI 2018. AISC, vol. 805, pp. 1–8. Springer, Cham (2019). https://doi.org/10.1007/978-3-319-99698-1_1
11. Kulkarni, N.: Effect of dynamic time warping using different distance measures on time series classification. Int. J. Comput. Appl. **975**, 8887 (2017)
12. Liu, Z., Jiang, P., Zhang, L., Niu, X.: A combined forecasting model for time series: application to short-term wind speed forecasting. Appl. Energy **259**, 114137 (2020)
13. Niennattrakul, V., Ratanamahatana, C.A.: Learning dtw global constraint for time series classification. arXiv preprint arXiv:0903.0041 (2009)
14. Rakthanmanon, T., et al.: Searching and mining trillions of time series subsequences under dynamic time warping. In: Proceedings of the 18th ACM SIGKDD International Conference on Knowledge Discovery and Data Mining, pp. 262–270. ACM (2012)
15. Sakoe, H., Chiba, S.: Dynamic programming algorithm optimization for spoken word recognition. IEEE Trans. Acoust. Speech Signal Process. **26**(1), 43–49 (1978)
16. Silva, D.F., Giusti, R., Keogh, E., Batista, G.E.: Speeding up similarity search under dynamic time warping by pruning unpromising alignments. Data Min. Knowl. Disc. **32**, 1–29 (2018). https://doi.org/10.1007/s10618-018-0557-y
17. Tan, C.W., Herrmann, M., Forestier, G., Webb, G.I., Petitjean, F.: Efficient search of the best warping window for dynamic time warping. In: Proceedings of the 2018 SIAM International Conference on Data Mining, pp. 225–233. SIAM (2018)
18. Zhou, M., Wong, M.H.: Boundary-based lower-bound functions for dynamic time warping and their indexing. Inf. Sci. **181**(19), 4175–4196 (2011)

Ensemble-Based Relationship Discovery in Relational Databases

Akinola Ogunsemi[1(✉)], John McCall[1], Mathias Kern[2], Benjamin Lacroix[1], David Corsar[1], and Gilbert Owusu[2]

[1] Robert Gordon University, Aberdeen, UK
{a.ogunsemi,j.mccall,b.m.e.lacroix,d.corsar1}@rgu.ac.uk
[2] BT Applied Research, Ipswich, UK
{mathias.kern,gilbert.owusu}@bt.com

Abstract. We performed an investigation of how several data relationship discovery algorithms can be combined to improve performance. We investigated eight relationship discovery algorithms like Cosine similarity, Soundex similarity, Name similarity, Value range similarity, etc., to identify potential links between database tables in different ways using different categories of database information. We proposed voting system and hierarchical clustering ensemble methods to reduce the generalization error of each algorithm. Voting scheme uses a given weighting metric to combine the predictions of each algorithm. Hierarchical clustering groups predictions into clusters based on similarities and then combine a member from each cluster together. We run experiments to validate the performance of each algorithm and compare performance with our ensemble methods and the state-of-the-art algorithms (FaskFK, Randomness and HoPF) using Precision, Recall and F-Measure evaluation metrics over TPCH and AdvWork datasets. Results show that performance of each algorithm is limited, indicating the importance of combining them to consolidate their strengths.

Keywords: Semantic relationship · Primary/Foreign key relationship · Data discovery · Database management · Ensemble-based discovery

1 Introduction

Data are one of the most important assets in the economy of the 21st century. Entire new industries rely on and are centred around the exploitation of large data sets, as many modern business processes generate millions or even billions of data records every day which are stored in databases. Understanding the relationship between data and gaining insight from data is central to their commercial success.

A user such as a business analyst may gain access to an existing database but expertise about how data is structured and how data tables relate to each other may not be provided, and little or no documentation exists. It could be that the technical and domain experts have moved on or left the business altogether,

© Springer Nature Switzerland AG 2020
M. Bramer and R. Ellis (Eds.): SGAI-AI 2020, LNAI 12498, pp. 286–300, 2020.
https://doi.org/10.1007/978-3-030-63799-6_22

or many different groups have contributed to the database over time without a single authority fully understanding the overall information. This is a significant roadblock to exploiting this data. This challenge has mostly been addressed through highly time-intensive human analysis and exploration by domain experts [5,6,11,22]. However, such an approach is limited due to time, cost and the amount of information that can be looked at, and is further likely to be error-prone [2,7,9]. Clearly, we need an automated mechanism to speed up the data discovery process.

In this paper, we investigate several relationship discovery algorithms that infer links between columns of tables and propose a framework that combines them into an overall framework. To the best of our knowledge, several approaches have been proposed to determine semantic relationships between database schemas and several variations have been reviewed with each having its strengths and weaknesses. See [1]. However, limited research work has been seen in exploring various ensemble strategies for combining several relationship discovery algorithms. One of these strategies was seen in [14] and this is in the space of schema matching which focuses on the manipulation of database schema elements for mapping [21].

Our motivation for combining several algorithms is to reduce the generalization error of the prediction produced by the individual algorithms [12]. Individual algorithms are diverse and independent so, the predictions made by a single algorithm may lead to imperfect discovery compared to a framework that combines several approaches [21].

Our proposed approach emphasizes recall and this is based on the premises that our methods discover different relationship types; primary/foreign key (explicit) and semantically equivalent (implicit) relationships. We only rely on the explicitly defined primary key/foreign key relationship as our gold standard. Thus, false positives (which are more likely to be semantically equivalent relationships) could be discovered due to the impact of the specified gold standard. This paper makes the following contributions;

- We investigated the problem of automatically discovering primary keys and foreign keys as well as semantically equivalent (implicit) relationships by ensemble methods.
- We used hierarchical clustering method as an ensemble framework to combine the prediction of individual discovery algorithms to better provide a comprehensive matching outcome.

The rest of this paper is structured as follows. Section 2 briefly explores some related work in relationship discovery. Section 3 defines the problem and describes the individual algorithms and their ensemble strategies. The experimental evaluations are provided in Sect. 4. Finally, a conclusion is given in Sect. 5.

2   Related Work

Several approaches have been proposed in the literature using different categories of data. For instance, Jiang and Naumann [11] proposed a holistic discovery of both primary key and foreign key (HoPF) as a subset of sets of unique column combinations and inclusion dependencies based on score function and several pruning rules. [22] proposed ten feature-based approach to automatically detect foreign keys using a machine learning model. In [6], K-Means clustering was used to solve multi-schema matching problem. They used a well-known TFIDF weighting to convert attributes to points in a vector space model and used cosine measure as a distance metric between attributes. [15] proposed a content based matching approach to determine the relationship between attributes which rely on the combined strengths of Google as a web semantic and regular expression as pattern recognition. [27] proposed an unsupervised solution that clusters set of columns to identify attribute relationships based on similar value characteristics using Earth Mover's Distance (EMD) as distance measures.

3   Ensemble-Based Discovery

3.1   Problem Definition

For a given database of n tables, $T = \{t_1, t_2, \cdots, t_n\}$, let $C = \{c_1, c_2, \cdots, c_\theta\}$ be the set of all columns of tables T where θ is the number of columns in the database. We define $t_i(c_i)$ as a table with an associated column where c_i is an i-th column of table t_i. Let $\Delta = \{(c_i, c_j) \colon \exists\ t_i(c_i) = t_i(c_j), (c_i, c_j) \in C \times C\}$ be a set of column pairs (c_i, c_j) of the same table. We define $g_k = (C_k, E_k)$ as a graph of inferred relationships between set of columns (nodes) C_k and $E_k \subseteq C_k \times C_k \subset (C \times C) \setminus \Delta$ as the set of edges of g_k. Columns c_i and c_j are nodes in C_k, and each pair of columns (c_i, c_j) represents an edge in E_k, such that $(c_i, c_j) \in C_k \times C_k$. Let $f_k \colon C \times C \to g_k$ be a given discovery algorithm that produces graph g_k.

Our task is to determine the relationships between database tables which forms a graph G. The relationships include both primary/foreign key and semantic relationships which are determined by different discovery techniques to produce graphs, whereby the graphs are combined, with appropriate ensemble methods, to produce a global graph. The discovery techniques exploit metadata/schema information and column values available in relational database model.

1. Input Parameters
    (a) C - A set of all columns of the tables in T in the database DB.
    (b) f_k – A suitable method for discovering table relationships.
2. Output Parameters
    (a) $g_k = (C_k, E_k)$ - A graph containing a set of column pairs (c_i, c_j) in C_k where $C_k \in C$.

3.2   Relationship Discovery Algorithms

Pseudo-Primary Key Discovery (Pri). Pri is important in an application area, where no explicit definition of primary and foreign key constraints is available [22]. Existing work in this area can be explored in [11,18,22,26]. We denote

A as the subset of C, $A \subseteq C$, which contains all columns with explicitly defined primary key columns in a database. Let B be defined as the subset of $C \setminus A$, $B \subseteq C \setminus A$, which are columns qualified as potential primary key candidates. The sets A and B do not share any columns. Let X be the union of A and B: $X = A \cup B$. We then calculate a graph g_k in which the nodes are columns from X plus their associated foreign key columns. Two column nodes are linked in the graph if they are in a primary/foreign key candidate relationship. We use the following four tests to infer B.

- Alphanumeric Datatypes Test: Columns with alphanumeric datatypes.
- Nullability Test: Non-null columns.
- Uniqueness Test: Columns with unique values.
- Word Character Test: Columns with letter, digit or underscore character.

We distinguish two cases in primary key/foreign key column pairs:

- Either a column is explicitly marked as a foreign key in the database itself,
- Or we need to establish that the second (foreign key) column only contain values that appear in the first (primary key candidate) column.

In Eq. (1), $values(c_i)$ denotes values in column c_i. $w(c_i, c_j)$ returns 1 if two columns c_i and c_j are in a (potential) primary/foreign key relationship, and 0 otherwise:

$$w(c_i, c_j) = \begin{cases} 1, & \text{if } c_i \subset A \text{ and } c_j \text{ is foreign key for } c_i \text{ and } t_i(c_i) \neq t_i(c_j) \\ 1, & \text{if } c_i \in B \text{ and } values(c_j) \frown values(c_i) \text{ and } t_i(c_i) \neq t_i(c_j) \quad (1) \\ 0, & \text{otherwise} \end{cases}$$

Name Similarity (NSim). Nsim is used to determine the linkages between tables by identifying the similarity between column names associated with each table. Several names used in identifying tables and columns are usually designated based on the nature of the business activities. Thus, column names may have inconsistent designations across tables. For instance, a column name "Customer Name", might be represented either as "CustName", "CustomerN" or "CstName". We used Jaro-Winkler to discover the similarity between two columns names (c_i and c_j) because it is a well-known algorithm used as far back in the 80s. This has currently been used in name similarity matching like entity matching [24]. See [10] and [25] for detailed mathematical definitions. We used java-string-similarity[1] library for our implementation. In Eq. (2), we define the $Score(c_i, c_j)$ function for all threshold dependent algorithms. The $Score(c_i, c_j)$ function returns 1 if a given $Metric$ produces a value greater than or equal to a given $Threshold$ and if c_i and c_j are not from the same table t_i. $Score(c_i, c_j)$ returns 0 otherwise. In the NSim algorithm, we implement $JWinkler(c_i, c_j)$ as the $Metric$ function. The value of $JWinkler(c_i, c_j)$ is a real number between the range of 0 and 1. If this value is greater than or equal to the $Threshold$, 1

---

[1] https://github.com/tdebatty/java-string-similarity.

is assigned to $Score(c_i, c_j)$ which allows us to add the two columns as nodes to a graph g_k and connect them in the graph.

$$Score(c_i, c_j) = \begin{cases} 1, & \text{if } Metric \geq Threshold \text{ and } t_i(c_i) \neq t_i(c_j) \\ 0, & \text{otherwise} \end{cases} \tag{2}$$

Usage-Based Approach (Usage). Usage uses a set of existing scripts from the database to infer relationship between tables. Scripts may include existing database logic such as procedures, functions, views or user queries. From these scripts, we extract all pairs of columns that co-occur in linking tables together. This approach was first introduced in [8]. Usage-based approach is suitable, in special cases, where column names are opaque or where there are no sufficient information about schema and data instance. However, it is often difficult to obtain suitable usage data [20]. We used General SQL Parser (GSP) library [2] to implement this approach. Let $S = \{s_1, \cdots, s_q\}$ be the set of existing scripts for a database. s_i denotes a single script and references a set of tables T_{s_i} in its logic. We define $T_{s_i} = \{t_{s_i1}, \cdots, t_{s_i\iota}\}$, where ι is the number of tables in T_{s_i}. If script s_i contains a link statement, e.g.. a join statement, between tables t_{s_ix} and t_{s_iy}, and more specifically links the referenced columns in t_{s_ix} and t_{s_iy} respectively, we then, infer a link between those two columns and add the two columns as nodes to graph g_k.

Cosine Similarity Approach (Cosine). Cosine uses vector representation to measure the cosine angle between two vectors. Cosine was used in [6] as a distance metric measure for clustering attributes. We adopt cosine similarity to represent each attribute/column as a vector using Term Frequency Inverse Document Frequency (TFIDF) weighting computation. TFIDF is a term weighting scheme for cosine computation. TFIDF is a product of a term frequency (TF) weight factor and an inverse document frequency (IDF) weight factor. We define the cosine similarity metric between a pair of columns as $CoSim(c_i, c_j)$. See detailed computation of cosine similarity $CoSim(c_i, c_j)$ in [23]. The cosine similarity value $CoSim(c_i, c_j)$ is a real number between 0 and 1 and it represents the $Metric$ function defined in Eq. (2). If the value is greater than or equal to the $Threshold$ in Eq. (2), we then assign 1 to $Score(c_i, c_j)$ or 0 otherwise. A $Score(c_i, c_j)$ of 1 will add the two columns as nodes to graph g_k and connect them in the graph.

Semantic Similarity in a Taxonomy (Sem). Sem exploits additional, external information to measure the similarity between a pair of words or concepts. The key resource used is a knowledge-based database, such as a business-specific ontology or a general-purpose database like WordNet [17], which encodes relations between concepts. For example, when column headers are described

---

[2] https://dpriver/www..com/.

slightly differently e.g.., "AUTOMOBILE_NO" can conceptually mean the same as "VEHICLE_ID". We used a knowledge based function in [16], to measure the similarity between a pair of columns. We define the knowledge metric as $Sem(c_i, c_j)$ which computes the average similarity score by combining resultant similarity scores of substrings of c_i and c_j. We define v_{ik} as the $k - th$ substring/term associated with the name for column c_i. The $SemSim(v_{ik}, v_{jk})$ metric in Eq. (3) is used in the $Sem(c_i, c_j)$ metric computation (see [16]) which returns a similarity score between a pair of terms v_{ik} and v_{jk} associated with the names of columns c_i and c_j respectively. A stopword (i.e, most common word in a language) term returns score 0. If both terms are not in the knowledge networks, name similarity $JWinkler(v_{ik}, v_{jk})$ is used. $JWinkler(v_{ik}, v_{jk})$ is also used for terms that are either adjectives or adverbs in the knowledge network. Lastly, if the pair of terms are both verbs or nouns in the knowledge networks, we then compute $sim_{Lin}(v_{ik}, v_{jk})$, otherwise score returns 0.

$$
SemSim(v_{ik}, v_{jk}) = \begin{cases} 0, & \text{if } v_{ik} \text{ or } v_{jk} = stopword \\ JWinkler(v_{ik}, v_{jk}), & \text{if } v_{ik} \text{or } v_{jk} \notin ontologies \\ sim_{Lin}(v_{ik}, v_{jk}), & \text{if } v_{ik} \text{ and } v_{jk} \in ontologies(noun) \\ sim_{Lin}(v_{ik}, v_{jk}), & \text{if } v_{ik} \text{ and } v_{jk} \in ontologies(verb) \\ JWinkler(v_{ik}, v_{jk}), & \text{if } v_{ik} \text{ or } v_{jk} \in ontologies(adv) \\ JWinkler(v_{ik}, v_{jk}), & \text{if } v_{ik} \text{ or } v_{jk} \in ontologies(adj) \\ 0, & \text{otherwise} \end{cases}
$$

$$(3)$$

We implemented $sim_{Lin}(v_{ik}, v_{jk})$ using Semantic Measures library [3]. See computation in [13]. It takes two concepts and returns their semantic relatedness value. Let $Sem(c_i, c_j)$ represents the $Metric$ function in Eq. (2). The $Score(c_i, c_j)$ function defined in Eq. (2) is assigned 1 if the $Sem(c_i, c_j)$ is greater than or equal to the $Threshold$ and if the column pair are not from the same table.

Soundex Similarity (Soundex). It is a phonetic algorithm that indexes a string by sound in English. It simply evaluates letters of a string and assigns a numeric value. Soundex is used in the context of identifying the relationship between two tables based on the phonetic similarity between their column names. See computation in [19]. We implemented Soundex using Apache Commons library [4] in Java. We denote the phonetic similarity as $Sdex(c_i, c_j)$. The value of $Sdex(c_i, c_j)$ is between 0 and 4. A $Sdex(c_i, c_j)$ value of 4 means that a pair of column names sound strongly similar and 0 means otherwise. $Sdex(c_i, c_j)$ computes the $Metric$ value in Eq. (2) to assign $Score(c_i, c_j)$ a score 0 or 1.

Value Ranges Similarity (Val). Val uses minimum and maximum values of column pairs to determine whether they are linked. Val works with numeric,

---

[3] https://www.semantic-measures-library.org/sml/index.php?q=downloads#sml.
[4] https://commons.apache.org/proper/commons-codec/download_codec.cgi.

strings or date datatypes. Two columns of the same datatype are similar if they have similar value range pattern. We denote a_i as a pair of minimum and maximum values $\langle min(c_i), max(c_i) \rangle$ for column c_i. Columns c_i and c_j are logically equivalent ($a_i \equiv a_j$), if a_i is similar to a_j or vice versa. The check $range(c_i, c_j)$ in Eq. (4) returns 1 for similar value ranges between two columns c_i and c_j or 0 otherwise. (c_i, c_j) is added to g_k if $range(c_i, c_j)$ is 1.

$$range(c_i, c_j) = \begin{cases} 0, & \text{if } datatype(c_i) \neq datatype(c_j) \text{ or } t_i(c_i) = t_i(c_j) \\ 1, & \text{if } a_i \equiv a_j \text{ and } t_i(c_i) \neq t_i(c_j) \\ 0, & \text{otherwise} \end{cases} \qquad (4)$$

Content-Based Similarity (Col). Col exploits and compares data instances to determine the relationship between columns pair. $content(c_i, c_j)$ returns 1 if the set of value samples in column c_j is a subset of unique values of column c_i, and 0 otherwise. (c_i, c_j) is added to graph g_k if $content(c_i, c_j)$ is 1.

$$content(c_i, c_j) = \begin{cases} 0, & \text{if } datatype(c_i) \neq datatype(c_j) \text{ or } t_i(c_i) = t_i(c_j) \\ 1, & \text{if } samplevalues(c_j) \subset values(c_i) \text{ and } t_i(c_i) \neq t_i(c_j) \\ 0, & \text{otherwise} \end{cases}$$
$$(5)$$

3.3   Ensemble Strategies

We used voting scheme and hierarchical clustering to find the best combination of graphs generated by the discovery algorithms.

Voting Scheme. The voting scheme checks if the individual graphs share common edges. It uses a weighting measure to determine the proportion of graphs that contain a pair of columns (c_i, c_j). Given, g_k and $P_{weighting}$, we can generate a global graph G. We defined w_k in Eq. (6) as a score that indicates whether a pair of columns (c_i, c_j) exists in graph g_k. w_k returns 1 if a pair of columns (c_i, c_j) is an element of $E_k \in g_k$ and 0 otherwise. We compute the weighted value of $p_{(c_i, c_j)}$ in Eq. (7) for each pair of columns (c_i, c_j) as the sum of scores of w_k divided by the number of graphs m. We then generate a global graph G by adding a pair of columns (c_i, c_j) to graph G where the obtained weighting value of $p_{(c_i, c_j)}$ is equal or greater than a given $P_{weighting}$.

$$w_k = \begin{cases} 1, & \text{if } (c_i, c_j) \in E_k \\ 0, & \text{Otherwise} \end{cases} \qquad (6)$$

$$p_{(c_i, c_j)} = \frac{\sum_{k=1}^m w_k}{m} \qquad (7)$$

Hierarchical Clustering. We used the clustering approach (hierarchical clustering) proposed in [3] to group together variables which are strongly related to each other into homogeneous clusters. Each variable represents a graph g_k. We used hierarchical clustering proposed in [3] to group the variables (graphs) into clusters based on how they are strongly linked. See [3] for detailed formulation of the hierarchical clustering method proposed in the study.

The rationale for this strategy is that members in each cluster contains similar prediction pattern. We can therefore, select a member of each cluster and combine with a selected member of another cluster to exploit diversity and reduce error in prediction.

We represent each graph g_k as a categorical variable Φ_k and we defined $\{\Phi_1, \cdots, \Phi_m\}$ as a set of Φ categorical variables where $\Phi_k \in \Phi$ and $k = 1, \cdots, m$. m is denoted as the total number of variables (number of graphs). Then, let x be a set of all pairs of columns in $(C \times C) \backslash \Delta$, such that $E_k \subset x$. Φ_k has the same dimension (number of column pairs) as x, and for each variable Φ_k, contains binary strings of 0 and 1. String 1 indicates that $(c_i, c_j) \in E_k$ and 0 otherwise.

Let $\mathcal{P} = (\mathcal{P}_1, \ldots, \mathcal{P}_q)$ be a partition into q clusters of Φ variables. q denotes the total number of clusters and $\mathcal{P}_l$ is the $l - th$ cluster of $\mathcal{P}$.

We generate $\{G_1, \ldots, G_\alpha\}$ as a set of graphs $\mathfrak{G}$ where G_i is the ith graph in $\mathfrak{G}$. We expect to obtain at least a graph from $\mathfrak{G}$ graphs which gives a strong and improved prediction of relationship between column pairs. We denote α as the total number of graphs (i.e, number of possible combination of variables from each cluster). This is expressed in the equation below;

$$\alpha = \prod_{l=1}^{q} |\mathcal{P}_l|$$

$|\mathcal{P}_l|$ denotes the number of Φ variables in cluster $\mathcal{P}_l$. Let Φ_{jl} be a variable in cluster $\mathcal{P}_l$, so that each graph $G_i \in \mathfrak{G}$ is produced by combining a set of q variables selected from each cluster using intersection operation. This is expressed below as follows;

$$G_i = \bigcap_{l=1}^{q} \Phi_{jl}$$

4 Experimental Evaluation

4.1 Dataset Description

The two datasets (TPCH[5] and AdvWork[6]) used for this paper are synthetic datasets. For ease of comparison, the TPCH used the same parameter setting used in [11]. We stored the individual datasets in an Oracle database. The characteristics of the two datasets are given in Table 1. Both synthetic datasets contain database views and procedures we used as existing database queries.

---

[5] https://www.tpc.org/tpch.

[6] https://github.com/Microsoft/sql-server-samples/releases/tag/adventureworks.

Table 1. Data Characteristics

Data	No of Tables	No of Columns	AvgNo of Columns per Table	MaxNo of Columns per Table	Total Rows	No of Queries	Primary keys	Foreign keys
TPCH	8	61	8	16	6,885,051	22	8	8
AdvWork	71	486	7.5	26	754,248	33	27	45

4.2 Experimental Set-Up

We implemented our algorithms in Java and performed experiments on an Intel Core i5 vPro 2.4 GHz CPU with 8 GB Ram. We first run experiments for threshold dependent algorithms to select appropriate thresholds required for an overall comparative analysis. The range of thresholds include; NSim (0.50–0.95), Soundex (1–4), Sem (0.50–0.95) and Cosine (0.50 and 0.95). Next, we explored the performance of individual algorithms based on mean completion time over 20 runs. We then combined their predictions based on voting scheme and hierarchical clustering. Finally, we compared performance with state-of-the-art algorithms (FaskFK [4], Randomness [26] and HoPF [11]). FastFK combines heuristic features with different rules to detect foreign keys, which assumes that each table pair can hold only one foreign key. Randomness algorithm uses a randomness metric to discover both single-column and multi-column foreign keys by using the earth-mover distance (EMD) to measure the data distribution similarity between foreign key candidates. HoPF uses score function and pruning rules for holistic discovery of both primary and foreign keys as a subset of sets of unique column combinations and inclusion dependencies.

4.3 Evaluation Metrics

We employ three standard evaluation metrics to measure the performance of individual algorithms; Precision, Recall and F-Measure. Let g_1 be a graph of actual relationships between set of columns (nodes) C_1 and E_1 be the set of edges of g_1. Let g_2 be another graph containing inferred relationships between columns discovered by a discovery algorithm with set of columns C_2 as nodes and E_2 as edges of g_2. Let $TP = E_1 \cap E_2$. TP represents true positives, a set of edges common to both E_1 and E_2 and $|TP|$ is the number of edges in TP. Let $FP \subseteq E_2 \setminus TP$ be a subset of $E_2 \setminus TP$ which represents false positives. FP and TP do not share common edges and $|FP|$ is the number of edges in FP. Let $FN \subseteq E_1 \setminus TP$ and $|FN|$ represents the number of edges in FN. Let $x = (C \times C) \setminus \Delta$ be all edges formed from all pairs of columns, such that E_1 and E_2 are both subsets of x. Then, we define TN (True negatives) as $TN = x \setminus (E_1 \cup E_2)$ and $|TN|$ is the number of edges in TN.

Precision is computed as $\frac{|TP|}{|TP| + |FP|}$ which evaluates the percentage of relevant outcomes discovered by our algorithms. We compute recall as $\frac{|TP|}{|TP| + |FN|}$. Recall evaluates the percentage of relevant outcomes that were discovered by a discovery algorithm over the total relevant outcomes. We then compute F-measure as $\frac{2 * Precision * Recall}{Precision + Recall}$ to measure the weighted harmonic mean of precision and recall.

4.4   Comparative Analysis

Discovery Completion Time. The mean completion time of individual algorithms is shown in Table 2. This involves 20 experimental runs over the TPCH dataset. Name similarity (NSim) algorithm records the lowest mean time of 4.25 ms with a minimum time 0 ms and maximum time 16 ms. On the other hand, content-based (Col) approach takes longer time than other discovery algorithms with recorded mean time of 2868283.3 ms (47.81 min). Figure 1 shows example of graphs generated by Sem (a) and Soundex (b) algorithms over the TPCH dataset.

Table 2. Completion Time of Discovery Algorithms in Milliseconds

Algorithms	MinTime	AveTime	MaxTime
Cosine	72	136.15	351
Pri	1228045	1501709.15	2926454
NSim	0	4.25	16
Col	2107575	2868283.3	7901629
Val	15671	16170.85	19454
Sem	3481	4491.35	8711
Soundex	3	5.95	34
Usage	144	342.2	1552

Comparison with Existing Techniques. We compared our results with the results already reported in [11]. The specified gold standard used for evaluation is based on primary/foreign key relationship. Performance is shown in Table 3. The best performance for the TPCH dataset results in f-measure of 1.00 which was achieved by Randomness. The Randomness performance is largely attributed to the assumption that true primary keys exist and are known. Randomness exactly matches the known primary keys to columns with the same names which makes it possible for the algorithm to achieve that score. Our methods exploit database information differently without any known assumptions about true primary key existence. Three of our methods (Sem, Usage, Cosine) outperformed the FastFK algorithm on TPCH dataset with respective f-measure scores 0.83, 0.80 and 0.73. The performance of the Usage based approach is highly dependent on the quality of existing queries. For instance, if the queries use all the true primary keys to link tables then f-measure of 1.00 is possible.

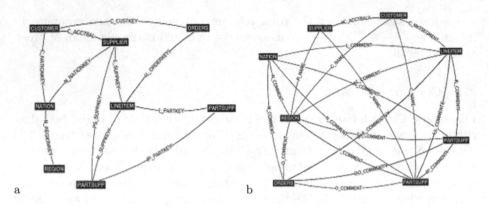

a   b

Fig. 1. Graph Example

In respect to the AdvWork dataset in Table 3, our algorithms could not achieve significant f-measure results apart from the Usage-based algorithm that achieved f-measure score of 0.23. The poor performance is largely attributed to

Table 3. Comparison of Proposed Discovery Algorithms, Ensemble Strategies and state of the art results already reported in [11]

Categories	Algorithm	TPCH			Algorithm	AdvWork		
		Precision	Recall	F-Measure		Precision	Recall	F-Measure
Individual Algorithms	Cosine	0.73	0.73	0.73	Cosine	0.02	0.86	0.04
	Pri	0.24	0.91	0.38	Pri	0.03	0.90	0.06
	NSim	0.22	1.00	0.37	NSim	0.02	0.83	0.04
	Col	0.15	0.91	0.26	Col	0.01	0.93	0.03
	Val	0.08	1.00	0.15	Val	0.01	0.04	0.02
	Sem	0.77	0.91	0.83	Sem	0.02	0.83	0.04
	Soundex	0.07	0.27	0.12	Soundex	0.02	0.83	0.04
	Usage	0.89	0.72	0.80	Usage	0.14	0.58	0.23
2-Clusters Combination	Sem_Pri	1.00	0.91	0.95	Sem_Pri	0.18	0.73	0.29
	NSim_Val	0.85	1.00	0.9	Cosine_Pri	0.19	0.76	0.30
	NSim_Pri	0.91	0.91	0.91	NSim_Pri	0.18	0.73	0.29
3-Clusters Combination	Sem_NSim_Pri	1.00	0.91	0.95				
	Sem_NSim_Col	1.00	0.82	0.90				
	Sem_NSim_Val	0.91	0.91	0.91				
Voting	PVote50	0.79	1.00	0.88	PVote75	0.18	0.80	0.29
	PVote62.5	0.85	1.00	0.92	PVote87.5	0.16	0.49	0.25
	PVote75	1.00	0.91	0.95				
State-of-the-Art	FastFK	0.56	0.90	0.69	FastFK	0.32	0.97	0.49
	Randomness	1.00	1.00	1.00	Randomness	0.90	0.41	0.56
	HoPF	0.88	0.88	0.88	HoPF	0.31	0.84	0.46

huge number of false positives discovered by our methods. These false positives are caused by the inherent semantic relationships which are not defined in the primary/foreign key relationship that we have used as gold standard in our evaluation. In terms of recall, Content-based (Col) and Primary key (Pri) algorithms achieved 0.93 and 0.90 respectively.

Overall, the diversity displayed by the individual algorithms are based on the characteristics of data. The algorithms have performed in different ways over the two datasets. However, the diversity of the independent algorithms can be exploited by combining their outcomes in different ways to improve performance.

Ensemble Performance. We used voting strategy and hierarchical clustering to combine the diversity of the outcomes produced by the individual algorithms and compare performance with the results of the state of the art algorithms reported in [11]. Voting thresholds are given as;
$P_{weighting} = (12.5\%, 25\%, 37.5\%, 50\%, 62.5\%, 75\%, 87.5\%, 100\%)$. We include results of the top three voting thresholds over the two datasets (TPCH and AdvWork) in Table 3. For TPCH dataset, the three top voting thresholds, 75%, 62.5% and 50% (i.e., PVote75, PVote62.5 and PVote50) achieve respective f-measure scores 0.95, 0.92 and 0.88, precision scores 1.00, .85 and 0.79 and recall scores 0.91, 1.00 and 1.00. The voting scheme could not reach the f-measure score (1.00) delivered by the Randomness algorithm, however, a 0.95 score was achieved which outperformed HoPF and FastFK.

In the AdvWork dataset, despite the poor performance of the individual approaches, the voting scheme helped in improving the performance. Although, this strategy could not outperform the selected state of the art algorithms. The reason for this is due to the existence of several semantic relationships which are not explicitly specified in the database structure. We only relied on the explicit specifications of primary key/foreign key relationships for our evaluation.

The drawback in the voting strategy is that the voting strategy takes all the discovery algorithms into consideration. This is quite expensive in terms of the computational time. For instance, based on Table 2, the total average completion time to implement a voting strategy will take about 4391143.2 ms (73.19 min). However, this could be addressed by using an appropriate sophisticated parallel computing approach which is beyond the scope of this paper.

In terms of the hierarchical clustering strategy, with the TPCH dataset, we evaluate two clusters and three clusters combinations. We obtain 15 unique combinations of algorithms with two clusters and 18 unique combinations with three clusters. The best performance in the two clusters combination for instance, is produced by Sem_Pri. Sem_Pri gives an f-measure score of 0.95 with precision score equal to 1.00. This means that no false positives were predicted with the combined efforts of both Sem and Pri algorithms. Sem_NSim_Pri obtains an f-measure score of 0.95 with precision score of 1.00. When comparing performance with state of the art algorithms, Sem_Pri and Sem_Nsim_Pri give better performance than HoPF and FastFK.

In the AdvWork dataset, two clusters were predicted by the clustering algorithm. We obtained top three unique combinations of the two cluster based on f-measure performance. The best performance is produced by the combination of Cosine_Pri with f-measure score 0.30, precision score 0.19 and recall score 0.76. The results reported by the state of the art algorithms outperformed the combined efforts of Cosine and Pri. See Table 3. We have earlier attributed the poor performance over the AdvWork dataset to lack of sufficient gold standard used in the study. We only relied on the primary/foreign key relationships which is specified in the database. An expert opinion would be needed for additional information about semantic relationship.

Overall, results show clearly that some specific algorithms are relevant when combined in certain ways. The Pri for instance, has the tendency of performing well when combined with algorithms like Sem, Nsim or Cosine irrespective of the data characteristics. However, the suitability of Pri is impaired due to speed considerations. Therefore, the choice of algorithms to combine depends largely on user's compromise on speed, reliability and sufficiency.

5   Conclusion

We investigated eight discovery algorithms and showed how their predictions can be combined to identify more comprehensive links between database tables involving both primary/foreign key and semantic relationships. The discovery algorithms identify potential links in different ways based on different levels of database information. In evaluating the performance of our approaches, based on two diverse datasets, we showed that different levels of schema information can be exploited and combined in a view to reduce the generalization error associated with each algorithm. We showed in our experiment that an appropriate combination strategy can be adopted to improve relationship discovery outcomes. The performance of individual discovery algorithm is limited, indicating the necessity to combine several algorithms to bring together their strengths. We compared precision, recall and f-measure with state of the art algorithms.

References

1. Alwan, A.A., Nordin, A., Alzeber, M., Abualkishik, A.Z.: A survey of schema matching research using database schemas and instances. Int. J. Adv. Comput. Sci. Appl. **8**(10) (2017)
2. Bellahsene, Z., Bonifati, A., Rahm, E.: Schema Matching and Mapping, Section 6. In: Data-Centric Systems. Springer, Heidelberg (2011). https://doi.org/10.1007/978-3-642-16518-4
3. Chavent, M., Kuentz, V., Liquet, B., Saracco, L.: ClustOfVar: an R package for the clustering of variables. arXiv preprint arXiv:1112.0295 (2011)
4. Chen, Z., Narasayya, V., Chaudhuri, S.: Fast foreign-key detection in Microsoft SQL server PowerPivot for excel. Proc. VLDB Endow. **7**(13), 1417–1428 (2014)
5. De Carvalho, M.G., Laender, A.H., GonçAlves, M.A., Da Silva, A.S.: An evolutionary approach to complex schema matching. Inf. Syst. **38**(3), 302–316 (2013)

6. Ding, G., Sun, T., Xu, Y.: Multi-schema matching based on clustering techniques. In: 2013 10th International Conference on Fuzzy Systems and Knowledge Discovery (FSKD), pp. 778–782. IEEE (2013)
7. Do, H.H.: Schema matching and mapping-based data integration (2006)
8. Elmeleegy, H., Ouzzani, M., Elmagarmid, A.: Usage-based schema matching. In: 2008 IEEE 24th International Conference on Data Engineering, pp. 20–29. IEEE (2008)
9. Hai, D.H.: Schema matching and mapping-based data integration. University of Leipzig (2005)
10. Jaro, M.A.: Advances in record-linkage methodology as applied to matching the 1985 census of Tampa, Florida. J. Am. Stat. Assoc. **84**(406), 414–420 (1989)
11. Jiang, L., Naumann, F.: Holistic primary key and foreign key detection. J. Intell. Inf. Syst. 1–23 (2019)
12. Kotu, V., Deshpande, B.: Data Science: Concepts and Practice. Morgan Kaufmann, Burlington (2018)
13. Lin, D., et al.: An information-theoretic definition of similarity. In: ICML, vol. 98, pp. 296–304. Citeseer (1998)
14. Maric, A., Gal, A.: Managing uncertainty in schema matcher ensembles. In: Prade, H., Subrahmanian, V.S. (eds.) SUM 2007. LNCS (LNAI), vol. 4772, pp. 60–73. Springer, Heidelberg (2007). https://doi.org/10.1007/978-3-540-75410-7_5
15. Mehdi, O.A., Ibrahim, H., Affendey, L.S.: An approach for instance based schema matching with Google similarity and regular expression. Int. Arab J. Inf. Technol. **14**(5), 755–763 (2017)
16. Mihalcea, R., et al.: Corpus-based and knowledge-based measures of text semantic similarity. In: AAAI, vol. 6, pp. 775–780 (2006)
17. Miller, G.A.: WordNet: a lexical database for English. Commun. ACM **38**(11), 39–41 (1995)
18. Papenbrock, T., Naumann, F.: A hybrid approach for efficient unique column combination discovery. Datenbanksysteme für Business, Technologie und Web (BTW 2017) (2017)
19. Pinto, D., Vilarino, D., Alemán, Y., Gómez, H., Loya, N.: The soundex phonetic algorithm revisited for SMS-based information retrieval. In: II Spanish Conference on Information Retrieval CERI (2012)
20. Rahm, E.: Towards large-scale schema and ontology matching. In: Bellahsene, Z., Bonifati, A., Rahm, E. (eds) Schema Matching and Mapping, pp. 3–27. Springer, Heidelberg (2011). https://doi.org/10.1007/978-3-642-16518-4_1
21. Rahm, E., Bernstein, P.A.: A survey of approaches to automatic schema matching. VLDB J. **10**(4), 334–350 (2001)
22. Rostin, A., Albrecht, O., Bauckmann, J., Naumann, F., Leser, U.: A machine learning approach to foreign key discovery. In: WebDB (2009)
23. Salton, G., Buckley, C.: Term-weighting approaches in automatic text retrieval. Inf. Process. Manag. **24**(5), 513–523 (1988)
24. Wang, Y., Qin, J., Wang, W.: Efficient approximate entity matching using Jaro-Winkler distance. In: Bouguettaya, A., et al. (eds.) WISE 2017. LNCS, vol. 10569, pp. 231–239. Springer, Cham (2017). https://doi.org/10.1007/978-3-319-68783-4_16
25. Winkler, W.E.: Frequency-based matching in Fellegi-Sunter model of record linkage. Bur. Census Stat. Res. Div. **14** (2000)

26. Zhang, M., Hadjieleftheriou, M., Ooi, B.C., Procopiuc, C.M., Srivastava, D.: On multi-column foreign key discovery. Proc. VLDB Endow. **3**(1–2), 805–814 (2010)
27. Zhang, M., Hadjieleftheriou, M., Ooi, B.C., Procopiuc, C.M., Srivastava, D.: Automatic discovery of attributes in relational databases. In: Proceedings of the 2011 ACM SIGMOD International Conference on Management of data, pp. 109–120. ACM (2011)

Intention-Aware Model to Support Agent Deliberation in a Large-Scale Dynamic Multi-Agent Application

Vince Antal, Tamás Gábor Farkas, Alex Kiss, Miklós Miskolczi,
and László Z. Varga[✉] [iD]

Faculty of Informatics, ELTE Eötvös Loránd University, Budapest 1117, Hungary
lzvarga@inf.elte.hu

Abstract. It is hoped that the traffic in the cities will be almost optimal when autonomous vehicles will dominate the traffic. We investigate the route selection of autonomous vehicles. We extend, implement and apply a formal model to support the trustworthy route selection of real-world autonomous agents. We trust a model, if the route selection strategy of the model selects routes which are close to the possible fastest all the time. The formal model extends the intention-aware online routing game model with parallel lanes, traffic lights and give way intersections. These extensions are needed for real-world applications. The actual parameters of the formal model are derived from real-world OpenStreetMap data. The large-scale real-world testing of the model uses the SUMO (Simulation of Urban MObility) open source simulator. The implemented intention-aware online routing game model can execute the route selection for each vehicle faster than real-time. Our hypothesis is that the extended intention-aware online routing game model produces at least as good traffic as the dynamic equilibrium route assignment. This hypothesis is confirmed in a real-world scenario.

Keywords: Autonomous vehicles · Route selection · Dynamic equilibrium

1   Introduction

When designing a dynamic multi-agent system, it is important to ensure that the resulting system will not produce unwanted extreme behaviour. This usually requires the application of some kind of deliberative agent architecture, because the agents must be prepared for future changes in a dynamic environment, and the agents must base their actions on the predicted actions of other agents. In order to avoid an unwanted extreme behaviour of the whole system, the agents must somehow coordinate their actions. If the multi-agent system consist of a large number of agents, then direct communication among all the agents is not realistic. In this case, the agents often use stigmergic communication [3] through the environment. An advanced version of stigmergic communication is when

© Springer Nature Switzerland AG 2020
M. Bramer and R. Ellis (Eds.): SGAI-AI 2020, LNAI 12498, pp. 301–314, 2020.
https://doi.org/10.1007/978-3-030-63799-6_23

the agents leave not only traces in the environment, but they also submit their intentions to the environment, which is then able to aggregate the intentions and make predictions [7]. Then the agents can use this prediction in their deliberation process to select their best action towards their goal.

Multi-agent systems are applied in many domains since their first industrial applications [13]. Currently, a typical application of large-scale dynamic multi-agent systems is the route selection of autonomous vehicles in a city traffic. This is a complex problem, not only because of the complexity of the road network, but also because the traffic changes with delay in response to the actions of the agents. When an agent selects a route to follow, then the agent may contribute to a congestion which will develop in the network sometime later. Agents are dynamically entering and departing the system. Real-time traffic data are available nowadays, but these data describe only the current travel times. There is uncertainty about the feasible decision of an agent, because the travel times on the roads will change by the time the agent gets there. This is because the departing of agents makes the travel faster, agents simultaneously selecting their route will influence each other's travel times, and agents entering the system later may also influence the travel times of the agents that are already on their trips.

We are interested in the route selection of autonomous vehicles, and we would like to know how the formal models for this problem can support the trustworthy decision making of real-world autonomous agents. We assume, that autonomous vehicles can safely avoid obstacles on their way, so we assume that in this sense they are trustworthy. We are interested in the trustworthiness of their route selection. If the route selection strategy of the model makes the agents select routes which are close to the possible fastest, then we can trust that model.

In Sect. 2, we shortly overview previous models of route selection, congestion sensitivity and prediction. In Sect. 3, we describe how we extend the intention-aware online routing game model with parallel lanes, traffic lights and give way intersections. In Sect. 4, we shortly describe the implementation and the test environment of the extended formal model. In Sect. 5, we describe a real-world scenario to be used for the evaluation of the extended intention-aware online routing game model. The experiments are evaluated in Sect. 6. Finally, we conclude the paper in Sect. 7.

2   Related Models

From a computer science point of view, the road traffic is a large-scale and open multi-agent system that tries to solve the *routing problem*. The routing problem is a network with traffic flows going from a source node to a destination node. The traffic is routed in a congestion sensitive manner. The participants of the traffic want to optimise their trips.

There are different formal models for the routing problem. A model describes the participants, the allowed actions of the participants, and the available information that they can use to select the best action. The participants are assumed to be rational, in the sense that each participant selects an action which is the best response to the expected actions of the other participants. A model involves a solution concept [12] which forecasts the possible outcomes of the problem if the participants are rational. The most common solution concept is the equilibrium concept. A basic assumption of traffic engineering is that the traffic flows are assigned to possible routes in accordance with an equilibrium, which is either a static equilibrium [4,27] or a dynamic equilibrium [16,20]. The dynamic equilibrium assumes that the agents of the system know exactly how long the travel time is going to be right ahead on all routes, and they always select the route with the fastest travel time.

2.1   Route Selection Models

Routing Game. From an algorithmic game theory point of view [17], the routing problem is a network with source routing, where end users simultaneously choose a full route to their destination and the traffic is routed in a congestion sensitive manner [22]. The solution concept of the routing game is the *static equilibrium* concept. If some restrictions are applied to the model, then the existence of equilibria and an upper limit on the price of anarchy are proved. The drawback of the classic game theory model is that it assumes full knowledge of the game, it describes static situations and decisions are on the flow level (i.e. the flows are the agents).

Evolutionary Routing Game. The evolutionary dynamics of games [30] is usually investigated in repeated games where the agents receive feedback by observing their own and other agents' action and cost, and in the next game they change their own action based on these observations to decrease their cost [5,11,23]. If the initial traffic flow assignment has at least some traffic flow on each path of the static routing game, and some assumptions hold, then the traffic flow assignment converges to the Nash equilibrium of the static routing game. The repeated routing game has similar limitations as the algorithmic game theory model: decisions are on the flow level.

Queuing Network. The *non-atomic queuing network* [9] is a way of investigating how non-atomic traffic flows evolve over time. The solution concept for the queuing model is the *dynamic equilibrium all the time* [9], which corresponds to the *Nash equilibrium over time* defined in [14]. The queuing model does not have load-dependent cost of the edge if the queue is empty and the inflow is below the maximum capacity, because in this inflow range the edge has a constant delay. Therefore the queuing model is not a full extension of the static routing game to the time dimension. Regarding the practical applicability for autonomous vehicles, the queuing model also has limitations. The queuing model assumes the idealistic situation where all the agents have complete knowledge of the current and the future states of all queues and edges. A queuing network with more than one flow is a complex system which may not reach a dynamic equilibrium over time.

Online Routing Game. The online routing game model [24] contains elements of the routing game model, the queuing model and the concept of online mechanisms [19]. The online routing game model may comprise other important aspects as well: feedback from the traffic network, intention-awareness and intention-aware prediction. In the online routing game model, the traffic flow is made up of individual agents who follow each other, and the agents of the traffic flow individually decide which path to select, depending on the real-time situation.

Intention-Aware Online Routing Game is a special type of online routing game, where the agents can perceive their environment, and in addition they also receive aggregated information about the intentions of other agents in the system. The agents communicate their intentions to a service. The service aggregates the data about the agent collective, and it sends a feedback to the agents [7]. The feedback is a forecast of future traffic durations, and the agents who are still planning their route use this information to make a decision. The *intention-aware* [29] and the *intention propagation* [8] approaches are based on this scheme. Many results in different dynamical games show that many games exhibit complex unpredictable behaviour, or in the best case, they converge to a cycle [18]. Intention-aware online routing games are complex games that tend to cycle around an equilibrium, and this fluctuation is measured empirically[26].

2.2 Congestion Sensitivity Models

The above route selection models contain one or two concepts of congestion sensitivity: the cost function and the queuing delay. These are more or less in line with real traffic travel times as a function of the traffic flow [2] as described in the Highway Capacity Manual (HCM) [1]. The travel time on a road can be approximated roughly with a linear function of the traffic flow up to the point when the traffic flow reaches the maximum capacity of the road and the road becomes jammed. If the road in under-saturated, then the cost function is a good model of the travel time on the road. If the road is over-saturated, then the maximum capacity and the queue is a good model of the additional travel delay on the road. The online routing game model contains both components.

Real city traffic has other congestion creating components as well: traffic light controlled and give way sign controlled intersections. Deterministic queuing models can predict the delay at traffic light controlled intersections when the traffic flow is below the capacity that can be served during a green interval per cycle [10]. This is in line with the HCM [1] recommendation. If the traffic flow is above the capacity of the traffic light controlled intersection, then the growing queue of the queuing model is dominant. The Webster model [28] is a stochastic delay model that attempts to account for the randomness of vehicle arrivals.

There are different delay models of give way sign controlled intersections [6,31]. The delay models heavily depend on the structure of the intersection (e.g. if onward going vehicles may block turning vehicles). The recommended [1] simplest solution is to model give way sign controlled intersections as traffic light controlled intersections where the green interval cycle is derived from the traffic intensity of the higher order road.

2.3 Prediction Models

The prediction method is a critical point of those online routing games that exploit intention-aware prediction. Two prediction methods were formalised in [25]: the detailed prediction method and the simple prediction method.

The **detailed prediction method** takes into account all the intentions (in this case route selections) already submitted to the central service of the intention-aware stigmergic environment. Then the detailed prediction method computes what will happen in the future if the agents execute the plans assigned by these intentions, and then it computes for each route in the network the predicted travel time by taking into account the predicted future travel durations. The prediction algorithm used in [29] is close to this detailed prediction method. The main difference is that the prediction algorithm of [29] uses probabilistic values, while the method in [25] is deterministic.

The **simple prediction method** also takes into account all the intentions already submitted to the central service of the intention-aware stigmergic environment. Then the simple prediction method computes what will happen in the future if the agents execute the plans assigned by these intentions. However, when the simple prediction method computes the predicted travel time for each route in the network, then it takes into account the predicted duration at the latest intention submission for each road. This way, the simple prediction method needs a little bit less computation, and the simple prediction method brings forward the predictions. The simple prediction method is an approximation and does not try to be exact. As time goes by, if no new prediction is generated for a road, then the simple prediction method "evaporates" the prediction for that road, like the bio-inspired technique of [8].

3   Intention-Aware Model for Real-World Traffic Routing

The existing route selection models are on an abstract level, and they can be applied only to simple route networks which are far from reality. Our goal is to extend an existing route selection model for real-world applications. The parameters of these extensions can be generated into the model from a real-world map.

The best starting model is the **intention-aware online routing game** model, because it has the concept of both the cost function and the queuing delay. In addition, the online routing game model captures the evolutionary dynamic inside the routing game. The traffic flow is made up of individual agents who follow each other, and the agents of the traffic flow decide individually on their actions (i.e. route selection) based on the real-time information. The reader is referred to the openly accessible article [24] for the formal description of the intention-aware online routing game model. In short, the online routing game model is the sextuple $<t, T, G, c, r, k>$, where $t = \{1, 2, ...\}$ is a sequence of time steps, T time steps give one time unit (e.g. one minute), G is a directed multi-graph representing the road network, c is the cost function of G with $c_e : R^+ \rightarrow R^+$ for each edge e of G, r is a vector of flows, and $k = (k^1, k^2, ...)$ is a sequence of decision vectors $k^t = (k_1^t, k_2^t, ...)$ made by the agents in time step t. Edges have FIFO property, and there is a minimum following distance Gap_e on the edges which determines the maximum capacity of the edge. If the incoming traffic flow exceeds this maximum capacity, then the agents are queued-up with time distance Gap_e. The cost function of an edge is given as $VarCost \times flow + FixCost$ where $flow$ is the traffic flow currently entering the road and $VarCost, FixCost$ are constants. $FixCost$ is the travel time on the edge for an agent that enters an empty edge.

We extend the intention-aware online routing game with three concepts: edges with parallel lanes, traffic light controlled intersections and give way sign controlled intersections. We implement these concepts in the **detailed prediction** and the **simple prediction** as well.

Edges with Parallel Lanes. We introduce parallel lanes into the online routing game model as parallel edges of the road graph. This is not a major change in the model, and it is able to represent the increased capacity between nodes. Although the vehicles can change lanes between nodes in real traffic, we allow lane changes only at intersections. Parallel edges increase the complexity of the route search. The number of possible routes between a source and a destination node will increase, but we reduce it by eliminating routes that include the same road more than once.

Traffic Light Controlled Intersections. We introduce traffic light controlled intersections into the online routing game model by changing the characteristic of the edges leading to a traffic light controlled intersection. The changes concern both the following distance Gap_e and the cost function.

If edge e is leading to a traffic light controlled node, and the following distance of the edge without the traffic light is Gap_e time steps, and $Green$ is the time of the green period of the traffic light cycle in seconds, and $Cycle$ is the total time of the traffic light cycle in seconds, then the following distance of the edge will be changed to $LightGap_e = Gap_e \times Cycle \div Green$. This way, the throughput capacity of the edge will decrease, and the queuing time on the edge may grow faster.

For the change in the cost function, we use the delay from the deterministic queuing model in [10], because our model is deterministic too. If the cost function of edge e is $c_e(flow) = VarCost \times flow + FixCost$ in seconds, and T time steps give one time unit in the model, and Red is the time of the red period of the traffic light cycle in seconds, then the cost function of the edge will be changed to

$$c_e(flow) = VarCost \times flow + FixCost + \frac{Red^2 \times \frac{T}{Gap_e}}{\left(\frac{T}{Gap_e} - flow\right) \times 2 \times Cycle}.$$ The last addition

in the equation is the additional delay as specified in Eq. (1) in [10], and in our case, the saturation flow rate is $T \div Gap_e$. The $T \div Gap_e - flow$ component in our equation is responsible for the sharp increase in the cost function when the incoming flow gets close to the saturation flow rate. We limit this sharp increase when the incoming flow reaches the capacity resulting from $LightGap_e$ (i.e. we replace $T \div Gap_e - flow$ with a constant if it is below a given positive value), because the maximum capacity and the growing queue in front of the traffic light is modelled with $LightGap_e$, as described in the previous paragraph.

Give Way Sign Controlled Intersections. We introduce give way sign controlled intersections into the online routing game model by changing the characteristic of the edge leading to a give way sign controlled intersection. If the vehicles on edge e have to give way to the vehicles on edge f, then we treat edge e as an edge leading to a traffic light controlled intersection, where the parameters of the "imagined traffic light" is derived from the traffic flow on edge f.

The parameters of the "imagined traffic light" is derived the following way. The cycle is the time difference of the vehicles on edge f, i.e. $Cycle = T \div flow_f$ where $flow_f$ is the current traffic flow on edge f. The green period is the time period when a vehicle can enter edge f, i.e. $Green = Cycle - Gap_f$. The red period is the time period when a vehicle can not enter edge f, i.e. $Red = Cycle - Green$.

4 Implementation and Test Installation of the Intention-Aware Model

The architecture of the implementation of the extended online routing game model and its test environment are shown in Fig. 1. Agents are associated with the vehicles. The environment of the vehicle agents is represented by the map and the prediction service. The map contains the road network, as well as the traffic rules, like allowed speed, yielding, traffic lights, etc. Our implementation is able to extract these data from the openly available OpenStreetMap[1] (OSM). Vehicle agents have horizontally layered hybrid agent architecture. The driving layer is responsible for the reactive behaviour, like following the road, keeping the distance from other cars, turning at crossings, etc. The route selection layer is responsible for the proactive behaviour, which is the planning of the route of the vehicle in accordance with the intention-aware online routing game model. The prediction agent receives the intentions of the vehicle agents and makes predictions of future travel durations.

The reactive behaviour layer of the vehicle agent would need real vehicles in the real-world, but we have no access to enough (or any) vehicles for a large-scale experiment. Therefore we used the SUMO (Simulation of Urban MObility) traffic simulation suite [15] to simulate the real-world behaviour of vehicles. SUMO is able to do microscopic traffic simulation. The main model of the microscopic traffic simulation is the car following model [21] which simulates real driving behaviours. The car following model assumes that a vehicle maintains a safe

---

[1] https://www.openstreetmap.org/.

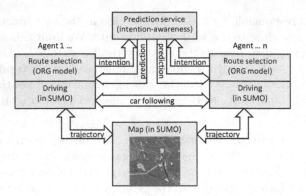

Fig. 1. The test installation of the online routing game (ORG) model with intention-awareness and simulated driving.

space and time gap between itself and the vehicle that precedes it. SUMO is an open source, highly portable, microscopic and continuous road traffic simulation package designed to handle large road networks. The SUMO system is responsible for both the two-dimensional view and for the micromanaging of the vehicles, such as changing lanes, keeping the required following distance and complying with the traffic rules.

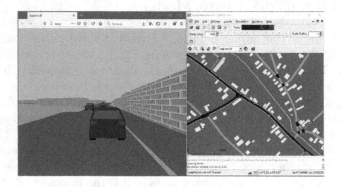

Fig. 2. The user interface of a simulation.

The user interface of the system during a simulation is shown in Fig. 2. The 3D View is on the left-hand side of the figure, and the SUMO simulator is on the right-hand side of the figure.

Importing the OSM Networks. Importing maps from OpenStreetMap is accomplished by using the OSM Web Wizard utility provided in the SUMO software package. Whereas a map exported from OSM only contains nodes (junctions) and edges (lanes), this utility both transforms the network to fit the

SUMO specifications and supplements it with additional data such as give way rules by means of calculations and estimations. Our model parses these SUMO-compatible network files, then it filters out the necessary elements to construct the road network. This preprocessing phase discards the superfluous elements, such as railroads or footpaths. Each junction in the SUMO-compatible network file contains a set of connections, that describes which outgoing lanes can be reached from an incoming lane. For each connection of a junction, there exists a so-called request, that both describes whether it is prohibited to pass this intersection without decelerating, and whether it conflicts with another connection. If the intersection is controlled by a traffic light, then the traffic light periods are defined in the Traffic Light System (TLS) descriptions for each connection.

5   Real-World Test Scenario

The intention-aware model was tested in different real-world scenarios. The scenarios were created from OSM using the OSM Web Wizard of SUMO to create the real-world environment for the SUMO simulator. The OSM Web Wizard automatically creates the traffic regulation parameters of the imported map, like the give way relations between lanes and the traffic light timings. Unfortunately the OSM maps, and the automatic settings of the OSM Web Wizard contain inaccuracies and they have to be checked manually.

In this paper we show a manually checked real-world test scenario shown in Fig. 3. This scenario contains parallel lanes, a give way controlled intersection and a traffic light controlled intersection. There are two traffic flows: flow $f2$ going from point A (top left corner in the figure) to point F, and flow $f1$ going from point B to point F. Vehicles of flow $f1$ have no other real choice in normal traffic situations than to select route (B, D, F), because the route (B, D, C, E, F) is too long. Vehicles of flow $f2$ have the options of route (A, C, E, F) or route (A, C, D, F). At the road intersection D, the vehicles coming from A must give way to vehicles coming from B. There is a tram terminal at point G, and a traffic light controls the passing of the vehicles going from D to F. The road from G to F has two lanes in the direction to F. There is no traffic light on the route (C, E, F), and the vehicles on this route do not need to give way to other vehicles, because we do not inject into the network other flows than $f1$ and $f2$. The vehicles coming from E and D do not need to give way to each other at F, because they continue their trips in parallel lanes. The routes of the vehicles of the flows are selected by the extended intention-aware online routing game model.

The test scenario simulated a 90 min long period. Several experiments were run at different traffic flow values. The flow values were constant in each experiment. The flow $f1$ ranged from 0 to 10 $car \div minute$ in steps of 2. The flow $f2$ ranged from 5 to 20 $car \div minute$ in steps of 5. The combination of these traffic flow values resulted in 24 experiments. The maximum flow value was 20, because this was about the maximum flow that these entry points could accept. The range of $f2$ was the double of $f1$, because the vehicles of $f2$ could choose

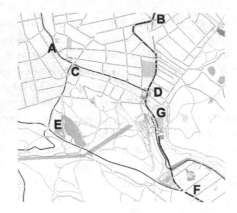

Fig. 3. The map in SUMO showing the real-world scenario of the experiment.

between two routes. The travel duration of every vehicle in the SUMO system was recorded in each experiment. The relative deviation, as well as the minimum, the maximum and the average of the travel durations of both traffic flow were computed in each experiment.

6   Performance in the Test Scenario

Our goal is to evaluate how good the intention-aware model selects the routes for the vehicles of flow $f2$ in the above test scenario. The ideal outcome is when the traffic is in dynamic equilibrium all the time during the experiment, i.e. none of the vehicles could have chosen another route to reduce its travel time.

Computing the dynamic equilibrium is a complex problem, and it is generally considered that the exact dynamic equilibrium cannot be reached, because there is randomness in real-world traffic. We used the "duaiterate" tool[2] of SUMO to compute the (approximate) probabilistic dynamic equilibrium of the real-world scenario. We iterated with this tool for each experiment until the relative deviation went below 0.001. Then we ran the resulting probabilistic traffic assignment in SUMO to measure and compute the relative deviation, as well as the minimum, the maximum and the average of the travel durations of flow $f2$. These were the reference values of the dynamic equilibrium for each experiment.

Our hypothesis is that the route selection of our intention-aware model brings the real-world system (represented by the SUMO simulation) close to the dynamic equilibrium all the time (which is approximated by the "duaiterate" tool).

The summary of the travel durations and the deviations for the different route selection methods in each experiment are shown in the diagrams of Fig. 4. If the routes are selected by the intention-aware model, then the maximum and the average travel durations are better than in the case of the "duaiterate" route

---

[2] https://sumo.dlr.de/docs/Demand/Dynamic_User_Assignment.html.

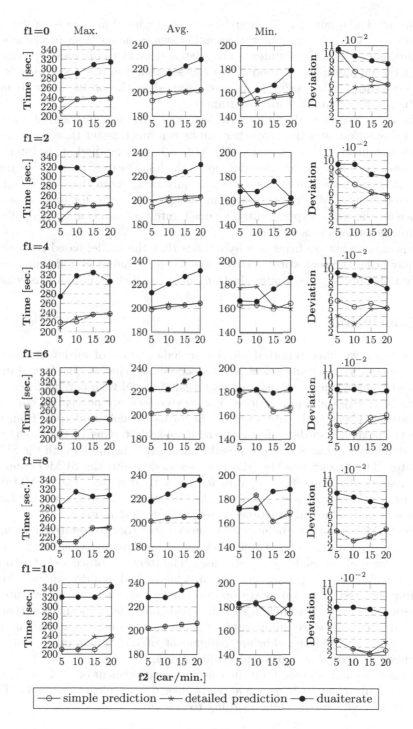

Fig. 4. The results of the experiments.

assignment. The minimum values are sometimes higher, but in most of the cases they are better in the case of the intention-aware model than in the case of the "duaiterate" route assignment. The relative deviations are also better in the case of the intention-aware model. We can see that the route selection of the intention-aware model performs at least as good as the probabilistic dynamic equilibrium of the "duaiterate" program.

The route selection of the intention-aware model runs interleaved with the SUMO simulation, and they together can be run much faster than real-time on an average laptop. This means that the route selection method of the intention-aware model can be applied in autonomous vehicles. The execution of the "duaiterate" program for a single experiment usually takes more than 30 min on the same laptop. The "duaiterate" program assigns the route for each vehicle in advance for the whole experiment. The duaiterate program cannot be applied in real-time in autonomous vehicles.

This experiment confirms our hypothesis that the model-based route selection may bring the real-world system close to the dynamic equilibrium, and in addition, the model-based route selection can be applied in autonomous vehicles.

7   Conclusion

In this paper we have reported on the implementation of an intention-aware model to support the route selection of autonomous vehicles. The formal model extends the intention-aware online routing game model with parallel lanes, traffic lights and give way intersections. These extensions are needed for real-world applications. The actual parameters of the formal model are derived from real-world OpenStreetMap data. Because the large-scale testing of the model with real autonomous vehicles was not possible, we tested the model with the SUMO simulator. The OpenStreetMap data is also loaded into the SUMO simulator which realistically simulates how vehicles follow their routes. The SUMO simulator uses car following models to drive the cars on their routes, while the formal model uses mathematical functions to select the fastest routes.

The SUMO simulator includes the "duaiterate" tool to iteratively compute a dynamic equilibrium of a traffic scenario. The dynamic equilibrium is the ideal outcome of rational agent behaviour. The iterative process of the "duaiterate" tool runs for long time, and it cannot be applied in autonomous vehicles. The implemented intention-aware online routing game model can execute the route selection for each vehicle faster than real-time. Our hypothesis is that the extended intention-aware online routing game model produces at least as good traffic as the dynamic equilibrium assignment of the "duaiterate" tool. This hypothesis was confirmed in a real-world scenario.

Further research will focus on the continuous adjustment of the formal model to the ongoing changes in the real-world, like e.g. accidents on roads. These adjustments could use machine learning techniques.

Acknowledgement. This work was supported by the European Union, co-financed by the European Social Fund (EFOP-3.6.3-VEKOP-16-2017-00002). The work of L.Z. Varga was supported by the"Application domain specific highly reliable IT solutions" project implemented with the support provided from the National Research, Development and Innovation Fund of Hungary, financed under the Thematic Excellence Programme no. 2020-4.1.1.-TKP2020 (National Challenges Subprogramme) funding scheme.

References

1. Highway capacity manual : a guide for multimodal mobility analysis. Transportation Research Board, Washington, D.C (2016)
2. Akçelik, R.: Speed-flow models for uninterrupted traffic facilities. Technical Report (2003). https://www.sidrasolutions.com/learn/publications/speed-flow-models-uninterrupted-traffic-facilities
3. Beckers, R., Holland, O.E., Deneubourg, J.L.: From local actions to global tasks: stigmergy and collective robotics. In: Artificial Life IV: Proceedings of the Fourth International Workshop on the Synthesis and Simulation of Living Systems. The MIT Press (1994). https://doi.org/10.7551/mitpress/1428.003.0022
4. Beckmann, M.J., McGuire, C.B., Winsten, C.B.: Studies in the Economics of Transportation. Yale University Press, London (1956)
5. Blum, A., Even-Dar, E., Ligett, K.: Routing without regret: on convergence to Nash equilibria of regret-minimizing algorithms in routing games. In: Proceedings of the 25th ACM Symposium on Principles of Distributed Computing, PODC 2006, pp. 45–52. ACM, New York (2006). https://doi.org/10.1145/1146381.1146392
6. Drilon, W.: Delay at unsignalized intersections. Transp. Res. Rec. J. Transp. Res. Board **2071**(1), 98–108 (2008). https://doi.org/10.3141/2071-12
7. Claes, R., Holvoet, T.: Traffic coordination using aggregation-based traffic predictions. IEEE Intell. Syst. **29**(4), 96–100 (2014). https://doi.org/10.1109/MIS.2014.73
8. Claes, R., Holvoet, T., Weyns, D.: A decentralized approach for anticipatory vehicle routing using delegate multi-agent systems. IEEE Trans. Intell. Transp. Syst. **12**(2), 364–373 (2011). https://doi.org/10.1109/TITS.2011.2105867
9. Cominetti, R., Correa, J., Olver, N.: Long term behavior of dynamic equilibria in fluid queuing networks. In: Eisenbrand, F., Koenemann, J. (eds.) IPCO 2017. LNCS, vol. 10328, pp. 161–172. Springer, Cham (2017). https://doi.org/10.1007/978-3-319-59250-3_14
10. Dion, F., Rakha, H., Kang, Y.S.: Comparison of delay estimates at under-saturated and over-saturated pre-timed signalized intersections. Transp. Res. Part B: Methodol. **38**(2), 99–122 (2004). https://doi.org/10.1016/s0191-2615(03)00003-1
11. Fischer, S., Vöcking, B.: On the evolution of selfish routing. In: Albers, S., Radzik, T. (eds.) ESA 2004. LNCS, vol. 3221, pp. 323–334. Springer, Heidelberg (2004). https://doi.org/10.1007/978-3-540-30140-0_30
12. Halpern, J.Y., Moses, Y.: A procedural characterization of solution concepts in games. J. Artif. Intell. Res. **49**, 143–170 (2014). https://doi.org/10.1613/jair.4220
13. Jennings, N.R., et al.: Using Archon to develop real-world DAI applications, Part 1. IEEE Expert **11**(6), 64–70 (1996). https://doi.org/10.1109/64.546585

14. Koch, R., Skutella, M.: Nash equilibria and the price of anarchy for flows over time. Theory Comput. Syst. **49**(1), 71–97 (2011). https://doi.org/10.1007/s00224-010-9299-y
15. Lopez, P.A., et al.: Microscopic traffic simulation using SUMO. In: 2018 21st International Conference on Intelligent Transportation Systems (ITSC). IEEE (2018). https://doi.org/10.1109/itsc.2018.8569938
16. Merchant, D.K., Nemhauser, G.L.: A model and an algorithm for the dynamic traffic assignment problems. Transp. Sci. **12**(3), 183–199 (1978). https://doi.org/10.1287/trsc.12.3.183
17. Nisan, N., Roughgarden, T., Tardos, E., Vazirani, V.V.: Algorithmic Game Theory. Cambridge University Press, New York (2007). https://doi.org/10.1017/CBO9780511800481
18. Palaiopanos, G., Panageas, I., Piliouras, G.: Multiplicative weights update with constant step-size in congestion games: convergence, limit cycles and chaos. In: Proceedings of 31st International Conference on Neural Information Processing Systems, pp. 5874–5884. Curran Associates (2017). https://doi.org/10.5555/3295222.3295337
19. Parkes, D.C.: Algorithmic Game Theory, Chap. Online Mechanisms, pp. 411–439. Cambridge University Press (2007). https://doi.org/10.1017/CBO9780511800481
20. Peeta, S., Ziliaskopoulos, A.K.: Foundations of dynamic traffic assignment: the past, the present and the future. Netw. Spat. Econ. **1**(3), 233–265 (2001). https://doi.org/10.1023/A:1012827724856
21. Pourabdollah, M., Bjarkvik, E., Furer, F., Lindenberg, B., Burgdorf, K.: Calibration and evaluation of car following models using real-world driving data. In: 2017 IEEE 20th International Conference on Intelligent Transportation Systems (ITSC). IEEE (2017). https://doi.org/10.1109/itsc.2017.8317836
22. Roughgarden, T.: Algorithmic Game Theory, Chap. Routing games, pp. 461–486. Cambridge University Press (2007). https://doi.org/10.1017/CBO9780511800481
23. Sandholm, W.H.: Potential games with continuous player sets. J. Econ. Theory **97**(1), 81–108 (2001). https://doi.org/10.1006/jeth.2000.2696
24. Varga, L.: On intention-propagation-based prediction in autonomously self-adapting navigation. Scalable Comput. Pract. Exp. **16**(3), 221–232 (2015). http://www.scpe.org/index.php/scpe/article/view/1098
25. Varga, L.Z.: Two prediction methods for intention-aware online routing games. In: Belardinelli, F., Argente, E. (eds.) EUMAS/AT -2017. LNCS (LNAI), vol. 10767, pp. 431–445. Springer, Cham (2018). https://doi.org/10.1007/978-3-030-01713-2_30
26. Varga, L.Z.: Dynamic global behaviour of online routing games. In: Weyns, D., Mascardi, V., Ricci, A. (eds.) EMAS 2018. LNCS (LNAI), vol. 11375, pp. 202–221. Springer, Cham (2019). https://doi.org/10.1007/978-3-030-25693-7_11
27. Wardrop, J.G.: Some theoretical aspects of road traffic research. Proc. Inst. Civil Eng. Part II **1**(36), 352–378 (1952)
28. Webster, F.V.: Traffic signal settings. Her Majesty's Stationery Office (1958)
29. de Weerdt, M.M., Stein, S., Gerding, E.H., Robu, V., Jennings, N.R.: Intention-aware routing of electric vehicles. IEEE Trans. Intell. Transp. Syst. **17**(5), 1472–1482 (2016). https://doi.org/10.1109/TITS.2015.2506900
30. Weibull, J.W.: Evolutionary Game Theory. MIT Press, Cambridge (1997)
31. Zhou, H., Hagen, L., Lin, P.S., Tian, Z.: Development of delay models for multi-lane two-way stop-controlled intersections. ITE J. (Inst. Transp. Eng.) **76**, 41 (2005)

Medical and Legal Applications

Combining Bandits and Lexical Analysis for Document Retrieval in a Juridical Corpora

Filipo Studzinski Perotto[1]([✉]), Nicolas Verstaevel[1], Imen Trabelsi[2], and Laurent Vercouter[2]

[1] Toulouse University, IRIT, 31000 Toulouse, France
{filipo.perotto,nicolas.verstaevel}@irit.fr
[2] Normandie University, INSA Rouen Normandie, LITIS, 76000 Rouen, France
{imen.trabelsi,laurent.vercouter}@litislab.fr

Abstract. Helping users to find pertinent documents within a big corpus through the use of simple queries on a search engine is a major concern in the information retrieval field. The work presented in this article combines the use of standard natural language processing methods to estimate the relevance of a document to a query with an online preference learning method to infer such kind of pertinence by analyzing the past behavior of other users making similar searches. The first contribution of this article is the proposition of a specific heuristic method, conceived for an open access online juridical corpus, to filter and interpret data collected from the user behavior while navigating on the search engine's query interface, on the list of results, and on the documents themselves. The second contribution is an original way for combining multiarmed bandit algorithms for learning pertinence from the user implicit feedback with natural language processing techniques in order to define a unique ranking for the search results.

Keywords: Document retrieval · Learning-to-Rank

1 Introduction

A document retrieval system (DRS) implements both a user interface and an engine to search over documents within a digital corpus. A DRS must: (a) find relevant documents to user queries and (b) evaluate the matching results, sorting them according to relevance. State-of-the-art DRS combine simple filtering techniques (from user given constraints concerning metadata and expression matching) with statistical analysis, natural language processing, and machine learning

This work is part of PlaIR 2.018, a project funded with the support from the European Union with the European Regional Development Fund (ERDF) and from the French Regional Council of Normandy. It is also partially supported by the C2C project, financed by French Regional Council of Occitanie to exploit both the semantic connections between documents and queries, and the feedback given by users in past interactions.

The work described in this article presents an original search engine architecture developed for a particular juridical digital corpus and query interface (described in Sect. 2) which includes:

(a) a specific way for filtering and interpreting user behavior data, collected by tracking user interactions with the search engine's query interface, the list of results, and the documents themselves;
(b) a domain-specific function for calculating user, document and query similarities;
(c) the use of advanced NLP techniques for calculating relevance between queries and documents, such as ontology-based matching and word-embedding;
(d) the use of multiarmed bandits algorithms for learning pertinence from behavior;
(e) a specific way for combining NLP and MAB in order to define a unique ranking for the search results.

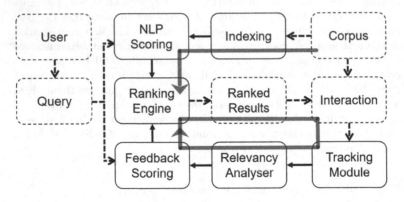

Fig. 1. Search engine modules. The top boxes represent the use of NLP modules for ranking document matches following lexical or even semantic text attributes; it is an offline process (the score of a document for a query does not change with time). The other boxes represent the online process of learning from the user feedback. Such modules analyze the user interaction with the list of results and with the documents themselves, trying to identify, from the user behavior, the evidences of relevance of a document for a query. Such evidence is then used as a reward, feeding a multiarmed bandit algorithm.

The structure of the search engine is illustrated in Fig. 1. The basic idea is to combine two strategies in order to better identify the relevance of documents to queries. The first strategy is the basis of any information retrieval system: the use of natural language processing techniques to analyze lexical and semantic matches. It corresponds to the top boxes in the Fig. 1, starting from the indexed corpus and matching with the query terms, which generates a linguistic relevance score. The second strategy is the differential of modern search engines: the use of user behavior in order to identify the relevance of a document based on implicit feedback. It corresponds to the middle and bottom boxes in the Fig. 1, forming a cycle where the implicit feedback collected by observing the interactions of users with the documents and with the ranked list of results feeds a multiarmed bandit algorithm that creates an alternative online ranking. Those two ways of scoring a document are then aggregated in a common ranking by the ranking engine.

The rest of the paper is organized as follows: Sect. 2 presents the targeted corpus of documents; Sect. 3 formalizes the problem in theoretical terms, and presents the background concepts concerning DRS and NLP; Sect. 4 overviews the use of multiarmed bandit algorithms for online preference learning; Sect. 5 presents the proposed architecture; Sect. 6 concludes the paper.

2   Corpus and Search Interface

We worked on a corpus extracted from the French Institute for the International Transportation Law (IDIT)[1]. Their virtual library, specialized in transportation jurisprudence, counts about 40000 documents, from which about 3000 are in open access. All the documents have been categorized by law experts and associated to specific keywords from a thesaurus containing about 2000 tokens. Around 35000 documents are French decisions of justice.

Each decision is associated with metadata such as the date of the decision, its country, type of court (tribunal, court of appeal, court of cassation - corresponding to the first, second or third degrees), associated themes (from thesaurus), etc. Due to domain specificity, the documents in the corpus have a regular structure. Every document of a given type of court can be divided into similar distinct, contiguous and non-overlapping segments, which always appear in the same order. In other words, each type of decision is segmented in a specific way. For example, the text of a decision from a court of appeal is divided into 4 segments:

header: where information like the name of the court, the judge, the city, the date, and the name of the disputing parts are declared;
facts: where the judge recalls the context of the disagreement, and the arguments claimed by the parts, as well as the verdict proffered by the lower court;
reasons: where the judge reproduces the arguments of the appellant for questioning the decision;
conclusion: where the judge declares and substantiates a new sentence, accepting or rejecting the plea;

Those documents are PDF files, but their contents are also available in plaintext format. After standard text pre-processing, each document is presented as

---

[1] www.idit.asso.fr.

an ordered collection of paragraphs. The paragraphs are divided into sentences and then tokenized into word-level terms to allow lexical analysis. The browsing navigation interface is composed of 4 frames or pages (query, results, abstract, and document) as illustrated in Fig. 2. The query interface frame is illustrated in Fig. 3. The list of results is illustrated in Fig. 4. The document is viewed online by the user through an interface similar to any classic PDF viewer as illustrated in Fig. 5.

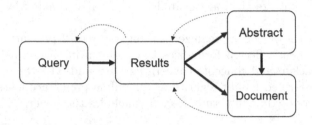

Fig. 2. Navigation between frames in the searching interface

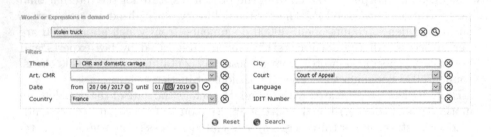

Fig. 3. The query interface

3   Background

Document research in a digital corpus corresponds to a browsing process driven by a user with specific information needs. Solving it requires the use of traditional information retrieval methods to estimate the most likely relevant documents to the user query. It can be improved by exploiting other elements like user profiles, browsing profiles and the semantic proximity of documents.

First of all, we need to formally define each entity involved in a document retrieval task.

3.1   Definitions

Let $D = \{d_1, \ldots, d_n\}$ be a corpus, consisting on a set of n documents, where each of its elements d_i is a document composed of metadata (e.g. date, geolocation,

Fig. 4. Ranked list of results interface. After executing the query, the website returns the results, ordered by the calculated relevance in the given time. The evidences learned from the interactions of the user with the list of results, as well as with the documents themselves, allow to improve the scoring for future queries. Searched terms are highlighted.

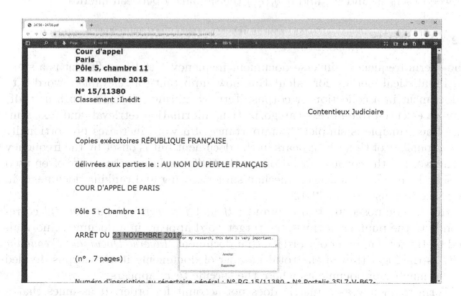

Fig. 5. The decision (a pdf document) is viewed online. The user can interact with the document (scrolling, selecting, etc.) and can also add private annotations (highlighted). All such actions are tracked in order to identify the interest of the user on the document, which helps to learn about its relevance to the query.

author, theme, type, etc.) and content (i.e. the structured sequence of words forming the text). Let $M = \{m_1, \ldots, m_{|M|}\}$ be the set of considered meta-attributes, and $m_{i,j}$ the value of attribute m_i on document d_j.

Let $W = \{w_1, \ldots, w_k\}$ be the complete set of k distinct words or terms appearing at least once in D, and $W_d \subset W$ the subset of those words that appears in document d. A query q is also a collection of terms but not necessarily limited to W.

Let $\phi_{w,d}$ be the relative frequency of a given word w on document d (usually called *tf* for *term frequency*), and ψ_w the proportion of documents where the word w appears in relation to the entire set of documents (usually called *df* for *document frequency*).

Let $R = \{r_1, \ldots, r_{|R|}\}$ be a set of anaphoric relationships (synonym, antonym, generalization, specialization, ...). An ontology O corresponds to the set of functions $\omega_r(w_1, w_2)$ indicating the strength of relation r between the words w_1 and w_2. Note that such relations can be symmetric (synonym, antonym) or asymmetric (general, specific).

Let $U = \{u_1, \ldots, u_z\}$ be a set of z users who have been interacting with the document retrieval search engine. Let Q_u be the history of queries made by a given user u, and $I_{u,d}$ the history of interactions between that user and a document d.

Let $\sigma(d_i, d_j)$ be a function that scores the similarity between documents d_i and d_j based on its lexical contents and metadata, $\sigma(u_i, u_j)$ the similarity between users u_i and u_j, and $\sigma(q_i, q_j)$ the similarity between queries.

3.2   Lexical Pertinence

The "term frequency · inverse document frequency" (tfidf) coefficient is a standard statistical method for calculating how important (or relevant) a word is to a document in a collection or corpus. Term weighting strategies (such as tfidf) play an essential role in text categorization, information retrieval, and text mining. The principle is simple: the importance of a word increases proportionally to the number of times it appears in the document but is offset by the frequency of the word in the corpus. Variations of the tfidf weighting scheme are often used by search engines as a central mechanism for scoring and ranking documents in response to a user query [2,13].

tfidf is composed by two operands: *tf* and *idf*. *Term Frequency (tf)* corresponds to the number of times the target word appears in a document, normalized by the total number of words in that document. *Inverse Document Frequency (idf)* is the logarithm of the total number of documents in the corpus divided by the number of documents where the specific term appears.

Term frequency as a metric does not account for order. It assumes that a document is just an order-ambivalent collection of tokens (bag-of-words), which could be represented by enumerating the number of times each token appears. In that bag-of-words model, each document can be represented by a vector of length k, where k is the total number of unique terms within the entire corpus (all documents) and each entry is the number of times that specific term appears in that document.

Inverse document frequency measures how informative a term can be within a corpus by weighing down the frequent terms while scaling up the rare ones. The standard tfidf coefficient τ, for a given word or term $w \in W$ and a given document $d \in D$, is defined in Eq. (1):

$$\tau_{w,d} = (1 + \log \phi_{w,d}) \cdot \log \frac{n}{\psi_w} \tag{1}$$

In such systems, term frequency, inverse document frequency, and document length normalization are important factors to be considered when a term weighting strategy is developed. Term length normalization is proposed to give equal opportunities to retrieve both lengthy documents and shorter ones. However, terms in very short documents could be assigned very high weights, resulting in a situation where shorter documents are ranked higher than lengthy documents that are more relevant to the user information needs. For that reason, in this research, we use the term weighting strategy proposed in [14] to alleviate the side effects of document length normalization.

To rank query results by lexical pertinence, the system must: (a) compute the tf and idf scores for every term, and then build the n length vector for each document, using the tfidf of each term; (b) considering the query, get a result set of matching documents; (c) compute a tfidf vector for the query; then, (d) calculate the similarity between the query vector and each document vector in the result set using *cosine similarity*; and (e) sort the documents by this score.

A document search engine must rank documents by their relevance to the query. For such a task, there is no unique and direct technical solution: it requires some examination of the corpus and data structures. If the documents are not just single text flows, but are structured and composed of known sections, different weights can be associated to the pertinence scores depending on the region the searched words are found. The same for textual metadata associated to the documents.

3.3 Similarity Metrics

We consider to analyse the similarity between elements inside the following categories of objects: user, query, and document, as indicated in Table 1:

Table 1. Different strategies for detecting similarity between entities. The table indicates what strategy can be applied to each kind of item.

Similarity	User	Query	Document
Lexical	No	Yes	Yes
Metadata	Yes	No	Yes
Feedback	Yes	Yes	Yes

Users and documents have associated metadata, and a first approach for measuring similarity is analyzing the proximity between such metadata values. Documents and queries, even if the last are very shorter, are composed by text. Therefore, a natural way for considering similarity is through lexical proximity, using NLP techniques. Finally, the feedback history can also be used for deducing an emerging similarity. The insight is that users producing similar queries and navigating through similar documents can be considered similar. Documents that are read by similar users during similar query sessions can be considered similar. Queries that are constructed by similar users and that lead to the reading of similar documents can be considered similar. Note, however, the circularity between such considerations. We are estimating a similarity between two objects based on the similarity between other objects related to it, which are also estimations.

3.4   User Feedback

In cooperation with NLP techniques, the architecture proposed in this paper makes use of learning techniques to infer the relevance between documents and queries using the user feedback. Depending on the problem, and on the existing user interface, an explicit feedback mechanism can be implemented (e.g. one to five stars, like/dislike, up/down, etc.). The drawback of such kind of explicit evaluation is that it introduces an additional effort that users are often unlikely to accept. They also involve modifying the website user interface, which can be undesirable. In addition, explicit evaluations can be biased or even misused by users.

The alternative is to get evidence on the relative importance of a query result by observing the user behavior [10]. Some interactions can produce particularly strong evidence about the importance of a document for a given user in her/his specific needs of information (e.g. a document clicked by the user after a query, in which she/he spent a long time scrolling and annotating its parts, that had been saved and printed, is probably a relevant document). Of course, several different information needs and browsing profiles can be expressed indistinctly by a same simple query. For that reason, the confidence concerning the estimated relevance of a document to a query increases with the number of observations.

For fine tracking user behavior on a web service, the most common strategy is the use of client side scripts (e.g. JavaScript functions incorporated to the webpage) that asynchronously send information of elementary user interactions with the pages, which is registered on a database on the server side [1]. The collected information generally comes from low-level actions (e.g. mouse movements, keyboard typing, link clicking, etc.). More abstract features must be inferred from such concrete data.

Implicit feedback (e.g., clicks, dwell times, etc.) provides an abundant source of data in human-interactive systems [11]. Contrarily to explicit feedback, implicit feedback means monitoring user behavior without intruding it. Implicit feedback features vary from simple ones, like view counting, to more sophisticated ones, like scrolling or mouse movement tracking. Due to its effortlessness, data can be obtained in much larger quantities for each user. On the other hand, they are inherently noisy, voluminous, and harder to interpret [11]. In addition, its inherent biases represent a key obstacle to be used effectively [6]. Beyond user-bias (e.g. some users tend to click in every result), the problem is the bias caused by the ranking itself. On a document retrieval system where most users are not experts on the domain, there is a tendency in accepting the ranking suggested by the system (i.e. the first results presented will be clicked more).

To avoid the disturbance caused by that bias (the user tendency for clicking on the first results, independent of their real relevance), a common feature calculated from low-level activity is the *relative click-through rate*. It consists in the ratio of the number of times a given result was clicked on, to the number of times it was displayed, pondered by its position on the results list. The pondering factor can be also adapted in function of the query profile (generic search of information vs. precise query). Other common features are the *effective dwell time* and the *pogo-sticking*. The first is the amount of time that a visitor spends on a given result after clicking on it, having focus on, or interacting with the document, and before closing it or coming back to the search results. The second is a negative evaluation, corresponding to the situation when a user bounces off an open document quickly (with few interaction) to return to the list of results looking for another document.

4   Learning-to-Rank

Most of the web search engines make the general assumption that users are often the best judges of relevance, so that if they select a particular search result, it is likely to be relevant, or at least more relevant than the presented alternatives [3]. Such engines rely on behavioral metrics to constitute their ranking factors. The basic strategy is using the collected click data on the query results to feed back into ranking. Infrequently clicked results should drop toward the bottom because they are probably less relevant, and frequently clicked results must bubble toward the top.

Online learning to rank can be viewed as a sequential decision-making problem where in each round the learning agent chooses a list of items and receives feedback in the form of clicks or other interactions from the user. Many sample-efficient algorithms have been proposed for this problem, assuming some specific click model relating rankings to user behavior [8].

Learning to rank is an important problem with numerous applications in web search and recommendation systems. The goal is to learn an ordered list of l items from a larger collection of size n that maximizes the satisfaction of the user, conditioned on a query. This problem has traditionally been studied in the offline setting, where the ranking policy is learned from manually-annotated relevance judgments. It has been observed that the feedback of users can be used to significantly improve existing ranking policies. This is the main motivation for online learning to rank, where the goal is to adaptively maximize the user satisfaction.

The standard click model in learning-to-rank is the cascade model (CM), built from the supposition that users scan the ranking from top to bottom, clicking on the first attractive item [7]. The system cannot observe what would have been the user's actions if the results have been placed in a different order. Such a problem is referred to as learning with partial feedback [5].

In the bandit setting with contextual information applied to ranking, an online algorithm receives a context (in the form of a feature vector) in time t and must select an action, whose quality is evaluated by a reward function. One of the first models had been presented by [12], an online learning algorithm that directly learn a diverse ranking of documents based on users' clicking behavior, able to minimize abandonment, or alternatively, maximize the probability that a relevant document is found in the top k positions of the ranking.

The learning-to-rank problem can be viewed as a regret minimization problem, where the goal is to asymptotically reduce the total number of bad-ranked items displayed over time. The trade-off between exploration and exploitation in that context comes from the necessary choice between presenting some unknown documents on the ranking list in order to collect information about those documents, or presenting the likely best items in order to ensure the user satisfaction [12]. Different bandit algorithms for the learning-to-rank task have been recently proposed in the literature, such as BanditRank [4] and TopRank [9].

5   Proposed Model

The standard approach for estimating the relevance of a document to a given search query is lexical correlation (tfidf), as indicated in previous sections. The relevance can be then modified using a MAB algorithm, based on the history of interactions, contextualized by the similarities between users and queries. The evidence of relevance must be interpreted from the user feedback.

In the query frame (Fig. 3), the feedback that can be analyzed concerns the construction of the query (typed or deleted words and expressions, and the time spent on it). In the list of results (Fig. 4), the frame that appears after the user launches the query, some feedback elements can be used for extracting evidence of relevance: the timestamp when each result snippet is shown to the user (after scrolling or changing to the next page of results), the total time that each snippet is visible to the user, if the user moves the mouse over the snippet, or reads a text tip, and finally, if the user clicks on the button to see the abstract of the decision (a kind of resume made by an expert, available on the website, which extends the snippet information) or to see the document (pdf) itself. Then, it is possible to collect the dwell time of (time spent on) an abstract or a document (Fig. 5), scroll percentage, counter of scrolling events or mouse pointer movements, print, copy or save actions, and particularly for the pdf documents, annotations and highlights made by the user, with corresponding timestamps.

The idea is that, the more the user interacted with a given document, the more it is likely to be relevant to her/his information need. In the subsequent MAB algorithm, the evidence of relevance is represented as a positive reward.

Some evidences can reveal the opposite: for example, interacting with the result snippet without opening the document, or opening the abstract and then closing it quickly. Such observed sequences of actions can indicate that the user paid attention to the document and decided to ignore it, which can be interpreted as an evidence of non relevance to the query. Table 2 distinguishes 4 categories adopted by the proposed mechanism for interpreting the observed evidences.

The proposed model analyzes query-document relevance based on multiple types of implicit feedback. Some feedback actions give evidence that a particular result was noticed by the user. It is the case for all interactions on the snippet (on the page of results). In fact, the opposite, a non-noticed (or completely ignored) result will not be impacted by feedback rewards. We consider in this case, that the user was searching for some specific document, and then the ignored ones do not need to be penalized. Other feedback actions indicate that the user paid attention to some result, e.g. reading the summary or the document. Such actions indicate the evidence of a potential importance of the document to the user and the query. However, the importance can only be confirmed by other actions indicating relevance, like saving the document or consistently annotating it.

The complete set of evidences considered for the specific target corpus is presented in Tables 3 and 4. The presence of each evidence increment the strength of the related parameter. The 4 parameters, $\alpha, \beta, \gamma, \delta$, are then heuristically combined as indicated in Eq. (2) in order to obtain a general evidence value ξ, which is returned as a reward to the MAB algorithm.

$$\xi = \alpha \cdot \beta \cdot (2\delta - \gamma) \tag{2}$$

Table 2. 4 different categories of evidences, with different consequences to the computation of relevance. Each category is associated to a parameter which measures the cumulated strength of the evidences.

Parameter	Interpretation	Consequence
α	Fruitful query evidences	Take feedback into account
β	Noticed result evidences	Take feedback into account
γ	Analyzed result evidences	Add small negative reward
δ	Relevant result evidences	Add big positive reward

Table 3. Tracking

Interface frame	Behavior	Threshold	Weight
Snippet	Display cumulated time	$\geq 10\,s$	$\beta \leftarrow \beta + 0.2$
	Mouse hover events Count	≥ 3 times	$\beta \leftarrow \beta + 0.4$
	Tip display cumulated time	$\geq 5\,s$	$\beta \leftarrow \beta + 0.4$
Abstract	See abstract click flag	true	$\gamma \leftarrow \gamma + 0.2$
	Get focus events count	≥ 3 times	$\gamma \leftarrow \gamma + 0.1$
	Focus cumulated time	$\geq 1\,min$	$\gamma \leftarrow \gamma + 0.1$
	Mouse hover events count	≥ 5 times	$\gamma \leftarrow \gamma + 0.1$
	Add to favorites flag	True	$\delta \leftarrow \delta + 0.1$
	Print flag	True	$\delta \leftarrow \delta + 0.1$
Document	See PDF document click flag	true	$\gamma \leftarrow \gamma + 0.2$
	Get focus events count	≥ 3 times	$\gamma \leftarrow \gamma + 0.1$
	Focus cumulated time	$\geq 1\,min$	$\gamma \leftarrow \gamma + 0.1$
	Mouse hover events count	≥ 7 times	$\gamma \leftarrow \gamma + 0.1$
	Copy events count	≥ 3 times	$\delta \leftarrow \delta + 0.1$
	Print flag	true	$\delta \leftarrow \delta + 0.1$
	Save flag	True	$\delta \leftarrow \delta + 0.1$
Annotations	Annotations count	≥ 2 annotations	$\delta \leftarrow \delta + 0.1$
	Selected text size	≥ 20 characters	$\delta \leftarrow \delta + 0.1$
	Annotation text size	≥ 50 characters	$\delta \leftarrow \delta + 0.1$
	Edition cumulated time	$\geq 1\,min$	$\delta \leftarrow \delta + 0.1$
	Modification events count	≥ 5 times	$\delta \leftarrow \delta + 0.1$

Table 4. Navigation evidence

Results with evidence of relevance	Query reformulated after	Weight
No	No	$\alpha = 0.5$
No	Yes	$\alpha = 0.0$
Yes	No	$\alpha = 1.0$
Yes	Yes	$\alpha = 0.5$

6   Conclusions

This paper proposed an architecture that combines lexical methods and bandit learning algorithms for producing a ranking of query-based searched documents within a particular juridical corpus, which is improved thanks to the user feedback. We described the interesting findings of an ongoing work. The next steps of this research include the use of synthetically generated data, and real collected data, in order to evaluate the quality of the proposed solution. In a first phase, a set of search problems and their corresponding relevant documents, previously prepared by an expert, is submitted as an exercise to different subjects, with different expertise levels, in order to observe their behavior during searching sessions. In such a preliminary phase, the goal is identifying what kind of evidences present greater correlation to document relevance. The intensity of the correlation can also suggest the weight of an evidence for deducing relevance, modifying the values presented in Tables 3 and 4. Based on such values, in a second phase we will be able to analyze the quality of ranking answers over time, comparing classic tfidf, as well as other state-of-the-art learning-to-rank methods against the proposed method.

References

1. Atterer, R., Wnuk, M., Schmidt, A.: Knowing the user's every move: user activity tracking for website usability evaluation and implicit interaction. In: Proceedings of the 15th International Conference on World Wide Web, pp. 203–212. ACM, New York (2006)
2. Croft, B., Metzler, D., Strohman, T.: Search Engines: Information Retrieval in Practice, 1st edn. Addison-Wesley, Boston (2009)
3. Enge, E., Spencer, S., Stricchiola, J., Fishkin, R.: The Art of SEO - Mastering Search Engine Optimization, 2nd edn. O'Reilly, Sebastopol (2012)
4. Gampa, P., Fujita, S.: BanditRank: Learning to rank using contextual bandits. CoRR abs/1910.10410 (2019)
5. Gentile, C., Orabona, F.: On multilabel classification and ranking with bandit feedback. J. Mach. Learn. Res. 15(1), 2451 2487 (2014)
6. Joachims, T., Swaminathan, A., Schnabel, T.: Unbiased learning-to-rank with biased feedback. In: Proceedings of the 10th ACM International Conference on Web Search and Data Mining, WSDM 2017, pp. 781–789. ACM, New York (2017)
7. Kveton, B., Szepesvári, C., Wen, Z., Ashkan, A.: Cascading bandits: learning to rank in the cascade model. In: Proceedings of the 32nd International Conference on International Conference on Machine Learning, ICML 2015, vol. 37, pp. 767–776. JMLR.org (2015)
8. Lattimore, T., Kveton, B., Li, S., Szepesvari, C.: TopRank: a practical algorithm for online stochastic ranking. In: Advances in Neural Information Processing Systems, Proceedings of NIPS 2018, vol. 31, pp. 3945–3954. PMLR (2018)
9. Lattimore, T., Kveton, B., Li, S., Szepesvari, C.: TopRank: a practical algorithm for online stochastic ranking. In: Bengio, S., Wallach, H., Larochelle, H., Grauman, K., Cesa-Bianchi, N., Garnett, R. (eds.) Advances in Neural Information Processing Systems, vol. 31, pp. 3945–3954. Curran Associates, Inc. (2018)
10. Mandal, S., Maiti, A.: Explicit feedbacks meet with implicit feedbacks: a combined approach for recommendation system. In: Aiello, L.M., Cherifi, C., Cherifi, H., Lambiotte, R., Lió, P., Rocha, L.M. (eds.) COMPLEX NETWORKS 2018. SCI, vol. 813, pp. 169–181. Springer, Cham (2019). https://doi.org/10.1007/978-3-030-05414-4_14
11. Peska, L.: Using the context of user feedback in recommender systems. In: Proceedings 11th Doctoral Workshop on Mathematical and Engineering Methods in Computer Science, MEMICS 2016, Telč, Czech Republic, 21–23 October 2016, pp. 1–12 (2016)

12. Radlinski, F., Kleinberg, R., Joachims, T.: Learning diverse rankings with multi-armed bandits. In: Proceedings of the 25th International Conference on Machine Learning, ICML 2008, pp. 784–791. Association for Computing Machinery, New York (2008)
13. Wu, H., Luk, R., Wong, K., Kwok, K.: Interpreting TF-IDF term weights as making relevance decisions. ACM Trans. Inf. Syst. 26(3), 13:1–13:37 (2008)
14. Zhu, D., Xiao, J.: R-tfidf, a variety of TF-IDF term weighting strategy in document categorization. In: Proceedings of 7th International Conference on Semantics, Knowledge and Grids, SKG 2011, pp. 83–90. IEEE, Washington, DC, USA (2011)

In-Bed Human Pose Classification Using Sparse Inertial Signals

Omar Elnaggar(✉), Frans Coenen, and Paolo Paoletti

University of Liverpool, Liverpool, UK
`omar.elnaggar@liverpool.ac.uk`

Abstract. Recent studies on sleep reveal its impact on the well-being of humans. Monitoring of in-bed body postures can provide clinicians with early indicators of a wide range of musculoskeletal disorders. Current work on sleep pose classification is directed at non-wearable technologies, with issues associated to limited body observability and concerns over personal privacy; or on wearable sensors that consider only a small number of sleep poses and thus have limited generalisation. This paper proposes a novel method for wearable-based human pose classification capable of classifying twelve benchmark sleeping poses. To overcome the scarcity of labelled inertial data, a new data augmentation technique is proposed to generate realistic synthetic datasets emulating real-world conditions. An Error-Correcting Output Codes model is used to employ a multi-class classifier based on an ensemble of Support Vector Machine based classifiers. For system validation, a computer graphics simulator was used to accurately emulate data recording of in-bed body postures, leveraging on a standard articulated body file format commonly used by commercial motion-capture technologies. Experiments show superior performance (as high as 100% classification accuracy), and resilience to noise contamination beyond what could be encountered in reality.

Keywords: Sleeping pose classification · Human pose classification · Wearable sensing · Data augmentation · Support Vector Machine

1 Introduction

Sleep is a recovery mechanism through which the human body is able to recuperate from daily activities. Recently, motivated by the impact sleep has on physical and mental well-being [1], the study of human sleep behaviour has attracted increasing attention. Multiple studies have demonstrated a correlation between chronic diseases and sleep disorders. Abnormal sleep behaviours can be categorised into *movement* and *stable state* disorders. Normally, in-bed body movements are essential for the prevention of *pressure ulcers* [2]; however, sleep can be associated with chronic irregular movements [3], such as *restless leg syndrome, periodic limb movement*, and *rapid eye movement*. Sleeping poses also determine, to some extent, various sleep parameters (e.g. waking episodes) [4]. For instance, prolonged sleep in

© Springer Nature Switzerland AG 2020
M. Bramer and R. Ellis (Eds.): SGAI-AI 2020, LNAI 12498, pp. 331–344, 2020.
https://doi.org/10.1007/978-3-030-63799-6_25

the supine position deteriorate the quality of sleep and leads to a higher chances of apnea in comparison with sleeping in either of the lateral positions [5]. In-bed body posture monitoring helps clinicians to diagnose common risk factors associated with sleep disorders, enabling their prevention or treatment, and possibly monitoring the success of treatment.

Work on human motion analysis has tended to focus on activity recognition [6,7]. Monitoring in-bed body postures is a classification problem involving *quasi-static* pose data, as the body pose remains mostly unchanged throughout sleeping time. Gathering sleeping pose data requires specialised trackers and algorithms. Non-wearable trackers prominently rely on either in-bed or imaging sensors. For example, in [8] 24 features were extracted from quadruple load cells placed under the bed legs to detect and classify in-bed motions using *Support Vector Machine* (SVM), *Random Forest*, and *XGBoost* techniques achieving an overall error rate of 8.5%. Leveraging recent advances in image processing and deep learning, sleep monitoring using infrared/depth cameras has achieved reasonably high performance. Two machine learning approaches were investigated in [9] to effectively recognise two poses of the head and body during sleep: (i) supervised classifiers, and (ii) *Convolutional Neural Networks* (CNNs).

The aforementioned non-wearable technologies are limited by a number of factors. Vision-based systems, for example, are associated with privacy issues and are limited by occlusions due to (say) blankets. Secondly, due to the limited observability, such systems often fail to differentiate between some postures, e.g. supine and prone body posture. Consequently, an emerging research direction employs wearable inertial sensors to track in-bed body postures.

This paper presents a novel approach for robust classification of twelve benchmark sleeping poses which can be applied to data collected via wearable sensors. A minimal parameterisation of the human pose is employed, where only the orientations of the four human body extremities are extracted by a proposed algorithm for robust limb tracking. Based on this minimal representation, an SVM was used to classify the data into the twelve poses. A novel limb calibration procedure exclusively determines the initial offset between each extremity limb, defined by its intrinsic anatomical axes of rotation, and the global reference frame. For validating the system, a computer graphics simulator was used to accurately emulate the motion capture of in-bed body postures. To replicate the non-ideal conditions that one would expect in a real-world scenario, we also propose a data augmentation technique to produce various realistic synthetic datasets at different *"jittering"* levels. Experiments demonstrated high system performance and robustness, even at levels of noise contamination beyond what can be expected from modern off-the-shelf inertial sensing technologies.

2   Related Work

Research on recognising human activities dominates the field of human motion analysis. In contrast, the limited reported work on static human pose classification have not reached the same level of maturity. This section first discusses general frameworks for activity recognition, since most of these approaches remain applicable to static pose classification; and then goes on to consider work on the classification of static body postures.

Work on human activity recognition tends to be based on pattern recognition [10]. Inertial data is sampled at a constant rate, features are extracted and then fed into an optional dimensionality reduction stage. Three categories of inertial data feature may be extracted [11,12]: (i) time-domain features, (ii) frequency-domain features, and (iii) time-frequency features. Dimensionality reduction, such as *principal component analysis* [13], can be used to reduce the dimensionality of feature vectors to enhance real-time performance. Finally, a classifier maps the feature vectors to their respective classes of human activity. Shallow classifiers, such as *shape k-nearest neighbours* [11], *shape SVM* [14], and *shape hidden Markov model* [12], often achieve recognition rates in the range of 83–96%.

To overcome some of the limitations of these approaches, including choice of relevant features and classifier, and scarcity of labelled data, *deep learning* has been exploited. An automatic feature extraction aided with deep learning was proposed in [15] as part of a combined classification-regression framework. The classifier was used to classify human activities, while the sensor-to-segment alignment was auto-calibrated by a regressor. An ensemble of augmentation methods was used in [16] to generate artificial spectrogram-based features to feed a deep *shape Long Short-Term Memory* network for human activity classification.

Recently, inertial sensors have been used for static human pose classification. In [17], an attribute-based zero-short learning scheme was proposed to classify 22 different poses, using a dense network of 31 (body intrusive) *Inertial Measurement Unit* (IMU) sensors, achieving a recognition accuracy of 81%. The scheme consisted of two primary steps: (i) CNN-based attribute learning to estimate the status parameters of selected body joints from raw sensor readings, and (ii) feed forward of the joint status parameters into a 1-nearest neighbour classifier for pose classification. In [2], three accelerometers attached to the ankles and chest were used to classify sleeping poses using a learning vector quantisation technique. Despite the system achieving 99.8% recognition accuracy for individual models, its generalisation performance dropped to only 83.6% for multi-subject models. Additionally, with one accelerometer coupled to the chest, a linear discriminant classifier was reported to recognise 99% of the sleeping poses [18]. However, this work only considered four sleeping poses: supine, prone, and left and right lateral. Moreover, these systems demonstrated poor generalisation performance across human subjects.

This paper addresses the aforementioned open issues. Firstly, the proposed approach is capable of classifying a set of twelve benchmark sleeping poses. Secondly, the sleeping poses are parameterised with the orientation of the four body extremities only, obviating the need for a dense network of inertial sensors. Thirdly, a new orientation data augmentation technique is proposed to compensate for the scarcity of labelled data. Fourthly, efficient limb calibration and orientation tracking algorithms are introduced to enable robust and simultaneous tracking of the four limb extremities in the inertial Earth frame. Finally, the realistic emulation of human motion capture using graphics simulation software provides a useful tool for use with respect to the wider research community.

3   Methodology

The proposed methodology first emulates the in-bed human postures using a virtual character, generated using computer graphics software, capable of providing data in the same format as standard motion capture platforms. Then, a complete pattern recognition system is proposed to extract and process an abstract parameterisation of the sleeping pose so as to classify the pose.

3.1   Virtual Human Motion Capture

The scarcity of labelled data is a major challenge when developing machine learning algorithms for human pose estimation. To tackle this challenge, a virtual human character was implemented in Blender©, a computer graphics software system capable of exporting human pose data in formats compatible with real motion caption platforms. An added bonus, when using such platforms, is easy visualisation of collected data and results. The process whereby this virtual human motion capture was conducted is briefly described below.

An open-source 3D human character model, the *Sky Body model*[1], was used with a human *rig*, i.e. a skeleton providing a standard framework for moving the body. Rigging human character models involves coupling the skeleton to the 3D model. Once coupled, the articulation of the armature results in mesh deformations over the surface of the 3D model. Each bone in the rig skeleton has six (translational and rotational) Degrees Of Freedom (DOFs) about its pivot axes, unless constrained. It is important to define the necessary parent-child relationships between successive bones along the skeleton to incorporate the segment connectivity assumption as a hard biomechanical constraint. In this paper, the *Meta-Rig* generic human skeleton was built using Blender and incorporated with all the required bone labelling and parenting relationships. To perform *character rigging*, i.e. to link the skeleton to the 3D model, four major steps were performed:

1. *Pose the character 3D model in the rest pose.* The rest pose is the default pose before applying any body movements or deformations. The calibration T-pose, with the character standing with both arms pointing out to the sides, was chosen as the rest pose.
2. *Align Meta-Rig with the character 3D model.* The bone sizes and orientations are made consistent with the body parts of the character 3D model.
3. *Bind the character 3D model and Meta-Rig together.* Determine the degree of deformational influence bones have on the vertices located within their proximity.
4. *Manually incorporate hard joint constraints within the Meta-Rig.* There are two types of joint constraints: (i) bounds on joint range of motion, and (ii) disabling one or more of the joint DOFs. For the scenario considered here, the former constraint type resulted in motion discontinuities during animation,

---

[1] https://cloud.blender.org/p/animation-fundamentals/5d69ab4dea6789db11ee65d1.

and therefore was discarded. The second category of constraints was applied to make elbows and knees hinge joints about their flexion/extension axes. This step ensures plausible human body poses during animation.

Although most of the literature has been focusing on a handful of main sleeping poses (e.g. supine, side lying, prone) [2,18,19], such a coarse classification is of limited use for the intended clinical purpose. Medical specialists suggested that the authors augment this set to the 12 sleeping poses shown in Fig. 1. Therefore, an animation clip with a total of 50 *keyframes* was produced, with each keyframe corresponding to a sleeping pose interleaved by a T-pose keyframe. Each sleeping pose was manually created to visually match the twelve benchmark poses and in particular the associated critical extremity limb orientations. A 15 frames/s animation was then created by maintaining each pose for 10 frames and then interpolating between poses for another 10 frames.

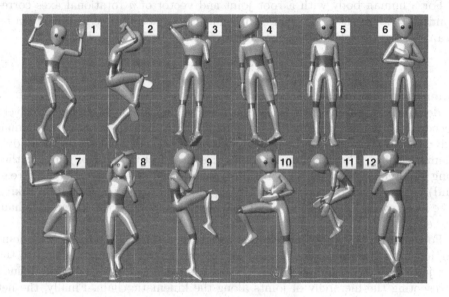

Fig. 1. The 12 sleeping poses considered.

Exporting the pose data of the virtual human character from Blender is required for subsequent processing and classification. The *BioVision*© *Hierarchy* (BVH) binary format was chosen because of its ability to encode skeleton motion data in a hierarchical format, and of its widespread use in the biomechanics community. BVH is the standard format used by commercial motion capture systems. However, BVH has two drawbacks: (i) it lacks the full definition of the initial pose (the initial pose offset term is unknown, therefore additional calibration was needed as explained in Sect. 3.2), and (ii) it only uses translational offsets to define child bones with respect to their parents (tracking the extremity limb orientations only requires the rotational displacements rather than the bone-to-bone rotational offsets).

3.2   Articulated Body Representation

This sub-section focuses on the underlying kinematic principles required to extract and express the pose of the human character model.

Human Pose Parameterisation

In general, the human body can be modelled with four joint types: (i) root, (ii) ball, (iii) saddle and (iv) hinge joints. A *root joint* has a total of six DOFs representing the combined triaxial translation and orientation, $\boldsymbol{\xi}$, of the overall human body. The root of the human body is typically chosen to be the far bottom end of the spine. *Ball joints*, e.g. the hip joint, do not allow for translational movements but have no rotational constraints. *Saddle joints* have two rotational DOFs, such as the *Carpometacarpal joint* lying at the base of the thumb. *Hinge joints*, e.g. knee, can only perform uni-axial rotations.

For a human body with a root joint and vector of n rotational axes corresponding to all of the body joints, the human pose at any time instant t can be parameterised by a D-dimensional state vector, $\boldsymbol{h}_t \in \mathbb{R}^D$ with $D = n + 6$

$$\boldsymbol{h}_t := (\boldsymbol{\xi}, \boldsymbol{\theta}); \qquad \boldsymbol{\xi} \in \mathbb{R}^6, \boldsymbol{\theta} \in \mathbb{R}^n \tag{1}$$

Kinematic Chains

By definition, a *parent joint* is a term used to describe a joint that relatively precedes another *child joint* in a kinematic chain, i.e. the root of the human body is always regarded as the parent joint of all branches making up the body's kinematic chain. Therefore, upper joints directly affect the pose of joints further along the kinematic chain. For instance, the motion of an extremity limb (e.g. hand) can be tracked only by quantifying the local pose transformation taking place at the wrist, in addition to all its parent joints along the kinematic chain (e.g. elbow).

Formulating this problem requires assigning a frame $\{F_i\}$ to each ith joint starting from the child joint ($i = 1$) all the way up the kinematic chain to the root joint ($i = D$). Then a *shape forward kinematics map* needs to be defined representing the hierarchy of joints along the kinematic chain. Finally, the net transformation of the child joint frame with respect to some fixed global frame $\{G\}$ needs to be tracked by concatenating all the hierarchical joint transformations according to the forward kinematics map:

$$^G\boldsymbol{H}_{F_1} = {}^{F_D}\boldsymbol{H}_{F_{D-1}} \ldots {}^{F_n}\boldsymbol{H}_{F_{n-1}} \ldots {}^{F_2}\boldsymbol{H}_{F_1} {}^G\boldsymbol{H}_{F_1}(0)$$

$$= \left(\prod_{Genealogy} {}^{F_i}\boldsymbol{H}_{F_{i-1}} \right) {}^G\boldsymbol{H}_{F_1}(0) \tag{2}$$

where $^{F_i}\boldsymbol{H}_{F_{i-1}}$ represent the group of all local homogenous transformation matrices of all joints along the kinematic chain for different values of i, and $^G\boldsymbol{H}_{F_1}(0)$ is the initial pose offset between the child frame and the fixed global frame at the calibration pose. Recall that a body joint can have a maximum of six DOFs about/along the intrinsic axes of the joint frame, therefore, the local joint homogeneous transformation matrix is defined as:

$$^{F_i}H_{F_{i-1}} = \prod_{j \in \{\hat{x},\hat{y},\hat{z}\}} H\left(j, \Delta\theta_j, \Delta\xi_j\right) \tag{3}$$

where the angular and translational displacements, if any, associated with each ith joint DOF is denoted by $\Delta\theta_j$ and $\Delta\xi_j$ respectively.

Virtual Calibration Procedure

It is clear from Eq. (2) that globally tracking a child joint frame requires its initial pose offset with respect to the fixed global frame. In real life, it is a common practice to assume that the offset term is simply an identity matrix for each extremity limb, i.e. the child and reference spatial frames are initially coincident [20]. However, this assumption precludes mutually tracking multiple child frames in the same reference frame, because each child frame has its own initial offset at the calibration pose.

Therefore, to globally track the orientation of extremity limbs, a virtual calibration procedure, outlined in Algorithm 1, needs to be applied to determine the initial orientation offsets between each limb frame and the global frame. This procedure requires pure positive rotations about each anatomical axis of each joint, one at a time, with an arbitrary angle. Then, the axis-angle representations, $\{\hat{\omega}, \theta\} \in \mathbb{R}^4$, of these local rotations are extracted to find the rotation matrix representing the orientation offset of each limb, where $\hat{\omega}$ represents a unit vector along the axis of rotation, and θ is the angle of rotation about $\hat{\omega}$.

Characterisation of Sleeping Poses and Limb Orientation Tracking

Analogous to pattern recognition systems, the characterisation of sleeping poses resembles the feature extraction phase, and involves finding characteristic patterns of features in the raw data associated with each sleeping pose. In this work, the body posture is parametrised by the orientation of the four extremity limbs (wrists and ankles) defined about their intrinsic anatomical axes. Kinematically speaking, one way to address this is to find the orientation of each child frame with respect to its parent frame [21], e.g. hand-to-forearm and foot-to-shin. Despite the simplicity of this tracking algorithm, it requires the calibration of both parent and child bones about each joint being tracked. In addition, since the child and parent frames are unlikely to be initially coincident, the initial non-zero orientation offset between both frames must be algorithmically nullified before computing the limb orientation.

Alternatively, some previous work (e.g. [22]) has used Euler angles to track the orientation of body segments since they are easy-to-compute and convenient. However, Euler-based tracking algorithms require the order of rotation as an input, making it unreliable for multi-DOF body joints; therefore, the associated estimation error are clearly unavoidable [23].

As shown in Algorithm 2, it is proposed that only the local transformation taking place at the child bone are considered. Given the pre-child skeleton trans-

---

Algorithm 1. Virtual Calibration Procedure

1: $Limbs \in \mathbb{R}^N$: the set of limbs to be calibrated
2: $h_0 \leftarrow$ Calibration Pose   % Save the Calibration Pose
3:
4: **procedure** CALIBRATELIMB($Limbs$, h_0)
5:     **for** each k in $Limbs$ **do**
6:         Perform a $+ve$ rotation about the local x-axis at $keyframe = 1$
7:         $h_2 \leftarrow h_0$
8:         Perform a $+ve$ rotation about the local y-axis at $keyframe = 3$
9:         $h_4 \leftarrow h_0$
10:         Perform a $+ve$ rotation about the local z-axis at $keyframe = 5$
11:         $h_6 \leftarrow h_0$
12:         Extract the initial orientation offset between the child and global frames
13:         ${}^G\boldsymbol{R}_{F_1}(0) := \begin{bmatrix} {}^G\boldsymbol{x}_{F_1}(0) & {}^G\boldsymbol{y}_{F_1}(0) & {}^G\boldsymbol{z}_{F_1}(0) \end{bmatrix} \leftarrow$ FINDCHILDFRAME(h_1, h_3, h_5)
14:         ${}^G\boldsymbol{H}_{F_1}(0) \leftarrow \begin{bmatrix} {}^G\boldsymbol{R}_{F_1}(0) & {}^G\boldsymbol{d}_{F_1} \\ \boldsymbol{0}_{1\times3} & 1 \end{bmatrix}$
15:         % ${}^G\boldsymbol{d}_{F_1}$ is the 3×1 Cartesian position of the child joint from the BVH file
16:     **end for**
17: **end procedure**
18:
19: **function** FINDCHILDFRAME(h_i, h_j, h_k)
20:     **for** each t in $\{h_i, h_j, h_k\}$ **do**
21:         ${}^G\boldsymbol{H}_{F_1} \leftarrow$ Equation 2
22:         ${}^G\boldsymbol{R}_{F_1} \leftarrow$ FINDROTATION$\left({}^G\boldsymbol{H}_{F_1}\right)$ % Single-axis rotation
23:         $\{\hat{\boldsymbol{\omega}}, \theta\}_t :=$ ROTMTX2AXISANGLE$\left({}^G\boldsymbol{R}_{F_1}\right)$
24:     **end for**
25: **end function**

---

formations available from the BVH file, the algorithm tracks the child bone orientation before and after applying the child bone's local transformation. Then, it breaks down this relative orientation term into its respective axis-angle representation. Compared to the aforementioned algorithms, this algorithm only requires the calibration of the child bone of each joint being tracked. Moreover, since it quantifies the local transformation taking place at each joint of interest, it does not need to compute the initial non-zero orientation offset relative to the parent joint.

Synthetic Dataset Formation

As discussed in Sect. 2, the scarcity of labelled inertial data is a frequently encountered challenge with respect to research on supervised human motion analysis. Indeed, the 12 keyframes corresponding to the sleeping poses are insufficient to train a classifier of good generalisation performance, hence an additional *data augmentation* step is necessary to create a data-rich dataset of the parameterised sleeping poses.

There are different means of augmenting temporal data, such as permutation, time-warping and scaling [24]. The proposed work leverages on *jittering*, which involves contaminating the input temporal signal with noise emulating additive sensor noise. A Gaussian noise, realised by the distribution $\mathcal{N}(0, \sigma^2)$, was used to perform the desired jittering where σ represents the standard deviation of the distribution. However, simply adding noise to the 4-element axis-angle representation does not provide realistic results, as mild levels of additive noise on the axis of rotation $\hat{\omega}$ may result in biomechanically infeasible poses.

Therefore, prior to data augmentation, the axis of rotation $\hat{\omega}$ is expressed into a spherical coordinate system $\{r_\omega, \theta_\omega, \phi_\omega\}$, where $r_\omega = 1$ is the unit radius, θ_ω is the polar angle measured from the positive z-axis ($0 \leqslant \theta \leqslant \pi$), and ϕ_ω is the azimuthal angle measured clockwise from the positive x-axis in the x-y plane ($0 \leqslant \phi \leqslant 2\pi$). Data augmentation is then performed by adding Gaussian noise to the orientation $\{\theta_\omega, \phi_\omega\}$ of the rotational axis and to the angle of rotation θ only, i.e.

$$^{aug}\theta_\omega(n) = \theta_\omega + \delta\theta_\omega(n)$$
$$^{aug}\phi_\omega(n) = \phi_\omega + \delta\phi_\omega(n)$$
$$^{aug}\theta(n) = \theta + \delta\theta(n) \tag{4}$$

with $\delta\theta_\omega, \delta\phi_\omega \sim \mathcal{N}(0, \sigma_\omega^2)$ and $\delta\theta \sim \mathcal{N}(0, \sigma_\theta^2)$. Here, $n \in \{1, \ldots, N\}$ identifies the nth sample in the augmented dataset, which contains N samples in total. This approach ensures bounded orientation changes.

By the end of the data augmentation phase, a synthetic dataset was formed with $N = 101$ data samples for each sleeping pose: 1 data sample for the refer-

---

Algorithm 2. Limb Orientation Tracking Algorithm

1: $h_0 \leftarrow$ Calibration Pose
2: $h_t \leftarrow$ Arbitrary Pose from Character Animation
3: $Limbs \leftarrow \{Wrist_{left}, Wrist_{right}, Ankle_{left}, Ankle_{right}\}$
4:
5: **procedure** LIMBORITATIONTRACKER(h_0)
6:     **for** each k in $Limbs$ **do**
7:         $^G H_{F_{child}}(0) \leftarrow$ CALIBRATELIMB($child, h_0$)
8:         % Find the child frame orientation after full-skeleton transformation
9:         $^G H_{F_{child_{post}}}(t) \leftarrow$ Equation (2)
10:        % Find the child frame orientation neglecting child bone transformation
11:        $^{FG} H_{F_{child_{pre}}}(t) = \left(\prod_{Root \leftarrow Parent} {}^{F_i} H_{F_{i-1}}\right) {}^G H_{F_{child}}(0)$
12:        % Quantify the local transformation taking place at the child joint
13:        $^{child_{pre}} H_{F_{child_{post}}}(t) = \left({}^G H_{F_{child_{pre}}}(t)\right)^{-1} {}^G H_{F_{child_{post}}}(t)$
14:        $^{child_{pre}} R_{F_{child_{post}}}(t) \leftarrow$ FINDROTATION$\left({}^{child_{pre}} H_{F_{child_{post}}}(t)\right)$
15:        $\{\hat{\omega}, \theta\} :=$ ROTMTX2AXISANGLE$\left({}^{child_{pre}} R_{F_{child_{post}}}(t)\right)$
16:     **end for**
17: **end procedure**

---

ence pose, 70 and 30 synthetic data samples for designated training and testing of the machine learning algorithm. Finally, the augmented axes of rotation are expressed as Cartesian coordinates so as to maintain the axis-angle representation in the synthetic dataset.

3.3 Classification of Sleeping Poses

For the proposed approach the SVM mechanism was chosen to classify the sleeping poses. This choice was motivated by SVM robustness to moderately noisy datasets, its ability to classify non-linearly separable classes and its efficiency during training in high-dimensional spaces [25].

To account for potential outliers in the presence of noise contamination, the *Soft Margin* SVM was adopted:

$$\min_{\boldsymbol{W},b} \quad \frac{1}{2}\|\boldsymbol{W}\|^2 + C \sum_{i=1}^{N} \xi_i$$
$$\text{s.t.} \quad y_i \cdot (\boldsymbol{W} \cdot \boldsymbol{X}_i + b) - 1 \geqslant -\xi_i \tag{5}$$
$$\xi_i \geqslant 0$$
$$i = 1, 2, \ldots, N$$

where $\boldsymbol{X}_i$ is the feature vector combining the orientations of all extremity limbs at a given i^{th} frame, $\boldsymbol{W} \in \mathbb{R}^m$ is the hyperplane dimensional weights, and b is the classifier scalar bias. The scalar hyper-parameters ξ_i and C were used to relax the optimisation constraints and to apply L_1 regularisation to the cost function of the SVM. The ξ_i hyper-parameter accepts some misclassification for the benefit of a smoother decision boundary, while C is an additional parameter that controls this trade-off. To enhance performance in the presence of non-linearly separable classes, the *kernel trick* [26] is employed to transform the feature space to a higher dimensional space where it would become possible to separate classes using a hyperplane. In particular, the Gaussian kernel was chosen as it can result in a more complex decision boundary, and theoretically, performs an infinite summation over increasing order polynomial kernels.

Although SVMs were originally designed for binary classification, they can be extended to address regression and multi-class classification problem [27]. Motivated by the work in [28], an *Error-Correcting Output Codes* (ECOC) model [29] was employed such that L binary SVM classifiers were combined to produce a k-class classifier (classes corresponding to the 12 sleeping poses). Briefly, the framework consists of two steps: (i) a coding step in which the combined output of all binary classifiers (codeword) is designed to be distinct in response to each input class, and (ii) a decoding step which assigns a class membership to a test data point based on codeword matching. Various configurations of binary classifiers could be deployed by different coding designs; however, for applications involving large numbers of classes ($k > 5$), it is common to investigate *one-against-all* or *one-against-one* coding designs since they are computationally and memory efficient. Lastly, the *Bayesian Optimisation* algorithm [30] was used to find the optimal hyper-parameters (ξ_i, C), and the ECOC coding design.

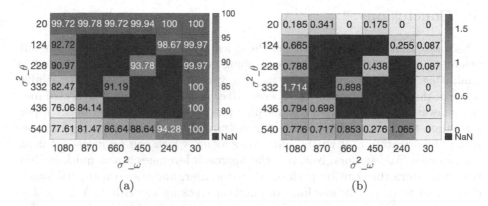

Fig. 2. Sleeping pose classification results: **(a)** mean classification accuracies, and **(b)** their respective standard deviations.

4 Experiments and Discussion of Results

As discussed in Sect. 3.2, both σ_ω^2 and σ_θ^2 were manually adjusted to evaluate the robustness of the classifier to various noise levels in the orientation data of the extremity limbs. Eventually, the upper and lower bounds of these two hyper-parameters were empirically determined. To define the 2D grid constructed by both hyper-parameters, each range was subdivided into five intervals. The performance evaluation experiments were performed using combinations of these discretised hyper-parameter values. Given each jittering setting, a new synthetic dataset was generated to train a multi-class SVM classifier for 10 consecutive experiments to reduce the effects of random error, where the mean and standard deviation of the pose classification accuracy were regarded as primal performance metrics as plotted in Fig. 2. Each time a classifier was trained, the Bayesian optimisation algorithm was executed for a maximum of 30 iterations.

From Fig. 2, over the entire range of values for σ_ω^2 and σ_θ^2, the mean classification accuracy remains well above 75% with a standard deviation of less than 2%. When both the augmented axis and angle of rotation are off by $\sigma_\omega = \pm 25.7°$ and $\sigma_\theta = \pm 18.2°$ respectively (i.e. with respect to the reference extremity limb orientations at each sleeping pose), the classifier is robust enough to correctly classify more than 91% of the test data points on average, with a standard deviation below 1%. It is worth noting that such noise levels are above what modern IMU sensors and sensor fusion algorithms provide, therefore it is expected that the algorithm will also perform well with respect to real experiments. In comparison to [2,18], the proposed approach classifies 12 sleeping poses instead of only 4 standard body poses, and achieves superior classification accuracy. Without the highly dense network of IMUs reported in [17], the proposed approach achieves a higher pose classification accuracy using the extremity limb orientations alone, which requires sparse sensors. Due to differences in the nature of the required raw data, a fair lateral comparison against this previous work was infeasible.

5   Conclusions

This paper has demonstrated that the orientation of extremity limbs are sufficient to effectively classify twelve sleeping poses. The study was validated by emulating in-bed human postures using a computer graphics simulator. Unlike state-of-the-art approaches, which uses either a dense network of wearable inertial sensors or classify only a few sleeping poses with limited generalisation performance, the presented approach demonstrated high classification performance using the orientation of wrists and ankles alone, which can be measured using off-the-shelf IMU sensors. Notably, the approach leverages a new quick calibration procedure that can be performed by the user, and uses a computationally cheap and memory-efficient limb orientation tracking algorithm. A novel data augmentation technique was used to synthesize datasets of limb orientation features, overcoming the challenge of labelled data scarcity. These datasets were used to train a multi-class SVM. The reported evaluation demonstrated that the proposed approach was robust at high levels of noise contamination beyond what can be expected using modern off-the-shelf inertial sensing technologies.

Acknowledgements. The authors would like to thank Dr Lyndon Mason and Prof Rahul Savani for their input in the definition of the clinical problem.

References

1. Deen, M.J.: Information and communications technologies for elderly ubiquitous healthcare in a smart home. Pers. Ubiquit. Comput. **19**(3–4), 573–599 (2015). https://doi.org/10.1007/s00779-015-0856-x
2. Fallmann, S., Van Veen, R., Chen, L., Walker, D., Chen, F., Pan, C.: Wearable accelerometer based extended sleep position recognition. In: IEEE 19th International Conference on e-Health Networking, Applications and Services (Healthcom), pp. 1–6 (2017). https://doi.org/10.1109/HealthCom.2017.8210806
3. Ibáñez, V., Silva, J., Cauli, O.: A survey on sleep questionnaires and diaries. Sleep Med. **42**, 90–96 (2018). https://doi.org/10.1016/j.sleep.2017.08.026
4. Nojiri, A., Okumura, C., Ito, Y.: Sleep posture affects sleep parameters differently in young and senior Japanese as assessed by actigraphy. Health **6**(21), 2934–2944 (2014). https://doi.org/10.4236/health.2014.621332
5. Pinna, G.D., et al.: Differential impact of body position on the severity of disordered breathing in heart failure patients with obstructive vs. central sleep apnoea. Eur. J. Heart Fail. **17**(12), 1302–1309 (2015). https://doi.org/10.1002/ejhf.410
6. Lara, Ó.D., Labrador, M.A.: A survey on human activity recognition using wearable sensors. IEEE Commun. Surv. Tutor. **15**(3), 1192–1209 (2013). https://doi.org/10.1109/SURV.2012.110112.00192
7. Lopez-Nava, I.H., Angelica, M.M.: Wearable inertial sensors for human motion analysis: a review. IEEE Sens. J. **16**(22), 7821–7834 (2016). https://doi.org/10.1109/JSEN.2016.2609392

8. Alaziz, M., Jia, Z., Howard, R., Lin, X., Zhang, Y.: In-bed body motion detection and classification system. ACM Trans. Sens. Netw. **16**(2), 131–1326 (2020). https://doi.org/10.1145/3372023
9. Akbarian, S., Delfi, G., Zhu, K., Yadollahi, A., Taati, B.: Automated non-contact detection of head and body positions during sleep. IEEE Access **7**, 72826–72834 (2019). https://doi.org/10.1109/ACCESS.2019.2920025
10. Bartlett, H.L., Goldfarb, M.: A phase variable approach for IMU-based locomotion activity recognition. IEEE Trans. Biomed. Eng. **65**(6), 1330–1338 (2018). https://doi.org/10.1109/TBME.2017.2750139
11. Preece, S.J., Goulermas, J.Y., Kenney, L.P., Howard, D.: A comparison of feature extraction methods for the classification of dynamic activities from accelerometer data. IEEE Trans. Biomed. Eng. **56**(3), 871–879 (2009). https://doi.org/10.1109/TBME.2008.2006190
12. Panahandeh, G., Mohammadiha, N., Leijon, A., Handel, P.: Continuous hidden Markov model for pedestrian activity classification and gait analysis. IEEE Trans. Instrum. Meas. **62**(5), 1073–1083 (2013). https://doi.org/10.1109/TIM.2012.2236792
13. Wu, D., Zhang, H., Niu, C., Ren, J., Zhao, W.: Inertial sensor based human activity recognition via reduced kernel PCA. In: Fortino, G., Wang, Z. (eds.) Advances in Body Area Networks I. IT, pp. 447–456. Springer, Cham (2019). https://doi.org/10.1007/978-3-030-02819-0_34
14. Kasebzadeh, P., Hendeby, G., Fritsche, C., Gunnarsson, F., Gustafsson, F.: IMU dataset for motion and device mode classification. In: International Conference on Indoor Positioning and Indoor Navigation (IPIN) (2017). https://doi.org/10.1109/IPIN.2017.8115956
15. Zimmermann, T., Taetz, B., Bleser, G.: IMU-to-segment assignment and orientation alignment for the lower body using deep learning. Sensors **18**(302), 1–35 (2018). https://doi.org/10.3390/s18010302
16. Eyobu, O.S., Han, D.S.: Feature representation and data augmentation for human activity classification based on wearable IMU sensor data using a deep LSTM neural network. Sensors **18**(9), 1–26 (2018). https://doi.org/10.3390/s18092892
17. Ohashi, H., Al-Naser, M., Ahmed, S., Nakamura, K., Sato, T., Dengel, A.: Attributes' importance for zero-shot pose-classification based on wearable sensors. Sensors **18**(2485), 1–17 (2018). https://doi.org/10.3390/s18082485
18. Zhang, Z., Yang, G.Z.: Monitoring cardio-respiratory and posture movements during sleep: what can be achieved by a single motion sensor. In: IEEE 12th International Conference on Wearable and Implantable Body Sensor Networks (BSN), pp. 1–6 (2015). https://doi.org/10.1109/BSN.2015.7299409
19. Cary, D., Briffa, K., McKenna, L.: Identifying relationships between sleep posture and non-specific spinal symptoms in adults: a scoping review. BMJ Open **9**(6), 1–10 (2019). https://doi.org/10.1136/bmjopen-2018-027633
20. Pons-Moll, G., Rosenhahn, B.: Model-based pose estimation. In: Moeslund, T., Hilton, A., Krüger, V., Sigal, L., et al. (eds.) Visual Analysis of Humans, pp. 139–170. Springer, London (2011). https://doi.org/10.1007/978-0-85729-997-0_9
21. Garg, R., et al.: Wrist kinematic coupling and performance during functional tasks: effects of constrained motion. J. Hand Surg. **39**(4), 634–642 (2014). https://doi.org/10.1016/j.jhsa.2013.12.031
22. Nam, H.S., Lee, W.H., Seo, H.G., Kim, Y.J., Bang, M.S., Kim, S.: Inertial measurement unit based upper extremity motion characterization for action research arm test and activities of daily living. Sensors **19**(8), 1–10 (2019). https://doi.org/10.3390/s19081782

23. Wu, G., et al.: ISB recommendation on definitions of joint coordinate systems of various joints for the reporting of human joint motion - part II: shoulder, elbow, wrist and hand. J. Biomech. **38**(5), 981–992 (2005). https://doi.org/10.1016/j.jbiomech.2004.05.042

24. Rashid, K.M., Louis, J.: Times-series data augmentation and deep learning for construction equipment activity recognition. Adv. Eng. Inform. **42**(100944), 1–12 (2019). https://doi.org/10.1016/j.aei.2019.100944

25. Smola, A.J., Schölkopf, B.: A tutorial on support vector regression. Stat. Comput. **14**(3), 199–222 (2004). https://doi.org/10.1023/B:STCO.0000035301.49549.88

26. Abe, S.: Two-class support vector machines. In: Singh, S. (ed.) Support Vector Machines for Pattern Classification. Advances in Pattern Recognition, pp. 21–106. Springer, London (2010). https://doi.org/10.1007/978-1-84996-098-4_2

27. Hastie, T., Tibshirani, R., Friedman, J.: The Elements of Statistical Learning: Data Mining, Inference, and Prediction. SSS. Springer, New York (2009). https://doi.org/10.1007/978-0-387-84858-7

28. Allwein, E.L., Schapire, R.E., Singer, Y.: Reducing multiclass to binary: a unifying approach for margin classifiers. J. Mach. Learn. Res. **1**, 113–141 (2000). https://doi.org/10.1162/15324430152733133

29. Dietterich, T.G., Bakiri, G.: Solving multiclass learning problems via error-correcting output codes. J. Artif. Intell. Res. **2**, 263–286 (1995). https://doi.org/10.1613/jair.105

30. Shahriari, B., Swersky, K., Wang, Z., Adams, R.P., De Freitas, N.: Taking the human out of the loop: a review of Bayesian optimization. Proc. IEEE **104**(1), 148–175 (2016). https://doi.org/10.1109/JPROC.2015.2494218

Maintaining Curated Document Databases Using a Learning to Rank Model: The ORRCA Experience

Iqra Muhammad[✉], Danushka Bollegala, Frans Coenen, Carol Gamble, Anna Kearney, and Paula Williamson

University of Liverpool, Liverpool, UK
`iqra.muhammad@liverpool.ac.uk`

Abstract. Curated Document Databases play a critical role in helping researchers find relevant articles in available literature. One such database is the ORRCA (Online Resource for Recruitment research in Clinical trials) database. The ORRCA database brings together published work in the field of clinical trials recruitment research into a single searchable collection. Document databases, such as ORRCA, require year-on-year updating as further relevant documents become available on a continuous basis. The updating of curated databases is a labour intensive and time consuming task. Machine learning techniques can help to automate the update process and reduce the workload needed for screening articles for inclusion. This paper presents an automated approach to the updating of ORRCA documents repository. The proposed automated approach is a learning to rank model. The approach is evaluated using the documents in the ORRCA database. Data from the ORRCA original systematic review was used to train the learning to rank model, and data from the ORRCA 2015 and 2017 updates was used to evaluate performance of the model. The evaluation demonstrated that significant resource savings can be made using the proposed approach.

Keywords: Learning to rank · Curated Document Databases

1 Introduction

There is an abundance of scientific research published in the form of academic papers; the number of published papers in most of the domains has increased in the recent years. This makes it challenging for researchers to maintain an overview of the published literature and to find relevant documents in their domain of interest. One solution is the use of Curated Document Databases (CDDs) which bring together, into a single scientific literature repository, all published work in a particular domain. One example of such a CDD is the Online Resource for Recruitment research in Clinical trials[1] database [6]. The ORRCA

---

[1] https://www.orrca.org.uk/.

© Springer Nature Switzerland AG 2020
M. Bramer and R. Ellis (Eds.): SGAI-AI 2020, LNAI 12498, pp. 345–357, 2020.
https://doi.org/10.1007/978-3-030-63799-6_26

database brings together abstracts of papers concerned with recruitment strategies for clinical trials. A manual systematic search process was used to create this database and a similar process is required to update the database on an annual basis. The manual search process for updating the ORRCA database requires substantial human resources. There is a growing need to regularly update this repository as the number of articles being published in the clinical trials domain is growing exponentially. A similar challenge is encountered when updating CDDs in the wider context.

This paper presents an approach to support the automated updating of CDDs. The proposed approach is founded on the use of machine learning, particularly the concept of learning to rank models [10,11]. The idea is to first obtain a collection of candidate documents from medical bibliographic databases. In the case of the ORRCA database, candidate documents were obtained by searching over various medical literature bibliographic databases. Then the next step is to apply a learning to rank mechanism on the set of candidate documents. One such approach was presented in Norman et al. [12] where a pointwise document ranking algorithm was proposed, the CN algorithm. In this paper, we propose to use the CN algorithm as a foundation and incorporate a Support Vector Regression (SVR) [12] mechanism to rank documents (abstracts). In this paper, this model was trained using the pre-2015 ORRCA database, and tested using ORRCA 2015 and 2017 updates. The evaluation demonstrated that significant resource savings can be made using the proposed approach.

The remainder of this paper is organised as follows. A brief literature review is given Sect. 2. Then, in Sect. 3, a review of the proposed approach is presented. Section 4 considers the necessary data pre-processing. The conducted evaluation of the approach is reported on in Sect. 5. The report is concluded in Sect. 6.

2   Literature Review

CDDs require regular updating. This updating process involves considerable human resource as it is typically conducted manually in the form of a systematic review of a candidate collection of documents. The resource required for such systematic review can be significantly reduced by pruning the set of candidates using document ranking. The main objective of document ranking, also referred to as a score-and-sort, is to compute a relevance score for each document and then generate an ordered list of documents so that the top k most relevant documents can be selected. Document ranking models can typically be categorised as being either: (i) probabilistic models or (ii) Learning to Rank Models (LRMs).

Probabilistic ranking models focus on document relevance by assigning a probabilistic value to each document [14]. The idea is to estimate the probabilistic relevance of each document with respect to some criteria (such as a query). Okami BM25 is an example of a probabilistic ranking model. Okapi BM25 is used as a baseline in many document ranking applications and it has been shown to substantially outperform alternatives [2].

LRMs use machine learning techniques to "learn" a ranking model. The majority of neural ranking models fall within two groups: (i) representation-based learning to rank models and (ii) interaction-based learning to rank models. Representation based model uses representations of queries and documents independent of each other [14]; while the query and document representations are closely related in interaction-based model, which is beneficial for relevance matching in the documents [2]. A number of such methods for updating curated databases in domain-specific settings, have been proposed including Voting Perceptrons, Lambda-Mart, Decision Trees, SVR, Waode, kNN, Rocchia, hypernym relations, Linear Models, Convolutional Neural Networks, Gradient Boosting Machines, Random Indexing and Random Forests [1,3,4,8,9,13,17]. Some of the most recently published works in learning to rank models in non-domain specific settings for documents are based on: (i) iterative learning on implicit feedback [15], (ii) transformers based re-ranking [10] and (iii) pre-trained sequence to sequence models [11] iv) BERT-based document ranking [16].

The work on iterative learning and implicit feedback in [15] involves implicit feedback from users to understand the intent of selecting a document, and this implict feedback has been used to improve the quality of the learning-to-rank model based on LambdaMART algorithm. The LETOR model in [15] was trained and tested on a community question answering dataset. Their proposed LETOR model is evaluated in two kinds of scenarios, the scenarios where training data is not available and the scenario when it is available.

The work in [10] proposed to use a model called PreTTR (Precomputing Transformer Term Representations), and the aim of using this LETOR model is to reduce the query-time latency by utilizing deep transformer networks and hence, this system can be used in real-time learning to rank scenarios. The model in [10] is based on pre-computed document term representations at indexing time without the use of a query and then merge the pre-computed representation with query representations at query time to get a final learning to rank score.

The work in [11] is about a pre-trained sequence-to-sequence model utilized for document ranking. This work in [11] is based on an encoder based approach and is different from classification based ranking models such as BERT. The encoder used in [11] s a sequence-to-sequence model and trained on relevance labels as target words and these target words can be referred to as relevance probabilities for ranking.

A BERT based ranking model in [16] is also one of the latest approaches in learning-to-rank in non-domain specific settings. The pre-trained BERT in [16] has been tested on two benchmark LETOR datasets: MS MACRO and TREC web track. Results from the use of a pre-trained BERT model on both of these benchmark datasets are encouraging and show that BERT makes use of surrounding contexts of words for document ranking. The results on the MS MARCO passage ranking task show that experimental results show that BERT-based ranking approach is equivalent with the previous classification based models. The BERT based ranking model was also tested on the TREC 2004 Robust

Track dataset and it demonstrated that a zero-shot transfer-based approach is better than the previous state-of-the-art models.

Learning to rank models have also been used in the domain of biomedical information retrieval. Some of the relevant works in the field of biomedical information retrieval include [5,7,12]. The work in [7] is based on the CLEF 2017 e-Health Lab Task 2. In [7], the goal is to effectively rank studies for title and abstract automated screening instead of doing manual Diagnostic Test Accuracy systematic reviews. In [7], the learning to rank model was trained on a benchmark collection of fifty such systematic reviews. Another similar work for screening automation of systematic reviews, involved the use of random forest classifier. In [7], the random forest classifier was trained on a dataset of 15 systematic reviews conducted by the Oregon Evidence Based Practice Center (EPC), Southern California EPC. The random forest classifier in [7] proved to get high recall and also helped the systematic review authors save time. In [9], word embeddings and logistic regression have been used to create a model for automation of screening citations when updating the network-meta analysis(NMA). In [9], the model was tested on four benchmark datasets from medical domains and demonstrated 100% sensitivity on two network-meta analysis benchmark datasets. The workload was reduced by 53% while screening articles for updating network-meta analysis in [9]. The work in [12] made use of a logistic regression based ranking model on a clinical outcomes articles dataset[2]. The screening automation using the logistic regression model resulted in a workload reduction of at least 75% and also only missed references around 2%. This ranking model has been used as the foundation for the work presented in this paper.

3   The Curated Document Database Update Approach

This section presents an overview of the proposed CDD update approach founded on a SVR Learning to Rank Model (LRM). A schematic of the approach is given in Fig. 1. The start point, top left, is an existing CDD such as the ORRCA CDD. Learning to rank algorithms require training data, both positive examples ("relevant" abstracts) and negative examples ("not relevant" abstracts). By definition CDDs do not include negative examples and thus the positive examples within the CDD need to be augmented with negative examples. For the evaluation presented later in this paper, the pre-2015 version of the ORRCA database was used and augmented with negative examples (irrelevant documents). This training data was then preprocessed so that it was in a format that allowed for the generation of the desired LRM; the nature of the pre-processing is discussed in more detail in Sect. 4 below. A SVR learning approach was used to generate the desired LRM. More specifically the SVR within the Scikit-learn Python machine learning library[3].

---

[2] http://www.comet-initiative.org/.
[3] Sklearn is a python based machine learning library that contains implementations for various machine learning algorithms.

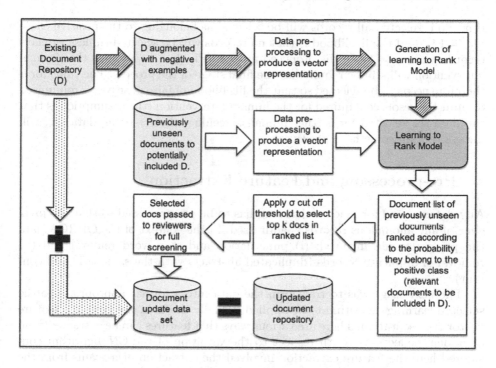

Fig. 1. Schematic of CN document collection update system

Once the model has been generated it can be applied to previously unseen data; in other words a collection of candidate documents for inclusion in the CDD. For the evaluation presented later in this paper, the 2015 and 2017 ORRCA update data collection were used (extracted from various medical repositories). SVR is a supervised machine learning model. This model is used to assign a probability value p to a previously unseen document, the probability that the unseen document belongs to the positive class. The probability that the document belongs to the negative class is then $p - 1$. A decision boundary, defined in terms of a threshold σ, is then required to assign an appropriate class label c to the previously unseen records. If $p > \sigma$ $c = relevant$; otherwise $c = not\ relevant$ (Eq. 1). The challenge is to identify an appropriate value for σ.

$$c = \begin{cases} relevant, & if\ p > \sigma \\ not\ relevant, & otherwise \end{cases} \tag{1}$$

For the ORRCA application considered here, the ranking model was trained using log loss[4]. Thus when using the resulting model, each previously unseen record is assigned a probability value between 0 and 1, which in turn can be used to perform a simple binary classification using a decision threshold σ $(0 \leq \sigma \leq 1)$.

---

[4] Logarithmic loss (related to cross-entropy) measures the performance of a classification model where the prediction output is a probability value between 0 and 1.

If $\sigma = 0$ is selected all records will be selected as belonging to the positive class; if $\sigma = 1$ is used the likelihood is that no records will be selected (unless we have records where $p = 1$). In the proposed process (Fig. 1) it is assumed that human intervention will still be required at the final stage of the process. The value for σ therefore needs to be selected so that the likelihood of false positives is minimised to limit the resource required for the human intervention (the assumption is that the data set selected for further human screening, the screening data set, will always contain some false positives).

4   Pre-processing and Feature Extraction

Any dataset used for machine learning has to be pre-processed so that the presence of any anomalous records is addressed. In the context of the ORRCA data the pre-processing involved: (i) punctuation and stop word removal and (ii) removal of duplicate records (duplicated abstracts with the same title and content).

The next stage was to transform the data into a format appropriate to the selected learning algorithm to be applied. Usually this is in the form of a feature vector representation. There are various ways that features can be extracted from document collections. With respect to the variation of the CN algorithm considered here the feature extraction involved the extraction of n-grams from the titles and abstracts of documents. An n-gram is defined as contiguous sequence of n words from a given sample of text. Three kinds of n-grams were extracted as potential features: unigrams, bigrams and trigrams. For each n-gram found in a document the Term-Frequency - Inverse Document Frequency (TF-IDF) value was calculated. The TF-IDF value is an indicator of how important a n-gram is to a particular document in a collection or corpus of documents. The TF-IDF value for a n-gram w, $tfidf(w)$, is calculated as shown in Eqs. 2, 3, and 4 where: (i) tf is term frequency, (ii) w is a given n-gram (iii) d is a document, (iv) $|d|$ is the size of the document d in terms of number of words, (v) D is the entire document collection $(d \in D)$ and (vi) $|D|$ is the size of D in terms of number of documents. Once the TF-IDF values have been calculated a threshold θ is required to decided which n-grams go into the vector representation. For the evaluation presented in Sect. 5, the default value of θ, present in Scikit-learn's SGD classifier was used. The ORRCA pre-2015 training dataset was unbalanced hence, in order to mitigate this imbalance between the number of positive and negative examples, the training weight for the positive examples was increased to 80.

$$tfidf(w) = tf(w) \times idf(w) \tag{2}$$

$$tf(w) = \frac{frequency\ count\ of\ w \in d}{|d|} \tag{3}$$

$$idf(w) = \frac{|D|}{total\ number\ of\ d \in D\ in\ which\ w\ appears} \tag{4}$$

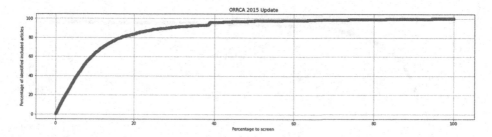

Fig. 2. Effort-recall curve for ORRCA 2015 dataset with both titles and abstracts, showing the percentage of articles screened versus the percentage of relevant articles identified.

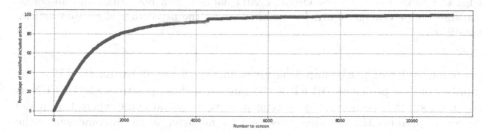

Fig. 3. Effort-recall curve for ORRCA 2015 dataset with both titles and abstracts, showing the number of articles screened versus the percentage of relevant articles identified.

5   Evaluation

This section an analysis of the proposed LRM-based CDD update approach. For the analysis, as already noted above, the ORRCA pre-2015 database augmented with negative examples was used as the training set and the 2015 and 2017 ORRCA updates as the test set. Some statistics concerning these two data set are given in Table 1. The objectives of the analysis were to:

1. Determine a most appropriate value for σ.
2. Measure the performance of the proposed CDD update approach with respect to: (i) effectiveness and (ii) time saving.

With respect to the first objective, effort-gain curves were used where the number of documents, or the percentage of documents, in the ranked list of documents selected for manual screening (the *effort*) was plotted against and number/percentage of true-positives identified (the *gain*). These curves tend to be exponential in nature, they feature an initial steep climb and then a flattening-off. The idea is that σ should be selected according to the location of the elbow between the climb and the flattening-off because this is the point where the "gain" to decrease compared to the "effort" required for manual screening. With respect to the second objective, the metrics used to measure effectiveness were

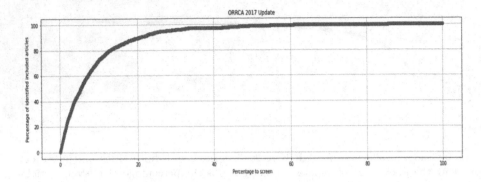

Fig. 4. Effort-recall curve for ORRCA 2017 dataset with both titles and abstracts, showing the percentage of articles screened versus the percentage of relevant articles identified.

precision and recall, calculated as given in Eqs. 5 and 6 where: (i) TP is the number of true positives, (ii) FP is the number of false positives and (iii) FN us the number of false negatives. A true positive is an outcome where the model correctly predicts the positive class. A true negative is an outcome where the model correctly predicts the negative class. A false negative is an outcome where the model incorrectly predicts the negative class. Recall that we wish to select a value for σ whereby the set of selected abstracts to be screened by a human is comprised of relevant abstracts (true positives)).

$$Precision = TP/(TP + FP) \tag{5}$$

$$Recall = TP/(TP + FN) \tag{6}$$

The resulting effort-gain curves are presented in Figs. 2, 3, 4, and 5. Figures 2 and 3 show the curves for the 2015 update, and Figs. 4 and 5 the curves for the 2017 update based on features from titles and abstracts of documents. For the effort-gain curves given in Figs. 2 and 4 the x-axis denote the percentage of candidate abstracts (thus both relevant and irrelevant abstracts) to be screened as a percentage of the total number of abstracts; whilst Figs. 3 and 5 show the same information but in terms of absolute numbers. Figure 8 and 9 shows the curves for the 2015 update and 2017 update based on features from titles of documents

Table 1. Statistical overview of the ORRCA training and test data

Database name	Positive examples		Negative examples		Total
	Num.	%	Num.	%	
Pre-2015 training dataset	4570	8.2	51460	91.8	56030
ORRCA 2015 update test dataset	1302	11.7	9797	88.3	11099
ORRCA 2017 update test dataset	1027	7.1	13458	92.9	14485

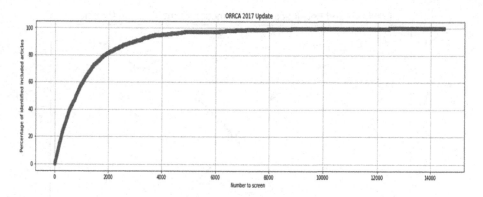

Fig. 5. Effort-recall curve for ORRCA 2017 dataset with both titles and abstracts, showing the number of articles screened versus the percentage of relevant articles identified.

only. For the effort-recall curves on datasets with features from titles of documents only, Figs. 8 and 9 the x-axis denote the percentage of candidate abstracts (thus both relevant and irrelevant abstracts) to be screened as a percentage of the total number of abstract.

Inspection of Fig. 2 that is based on features from both titles and abstract of documents for the 2015 update indicates that 97% of relevant abstracts can be identified by considering the top 45% of abstracts in the ranked document list. From Fig. 3 this equates to the top 1,500 abstracts in the ranked document list. Similarly, inspection of Fig. 4 for the 2017 update, indicates that identification of 97% of relevant abstracts requires consideration of the top 40% of abstracts in the ranked document list; and that, from Fig. 5, this equates to the top 6000 abstracts. Thus screening the top 40%–45% of abstracts in the ranked abstracts list would result in a loss of roughly 3% of the relevant abstract; which, it is argued here, is an acceptable compromise (trade-off) between effectiveness and efficiency. Selection of the top 40%–45% abstracts, in this case, would equate to a σ threshold of $\sigma = 0.3$.

Inspection of Fig. 8 that is based on features from titles only for the 2015 update indicates that 97% of relevant abstracts can be identified by considering the top 6000 of abstracts in the ranked document list. Similarly, inspection of Fig. 9 that is based on features from titles only for the 2017 update also indicates that 97% of relevant abstracts can be identified by considering the top 8000 of abstracts in the ranked document list. This indicates that screening with titles of documents only, is not a feasible option for identification of relevant documents in a ranked list of documents, whereas screening with both titles and abstracts is a more practical option for automatic screening of documents.

In order to estimate the time saved by automating the manual screening process, the assumption is made that the screening rate of an experienced screener is one abstract per minute. Using $\sigma = 0.3$, and considering the 2015 ORRCA update, this will result in 5099 (11099 − 6000 = 5099) abstracts

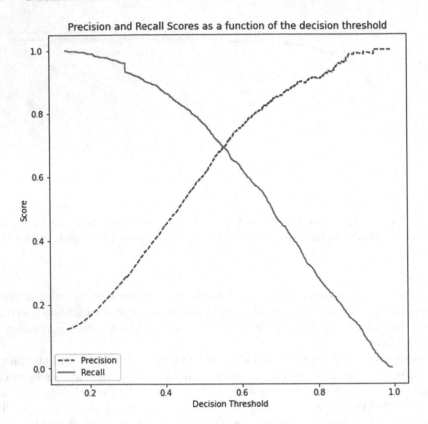

Fig. 6. Precision-recall curve for ORRCA 2015 dataset with both titles and abstracts, showing the values of decision thresholds σ on x-axes and the value of precision and recall on y-axes

being excluded, equating to a time saving of $5099 \div 60 = 85.0\,\text{h}$ (assuming an experienced screener for the abstract screening process). With respect to the 2017 ORRCA Update, by selecting $\sigma = 0.3$ 8485 abstracts would be excluded $(14485 - 6000 = 8485)$ equating to a time saving of $8485 \div 60 = 141.4\,\text{h}$.

Figures 6 and 7 show the precision-recall curve for the ORRCA 2015 and 2017 updates respectively. In these figures σ is plotted on the x-axis and the precision/recall score on the y-axis. Each figure features two curves, one for precision and one for recall. As noted earlier there is a trade off between the number of relevant abstracts and the number of irrelevant abstracts in the data set identified for screening depending on the selected value for σ. This is illustrated in the figure. From Fig. 6 and 7, in order to achieve a recall of 1 (identification of all relevant abstracts) $\sigma = 0.2$ would be required. Given, from the foregoing, after screening the first 40%–45% of the candidate abstracts, equivalent to a $\sigma = 0.3$ and identifying 97% of the relevant abstracts, we would be prepared to accept a loss of 3%; this is argued to be an acceptable trade-off in an automated systematic review system.

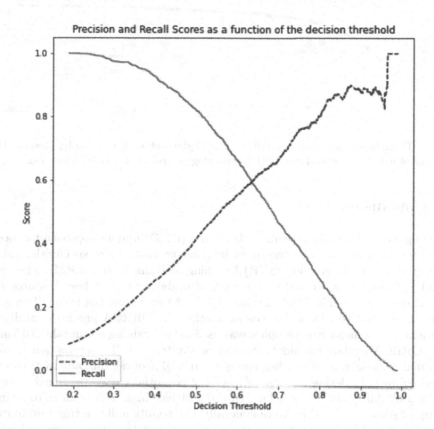

Fig. 7. Precision-recall curve for ORRCA 2017 dataset with both titles and abstracts, showing the values of decision thresholds σ on x-axes and the value of precision and recall on y-axes

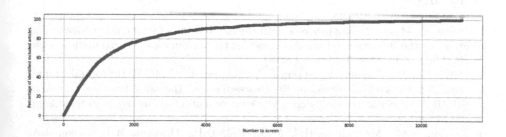

Fig. 8. Precision-recall curve for ORRCA 2015 dataset with titles only, showing the number of articles screened versus the percentage of relevant articles identified.

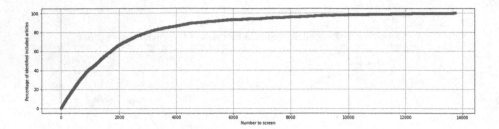

Fig. 9. Precision-recall curve for ORRCA 2017 dataset with titles only, showing the number of articles screened versus the percentage of relevant articles identified.

6   Conclusion

In this paper, a Curated Document Database (CDD) update approach has been presented founded on the concept of learning to rank, more specifically using a Support Vector Regression (SVR) Learning to Rank Model (LRM). The proposed approach was applied to the task of updating the Online Resource for Recruitment research in Clinical trials (ORRCA) database, but is equally applicable to alternative CDDs. For the evaluation the ORRCA pre-2015 database, augmented with negative examples, was used as the training set and the 2015 and 2017 ORRCA update candidate dataset as the test set. The evaluation results obtained demonstrate that, when using $\sigma = 0.3$, 97% of relevant abstracts can be identified by considering the top 40%–45% of potential abstracts ranked according to probability that they belong to the positive class. This equates to a time saving of some 85 to 141 h. More generally, the results indicate that automated screening can be used to reduce the workload and the time associated with CDD updating. In future, the plan is to use entity embeddings and BERT based learning-to-rank models for CDD updating.

References

1. Beller, E., et al.: Making progress with the automation of systematic reviews: principles of the international collaboration for the automation of systematic reviews (ICASR). Syst. Rev. **7**(1), 1–7 (2018)
2. Dehghani, M., Zamani, H., Severyn, A., Kamps, J., Croft, W.B.: Neural ranking models with weak supervision. In: Proceedings of the 40th International ACM SIGIR Conference on Research and Development in Information Retrieval, pp. 65–74 (2017)
3. Dowell, K.G., McAndrews-Hill, M.S., Hill, D.P., Drabkin, H.J., Blake, J.A.: Integrating text mining into the MGI biocuration workflow. Database J. Biol. Databases Curation (2009)
4. Howard, B.E., et al.: Swift-review: a text-mining workbench for systematic review. Syst. Rev. **5**(1), 87 (2016)
5. Kanoulas, E., Li, D., Azzopardi, L., Spijker, R.: CLEF 2017 technologically assisted reviews in empirical medicine overview. CEUR Workshop Proc. **1866**, 1–29 (2017)

6. Kearney, A., et al.: Development of an online resource for recruitment research in clinical trials to organise and map current literature. Clin. Trials **15**(6), 533–542 (2018)

7. Khabsa, M., Elmagarmid, A., Ilyas, I., Hammady, H., Ouzzani, M.: Learning to identify relevant studies for systematic reviews using random forest and external information. Mach. Learn. **102**(3), 465–482 (2015). https://doi.org/10.1007/s10994-015-5535-7

8. Krallinger, M., et al.: The protein-protein interaction tasks of biocreative iii: classification/ranking of articles and linking bio-ontology concepts to full text. BMC Bioinform. **12**(Suppl. 8), S3 (2011)

9. Lerner, I., Créquit, P., Ravaud, P., Atal, I.: Automatic screening using word embeddings achieved high sensitivity and workload reduction for updating living network meta-analyses. J. Clin. Epidemiol. **108**, 86–94 (2019)

10. MacAvaney, S., Nardini, F.M., Perego, R., Tonellotto, N., Goharian, N., Frieder, O.: Efficient document re-ranking for transformers by precomputing term representations. arXiv preprint arXiv:2004.14255 (2020)

11. Nogueira, R., Jiang, Z., Lin, J.: Document ranking with a pretrained sequence-to-sequence model. arXiv preprint arXiv:2003.06713 (2020)

12. Norman, C.R., Gargon, E., Leeflang, M.M.G., Névéol, A., Williamson, P.R.: Evaluation of an automatic article selection method for timelier updates of the comet core outcome set database. Database J. Biol. Databases Curation (2019)

13. O'Mara-Eves, A., Thomas, J., McNaught, J., Miwa, M., Ananiadou, S.: Using text mining for study identification in systematic reviews: a systematic review of current approaches. Syst. Rev. **4**(1), 5 (2015)

14. Pandey, G.: Utilization of efficient features, vectors and machine learning for ranking techniques. JYU Dissertations (2019)

15. Pereira, M., Etemad, E., Paulovich, F.: Iterative learning to rank from explicit relevance feedback. In: Proceedings of the 35th Annual ACM Symposium on Applied Computing, pp. 698–705 (2020)

16. Qiao, Y., Xiong, C., Liu, Z., Liu, Z.: Understanding the behaviors of BERT in ranking. arXiv preprint arXiv:1904.07531 (2019)

17. Suominen, H., et al.: Overview of the CLEF ehealth evaluation lab 2018. In: Bellot, P., et al. (eds.) CLEF 2018. LNCS, vol. 11018. Springer, Cham (2018). https://doi.org/10.1007/978-3-319-98932-7_26

What Are We Depressed About When We Talk About COVID-19: Mental Health Analysis on Tweets Using Natural Language Processing

Irene Li[1($\boxtimes$)], Yixin Li[1], Tianxiao Li[1], Sergio Alvarez-Napagao[2],
Dario Garcia-Gasulla[2], and Toyotaro Suzumura[2]

[1] Yale University, New Haven, USA
irene.li@yale.edu
[2] Barcelona Supercomputing Center (BSC), Barcelona, Spain

Abstract. The outbreak of coronavirus disease 2019 (COVID-19) recently has affected human life to a great extent. Besides direct physical and economic threats, the pandemic also indirectly impact people's mental health conditions, which can be overwhelming but difficult to measure. The problem may come from various reasons such as unemployment status, stay-at-home policy, fear for the virus, and so forth. In this work, we focus on applying natural language processing (NLP) techniques to analyze tweets in terms of mental health. We trained deep models that classify each tweet into the following emotions: anger, anticipation, disgust, fear, joy, sadness, surprise and trust. We build the EmoCT (Emotion-Covid19-Tweet) dataset for the training purpose by manually labeling 1,000 English tweets. Furthermore, we propose an approach to find out the reasons that are causing sadness and fear, and study the emotion trend in both keyword and topic level.

Keywords: Deep learning · Mental health · Natural language processing · Topic modeling

1 Introduction

Mental health is becoming a common issue. According to World Health Organization (WHO), one in four people in the world will be affected by mental or neurological disorders at some point in their lives.[1] A large emergency, such as the coronavirus disease 2019 (COVID-19), would especially sharply increase people's mental health problems, not only from the emergency itself, but also from the subsequent social outcomes such as unemployment, shortage of resources and financial crisis. Almost all people affected by emergencies will experience psychological distress, which for most people will improve over time.[2] In order

---

[1] https://www.who.int/whr/2001/media_centre/press_release/en/.
[2] https://www.who.int/news-room/fact-sheets/detail/mental-health-in-emergencies.

© Springer Nature Switzerland AG 2020
M. Bramer and R. Ellis (Eds.): SGAI-AI 2020, LNAI 12498, pp. 358–370, 2020.
https://doi.org/10.1007/978-3-030-63799-6_27

to help the society get prepared in response to surging mental problems during and after COVID-19 emergency, we need to understand people's general mental status as a first step.

Language, as a direct tool for people to convey their feelings and emotions, can be very helpful in the estimation of mental health conditions. Due to the recent impact of COVID-19, a large number of people move their works online, making some users are more active than usual on their social media accounts. Previous works have been conducted to utilize natural language processing (NLP) methods to process internet-based text data such as posts, tweets, and text messages on mental health problems [2, 4, 6, 9].

There are mainly two challenges in working with tweets using NLP methods. The first challenge is the large number of new posts online but restricted availability of APIs. There may be up to 90 or even 100 million tweets per day [4], so most of research is conducted on random samples [10, 12, 14]. We are interested in a million-level of tweets and also in a larger time span. Another challenge is the lack of labeled dataset for COVID-19. Though there exist labeled Twitter dataset for sentiment and emotions [7, 8, 10], due to the domain discrepancy, we still wish to have a manually-labeled dataset for training to have a better performed model. The work by [9] applies principal component analysis (PCA) to predict emotions. The method by [1] is to use k-Nearest Neighbors and Naive Bayes classifier to do classification on tweets. Very recently, many types of contextualized word embeddings are proposed and substantially improved the performance on many NLP tasks. A new language representation model, BERT [5], was proposed and obtains competitive results on up to 11 NLP tasks like classification. In this work, we apply a pre-trained BERT and fine-tune on our labeled data, providing in-depth analysis of mental health.

Our contributions are three-fold: we build the **EmoCT** (**E**motion-**COVID19-T**weet) dataset for classifying COVID-19-related tweets into eight emotions; then, we propose two models to do both single-label and multi-label classification respectively based on a multilingual BERT model, which are capable to predict on up to 104 languages and achieving promising results on English tweets; further analysis on case studies provide clues to understand why and how the public may feel fear and sad about COVID-19, and we also provide the study of emotion trend in both keyword and topic level.

2 Dataset

We applied Twitter API[3] to conduct a crawler with a list of keywords:coronavirus, covid19, covid, COVID-19, covid_19, confinamiento, flu, virus, hantavirus, fever, cough, social distance, lockdown, pandemic, epidemic, conlabelious, infection, stayhome, corona, épidémie, epidemie, epidemia, 新冠肺炎, 新型冠病毒, 疫情, 新冠病毒, 感染, 新型コロナウイルス, コロナ. Each day, we are able to crawl 3 million tweets in free text format from different languages. Due to the high

---

[3] https://developer.twitter.com/en/docs/tweets/data-dictionary/overview/intro-to-tweet-json.

capacity, we look at the tweets from March 24 to 26, 2020 to get language and geolocation statistics. Among these tweets, 8,148,202 tweets have the language information (`lang` field of the `Tweet` Object in Tweet API), and 76,460 tweets have the geographic information (`country_code` value from the `place` field if not `none`). We show the geolocation distributions in Fig. 1. Besides, Fig. 2 shows the language distribution of 8,148,202 tweets from 24 to 26 March, 2020 from the `lang` field of the tweet object.

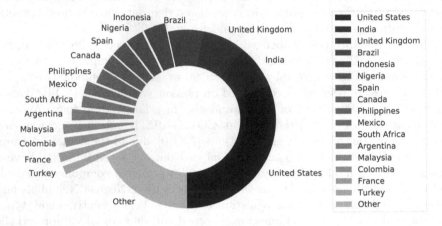

Fig. 1. Geolocation distribution on 76,460 tweets.

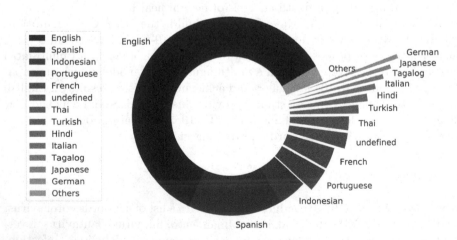

Fig. 2. Language distribution on 8,148,202 tweets.

To investigate the problem of mental health, we come up with the task of emotion classification on COVID-19-related tweets. We built **EmoCT** (**E**motion-**C**ovid19-**T**weet) dataset. We randomly annotated 1,000 English tweets selected from our crawled data. Following the work of EmoLex [11], we classify each tweet into the following emotions: anger, anticipation, disgust, fear, joy, sadness, surprise and trust. Each tweet is labeled as one, two or three emotion labels. For each emotion, we made sure that the primary label appeared in 125 tweets, and there is no number control in the secondary and tertiary label. We then split into 100/25 for each emotion as the training/testing set. We release two versions of the dataset: single-labeled version where only the primary label is kept for each example, and multi-labeled version where all the labels are kept. In this way, both single-label classification and multi-label classification can be conducted. We release the dataset to the public.[4]

3   Classification

Single-Label Classification. We first attempt to do a single-label classification task based on the single-labeled version of EmoCT. We apply a pre-trained multilingual version BERT model.[5] We take the output of the [CLS] token and add a fully-connected layer, which is fine-tuned using the labeled training examples (BERT). We set the learning rate to be 10^{-5} and number of epochs to be 20. Besides, we also fine-tune with the MLM (masked language model) on 1,181,342 unlabeled tweets randomly selected from our crawled data, and then trained on EmoCT (BERT(ft)). Table 1 shows the performance of the two models. As we can see, both models have competitive results on accuracy and F1, and BERT(ft) performs slightly better than BERT, so we take this model as our main model for analysis in later sections.

Table 1. Single-label classification results on EmoCT single-labeled version.

Method	Accuracy	F1
BERT	0.9549	0.9545
BERT(ft)	0.9562	0.9558

Table 2. Multi-label classification results on EmoCT multi-labeled version.

Method	Average precision	Coverage error	Ranking loss
BERT	0.6415	3.2261	0.2325
BERT(ft)	0.6467	3.1256	0.2159

Multi-label Classification. We also perform multi-label classification on the multi-labeled version of EmoCT. In this setting, each tweet has up to three labels

---

[4] https://github.com/IreneZihuiLi/EmoCT.
[5] https://github.com/huggingface/transformers: bert-base-multilingual-cased model.

Table 3. AUROC for each label of multi-label Classification on EmoCT multi-labeled version, as well as the micro average over all classes.

	BERT	BERT(ft)
Anger	0.7473	0.7397
Anticipation	0.6173	0.6897
Disgust	0.8222	0.8364
Fear	0.7010	0.7344
Joy	0.8380	0.8430
Sadness	0.7394	0.6809
Surprise	0.8620	0.8676
Trust	0.7919	0.8228
Micro-Avg.	0.7778	0.7891

out of eight, and we assume the labels are independent. We build a single-layer classifier with the activation function to be Sigmoid, which receives BERT output and predicts the possibility of containing each of the eight labels (BERT). The model uses binary cross-entropy loss and is trained for 10 epochs with learning rate 10^{-5}. Similarly, we also compare with a fine-tuned version as did in the previous model (BERT(ft)). For evaluation, we use example-based evaluation metrics mentioned in the work of [15] in Table 2. We could see that the two models achieve relatively low scores, probably due to the small-scale training data. We leave the improvement of this model as future work. In Table 3, we show the area-under-curve (AUC) of the response operating characteristic (ROC) curve for each class and their micro average. It can be noticed that both models are not performing so well by looking at the average score, and they are not very confident on certain classes like *anticipation*, and we leave it as future work.

4   Correlation

Due to the outbreak of coronavirus emergency, the two emotions *sad* and *fear* are more related to severe negative sentiments like depressed. To understand why the public may feel fear and sadness, we then attempt to analyze words and phrases that have a high correlation with both emotions. We apply our BERT(ft) model from the single-label classification task to predict the emotion label on randomly-picked 1 million English tweets data on April 7, 2020. Note that we keep only the tweets labeled as fear and sadness.

4.1   Attention Weight

When predicting the emotion label for each tweet, we take the last attention layer of the model and collect the top 3 tokens which have the maximum attention

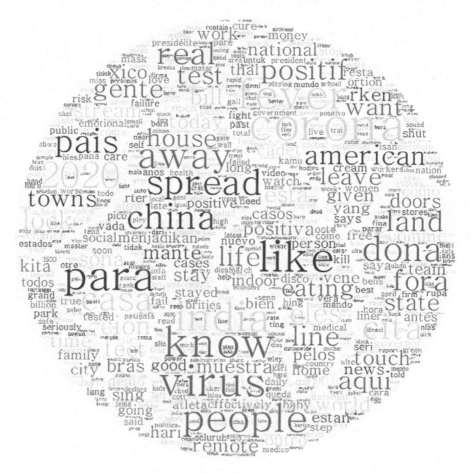

Fig. 3. Wordcloud from attention.

weights. Finally we rank the tokens by frequency and plot the wordcloud[6] of the top 500 tokens after filtering some stopwords in Fig. 3. A drawback of this method is that the tokens are split, so we can see some keywords that may not be meaningful without contexts, for example: *like, know* and *2020*. However, we can get some reasonable keywords: *fever, corona, spread, virus* and so on. Such words appear with a high frequency in the tweets labeled as fear and sadness, which may explain what and why people are feeling fear or sad. Note that this method can handle multiple language input as the pre-trained BERT model supports 104 different languages, though training was conducted on an English corpus.

---

[6] Visualization tool: https://wordart.com/. Invalid for a few languages.

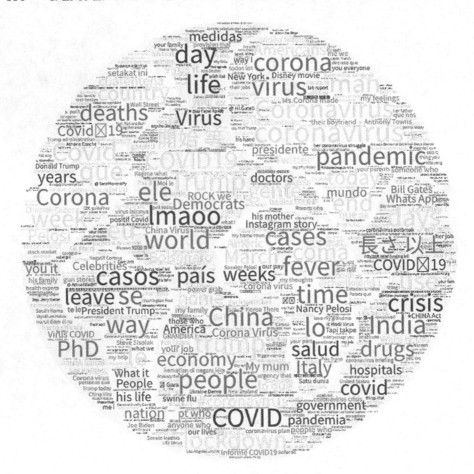

Fig. 4. Wordcloud from POS tagging.

4.2 POS Tagging

Intuitively, we assume that nouns are more meaningful in a tweet, making it possible and easier to understand the reasons why it is labeled as fear or sadness. As a comparison, we look at the Part-of-Speech (POS) tag of each token in the tweets and keep the nouns and noun phrases only. We apply the Stanza Python library to do POS tagging [13] and we include supporting to six languages including English, Spanish, Portuguese, Japanese, German and Chinese. Similarly, we plot the top 500 keywords and phrases based on frequency in Fig. 4. There are some informative keywords and phrases captured: *pandemic*, *China*, *economy*, 開始 (means *starting* in English), *President Trump*, *White House* and so on. While working on the analysis, we saw other meaningful phrases such as *gun stores*, *school closings*, and *health conditions* which has a lower frequency and may not be visible.

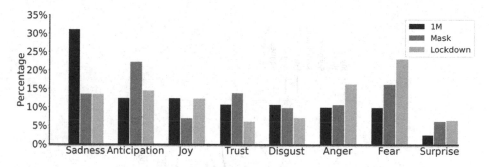

Fig. 5. Comparison of emotion distribution.

5 Emotion Trend Analysis

The emotion trend among different keywords or topics is also very important, as it potentially may show the public attitude change within a period of time. Similarly, we provide analysis only on the English tweets.

5.1 Emotion Trend with Keywords

We still choose the single-label classification BERT(ft) model to do prediction. We provide a case study on two keywords: *mask* and *lockdown*. We first pick 1 million tweets randomly from the data of March 29th, 2020. By filtering on the keywords, we found 8,071 tweets that contain the word *mask*, and 31,140 tweets that contain the word *lockdown*. Figure 5 shows the comparison of emotion distribution among 1 million samples (1M), tweets with *mask*, and tweets with *lockdown*. In the 1M group, most tweets are classified into negative classes like fear, anger and sadness. But when people are talking about masks, more tweets are classified into anticipation and trust, which is sometimes more neutral and positive. For the tweets talking about lockdown, there is no significant difference with that of 1M.

To further analyze the trends, we select the data of two weeks (March 25, 2020–April 7, 2020), and apply the same model to predict the emotion labels on all the tweets we crawled (around 3 million each day) that contains the two mentioned keywords respectively. There is no significant change for the emotion distribution in all the data. However, we found the dominating emotions and variations of the change are closely related to the topic. In Fig. 6 and 7, we illustrate the emotion trend for each single day of the selected keywords. The high variation (plot in solid lines in the figures) showed up in *sadness*, *anger* and *anticipation* for the tweets that contain the word *mask* in Fig. 6, and *disgust*, *sadness* for the tweets that contain the word *lockdown* in Fig. 7. Especially, for the *lockdown* tweets, the percentage of *disgust* emotion had a significant increase on March 27 and dropped on the next two days, as marked with the black asterisks. To further investigate, we looked at the news in March 27, which included U.S. as the first country to report 100,000 confirmed coronavirus cases,

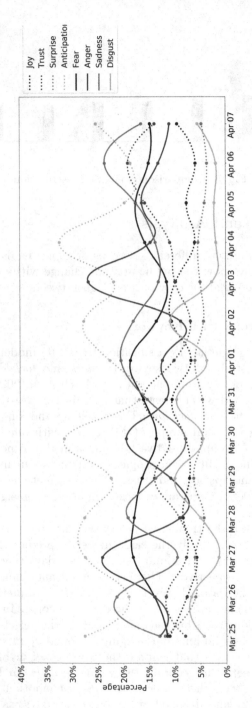

Fig. 6. Emotion trend on the word *mask* from March 25, 2020 to April 7, 2020.

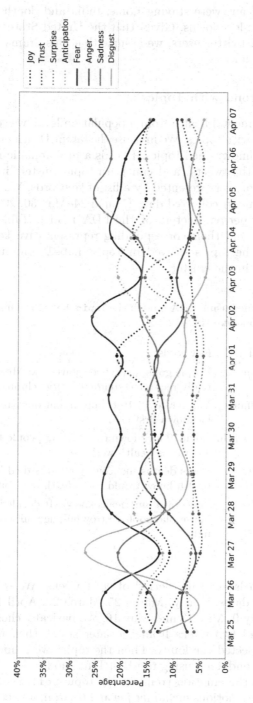

Fig. 7. Emotion trend on the word *lockdown* from March 25, 2020 to April 7, 2020.

and 9 in 10 Americans were staying home; India and South Africa joined the countries to impose lockdowns. Given that the United States, India and Brazil have large group of twitter users, we assume that this dramatic change may be triggered by those news.

5.2   Emotion Trend with Topics

To understand the mental health from a population level, we compare and study the emotion trends with topics. We first use the latent Dirichlet allocation (LDA) [3] model to learn fine-grained topics. LDA is a probabilistic model for discrete data (in our case, the tweets) and can learn topic clusters in an unsupervised way, where each topic is represented by a list of keywords. We sampled ten days' data randomly from our collected data (March 24–May 30, 2020) and tried with different sets of hyper-parameters of the LDA model. Table 4 shows the five fine-grained topics and their corresponding representative keywords. We then manually labeled the topics showed in `Topic Label` column by summarizing from the keywords in the cluster.

Table 4. Topics learned using LDA model: the `Topic Label` are manually summarized from the learned top `Keywords`.

ID	Topic Label	Keywords
1	Activities, life	People going everybody parties kickbacks majority really recover restaurant overwhelming spreads
2	Breaking affairs	Murder covid-19 trump urgent doctors deaths lives lockdown first crisis
3	Individual health	Covid19 lockdown care testing people time fever americans health work
4	Public health	Cases deaths like county months died lockdown health know would state death next breaking
5	Politics	Lockdown americans know left decided tired country house playbook destroy 69-page misleading crowd fight

We looked at a larger time period of eight weeks. We selected the data in from the following dates: (Early) March 25, March 29, April 1 and April 5; and (Later) May 6, May 9, May 13 and May 16. We basically chose two weeks from the early stage and two weeks from the later stage, then from each week, 2 days' data were selected randomly. Then the topics were inferred and emotion classification was conducted using the BERT(ft) model.

Figure 8 shows the emotion trend in the topic `politics`. There is a slight drop in the positive emotions including *joy* and *trust*; more people are feeling *fear* and *anger*, but less are feeling *disgust* and *sadness* in the later stage. Figure 9 shows the results for `individual health` where we see that an improvement happened in the joy emotion but still the top three emotions are *fear*, *anger* and *sadness*. In general, from the population level, we notice that many of the tweets are classified as a negative feeling than positive ones. From our data and analysis, we conclude that the COVID-19 pandemic potentially have had impacts on mental health on many perspectives like health conditions and the society (i.e., politics).

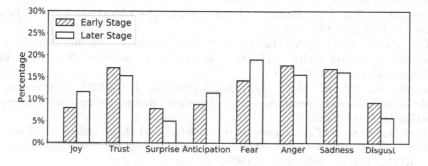

Fig. 8. Emotion trend on Politics.

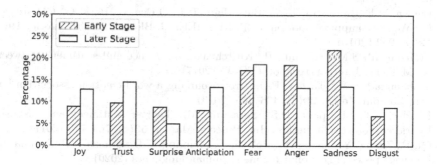

Fig. 9. Emotion trend on Individual Health.

6   Conclusion and Future Work

In this work, we build the EmoCT dataset for classifying COVID-19-related tweets into different emotions to study the mental health problem. Based on this dataset, we conducted both single-label and multi-label classification tasks and achieved promising results. To understand the reasons why the public may feel sad or fear, we applied two methods to calculate correlations of the keywords and conducted some analysis to study the emotion trend. In the future work, we will study more in-depth analysis to better understand how COVID-19 affect on mental health. Besides, it will be helpful for us to have a correct estimates of the COVID-19 effects on people's long term mental health.

References

1. Abidin, T.F., Hasanuddin, M., Mutiawani, V.: N-grams based features for Indonesian tweets classification problems. In: 2017 International Conference on Electrical Engineering and Informatics (ICELTICs), pp. 307–310. IEEE (2017)
2. Althoff, T., Clark, K., Leskovec, J.: Large-scale analysis of counseling conversations: an application of natural language processing to mental health. Trans. Assoc. Comput. Linguisti. **4**, 463–476 (2016)
3. Blei, D.M., Ng, A.Y., Jordan, M.I.: Latent Dirichlet allocation. J. Mach. Learn. Res. **3**(Jan), 993–1022 (2003)
4. Calvo, R.A., Milne, D.N., Hussain, M.S., Christensen, H.: Natural language processing in mental health applications using non-clinical texts. Nat. Lang. Eng. **23**(5), 649–685 (2017)
5. Devlin, J., Chang, M.W., Lee, K., Toutanova, K.: BERT: pre-training of deep bidirectional transformers for language understanding. arXiv preprint arXiv:1810.04805 (2018)
6. Dini, L., Bittar, A.: Emotion analysis on Twitter: the hidden challenge. In: Proceedings of the Tenth International Conference on Language Resources and Evaluation (LREC 2016), pp. 3953–3958 (2016)
7. Go, A., Bhayani, R., Huang, L.: Twitter sentiment classification using distant supervision
8. Hasan, M., Rundensteiner, E., Agu, E.: Emotex: detecting emotions in Twitter messages (2014)
9. Larsen, M.E., Boonstra, T.W., Batterham, P.J., O'Dea, B., Paris, C., Christensen, H.: We feel: mapping emotion on Twitter. IEEE J. Biomed. Health Inform. **19**(4), 1246–1252 (2015)
10. Mohammad, S.M., Sobhani, P., Kiritchenko, S.: Stance and sentiment in tweets. ACM Trans. Internet Technol. (TOIT) (2017)
11. Mohammad, S.M., Turney, P.D.: Crowdsourcing a word-emotion association lexicon. Comput. Intell. **29**(3), 436–465 (2013)
12. Pandey, A.C., Rajpoot, D.S., Saraswat, M.: Twitter sentiment analysis using hybrid cuckoo search method. Inf. Process. Manag. **53**(4), 764–779 (2017)
13. Qi, P., Zhang, Y., Zhang, Y., Bolton, J., Manning, C.D.: Stanza: a Python natural language processing toolkit for many human languages (2020)
14. Ritter, A., Clark, S., Etzioni, O., et al.: Named entity recognition in tweets: an experimental study. In: Proceedings of the Conference on Empirical Methods in Natural Language Processing, pp. 1524–1534. Association for Computational Linguistics (2011)
15. Zhang, M., Zhou, Z.: A review on multi-label learning algorithms. IEEE Trans. Knowl. Data Eng. **26**(8), 1819–1837 (2014)

Short Application Stream Papers

Using Sentence Embedding for Cross-Language Plagiarism Detection

Naif Alotaibi[✉] and Mike Joy

Department of Computer Science, University of Warwick, Coventry, UK
{naif.alotaibi,m.s.joy}@warwick.ac.uk

Abstract. The growth of textual content in various languages and the advancement of automatic translation systems has led to an increase of cases of translated plagiarism. When a text is translated into another language, word order will change and words may be substituted by synonyms, and as a result detection will be more challenging. The purpose of this paper is to introduce a new technique for English-Arabic cross-language plagiarism detection. This method combines word embedding, term weighting techniques, and universal sentence encoder models, in order to improve detection of sentence similarity. The proposed model has been evaluated based on English-Arabic cross-lingual datasets, and experimental results show improved performance when compared with other Arabic-English cross-lingual evaluation methods presented at SemEval-2017.

Keywords: Plagiarism detection · Semantic similarity · Cross-Language · English · Arabic

1 Introduction

Development of the Internet and information technology have increased the availability of digital libraries and automatic machine translation tools, where a text easily translates from one language to another language, and these have increased instances of plagiarism. Plagiarism occurs by copying words, phrases or ideas from someone else without giving acknowledgment to original work [8].

Zu Eissen et al. [20] presented a taxonomy of plagiarism, which was enriched by Alzahrani et al. [3], who classified plagiarism into *literal* and *intelligent* plagiarism. Literal plagiarism is word-for-word repetition of a phrase or transcription of a section of someone else's work. There are three types of this form, which are an *exact copy, near copy* and *modified copy*. Whereas, intelligent plagiarism is the changing of content in original text by modifying sentence structure such as paraphrasing or translating text into another language, and is referred to as *cross-language plagiarism*. Identification of translated plagiarism is more challenging than other types of plagiarism since each language has its own structure.

There exist a number of plagiarism detection approaches that are able to capture exact copy and simply modified plagiarism. However, these systems cannot effectively

© Springer Nature Switzerland AG 2020
M. Bramer and R. Ellis (Eds.): SGAI-AI 2020, LNAI 12498, pp. 373–379, 2020.
https://doi.org/10.1007/978-3-030-63799-6_28

detect more extensively disguised cases of plagiarism, including paraphrases and cross-language plagiarism. Eisa et al. [6] noted that existing methods are still struggling with the serious issues in identifying linguistic changes like substituting vocabulary by their synonyms. This paper proposes an English-Arabic cross-lingual plagiarism detection model, that is based on semantic sentence similarity. Effectiveness of word embedding and universal sentence encoding for representing sentence vectors are examined, and a model is proposed based on combining these approaches and using combinations of POS and TFIDF weighting schemes.

Several studies have been conducted on cross-lingual plagiarism detection. For example, a Cross-Lingual Alignment-based Similarity model (CL-ASA), that was presented in [4] used a parallel corpus to create a bilingual statistical dictionary. Another study based on comparable corpora was introduced in [9] and used a Cross-Language Explicit Semantic Analysis (CL-ESA) model that can be applied to corpora that contain texts that are written about similar topics in various languages. There has been little published research on Arabic-English cross-language plagiarism detection. Aljohani and Mohd [2] proposed an Arabic-English cross-lingual detection method based on winnowing algorithm, and used Google Translate to translate the texts. Although this model was able to detect literal plagiarism cases, it could not detect the cases of rewriting words using their synonyms. To overcome this, Hattab [10] employed Latent Semantic Indexing (LSI) to construct a cross-lingual semantic vector space in order to identify context similarity. The author used a parallel corpus to convert the source documents into target text instead of using direct translation, using cosine measurement to calculate degree of similarity. The method gave good results in the cases of replacing words, however the computational procedure of LSI is relatively expensive. Another study [1] introduced a technique based on key phrase extraction from suspect documents and then translated these phrases via machine translation. Thereafter, the similarity between these phrases was measured by a combination of three techniques: cosine similarity, longest common subsequence (lcs) and n-grams. Even though the model worked quite well, computational complexity of using the lcs method has an impact on the overall performance. Recently, Ezzikouri et al. [7] have applied a fuzzy semantic based similarity approach in order to capture cross language plagiarism cases utilizing WordNet and the algorithm that proposed in [18] in order to compute semantic similarity between two words.

On the other hand, word embedding is an approach to provide a distributed representation of vocabularies. There are number of methods which have been introduced to generate word embedding from text data, for example, two methods were offered in [12] to build the words representations model: (i) Continuous bag-of-words (CBOW) and (ii) skip-gram (SKIP-G). The CBOW model predicts the current word based on surrounding words, whereas the second model uses the current word to predict the neighboring words. Furthermore, the Universal Sentence Encoder embeds sentences into vector representations which capture rich semantic information that can be used in variety of natural language processing (NLP) applications, like classification and plagiarism detection [19]. The proposed model for detecting English-Arabic cross-lingual plagiarism is based on analyzing features of sentences using word embedding and multilingual universal sentence encoder (MUSE) models.

2 Proposed Method

The key idea for the proposed plagiarism detection technique for English-Arabic pairs of texts is based on sentence level comparisons. The proposed model is based on word embedding, term weighting, and MUSE. There are two steps in order to represent sentence vectors. Firstly, we combine word embedding and mixing parts of speech (POS) with the Term Frequency Inverse Document Frequency (TFIDF) weighting method, which we name CL-WE-Tw, and is based on machine translation. The second step is to combine the MUSE model with the CL-WE-Tw method in order to enhance detection of sentence similarity. Figure 1 illustrates the framework for the proposed method, and the main processes are shown in the following section.

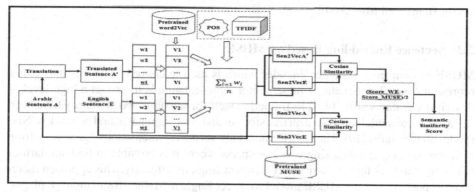

Fig. 1. Proposed framework for English-Arabic cross-language plagiarism detection

2.1 Sentence Embedding Based on CL-WE-Tw Model

Representation of sentences based on word embedding and term weight schemes is a useful way to extract features of each sentence, thus enhancing the ability to compute sentence similarity. Word embedding captures semantic and syntactic features of the language [13]. Term weighting schemes such as TFIDF and POS are methods to assign for each term its weighted contribution in the text. The key idea of TFIDF is to find relations of a word in a document to other documents in the corpus, and it is used to reduce the influence of the most common words such as "is", "the" and "a". According to [14], the TFIDF weighting scheme is integrated traditionally with information retrieval for enhancing textual retrieval performance. In terms of the POS weighting approach, which is beneficial to understand the sentence representation, POS is able to take into account ambiguity problems, such as the word "train" which can be a noun or a verb. The usefulness of combining the POS weighting scheme with information retrieval is to improve retrieval performance [11]. As a result, the proposed method integrates word embedding with both POS and TFIDF in order to represent sentences and then compute the similarity between two sentence vectors. Each word is represented as a vector and is weighted by mixing the TFIDF and POS weights. The weighted average of all word vectors is used to construct the corresponding sentence vector, as shown in Eq. 1.

$$Sv = \frac{1}{n} \sum_{i=1}^{n} vi * (TFIDF * POS(wi)) \tag{1}$$

Where Sv is sentence vector, vi is a function that finds word vector, wi is the ith word of text. After getting each sentence vector, cosine similarity is applied to compute similarity between two texts according to Eq. 2:

$$Ss = \frac{VE.VA'}{\|VE\|.\|VA'\|} \tag{2}$$

Where VE is the first sentence vector (in English sentence) and VA' is the sentence vector (translated from Arabic).

2.2 Sentence Embedding Based on MUSE

MUSE is a universal sentence encoder which is used to convert sentences into vector representations. The benefit of these vector representation is to extract a high level of descriptive features [19]. Two pre-trained models for semantic text similarity have been released, these models are based on transformer and convolutional neural network (CNN) model architectures [19]. The MUSE model allows the representation of sentences from different languages into a single vector space, where it is possible to find similarities between sentences that are written in different languages directly. This approach therefore proposes to use the MUSE model to detect English-Arabic cross-language plagiarism, performing a direct comparison between English and Arabic sentences and then applying cosine similarity between them to measure the degree of similarity.

2.3 Overall Sentence Similarity

As CL-WE-Tw and MUSE models are two important components for interpreting sentence meaning, the overall sentence similarity is measured by a combination of sentence similarity based on the CL-WE-Tw and MUSE models.

$$Sim_{sentence} = \frac{(s_{we} + s_{muse})}{2} \tag{3}$$

In Eq. 3, s_{we} is the result is obtained by sentence embedding based on CL-WE-Tw while s_{muse} is obtained based on the MUSE model. After obtaining the similarity score between the pair of sentences based on the proposed model, it can be judged whether this pair is plagiarized or non-plagiarized. Namely, if the degree of similarity exceeds a predefined threshold α, the pair of sentences is considered plagiarized.

3 Experiment and Results

In order to assess the proposed model, STS Test and Microsoft Research Video Description Corpus (MSRvid) datasets drawn from the Semantic Textual Similarity (STS) shared task from SemEval-2017 (STS Cross-lingual Arabic-English), released in [5], are used to assess the performance of the model. The total size of these datasets is 985 pairs of sentences, each pair of sentences having been labelled by humans on an integer scale from 0–5 (5 means exactly similar, whereas 0 indicates that the two sentences in the pair are completely different). The Pearson correlation coefficient P between the human rating and the predicted value of the model is used to assess the performance of the proposed model.

The proposed model consists of two components, the first is machine translation and the second is applying monolingual semantic analysis based on word embedding and mixing TFIDF with POS weightings. A pre-processing phase is required for making text is ready for further evaluation, and consists of the following steps. Firstly, all sentences are translated from Arabic into English via the Google Translation API. Secondly, Natural Language ToolKit (NLTK) is used for tokenization, POS tagging, removing punctuation marks, and normalization. After the texts are pre-processed, Mikolov et al.'s [13] pre-trained word2vec model, which is efficient to extract semantic and syntactic features, is used to generate a vector for each word in each sentence. The word2vec model was trained on a Google News dataset of about 100 billion words. On the other hand, the second component of the proposed model, which is based on MUSE model, is not required for the pre-processing steps. After representing sentence vector, the degree of the similarity between the pair of sentences is calculated using cosine similarity.

A number of experiments have been done in order to examine the performance of representing sentence embedding based on the CL-WE-Tw and MUSE models then measuring semantic similarity between two sentence vectors. Table 1 shows the results of the proposed model.

Table 1. Assessment results of proposed model

Datasets Methods	STS Test	MSRvid
Word2vec Model		
Average all vectors	0.6204	0.7269
Average all vectors & TFIDF	0.6693	0.7718
Average all vectors & POS	0.6801	0.7460
CL-WE-Tw	0.6902	0.7732
MUSE Model		
MUSE model	0.78	0.7977
Combination of CL-WE-Tw and MUSE Models		
((CL-WE-Tw) + (MUSE model))/2	0.8147	0.837

As displayed in Table 1, integrating the word2vec model with the POS and TFIDF weighting scheme achieves good results on both the STS test dataset and the MSRvid dataset with Pearson correlations of 0.6902 and 0.7732 respectively. Computing similarity between the two sentence vectors based on the MUSE model achieves the highest results for both datasets with correlations of 0.78 and 0.7977 respectively. Interestingly, combining the CL-WE-Tw and MUSE models achieved better performance than using them individually.

The proposed models have been compared with the ECNU [16], BIT [17] and HCTI [15] methods that obtained the best results on the STS Test dataset. Table 2 presents the comparative evaluation.

Table 2. Comparative evaluation

Models	Pearson correlation coefficient
The proposed model	0.8147
ECNU	0.7493
BIT	0.7007
CL-WE-Tw	0.6902
HCTI	0.6836

As shown in Table 2, the proposed model based on sentence embedding obtains the highest performance with a correlation of 0.8147.

4 Conclusion

This paper proposed a technique for detecting cross-lingual plagiarism based on combining word embedding, term weighting and the MUSE models. According to the results of the experiments, the proposed model is competitive when compared against other participating approaches in the SemEval-2017 Arabic-English cross-lingual evaluation task. For future work, we will explore the use of machine learning algorithms (e.g., decision tree and random forest) and neural network architectures (e.g., LSTM and RNN) in order to enhance cross-lingual plagiarism detection.

References

1. Alaa, Z., Tiun, S., Abdulameer, M.: Cross-language plagiarism of Arabic-English documents using linear logistic regression. J. Theor. Appl. Inf. Technol. **83**(1), 20–33 (2016)
2. Aljohani, A., Mohd, M.: Arabic-English cross-language plagiarism detection using winnowing algorithm. Inf. Technol. J. **13**(14), 23–49 (2014)
3. Alzahrani, S.M., Salim, N., Abraham, A.: Understanding plagiarism linguistic patterns, textual features, and detection methods. IEEE Trans. Syst. Man Cybern. Part C Appl. Rev. **42**(2), 133–149 (2011)
4. Barrón-Cedeno, A., Rosso, P., Pinto, D., Juan, A.: On cross-lingual plagiarism analysis using a statistical model. In: PAN, pp. 1–10 (2008)
5. Cer, D., Diab, M., Agirre, E., Lopez-Gazpio, I., Specia, L.: Semeval-2017 task 1: semantic textual similarity-multilingual and cross-lingual focused evaluation. In: Proceedings of the 11th International Workshop on Semantic Evaluation (SemEval-2017), pp. 1–14 (2017)

6. Eisa, T.A.E., Salim, N., Alzahrani, S.: Existing plagiarism detection techniques: a systematic mapping of the scholarly literature. Online Inf. Rev. **39**(3), 383–400 (2015)
7. Ezzikouri, H., Oukessou, M., Youness, M., Erritali, M.: Fuzzy cross language plagiarism detection (Arabic-English) using WordNet in a big data environment. In: 2nd International Conference on Cloud and Big Data Computing, pp. 22–27. ACM (2018)
8. Gipp, B.: Citation-based Plagiarism Detection, pp. 57–88. Springer, Wiesbaden (2014). https://doi.org/10.1007/978-3-658-06394-8_4
9. Gabrilovich, E., Markovitch, S.: Computing semantic relatedness using Wikipedia-based explicit semantic analysis. IJCAI **7**, 1606–1611 (2007)
10. Hattab, E.: Cross-language plagiarism detection method: arabic vs. english. In: 2015 International Conference on Developments of E-Systems Engineering (DeSE), pp. 141–144. IEEE (2015)
11. Lioma, C., Blanco, R.: Part of speech based term weighting for information retrieval. In: Boughanem, M., Berrut, C., Mothe, J., Soule-Dupuy, C. (eds.) ECIR 2009. LNCS, vol. 5478, pp. 412–423. Springer, Heidelberg (2009). https://doi.org/10.1007/978-3-642-00958-7_37
12. Mikolov, T., Chen, K., Corrado, G., Dean, J.: Efficient estimation of word representations in vector space. arXiv preprint arXiv:1301.3781 (2013)
13. Mikolov, T., Sutskever, I., Chen, K., Corrado, G.S., Dean, J.: Distributed representations of words and phrases and their compositionality. In: 26th International Conference on Neural Information Processing Systems, vol. 2, pp. 3111–3119 (2013)
14. Salton, G., Buckley, C.: Term-weighting approaches in automatic text retrieval. Inf. Process. Manage. **24**(5), 513–523 (1988)
15. Shao, Y.: HCTI at SemEval-2017 Task 1: use convolutional neural network to evaluate semantic textual similarity. In: Proceedings of the 11th International Workshop on Semantic Evaluation (SemEval-2017), Vancouver, pp. 130–133 (2017)
16. Tian, J., Zhou, Z., Lan, M., Wu, Y.: ECNU at SemEval-2017 task 1: leverage kernel-based traditional NLP features and neural networks to build a universal model for multilingual and cross-lingual semantic textual similarity. In: Proceedings of the 11th International Workshop on Semantic Evaluation (SemEval-2017), Vancouver, pp. 191–197 (2017)
17. Wu, H., Huang, H.Y., Jian, P., Guo, Y., Su, C.: BIT at SemEval-2017 task 1: using semantic information space to evaluate semantic textual similarity. In: Proceedings of the 11th International Workshop on Semantic Evaluation (SemEval-2017), Vancouver, pp. 77–84 (2017)
18. Wu, Z., Palmer, M.: Verbs semantics and lexical selection. In: Proceedings of the 32nd annual meeting on Association for Computational Linguistics, pp. 133–138 (1994)
19. Yang, Y., et al.: Multilingual universal sentence encoder for semantic retrieval. arXiv preprint arXiv:1907.04307 [CS.CL] (2019)
20. Meyer zu Eissen, S., Stein, B., Kulig, M.: Plagiarism detection without reference collections. In: Decker, R., Lenz, H.-J. (eds.) Advances in Data Analysis. SCDAKO, pp. 359–366. Springer, Heidelberg (2007). https://doi.org/10.1007/978-3-540-70981-7_40

Leveraging Anomaly Detection for Proactive Application Monitoring

Shyam Zacharia(✉) iD

British Telecom, Bengaluru, India
shyam.zacharia@bt.com

Abstract. Anomaly detection is one of the popular research fields in Machine Learning. Also, this is one of the key techniques in system and application monitoring in Industry. Anomaly detection comprises of outlier detection and identifying novelty from the data - it is a process to understand the deviation of an observation from existing observations [12] and identifying the new observations. Carrying out anomaly detection in an enterprise application is a challenge as there are complex processes to gather and analyze functional and non-functional logs of unlabeled data. In this paper we are proposing an unsupervised learning process with log featurization incorporating time window to detect outliers and novel errors from enterprise application logs.

Keywords: Anomaly detection · Outlier detection · Novelty detection

1 Introduction

Application monitoring with a real-world dataset is a complex task as huge quantities and a variety of log information are getting generated in every minute. The log information can be functional (application functionality logs) and non-functional (system operation logs, performance logs, security logs etc.), and these are unlabeled information. There exist plenty of anomaly detection algorithms in different categories for addressing the need. The log information is dynamic in nature as it is generated during a process journey and depends upon the data values in each step. And new logs will also be added during each cycle of application development. Rule based log capturing and anomaly detection methods will have enormous issues in these situations, as rules cannot cope with these frequent and dynamic changes. Our proposed method can capture the log in the same format and can also find the outliers and novel errors in the logs. We consider outliers as the errors which are deviant from the normal concentrated observation of data. We also define novel errors as errors which are not seen in the training data.

In this paper, we address the problem of anomaly detection from the log dataset by converting the log information to appropriate featurization and applying different unsupervised anomaly detection algorithms. The end-to-end strategic approach to tackle outlier and novelty detection within enterprise application logs is introduced in this paper.

The paper is organized as follows: In Sect. 2, we will highlight the related work in this area. Section 3 describes the proposed approach to the problem, and Sect. 4 contains

© Springer Nature Switzerland AG 2020
M. Bramer and R. Ellis (Eds.): SGAI-AI 2020, LNAI 12498, pp. 380–385, 2020.
https://doi.org/10.1007/978-3-030-63799-6_29

experiment results and benefits. Section 5 concludes the paper and presents future work. Acknowledgements for the paper follow.

2 Related Works

The mechanism to capture operational logs has been in existence since a long time. But most of the techniques were using a regex expression to parse the log file [8–10] to build the features from the logs and those patterns were used for detecting the outliers. Here the outlier detection is subjective to specific functionality. There are ways to incorporate the operational procedure along with the log information to identify anomalies [3, 11]. As mentioned, there exist plenty of Anomaly detection algorithms to identify the outlier and novelty. Some of the example algorithms are mentioned in [1, 2, 4, 5]. In the proposed approach we are portraying the anomaly detection by considering only the text information of functional or non-functional process logs.

3 Proposed Approach

For most of the addressed enterprise applications, the logs are generated in text format. This text format will be in accordance with the style of each application's logging procedures. In order to debug the errors, the entities such as time stamps, error codes, error messages and other related details are present in the log file. Some of these errors can be ignored as they will not cause any harm to the functionality of the application. But there are threatening errors which need to be addressed quickly to ensure application functionality.

We have considered three different types of logs generated by three different types of application/servers for our experiments, namely Siebel CRM (Customer Relationship Management) logs, Apache server logs and, WebLogic server logs. In each of these applications, we have followed the same approach and obtained consistent results at the end. The detailed overview will be mentioned based on the process we followed with the Siebel Application, but the same methods can be applied for all kinds of application logs.

3.1 Outlier Detection

An outlier is an observation which deviates from the course of other observations [12] or appears inconsistent with the remainder of the dataset [13]. As per [1–3] there are multiple ways to identify outliers. In the proposed method, we are using unsupervised outlier detection methods as we have the application log as input, which is not labelled. In the log details, we have functionality related errors which can originate from system issues in addition to data issues, programming issues, etc. In the non-functional logs there are issues such as server related - both hardware and software issues, network related issues, operational issues, performance issues, etc. The log files contain informational logging, warning contents and error contents. Our aim is to identify and isolate errors which appear inconsistent with previous appearances.

3.2 Novelty Detection

Novelty detection is an unsupervised learning technique to identify novel errors from the logs. The errors which have not occurred in training data are captured by this method. These novel errors will arise in case of addition of new functionality in the application, during system revamp, or in application upgrade scenarios.

These new errors in test data can be captured during our feature vector conversion, which is done using a Word2Vec [7] model. The log entry tokens which are not part of Word2Vec model are the actual novel errors. The words in these errors, unknown to the already formed Word2Vec model, are mapped to default vector values and concatenated to form the sentence feature vector which is then passed to the anomaly detection algorithm.

3.3 Implementation and Model Training

The approach in Fig. 1. has been taken for model training and prediction.

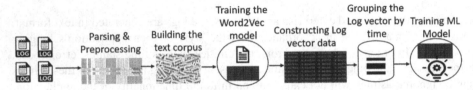

Fig. 1. Machine learning model training steps

- **Removing the log information for the known issues:** All the log files generated in certain time period, for example in past one month, must be collected for building the training data. Only those log files generated when the application was working normally are utilized. In addition, only the logs which are captured with minimum log level settings are used for training purposes.
- **Parsing and preprocessing the log files:** The relevant information such as event type, event subtype, time stamp and log message need to be parsed from each log file. Only the logs which are of the type 'Error' are then extracted for further processing, excluding information and warning related entries. Stop words and punctuation are also removed as part of the text cleaning process.
- **Building the text corpus:** With the cleaned data, a new text corpus is created by tokenizing each word from the sentence list from the log files.
- **Training the Word2Vec model:** The Word2Vec [7] model is built using the previously constructed corpus text data. The Gensim [6] package has been used for the purpose.
- **Constructing the feature vector data:** In order to construct the feature vectors in each log entry, the vector values equivalent to the preprocessed event type, event subtype and log message are concatenated. Each of these sub item vectors are the average of word vectors in each item.

- **Bucketizing the data with time window:** The records need to be bucketized based on the time window, in order to calculate the error count in each time window. With the timestamp in the log data, the log record count is calculated within each time window.
- **Training the Machine Learning Model:** The bucketized data is used as an input to build the machine learning model. We have tried different unsupervised algorithms to get the best results. The experiment results are shown in the next section.

4 Experiment Results and Application

Siebel Application component logs are used as training data to detect outlier and novel errors. From the component logs, event type, event sub type and error log are extracted and use to form the feature vector. Each of this individual concatenated feature vector has dimension of size 10. After grouping based on time window, the error count is taken and concatenated with the feature vector. The model is then trained to predict whether an error is present for each feature vector created. Training Data details are given in Table 1.

Table 1. Data details for building the model

#Samples	#Dimension	Outlier perc
459	31	27.27

We have run the experiment with ten different algorithms [Angle-based Outlier Detector (ABOD) [16],Cluster based Local Outlier Factor(CBLOF) [17], Feature Bagging(FB) [18], Histogram-base Outlier Detection (HBOS) [19], Isolation Forest(IF) [20], K Nearest Neighbors (KNN) [21], Local Outlier Factor (LOF) [5],Minimum Covariance Determinant (MCD) [22], One-class SVM (OCSVM) [15], Principal Component Analysis (PCA) [23]. We have used area under receiver operating characteristic (ROC) curve [24] and Precision @ rank n (P@N) [25] as evaluation metrics. The ROC performances and P@N performances (average of 10 independent trials) of each algorithm are shown as results in Table 2. The experiment conducted with the help of PyOD [14] package.

Table 2. ROC Performance and Precision @N Performance (average of 10 independent trials)

Algorithms	ABOD	CBLOF	FB	HBOS	IForest	KNN	LOF	MCD	OCSVM	PCA
ROC	0.12	0.916	0.833	0.708	0.733	0.9583	0.917	0.717	1	0.625
P@N	0.625	0.875	0.875	0.857	0.875	0.875	0.875	0.875	1	0.875

From Table 2 it can be seen that the OneClass SVM is doing a better job in predicting both outlier and novel errors from the input data. As per [15] OneClass SVM is able to detect the error distribution from existing distribution, and the errors which are novel to the underlying error distribution. The error message tokens which did not exist in the Word2Vec corpus model, are the actual novel errors which are detected in the OneClass SVM.

Real World Application: We have implemented the OneClass SVM based anomaly detection in our enterprise application such as Siebel CRM, and other various applications using WebLogic servers. The implementation allows us to detect the outlier errors in the application, which help in proactively identifying the issues and resolving it in quicker way. Also, during the release cycle or in system upgrade time, we could easily identify novel errors and fix them without impacting the customer.

5 Conclusion

Enterprise level application log anomaly detection was attempted with the different algorithms and it was found that OneClass SVM yielded promising results in the feature vector approach. The outlier data and novel data together were difficult to capture in most of the anomaly detection algorithms as per their design. OneClass SVM was the most successful in detecting both types of errors, scoring the highest in both evaluation metrics. Additionally, this process helps in finding application related problems in a systematic way. In future there is scope of reducing the training time of the process in a more optimized approach.

Acknowledgement. This work has been conducted using the resources and data in British Telecom. I thank all the reviewers and supporters who helped me in accomplishing this task. I also express my sincere gratitude to BT Research and to my Managers for their extended help.

References

1. Wang, H., Bah, M., Hammad, M.: Progress in outlier detection techniques: a survey. IEEE Access. **7**, 107964–108000 (2019). https://doi.org/10.1109/access.2019.2932769
2. Akoglu, L., Tong, H., Vreeken, J., Faloutsos, C.: Fast and reliable anomaly detection in categorical data. In: Proceedings of the 21st ACM International Conference on Information and Knowledge Management - CIKM '12 (2012). https://doi.org/10.1145/2396761.2396816
3. He, S., Zhu, J., He, P., Lyu, M.: Experience report: system log analysis for anomaly detection. In: 2016 IEEE 27th International Symposium on Software Reliability Engineering (ISSRE) (2016). https://doi.org/10.1109/issre.2016.21
4. Baur, C., Wiestler, B., Albarqouni, S., Navab, N.: Deep autoencoding models for unsupervised anomaly segmentation in brain MR images. In: Crimi, A., Bakas, S., Kuijf, H., Keyvan, F., Reyes, M., van Walsum, T. (eds.) BrainLes 2018. LNCS, vol. 11383, pp. 161–169. Springer, Cham (2019). https://doi.org/10.1007/978-3-030-11723-8_16
5. Breunig, M., Kriegel, H., Ng, R., Sander, J.: LOF. Proceedings of the 2000 ACM SIGMOD International Conference on Management of Data - SIGMOD '00 (2000)
6. Gensim Home Page. https://radimrehurek.com/gensim/models/word2vec.html. Accessed 25 Jun 2020

7. Mikolov, T., Sutskever, I., Chen, K., Corrado, G., Dean, J.: Distributed representations of words and phrases and their compositionality. In: Advances in Neural Information Processing Systems, pp. 3111–3119 (2013)
8. Xu, W., Huang, L., Fox, A., Patterson, D., Jordan, M.: Detecting large-scale system problems by mining console logs. In: Proceedings of the ACM SIGOPS 22nd Symposium on Operating Systems Principles - SOSP '09 (2009)
9. Yamanishi, K., Maruyama, Y.: Dynamic syslog mining for network failure monitoring. In: Proceeding of the Eleventh ACM SIGKDD International Conference on Knowledge Discovery in Data Mining - KDD '05 (2005)
10. Nagaraj, K., Killian, C., Neville, J.: Structured comparative analysis of systems logs to diagnose performance problems. NSDI, pp. 353–366 (2012)
11. Ghanbari, S., Hashemi, A.B., Amza, C.: Stage-aware anomaly detection through tracking log points. In: Proceedings of the 15th International Middleware Conference, pp. 253–264 (2014). https://doi.org/10.1145/2663165.2663319
12. Hawkins, D.: Identification of Outliers. Chapman and Hall, London (1980)
13. Barnett, V., Lewis, T.: Outliers in Statistical Data. Wiley, New York (1994)
14. Zhao, Y., Nasrullah, Z., Li, Z.: PyOD: a python toolbox for scalable outlier detection. J. Mach. Learn. Res. 20(96), 1–7 (2019)
15. Schölkopf, B., Platt, J., Shawe-Taylor, J., Smola, A., Williamson, R.: Estimating the support of a high-dimensional distribution. Neural Comput. 13, 1443–1471 (2001)
16. Kriegel, H.P., Schubert, M., Zimek, A.: Angle-based outlier detection in high-dimensional data. In: Proceedings of the 14th ACM SIGKDD International Conference on Knowledge Discovery and Data Mining, pp. 444–452 (2008)
17. He, Z., Xu, X., Deng, S.: Discovering cluster-based local outliers. Pattern Recogn. Lett. 24, 1641–1650 (2003)
18. Lazarevic, A., Kumar, V.: Feature bagging for outlier detection. In: Proceedings of the Eleventh ACM SIGKDD International Conference on Knowledge Discovery in Data Mining, 157–166 (2005)
19. Goldstein, M., Dengel, A.: Histogram-based outlier score (hbos): aa fast unsupervised anomaly detection algorithm. KI-2012: Poster and Demo Track, pp. 59–63 (2012)
20. Liu, F.T., Ting, K.M., Zhou, Z.H.: Isolation forest. In: 2008 Eighth IEEE International Conference on Data Mining, pp. 413–422 (2008). https://doi.org/10.1109/icdm.2008.17
21. Angiulli, F., Pizzuti, C.: Fast outlier detection in high dimensional spaces. In: European Conference on Principles of Data Mining and Knowledge Discovery, pp. 15–27 (2002)
22. Hardin, J., Rocke, D.: Outlier detection in the multiple cluster setting using the minimum covariance determinant estimator. Comput. Stat. Data Anal. 44, 625–638 (2004)
23. Shyu, M.L., Chen, S.C., Sarinnapakorn, K. and Chang, L.: A novel anomaly detection scheme based on principal component classifier. Miami Univ Coral Gables Fl Dept of Electrical and Computer Engineering (2003)
24. Hanley, J., McNeil, B.: The meaning and use of the area under a receiver operating characteristic (ROC) curve. Radiology 143, 29–36 (1982)
25. Craswell, N.: Precision at n. Encyclopedia of Database Systems, pp. 2127–2128 (2009)

Using Active Learning to Understand the Videoconference Experience: A Case Study

Simon Llewellyn[1](✉), Christopher Simons[2]⬤, and Jim Smith[2]⬤

[1] VQ Communications, Byron House, Chippenham, Wiltshire SN14 6RZ, UK
sllewellyn@vqcomms.com
[2] University of the West of England, Bristol BS16 1QY, UK
{chris.simons,james.smith}@uwe.ac.uk
https://www.vqcomms.com/
https://www.uwe.ac.uk/

Abstract. Videoconferencing is becoming ubiquitous, especially so during the COVID-19 pandemic. However, user experience of a videoconference call can be variable. To better understand and classify the performance of videoconference call systems, this paper reports a case study in which active learning - an interactive form of machine learning in which system engineers provide labels for instances of feature data - is applied to videoconference call logs. Investigations reveal that although system engineers have differing videoconference domain knowledge and so provide a wide range of labels, the active learning approach produces promising results in terms of model scale, accuracy and confidence reflecting the subjectivity of engineers' experience.

Keywords: Videoconference · Active learning

1   Introduction

The amenity of videoconferencing (VC) has increased significantly in recent years, especially so during the current COVID-19 pandemic as VC systems have become readily available and ubiquitous. However, a number of authors have reported that the quality of the VC experience can vary greatly depending a range of factors. Calyam et al. [1] suggest ways to measure the quality of experience (QoE) in VC, while Reichl et al. [7] propose a comprehensive framework for QoE and user behaviour modelling. Recently, Schmitt et al. [8] report efforts to promote individual QoE within multi-party VC. While such reports indicate promising results, understanding of the VC experience remains incomplete. To address this, the University of the West of England (UWE) and VQ Communications (VQ) are collaborating to investigate the application of active learning - an interactive form of machine learning (ML) - in understanding and predicting the user experience of the company's VC systems. This paper discusses some the challenges faced by the project, the approaches proposed to address those challenges, and then reports initial findings of the investigation.

© Springer Nature Switzerland AG 2020
M. Bramer and R. Ellis (Eds.): SGAI-AI 2020, LNAI 12498, pp. 386–392, 2020.
https://doi.org/10.1007/978-3-030-63799-6_30

2   Challenges Arising

Because user experience depends on perception and judgement, it is too simplistic to generally categorise VC calls as 'good' or 'bad'. Users will differ in their subjective context, their roles (e.g. system manager vs. caller) and hence in their choice of labels to describe their experience, so to avoid prejudice, it is necessary to find ways to map these *post-hoc*. A second challenge from the active learning perspective, is the absence, for commercial reasons, of 'benchmark' datasets.

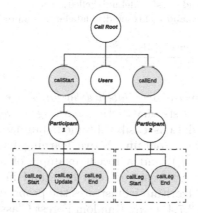

Fig. 1. Example hierarchy of a 2-participant call. Shaded circles represent CDRs, dash boxes highlight callLegs.

VQ system logs contain rich and detailed information, but the consequent size makes them hard to understand by systems engineers. In this case study, VQ software systems manage Cisco Meeting Server platforms [2] which produce Call Detail Records (CDRs) [3]. Typically, CDRs represent events within a *call*, and maps out its structure. Majority of these CDRs combine to show the call *legs*, one (or more in the case of problems and/or re-connection) for each call participant (see Fig. 1 for a simple example). *callStart* and *callEnd* information is recorded for each call, as well as *callLegStart*, *callLegUpdate* and *callLegEnd* information. Timing information is recorded for significant events. *callLegEnd* records also contain (i) reason codes to explain why the leg ended, and (ii) alarm codes where poor system performance is detected.

3   Proposed Approach

3.1   Active Learning

According to Settles [9], *"the key idea behind active learning is that a machine learning algorithm can achieve greater accuracy if it allowed to choose the data from which it learns. An active learner may pose queries, usually in the form*

Algorithm 1. Proposed algorithm for application of Active Learning

---

Require: unlabelled_data
Ensure: model, predictions, confidences, training_set, training_labels
1: **while** termination condition not reached **do**
2:    index = get_next_item_to_label_from_unlabelled_data()
3:    label = ask_user_for_item_label(index)
4:    add unlabelled_data[index] to training_set
5:    add label to training_labels
6:    model.train(training_set,training_labels)
7:    predictions = model.predict(unlabelled_data)
8:    confidences = get_confidences(model,unlabelled_data)
9:    accept_predicted_labels_above_threshold(unlabelled_data,predictions,confidences)
10: **end while**
11: **return** training_set,training_labels

---

of unlabelled data instances to be labelled by an oracle (e.g., a human anno-tator)." Settles also suggests that active learning is well-motivated for problems where unlabelled data is easily obtained, but labels are difficult, time-consuming, or expensive to obtain. Active learning has been widely applied in such situations (e.g. [4]), and a recent example of active learning embedded within human-machine 'teaming' can be found in [5]. Inspired by these promising approaches, Algorithm 1 illustrates the proposed approach, which was implemented in Python 3.7.4, using Random Forest Classifier as the model from Scikit-Learn 0.23.1.

In line 2 of Algorithm 1 the next item chosen for labelling was the one with the smallest margin between first and second most confident class predictions. Users are shown selected information for a call e.g. length, alarm values and are free to provide whatever they consider to be a meaningful label. Thus the proposed approach allows the `model` to incorporate either (i) categorical labels of VC calls, e.g. 'good', 'demonstration', 'catastrophic', or (ii) ordinal labels, e.g. a ranking scheme such as $[1, 2, \ldots, 5]$, corresponding to classification or regression tasks.

The `model` component in Algorithm 1 produces `predictions` for each CDR instance of `unlabelled_data` and the `training_set` overall, and `confidences` for `predictions`. The code is instrumented to allow examination of the accuracy of `predictions` and their corresponding levels of `confidences` as active learning and system engineers try to learn about VC calls. As some system engineers might provide a more complex labelling scheme than others, data is captured to enable comparison of what labels different engineers provide.

3.2   Data Features

It was made clear by VQ that customers systems are unique in terms of infrastructure and user behaviour. Therefore data was compiled from existing customers, and VQ's own internal system. This variety of sources made it possible to look for commonality between different systems.

First the log files are parsed into separate calls, and call trees created. Four 'views' were used to group features representing different aspects of a call i.e.

- Connection: e.g. *maxNumActiveCallLegs*,
- Participant: e.g. *numCallLegs, numCallLegUpdates*
- Alarms: e.g. *packetLoss, excessiveJitter*
- Time-Deltas: e.g. *callLegStart→callLegUpdate*

Most features map naturally onto a few integers. For those based within a continuous range (e.g. time-delta), we model the distribution as the sum of n (typically 10–12) Gaussian/Poisson curves, so creating a discretisation into n bins that reflects the underlying data. The feature dataset and CDRs used in this investigation are available at [6].

4   Outcomes

Five system engineers with varying degrees of domain knowledge participated in active learning with 6 datasets; two datasets each from three live production VQ systems. The smallest dataset comprised 42 calls and the largest 21,270. Results shown in Table 1, Figs. 2 and 3 are selected tests taken from a single dataset containing 164 calls judged to be illustrative of all the datasets investigated.

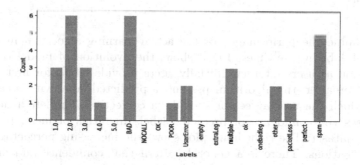

Fig. 2. Comparison of labelling schemes. Plot shows all the calls labelled as 'bad' by one user, and reports the corresponding labels applied by other users

Figure 2 shows a histogram of the frequencies of various labels users assigned to the calls classified as 'Bad' during test 6. A variety of labels is noted; no two participants provided identical sets of labels. However, labels do appear to reflect semantic similarities to 'Bad' e.g. 'BAD', '2' (out of 5), 'spam'.

Table 1. User entered labels for test data set.

Test	User entered labels
1	['1', '2', '3', '4', '5']
2	['UserError', 'DEMO', 'BAD', 'NOCALL', 'POOR', 'OK', 'Test', 'Demo']
3	['UserError', 'Bad', 'OK', 'Test', 'Poor', 'NoCall']
4	['multiple', 'ok', 'packetLoss', 'extraLeg', 'empty', 'spam']
5	['spam', 'perfect', 'onebadleg', 'other']

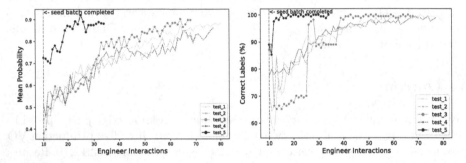

Fig. 3. Evolution of Active Learning Systems in response to number of labels provided. Left: system's mean confidence in its predictions. Right: percentage of correct classifications.

To examine the performance of the active learning algorithm in response to different labelling schemes, Fig. 3 shows the evolution of model confidence and precision as users interact. Initially, users provide labels for first 10 interactions. Thereafter, the algorithm presents a predicted label with a confidence level, to which the user agrees or provides a corrective. The left hand plot in Fig. 3 shows the confidence of predicted labels in terms of mean probability across the dataset. The right hand plot shows the increasing percentage of correct classifications. There is a general pattern that confidence and prediction accuracy increase (albeit non-monotonically) with the number of interactions. Naturally, there are differences in the rate of learning for each test, but learning appears both *effective* - high classification accuracies are reached, and for different numbers of classes, and *efficient* - these levels are reached by approximately 40 interactions.

The active learning algorithm terminates when all calls in the training set are labelled and have at least 95% confidence probability. However, we observe that this sometimes required many interactions (81 in Test 1), which may bring about a loss of focus and attention in the form of user fatigue. This suggests that an alternative stop condition may be useful.

It is interesting to observe test case 5 in which algorithm performance is superior to all other tests. We also observe (from Table 1) that the set of labels used in test case 5 is smaller than any other. We conclude that the use of a non-ambiguous and simple set of labels appears to be the most effective approach as it tends to correspond to a more learnable problem. In test case 1, however, with user labels $[1, 2, \ldots, 5]$, learning is less effective and it may be easier to learn labels as a regression problem when users provide ratings (e.g. see [10]). It is also interesting to note some jumps in model accuracy for test cases. We speculate that during early user interactions, the relative proportions of labels provided was not even, making prediction difficult. Once appropriate labels were provided, a jump in accuracy can be observed.

5 Conclusion

In this case study, we have found that although system engineers have a range of domain knowledge and so provide different labels, active learning produces promising results in terms of model accuracy and confidence, and reflects system engineers' VC understanding. Initial findings suggest our implementation of active learning appears to scale well, handling datasets of up to approximately 20,000 calls. However, with larger datasets, the number of engineer interactions with the active learning algorithm can increase, with the possibility of user fatigue causing lack of focus in learning. Future work will aim to address this by reexamining the algorithm's stop condition. During the current COVID-19 pandemic, user experience in VC systems has become crucial. Active learning systems, such as those described in this case study, appear well suited to provide flexible and effective machine learning shedding light on the user VC experience.

Acknowledgement. This work is supported by grant KTP 11049 from Innovate UK, part of UK Research and Innovation.

References

1. Calyam, P., Haffner, M., Ekici, E., Lee, C.-G.: Using Active Learning to Understand the Videoconference Experience. In: Krishnaswamy, D., Pfeifer, T., Raz, D. (eds.) MMNS 2007. LNCS, vol. 4787, pp. 14–25. Springer, Heidelberg (2007). https://doi.org/10.1007/978-3-540-75869-3_2
2. Cisco: Cisco Meeting Server. https://www.cisco.com/. Accessed 8 June 2020
3. Cisco: Call Detail Records Guide, 2.6 edn., January 2020. https://www.cisco.com/c/dam/en/us/td/docs/conferencing/ciscoMeetingServer/Reference_Guides/Version-2-6/Cisco-Meeting-Server-CDR-Guide-2-6-and-later.pdf. Accessed 8 June 2020
4. Fu, Y., Zhu, X., Li, B.: A survey on instance selection for active learning. Knowl. Inf. Syst. **35**(2), 249–283 (2013)
5. Legg, P., Smith, J., Downing, A.: Visual analytics for collaborative human-machine confidence in human-centric active learning tasks. Hum. Centric Comput. Info. Sci. **9**(1), 5 (2019)
6. Llewellyn, S.: Anonymised feature dataset and Call Detail Records (CDRs). www.dropbox.com/sh/p7nh77qrvwkk5cb/AACYxjHCzoSM90ixomIjEk4ma?dl=0

7. Reichl, P., et al.: Towards a comprehensive framework for QoE and user behavior modelling. In: 2015 Seventh International Workshop on Quality of Multimedia Experience (QoMEX), pp. 1–6. IEEE (2015)
8. Schmitt, M., Redi, J., Bulterman, D., Cesar, P.S.: Towards individual QoE for multiparty videoconferencing. IEEE Trans. Multimed. **20**(7), 1781–1795 (2017)
9. Settles, B.: Active Learning Literature Survey, Computer Sciences Technical report, 1648th edn. University of Wisconsin-Madison, USA (2010)
10. Smith, J., Legg, P., Matovic, M., Kinsey, K.: Predicting user confidence during visual decision making. ACM Trans. Interact. Intell. Syst. **8**(2) (2018)

An Application of EDA and GA for Permutation Based Spare Part Allocation Problem

Nouf Alkaabi[1](✉), Siddhartha Shakya[1](✉), Adriana Gabor[2](✉),
Andrzej Stefan Sluzek[3](✉), Beum Seuk Lee[4](✉), and Gilbert Owusu[4](✉)

[1] Emirates ICT Innovation Center (EBTIC), Khalifa University, Abu Dhabi, United Arab Emirates
{nouf.alkaabi,sid.shakya}@ku.ac.ae
[2] Department of Applied Mathematics, Khalifa University, Abu Dhabi, United Arab Emirates
adriana.gabor@ku.ac.ae
[3] Department of Electrical and Computer Engineering, Khalifa University, Abu Dhabi, United Arab Emirates
andrzej.sluzek@ku.ac.ae
[4] British Telecom, London, UK
{rom.lee,gilbert.owusu}@bt.com

Abstract. Enterprise Resource management is crucial to the success of any service organizations. Having right resource at the right time at the right place can make a big difference to the quality of their service offering. This paper focuses on spare parts management in a telecom industry as part of the enterprise resource management problem. The traditional way of moving the spare parts within the network is done manually by expert planners. However, this is not efficient as they may not have a global view of supply and demand, considering a large number of spares and potential locations that have to be taken into account when making distribution decisions. We investigate two evolutionary algorithms to solve this problem. The objective is twofold: 1) to identify and implement a permutation based Estimation of Distribution Algorithm for this problem, 2) to perform detail experimental analysis and compare the performance EDA to that of GA, with the goal of enhancing existing spare management software.

Keywords: Genetic algorithm · RK-EDA · Resource management

1 Introduction

Resource management is one of the key challenges for any service organization since it contributes to the organization's performance, profitability, cost, quality of service, and customer satisfaction [1]. Spare parts are one of the key resources that has to be managed carefully in any large organization. The process of regularly moving spare parts to the right locations must be automated. This paper considers a telecom service organization with a large inventory of spare parts that need redistribution in order to reduce the travel distance required to install the spare parts. Given the number of spares, the number of deployed items and the number of faults (if any) for each site, usually, expert planners

© Springer Nature Switzerland AG 2020
M. Bramer and R. Ellis (Eds.): SGAI-AI 2020, LNAI 12498, pp. 393–399, 2020.
https://doi.org/10.1007/978-3-030-63799-6_31

based on their technology and network assessment decide to move spare parts from one site to another. However, they may not have a global view of hundreds of different spares, at thousands of different locations and places where the spares are required. This could lead to suboptimal assignments of spares. This paper investigates two different evolutionary algorithms (EA) [2] to solve the spare allocation problem. Particularity, we implemented a permutation based version of a Genetic Algorithm (GA) [3], and a permutation based Estimation of Distribution Algorithm (EDA) [2] called Random Key EDA (RK-EDA) [4]. It is known that GA struggles with problems where there is complex dependency between decision variables. EDAs are supposed to handle the GA's drawback by representing the dependencies among variables in a probabilistic model and use that to help evolve the solution [2]. RK-EDA is one of the recent EDAs that is used to solve permutation based problems. The rest of the paper is organized as follows. Section 2 presents a literature survey of similar works in other domains and presents a mathematical formulation of the spare optimization problem. Section 3 details the evolutionary algorithm approach to solve the problem and describes two implemented EAs. Section 4 elaborates on the experimental setting and on the obtained results. Finally, Sect. 5 provides the main outcomes and conclusions of our work.

2 Background and Problem Formulation

Different approaches have been used in literature to find optimal locations within a given geographical distance. In [5] Tabu Search (TS), Simulated Annealing (SA) [6], GA, and Hybrid hill-climbing were used in order to find the optimal locations for an emergency medical services. The authors of [7] and [8] focus on the Maximal Covering Location Problem (MCLP) which maximizes the coverage within a given distance with a fixed number of facilities. Facilities location problems were also considered in [9–13], where different techniques were used, such as 0-1 Mixed Integer Programming, quadratic programming, and heuristics methods such as TS, SA, and GA.

The problem domain considered in our case is specific to telecom industries and hence has its characteristic, constraints and objectives. Previous work on this topic has applied a GA and some results comparing its performance against manual approach used by planners was presented in [3]. We extend this approach further, with the view to

1. Investigate the performance of an EDA for this problem.
2. Perform rigorous experimental analysis to compare the performances of GA and EDA on many instances of the problem

Following [3], the process of moving spares is divided into three steps:

1. S1 - Self-assignment
2. S2 - Near assignment
3. S3- Far assignment

In the Self-assignment step we check if a site with specific type of spare parts also has any deployed and working items of that type on the site. If the check is positive, the required spares are kept in that site so that they can be used if fault occurs at that site. The near assignment involves checking if the sites with deployed items are within 30 min of travel from the site with spares, and if so, the spares are not moved but instead, their allocation to the deployed item is assumed.

In the far assignment, the sites with remaining deployed items are considered. This is where EA will be used to find the best allocations out of many possible allocations ensuring that the travel time to move spares is minimized and their coverage to the most demanding locations is maximised. Following [3], we define this step as an optimisation process with the objective to minimise travel distance for moving spares, maximise coverage of spares based on deployed items, and maximise coverage of spares based on past repair history, formulated as:

$$\min_{K_i} f(K_i) = \frac{\alpha \times uncoverd(K_i) + \beta \times travel(K_i)}{\gamma \times fault(K_i)} \tag{1}$$

where, for each spare type i, we define its possible movement as a matrix K_i, where each element of matrix $k_{i,ab}$ denotes the number of spare type i, moved from location $a \in J$ to location $b \in J$. $uncoverd(K_i)$ represents the number of deployed items of type i that do not have spares allocated by the movement K_i. $travel(K_i)$ represents the total travel time with assignment K_i. $fault(K_i)$ represents the total past faults in the location where spares were moved with assignment K_i. α, β, γ are respective weights for deployed item, travel time, and past faults that can be configured to give a greater importance to specific objectives. The details of each term are not included here due to the space limitation. Interested readers are, however, are referred to [3].

3 EA Approach to Solve the Problem

We use a permutation-based representation to model the problem presented in [3], where each solution $X = \{x_1, x_2, ..., x_n\}$ represents the order of location in which the spares should be allocated. Here, n is the total number of the locations that have at least one deployed item and are much smaller than the size of the matrix K_i. The evaluation of a solution X is performed by simulating the allocation, where the spares from the nearest possible site are allocated to the locations x_i according to their orders in X. Once the allocation is completed, we get a matrix of allocation K_i, which is then used in Eq. (1) to calculate the fitness of the solution $f(X)$. The objective for GA and RK-EDA is then to find the best permutation of locations with deployed items which minimizes $f(X)$. GA workflow:

1. Generate a population of solutions P of size p_s by performing a random permutation of the locations with deployed items.
2. Evaluate each X in P by running a simulation as described in Sect. 4
3. Create a breeding pool by selecting S solutions from P
4. Perform a permutation-based crossover from the solutions in the breeding pool to generate new solutions
5. Perform a permutation based mutation on new solutions where a random subset of elements from a solution is randomly shuffled

6. Replace P with a new solution and go to the Step 2 until terminated.

RK-EDA workflow:

1. Initialize parameters σ, t_s, p_s
2. Generate an initial population P of size p_s by performing a random permutation of the locations with deployed items
3. For $g = 1$ to $MaxGen$ do

    a. Evaluate each X in P by simulating and rescaling them according to the value of each x_i in X as described in Sect. 4
    b. Select the best $t_s < p_s$ solution to some S
    c. Calculate μ_s, a set of means for each x_i in X using set S
    d. Set $c = 1 - \frac{g}{MaxGen}, \sigma_g = \sigma * c$
    e. Sample $N(\mu_s, \sigma_g)$ to generate a population of size p_s to replace P with

4. Output the best solution found so far

In step 3a of RK-EDA, each variable x_i in the solution X will be ranked based on their values to maintain a permuation representation in the solution, and normalized to a number betwen zero and one, to minimize the redundancy and improve the information captured by the probabilistic model [4]. As it can be noticed, unlike GA, RK-EDA does not have crossover or mutation operators for its variation. Instead it estimates a normal distribution $N(\mu_s, \sigma_g)$ of the best solutions in the population S and samples from it to generate a new population.

4   Experimental Results

Three types of spare part items were chosen for our experiments, labeled as Item A, Item B and Item C. A large number of experiments were performed with these three items and with many different setting for the weights of the objective function (β, α, γ from Eq. (1)) and also turning on and off the three steps in the optimization as described in Sect. 2 (S1, S2 and S3). To find the best parameter settings, experiments were performed with many different parameters configurations of GA and RK-EDA for each of the three instances, and for each of the weight and optimization step settings. The population size p for both algorithms was set to $c \times l$, where l is the length of the solution string and c is a parameter that was set to 3. i.e., the population size was set to 3 times the solution length. The solution length l represents the number of risky sites, i.e. the sites with deployed items but with fewer spares than required. The maximum generation was set to $b \times p$, where p is the population size, and b was fixed to 2. In GA, tournament selection was used with the tested range of crossover probability, cp being 0.5, 0.6, 0.7, and 0.8, and the tested range of the mutation probability, mp, being 0.0001, 0.001, 0.01, and 0.1. In RK-EDA, the tested variances, v, were 0.01, 0.05, 0.1, and 0.2, and the tested selection size ratios, ss, were 0.1, 0.3, 0.5, and 0.8. Since both of the algorithms are stochastic, we ran each algorithm 10 times for each combination, and recorded the mean fitness, and the best fitness out of 10 runs. Table 1 and 2 summarizes the results of the experiments. Table 1 shows the best average fitness (Avg Fit) together with its corresponding standard deviation (Stdev) found by GA and RKEDA out of a different combination of algorithm parameters and for a different combination of items, weights and optimization steps. Also, the algorithm parameter combination that achieved the best mean fitness is shown. Similarly, Table 2 shows the best overall fitness found by GA and RKEDA for different combinations.

Table 1. Best average fitness together with corresponding standard deviation found by GA and RKEDA with algorithm parameters that achieved respective results.

	Weights			Steps			RKEDA				GA			
Item	β	α	γ	S1	S2	S3	Avg Fit	Stdev	ss	v	Avg Fit	Stdev	cp	mp
A	1	0	0	×	×	✓	44605	588	0.1	0.05	**44211**	330	0.7	0.1
B	1	0	0	×	×	✓	**24423**	134	0.3	0.1	24472	134	0.7	0.001
C	1	0	0	×	×	✓	20053	248	0.5	0.1	**19744**	220	0.8	0.01
A	1	1	1	✓	✓	✓	45577	382	0.5	0.1	**45510**	320	0.8	0.1
B	1	1	1	✓	✓	✓	22593	88	0.5	0.2	**22523**	36	0.7	0.1
C	1	1	1	✓	✓	✓	18690	110	0.5	0.1	**18452**	41	0.8	0.001
A	1	1	1	×	×	✓	45161	653	0.1	0.05	**44412**	503	0.7	0.1
B	1	1	1	×	×	✓	**24699**	82	0.1	0.2	24745	62	0.7	0.01
C	1	1	1	×	×	✓	20886	139	0.1	0.1	**20683**	209	0.8	0.01
A	1	0	0	✓	✓	✓	45987	733	0.3	0.1	**45731**	1154	0.8	0.1
B	1	0	0	✓	✓	✓	22299	1103	0.1	0.2	**22269**	28	0.6	0.1
C	1	0	0	✓	✓	✓	17991	120	0.1	0.1	**17817**	135	0.8	0.001

It can be noticed from Table 1 that, for most of the tested instances, the GA was able to find a better solution than RK-EDA, with GA outperforming RK-EDA in 10 instances, RK-EDA was better in 2 instances, and for 6 instances, the results were exactly the same (which is not included in the table due to the space limitation). Also, this can be further noticed in Table 2, where GA was able to find the best quality solution for 8 out of 18 instances tested. The better results are highlighted in bold. This suggests that GA is able to better explore the search space, particularly for the cases where the distance weight was turned on (with $\beta = 1$). For the cases where the distance was ignored (with $\beta = 0$), both algorithms were able to find an optimal solution all the time, suggesting that the search space in such a case is smaller and it is easier for the algorithms to converge to an optimal solution (the results for $\beta = 0$ cases is omitted due to the space limit, and the results were same for both algorithms)

Table 2. Best overall fitness found by GA and RKEDA with algorithm parameters that achieved respective result.

Item	Weights			Steps			RKEDA			GA		
	β	α	γ	S1	S2	S3	Best Fit	ss	v	Best Fit	cp	mp
A	1	0	0	×	×	✓	43867	0.1	0.05	**43568**	0.7	0.0001
B	1	0	0	×	×	✓	24244	0.8	0.1	24244	0.8	0.01
C	1	0	0	×	×	✓	19626	0.5	0.1	**19498**	0.5	0.01
A	1	1	1	✓	✓	✓	44550	0.5	0.1	44550	0.7	0.001
B	1	1	1	✓	✓	✓	22506	0.1	0.2	22506	0.7	0.1
C	1	1	1	✓	✓	✓	18378	0.5	0.1	**18370**	0.5	0.0001
A	1	1	1	×	×	✓	44053	0.3	0.05	**43949**	0.6	0.1
B	1	1	1	×	×	✓	24535	0.5	0.05	**24525**	0.5	0.0001
C	1	1	1	×	×	✓	20494	0.1	0.05	**20357**	0.8	0.1
A	1	0	0	✓	✓	✓	44448	0.3	0.1	**43453**	0.8	0.1
B	1	0	0	✓	✓	✓	22243	0.3	0.05	22243	0.5	0.01
C	1	0	0	✓	✓	✓	17740	0.5	0.1	**17672**	0.6	0.1

5   Conclusion and Future Work

In this paper, we focused on the problem of finding the optimal spares distribution using evolutionary algorithms. Particularly, a GA and an EDA called RK-EDA were deployed and extensively analyzed with various parameters for many different instances of the problem. The comparisons of the results have shown that for most of the tested instances, GA was able to find better solutions, while RK-EDA was better in a few instances. The algorithm tested are incorporated into a tool built for our telecom partner, whose data is used in the experiments presented. The results of the automated planning of spare distribution using the built tool has been proven effective in the real world scenario, leading to operational efficiencies. For future work, other permutation based EAs and EDAs can be further explored to find algorithms that may perform better on this problem. One could also investigate whether other problem representations than permutation based are more suitable for standard versions of these EAs.

References

1. Shakya, S., Kassem, S., Mohamed, A., Hagras, H., Owusu, G.: Enhancing field service operations via fuzzy automation of tactical supply plan. In: Owusu, G., O'Brien, P., McCall, J., Doherty, N.F. (eds.) Transforming Field and Service Operations, pp. 101–114. Springer, Heidelberg (2013). https://doi.org/10.1007/978-3-642-44970-3_7
2. Larrañaga, P., Lozano, J.A.: Estimation of Distribution Algorithms: A New Tool for Evolutionary Computation. Kluwer Academic Publishers, Netherlands (2002)

3. Shakya, S., Seuk Lee, B., Di Cairano-Gilfedder, C., Owusu, G.: Spare parts optimization for legacy telecom networks using a permutation-based evolutionary algorithm. In: IEEE CEC (2017)
4. Ayodele, M., McCall, J., Regnier-Coudert, O.: RK-EDA: a novel random key based estimation of distribution algorithm. In: Handl, J., Hart, E., Lewis, P.R., López-Ibáñez, M., Ochoa, G., Paechter, B. (eds.) PPSN 2016. LNCS, vol. 9921, pp. 849–858. Springer, Cham (2016). https://doi.org/10.1007/978-3-319-45823-6_79
5. Li, X.: Covering models and optimization techniques for emergency response facility location and planning: a review. Math Meth Oper Res 74, 281–310 (2011)
6. Kirkpatrick, S., Gelatt, C.D., Vecchi, M.P.: Optimization by simulated annealing. Sci. Number 220(4598), 671–680 (1983)
7. Church, R.L., et al.: The maximum covering location problem. Papers Reg. Sci. Assoc. 32, 101–118 (1974)
8. Alsalloum, O.I.: Extensions to emergency vehicle location models. Comput. Oper. Res. 33, 2725–2743 (2006)
9. Cohen, M., Lee, H.: Resource deployment analysis of global manufacturing and distribution networks. J. Manuf. Oper. Manage. 2, 81–104 (1989)
10. Hodder, J., Dincer, M.: A multifactor model for international plant location and financing under uncertainty. Comput. Oper. Res. 13(5), 601–609 (1986)
11. Drezner, Z., et al.: On the logit approach to competitive facility location. J. Reg. Sci. 38 (2), 313 (1998). 15
12. Drezner, T., et al.: Solving the multiple competitive facilities location problem. Eur. J. Oper. Res. 142(1), 138–151 (2002)
13. Arostegui, M., et al.: An empirical comparison of tabu search, simulated annealing, and genetic algorithms for facilities location problems. Int. J. Prod. Econ. 103(2006), 742–754 (2006)

Do You Remember Me? Betty the Conversational Agent

Collette Curry(✉) ⓘ, James D O'Shea, and Keeley Crockett ⓘ

Department of Computing and Maths, Manchester Metropolitan University, Manchester, UK
drccurry@btinternet.com, {j.d.oshea,k.crockett}@mmu.ac.uk

Abstract. In this paper we introduce a conversational agent reminiscence companion system called Betty. Betty increases subjective wellbeing (SWB) by engaging with people and by collecting information during one-to-one conversations, then using this data in further personalised conversations with each individual. Results have shown a positive effect on SWB, and improvement in normal age-associated memory loss (NM) was evident through increased everyday interaction with Betty.

Keywords: Conversational agent · Subjective wellbeing · Reminiscence

1 Introduction

In this paper we introduce the development of Betty, a reminiscence themed conversational agent. Throughout development of Betty, a series of experiments were conducted, and results suggested an increase in SWB and improvement in NM in participants aged 65 years and older.

1.1 Ageing Population Growth

In 2017, 18.2% of the United Kingdom (UK) population were aged 65 years or older. More than a quarter of UK residents will be 65 years or over within the next 50 years [1]. As the population ages, normal ageing memory impairment problems will become more acute [2]. Improving memory impairment reduces distress for individuals and enhances their wellbeing and independence [3, 4].

The quality of life and moods in old age can be improved by increasing Subjective Wellbeing [5]. Moods are subjective states of mind that are typically described and quantified using self-reporting measures [6].

1.2 Conversational Agent Framework

A suitable methodology was followed to create Betty. The first factor considered was 'What is such a system going to offer?'. Betty would provide information, answer questions, provide companionship and discuss different reminiscence domain themed topics.

© Springer Nature Switzerland AG 2020
M. Bramer and R. Ellis (Eds.): SGAI-AI 2020, LNAI 12498, pp. 400–404, 2020.
https://doi.org/10.1007/978-3-030-63799-6_32

The direction of the interaction would be dual, so that the user and also Betty could introduce topics into the conversation. Betty would maintain the conversation through an Eliza layer and new content would be added to the personal ontology knowledge base saved for each user. Betty would allow some 'small-talk' and would steer the conversation when required. The handling of unknown or unexpected user input needed to be addressed and handling such content was built into the system. This was to ensure that an appropriate response was given at all times. This also allowed errors to be captured and to be handled by Betty and conversation continue uninterrupted.

Each participant would log in to access their personal ontology, which would build up over time, and to access a 'Learn' mode which would be set to run for either a set period of time during experimental studies, or until the user ended the current conversation. A modular approach was adopted in terms of themed reminiscence ontology inclusion. Content for the initial themed reminiscence ontology was gathered during group discussions, use of a questionnaire and also from the experimental conversational logs.

2 Related Work

There are many themed chatbots and conversational agents but none within the reminiscence domain. Systems are generally constructed by teams of people working on scripted replies and responses to input. There is a specific goal in mind when the system is produced. This could be to inform on a product or service or to give information about a set domain.

3 Developing Betty

Betty was developed to engage older people in conversation using reminiscence. Intended use of this system was to act as a personal companion that could allow conversation at any time of the day or night. Betty was non-judgemental, was never tired, and was always available to talk to. Conversations could be carried out and freely revisited at any time [7].

3.1 Components of the System

Components and functions of the system included the following.

Eliza Layer.
This layer kept the conversation on track and offered general conversation content to promote discussion. Conversation was sustained and continued throughout each session. Content that was recognised was redirected to the 'rule matcher', whilst unknown content was collected, added to the system and increased each personal ontology. If the system was in 'learn' mode, the system learned new content and reused the learnt content in further conversation with each individual. In general mode, the Eliza layer remembered the previous 25 iterations only, so giving an impression of recalling what had been said recently.

Rule Matcher.
User input through conversation was checked by the rule matcher which accepted the input and returned an appropriate response. The rules consisted of different topics and concepts. There were more than 20,000 rules mapped to the Reminiscence Ontology and WordNet.

Reminiscence Ontology.
This themed domain promoted recall and continued reminiscence engagement during conversation. Some subjects were commonly referred to, such as, 'Sixties cars', 'Schooldays', 'Family', 'Weather', and 'Sixties Music'. The reminiscence ontology is the knowledgebase for the themed conversation and also for subsequent threads. It allowed for shorter lines of programmed code. This was achieved by referencing the contents as a dictionary of terms back within the script. Data was contained as a hierarchy of tagged classes which were mapped to WordNet. The system automatically acted upon these tagged classes associations. Reminiscence domain known classes were split into attributes and roles. An ontology search algorithm processed user input, searching for named classes that were a match to detected keywords, it then further refined user input by identifying related terms. A number of subset assertions restricted the number of possible meanings and therefore resulted in more accurate and appropriate matched responses. Starting conversation is sometimes difficult for people, so having a supply of themed subjects to talk about helped participants. Scripted historical stories were incorporated to promote engagement and elicit more reminiscence data. These included events from the war years; the fifties and sixties; music and bands in the past; cars; sports, and famous people from the past.

WordNet.
A widely used resource in natural language processing. Betty was mapped to WordNet by identifying concepts then converting them to readable text files, sorted alphabetically with dates numbered. Within the companion system, WordNet was invoked by calling a keyword. For example, the conversation input could read "I remember the coalman bringing the coal", system reacted to the keyword 'coalman'. Found the definition and returned this internally to the system that then interrogated the reminiscence ontology and found more information about 'coalman'. The system replied, 'Did the coalman put the coal in the coal hole?', or 'Did the coalman bring the coal in a big sack?'.

Conversation Manager.
Accepts conversational input and passes it to the 'Eliza' layer or direct to the 'rule matcher'. When the conversation was a return conversation, Betty invoked past conversation, if two of these were refused by the person having the conversation, then the conversation manager returned the conversation to the Eliza layer and attempted to continue the conversation.

Spell Checking.
This attempted to correctly understand what had been input, even when spelled incorrectly. The input was checked, and the correct response then returned. The Eliza layer was invoked by unknown input to attempt to elicit further information which could then

be interpreted, and a correct reply given. A glossary of terms from the past was included within the spell checker.

Short-Term Memory.
Utilised the Eliza layer and allowed limited interactive unscripted conversation. The input was saved as a re-writable file that was progressively overwritten as new input was received.

Long-Term Memory and the Personal Ontology.
Some content was shared with others via the reminiscence ontology which increased through user conversations. An example would be a conversation about 'cleaning the step with a donkey stone'. Imagine that 'donkey stone' was unknown to Betty, so when added to the reminiscence ontology, it and its definition would be available to all people. Other conversation was stored as a personal ontology and was not available to anyone else.

3.2   The System in Operation

Betty incorporated some standard components of conversational agents; novel features were also included. A generic diagram of the system in operation is illustrated in Fig. 1.

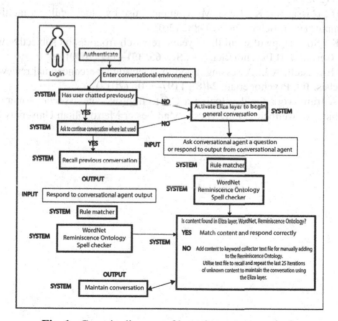

Fig. 1. Generic diagram of how the system worked.

4 Conclusions

There was strong evidence to suggest that a CA used as a conduit for reminiscence is successful if used to improve NM and to increase SWB in participants. Application of the ontology of reminiscence has informed the knowledge of Betty and provided a way of including reminiscence within conversation. Further modular ontologies can be compiled and added to expand the conversational topics and therefore allow more conversational themes to be explored by the participants conversing with Betty. The development of modular ontologies using new methods, combined with a novel scripting mechanism has shortened the time spent scripting Betty. The benefits of the use of a CA in the way described might include improved user memory, lack of isolation and new methods of social interaction in older people [7].

References

1. Coates, S.: Overview of the UK population: November 2018. Office for National Statistics (2018)
2. Morse, A.: Improving Dementia Services in England: An Interim Report. National Audit Office (2010)
3. Dorin, M.: Online education of older adults and its relation to life satisfaction. Educ. Gerontol. **33**, 127–143 (2007)
4. Wagner, J.H., Hassanein, K., Head, M.: Computer use by older adults: a multi-disciplinary review. Comput. Hum. Behav. **26**, 870–882 (2010)
5. George, L.K.: Still happy after all these years: research frontiers on subjective well-being in later life. J. Gerontol. B Psychol. Sci. Soc. Sci. **65**, 331–339 (2010)
6. Brown, L.J.E., Astell, A.J.: Assessing mood in older adults: a conceptual review of methods and approaches. Int. Psychogeriatr. **24**(8), 1197–1206 (2012)
7. Curry, C.: A framework for developing a CA to improve age associated memory loss and increase subjective wellbeing, PhD Thesis, Manchester Metropolitan University (2018)

Author Index

Printed in the United States
By Bookmasters